THE
OLD
WEST
SOURCEBOOK

Traveler's
GUIDE

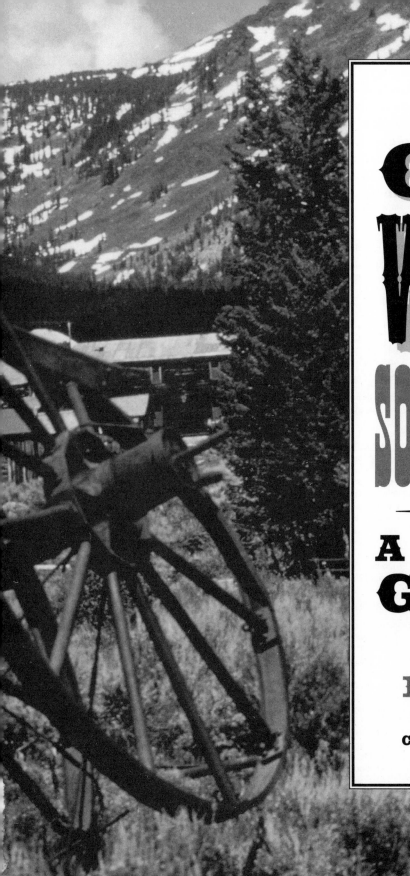

THE OLD WEST

SOURCEBOOK

A Traveler's
GUIDE

CHUCK LAWLISS

Crown Trade Paperbacks
New York

BOOKS BY CHUCK LAWLISS

The Civil War Sourcebook
The Submarine Book
The New York Theatre Sourcebook
The Marine Book
Gold, Ghost Towns & Gamblers
Hawaii for the Sophisticated Traveler
Great Resorts of America
Country Inns of America: The Mississippi

Published by Crown Publishers, Inc., 201 East 50th Street, New York, New York 10022. Member of the Crown Publishing Group.

Random House, Inc. New York, Toronto, London, Sydney, Auckland

Crown Trade Paperbacks and colophon are trademarks of Crown Publishers, Inc.

Manufactured in the United States of America

Design by Lauren Dong

Library of Congress Cataloging-in-Publication Data
Lawliss, Chuck.
The old west sourcebook: a traveler's guide / Chuck Lawliss.
p. cm.
Includes index.
1. West (U.S.)—Guidebooks. 2. Historic sites—West (U.S.)—Guidebooks.
3. West (U.S.)—History, Local. I. Title.
F595.3.L38   1993
917.8'0433—dc20   92-40763
                               CIP

ISBN 0-517-88032-6-Pbk.
10 9 8 7 6 5 4 3 2 1
First Edition

PHOTOGRAPH CREDITS

Travel Montana Department of Commerce, i (J. Wylder), ii (G. Wunderwald)
National Archives, 2, 21, 22 *(left)*, 23 *(bottom)*, 24, 27–30, 38, 43, 47, 52 *(top)*, 53, 55, 62, 67, 70, 72, 91, 99, 114, 115, 117, 118, 120, 125, 131, 135 *(bottom)*, 136 *(top)*, 145, 158, 162, 167, 172, 183, 184, 198 *(top)*, 201, 204, 206, 210, 212, 219, 221 *(top)*, 223, 226, 230, 233, 234, 236, 250, 254, 257, 258, 275, 292–94
South Dakota Tourism, 10, 22 *(right)*, 23 *(top)*, 25, 26, 32
North Dakota Tourism Promotion, 15, 18
Library of Congress, 16, 50, 56, 68 *(top)*, 83, 85, 93, 96, 98, 103 *(top)*, 104, 128, 130, 136 *(bottom)*, 138, 139, 143 *(top)*, 146, 153, 156, 159, 169, 173, 180, 220, 221 *(bottom)*, 247, 260, 266, 269 *(right)*, 283, 284
Paul Horsted, 31
Nebraska Department of Economic Development, 39–41 (Cindy Evert), 44, 46
Kansas Department of Commerce/Travel & Tourism Development Division, 52 *(bottom)*, 58, 63
Texas Tourist Agency/Texas Department of Commerce: 64, 90, 92 (Richard Reynolds); 89, 95, 100, 102, 103 *(bottom;* Elizabeth Grivas), 106
Oklahoma Tourism (Fred W. Marvel), 68 *(bottom)*, 69, 73, 74, 76
Colorado Tourism Board, 108, 148
Wyoming Travel Commission/Wyoming, 135 *(top and middle)*, 137, 140, 143 *(bottom)*
Utah State Historical Society, 165, 171, 174–76
Nevada Commission on Tourism, 179, 185, 186, 187
New Mexico Economic and Tourism Department (Mark Nohl), xii, 188, 193, 195–97, 198 *(bottom)*, 199, 202, 205, 208, 209, 215, 216
Arizona Office of Tourism, 228, 229, 237
State of Washington Tourism Division, 238, 243, 244, 249
California Office of Tourism, 267, 271, 279, 280, 281 (Tom Myers), 282, 286, 288 (Tom Myers), 290 (K. Hansgen), 297 (Michel Olsen)

MAP CREDITS

Pages x–xi, copyright © 1961 by American Heritage Publishing Company/Simon & Schuster, Inc., from *The American Heritage Book of Indians* by editor Alvin M. Josephy, Jr. (pp. 406-407).
Page 5, copyright © 1979 by Hammond, Inc., from *Medallion World Atlas* (p. U-23).
Page 6, copyright © 1979 by Hammond, Inc., from *Medallion World Atlas* (p. U-20).
Pages 12, 36, 66, 110, 190, 203, 240, 264, copyright © 1993 by Fodor's Travel Publications, Inc.
Page 112, copyright © 1977 by American Heritage Publishing Company/Bonanza Books, from *American Heritage History of the Indian Wars* by Robert M. Utely and Wilcomb E. Washburn (p. 297).
Page 119, copyright © 1977 by American Heritage Publishing Company/Bonanza Books, from *American Heritage History of the Indian Wars* by Robert M. Utely and Wilcomb E. Washburn (p. 273).
Page 149, copyright © 1981 by Northland Press, from *Ancient Ruins of the Southwest* by David Grant Noble (p. 24).
All used with permission.

Contents

Introduction

Like most boys, I grew up in the Old West, the Old West of my imagination. I turned a Vermont village into a rip-roarin' cow-town where I lived out my fantasies. It began when Santa brought me an Indian suit, complete with feathered headdress, a small bow, and arrows tipped with rubber suction cups. Later I was a cowboy and strapped on a pair of pistols that fired caps. When I had to come indoors, I listened to western serials on the radio. I was a Ralston Straight Shooter, and Tom Mix personally sent me a decoder ring that turned my finger green. I rode with the Lone Ranger. I drove a twenty-mule team in Death Valley. Saturday afternoons I went to the movies—a "B" feature, a cartoon, a serial, and a *western!* I liked Hopalong Cassidy, Wild Bill Elliott, and Lash LaRue; I frowned on cowboys who sang and hung around with girls.

My love affair with the West survived puberty, and my taste in westerns improved: John Wayne in *Stagecoach;* Gary Cooper in *High Noon;* Alan Ladd in *Shane;* Clint Eastwood in *High Plains Drifter.* They, rather than Sartre, defined existentialism for me. I was not alone. My father told me that his fondest boyhood memory was of being taken by his father to see Buffalo Bill's Wild West Show. Even the urbane Edward R. Morrow owned a Colt *Peacemaker,* practiced the fast draw, and like to plink tin cans.

When I became a travel writer, I jumped at every opportunity to go to the West. I went first to the places I knew from the movies—Tombstone, Dodge City, the Alamo, Monument Valley. Later I visited the Anasazi ruins of the Four Corners, California's Mother Lode country, and the ghost towns of the Rockies. I had a grand time, but there was a hit or-miss quality to my travels, and I had trouble separating western fact from western fiction. Any western history I had studied had gone the way of the Periodic Table and irregular French verbs.

I began a fresh study of the West, and its richness, diversity, and cast of characters amazed me. More important, it put the places I had seen into a new perspective. Now I could visit the Little Big-horn and relate Custer to the Sioux campaign, the Black Hills gold rush, and the whole tragedy of the Indian Wars. The Golden Spike in Utah became more than the completion of the first transcontinental railroad. It spoke to me of the shrewdness of California's Big Four, the gangs of Chinese laborers who laid the tracks, and the role of the Iron Horse in taming the West.

I began to think my experiences might be helpful to people like me, travelers who wanted to see *and* understand the West. Some problems arose. When did the Old West end? I chose 1912, when Arizona became the last western territory to become a state. An arbitrary choice. The Old West was fading when the Golden Spike was driven, almost gone when the smoke cleared at Wounded Knee. Or I could have chosen 1917, the year Buffalo Bill died.

More difficult was deciding what to include. The Old West was a lot more than cowboys and Indians and soldiers. It also was explorers and missionaries, trappers and prospectors, lawmen and outlaws, sodbusters and railroad tycoons, buffalo hunters and gamblers, lumberjacks and layabouts. And what a melting pot it was! The Spanish and Mexicans settled the Southwest. The Chinese were miners and railroad workers. Russian emigrants introduced winter wheat to the Great Plains. Blacks were buffalo soldiers.

All of this and more found its way into this work, *The Old West Sourcebook*. As a guidebook it contains the essential information about the historic sites in the seventeen Western states, plus a lot of other places of interest: ghost towns, ranches, museums, libraries, art galleries, every place that helps illuminate the Western experience. There are fascinating things to do: panning for gold, taking short trips with Native American guides, searching for buried treasure. There are listings of places to stay, and tips on visiting pueblos and reservations.

As a sourcebook, it has a chronology of the important dates in Western history, as well as essays on a number of aspects of the West, from bonanza farms to ladies of the evening, from cowboy music to the life of a trapper. For spice there is a generous sprinkling of quotes from myriad sources, and a multitude of historic photographs.

The book explores the myth and the mythmakers. Dime novels. Wild West shows. Western movies and TV shows. Cowboy fashion. The Noble Savage. Indian captivity legends. All are here for good reason. The Old West never really died; it lives on in our imagination.

Notes for the Visitor

VISITING NATIONAL PARKS AND MONUMENTS

Much of the significant history of the Old West is preserved on properties managed by the National Park Service. Visiting these properties is a high point of a Western vacation. Most offer a wide range of services: ranger-led tours, orientation films, exhibits, living-history programs, and campfire talks. Rangers know the properties intimately, and visitors should feel free to ask questions.

It is prudent to phone ahead, particularly if you are coming from a distance. Find out what programs will be offered while you are there. Check to see if adverse weather might close the property. Make reservations if necessary.

Dress appropriately and carry proper equipment. This may include long pants, jackets or sweaters, a hat, and sturdy shoes or hiking boots. Sunscreen and a container of water are musts for desert areas in the summer. Many parks offer hiking and back-country camping and may require hikers to register and file an itinerary. Obey the restrictions on camp and cooking fires.

Few properties have food facilities, but almost all have picnic areas. Picnicking while surrounded by history is a delight.

Do not disturb a site. Everything on the site, even the stones on the ground, is part of the historical environment, a precious national resource preserved for future generations. And don't litter. The golden rule at Park Service properties is "Take only pictures, leave only footprints."

Most properties charge a small admission; if you plan to visit several properties, you will save money by obtaining one of the three types of passes offered by the Park Service. All admit the holder and the people in his or her car, or the immediate family if arriving by bus.

Golden Eagle Passport. Available for $25 to people under age sixty-two. Valid from January 1 to December 31. May be purchased at the properties that charge entrance fees or by mail from the Park Service.

Golden Age Passport. Free, lifetime pass for people age sixty-two or older. Also provides a 50 percent discount on fees for camping, boat launching, and parking. Golden Age Passports must be picked up in person at a national park or a national park service office, and require proof of age.

Golden Access Passport. Carries the same privileges as the Golden Age Passport. Available to handicapped persons who are eligible for federal benefits as a result of disability.

For further information, write the National Park Service, Washington, D.C. 20240, or telephone 202/343-4747.

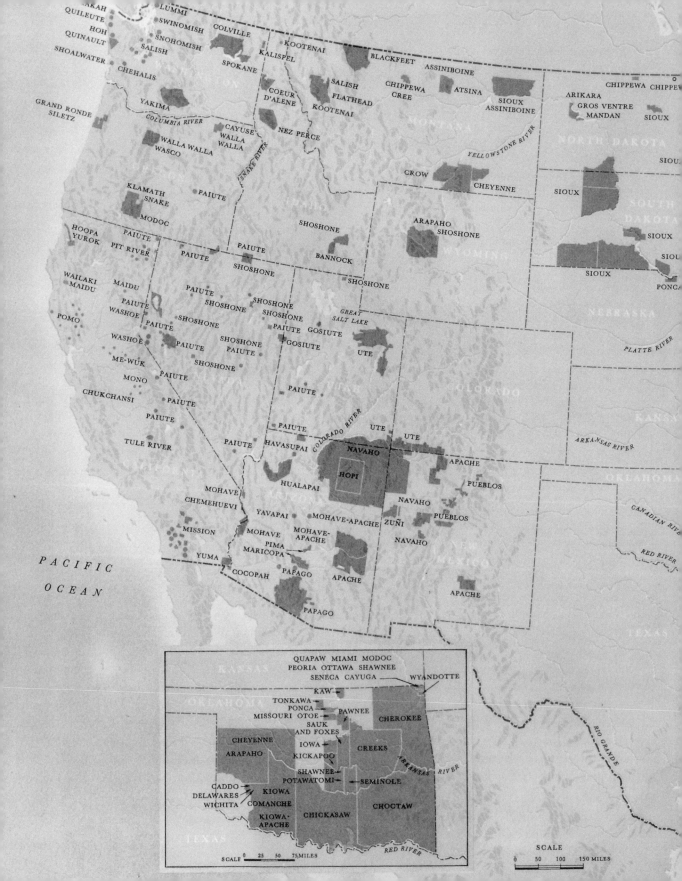

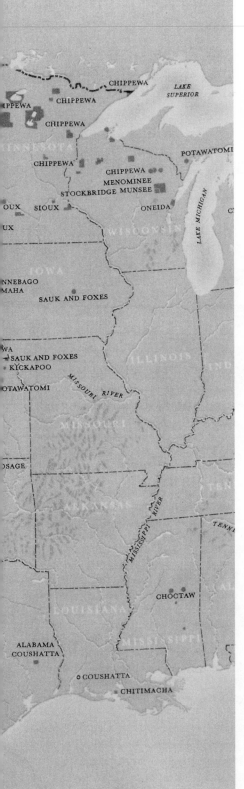

VISITING INDIAN RESERVATIONS

- Visitors to reservations are guests and should behave like guests.
- Alcohol and drugs are prohibited by tribal and federal law.
- Photographing, sketching, and recording are strictly prohibited, unless permission is granted by a tribal office. A fee may be involved. If photography is prohibited, do not carry a camera; it may be confiscated by tribal police.
- If photography is allowed, ask permission of residents before taking their picture.
- If you plan to spend the night on a reservation, obtain permission from the tribal office.
- Disturbing a site or removing artifacts is an offense punishable by both civil and tribal law.
- Observe posted speed limits. The maximum speed is fifty-five miles per hour. Watch for livestock on the roads and highways, especially at night.
- Many reservations have limited wheelchair access. Call the tribal office in advance of your trip to avoid disappointment.

VISITING GHOST TOWNS

- Some so-called ghost towns have become tourist attractions—Virginia City, Nevada; Tombstone, Arizona; Deadwood, South Dakota; Columbia, California. Others still have some people living there. They are simply mining towns that have seen better days—Georgetown, Colorado; Jerome, Arizona; Rough and Ready, California; White Oaks, New Mexico. True ghost towns are deserted, ramshackle, remote, and potentially dangerous.
- The roads to true ghost towns are invariably in poor repair. Some are closed in the winter. Others can be traveled only in four-wheel-drive vehicles. Inquire about road conditions before you set out.
- Plan your ghost town excursion. Leave sufficient time to get home before dark. Bring your own food and water.
- Be careful entering abandoned buildings. Old buildings collapse. Rotted floors give way. Snakes like abandoned buildings on hot days.
- Respect what you see. Ghost towns are legacies that belong to us all. Abandonment does not excuse destroying or looting old buildings, littering, or graffiti. Take only pictures, leave only footprints.

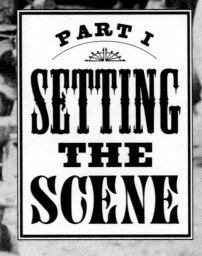

PART I

SETTING THE SCENE

A wagon train on the Santa Fe Trail in a rare 1872 photograph.

1

A Chronology of the Old West

25,000 B.C.	Aboriginal Asian peoples arrive in North America.
12–10,000 B.C.	Early man is entrenched in the Southwest.
7000 B.C.	Beginning of Desert Archaic Period.
A.D. 1–1300	Pithouse-Pueblo Period.
1300–1400	Drought forces the Anasazi to abandon their cliff dwellings.

1521	Conquest of Mexico; Cortez assumes control.
1536	After wandering through the Southwest, Cabeza de Vaca returns to Mexico with tales of cities of gold.
1539	Friar Marcos de Niza is the first white man to visit Arizona.
1540	Coronado leaves Mexico to hunt for gold in the Southwest.
	The De Soto expedition goes as far as Oklahoma.
1541	Coronado is the first white man to visit pueblos in New Mexico.
1542	Portuguese navigator Juan Rodríguez Cabrillo lands at San Diego.
1548	Captain James Cook, seeking the Northwest Passage, charts part of the Oregon coastline.

1579	Francis Drake claims California for Britain.
1598	Juan de Onate establishes San Gabriel in New Mexico.
1610	Don Pedro de Peralta founds Santa Fe.
1680	The Pueblo Revolt occurs.
1602	Sebastián Viscaíno explores the California coast.
1682	The Spanish establish the first permanent settlement in Texas at Ysleta, near present-day El Paso.
1685	A short-lived French colony is founded at Matagorda Bay, Texas.
1692–94	Diego de Vargas reconquers New Mexico.
1706	Juan de Ulibarri claims Colorado for Spain.
1743	Louis-Joseph and François Vérendrye explore South Dakota, seeking a water route to the Pacific.
1769	The Spanish build Mission Basilica San Diego de Alcalá, the first California mission.
1775	The American Revolution begins.
	The Spanish ship *San Carlos* is the first to sail through the Golden Gate.
1776	Fort Tucson is established in Arizona.
	Franciscan friars Escalante and Dominguez explore Utah.
	The Presidio is established in San Francisco.

A gold strike in the 1870s in Deadwood Gulch, South Dakota, attracted people such as Wild Bill Hickok and Calamity Jane. Soon 25,000 people were digging in the hillsides.

1781	Los Angeles is founded.
1783	Britain recognizes American independence.
1792–04	Captain George Vancouver explores the coast of Washington.
1803	The Louisiana Purchase adds to the United States French territory from the Gulf of Mexico to the Northwest. The Lewis and Clark expedition begins its exploration of the West.
1805	Lewis and Clark explore Oregon and Washington.
1807	Fur trapper John Colter explores the Yellowstone area in Wyoming.
1808	John Jacob Astor organizes the American Fur Company.
1810	Mexico revolts against Spanish rule.
1811	John Jacob Astor establishes a trading post at Astoria, Oregon.
1812	The Russians build Fort Ross, fifty miles north of San Francisco.
	A Scottish party makes the first permanent settlement in North Dakota, at Pembina.
1817	Fort Pierre is established as the first permanent settlement in South Dakota.
1818	The United States obtains the northeast part of North Dakota in a treaty with Britain.
1821	Led by Stephen Austin, the first Americans settle in Texas.
1822	Mountain man James Bridger makes the first expedition into the Rockies.
1823	Mexico becomes a republic.
	The first permanent settlement in Nebraska is established at Bellevue.
1824	James Bridger discovers the Great Salt Lake.
	Congress creates the Bureau of Indian Affairs.
1827	Fort Leavenworth is established in Kansas to protect travelers on the Santa Fe and Oregon trails.
1830	The Indian Removal Act is passed.
	George Catlin becomes the first important artist to paint the American Indians.
1831	The First Missouri steamboat reaches Pierre, South Dakota.
1833	Bent's Old Fort is built in New Mexico.
1834	The Indian Territory is created in present-day Oklahoma.

	Fort Laramie becomes the first trading post in Wyoming.
1835	The Texas Revolution begins.
1836	The Alamo falls to Mexican forces, and all its defenders are slain.
	Texans under Sam Houston defeat the Mexican army and capture General Santa Anna at the battle of San Jacinto.
	Texas becomes a republic.
1838	Cherokees begin the Trail of Tears, a 1,200-mile forced march from the East to present-day Oklahoma.
1843	John C. Frémont begins his exploration of the West.
	The California Trail opens.
1845	DECEMBER 29: Texas is admitted to the Union.
1846	The Mexican War begins.
	The Black Bear Revolt begins in California.
	The American flag is raised at Monterey, California.
	The United States, in a treaty with Britain, obtains the Oregon Territory, south of the 49th parallel.
	The first permanent settlement in Idaho is established by Mormons.
	The Donner Party is trapped in the Sierra Nevada when winter descends.
1847	JULY 24: Brigham Young and the Mormons arrive at the Great Salt Lake.
	Samuel Colt, with Texas Ranger Captain Sam Walker, develops the revolver.
1848	JANUARY 24: John Marshall discovers gold at Sutter's Mill.
	The Treaty of Guadalupe Hidalgo ends the Mexican War; the United States gets more than one-half million square miles, including what will become the states of California, Nevada, Utah, most of New Mexico and Arizona, and parts of Wyoming and Colorado. Texas is also ceded to the United States.
	A Mormon trading post at Genoa is the first permanent settlement in Nevada.
	AUGUST 14: Oregon is organized as a territory.
1848	The State of Deseret, incorporated by the

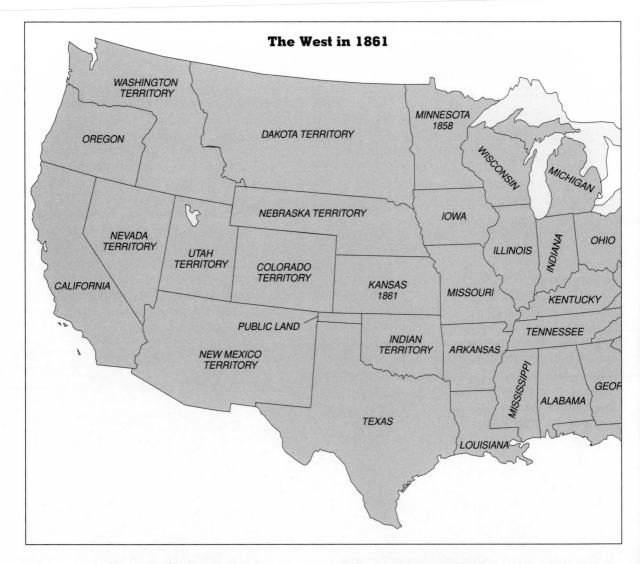

The West in 1861

Mormons, includes Utah, most of Nevada and Arizona, and parts of Oregon, Idaho, Wyoming, Colorado, New Mexico, and California.

1850 SEPTEMBER 9: California is admitted to the Union; New Mexico and Utah are organized as territories.

1853 MARCH 2: Washington is organized as a territory. The Gadsden Purchase from Mexico adds territory to Arizona and New Mexico.

1854 MAY 30: Nebraska and Kansas are organized as territories.

1858 Abolitionist John Brown leads a massacre of proslavery adherents at Pottawatomie Creek in Kansas.

Gold is discovered in Colorado.

1859 FEBRUARY 14: Oregon is admitted to the Union.

AUGUST 9–10: The Battle of the Big Hole occurs in Montana.

The Pike's Peak gold rush begins in Colorado.

The Comstock Lode is discovered in Nevada.

Painter Albert Bierstadt makes his first trip to the West.

1861   FEBRUARY 28: Colorado is organized as a territory.

APRIL 12: The South fires on Fort Sumter, and the Civil War begins.

APRIL 30: Federal troops evacuate Indian Territory troops.

Nevada is organized as a territory.

MARCH 2: South Dakota is organized as a territory.

1860   Gold is discovered in Idaho.

1861   JANUARY 29: Kansas is admitted to the Union.

MARCH 2: North Dakota and Nevada are organized as territories.

Denver is incorporated as a city.

1862   Gold is discovered in Montana.

Congress passes the Homestead Act.

1863   FEBRUARY 24: Arizona is organized as a territory.

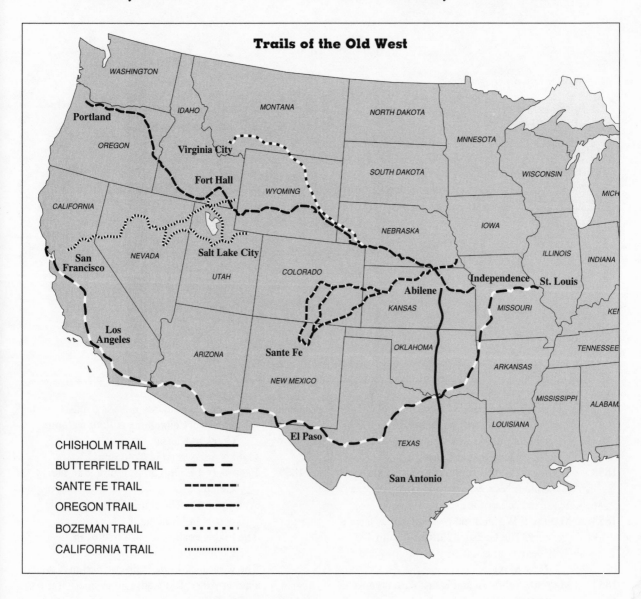

Trails of the Old West

CHISHOLM TRAIL

BUTTERFIELD TRAIL

SANTE FE TRAIL

OREGON TRAIL

BOZEMAN TRAIL

CALIFORNIA TRAIL

MARCH 3: Idaho is organized as a territory.

The Bozeman Trail opens from Colorado to the Nevada gold fields.

Charles Crocker, Mark Hopkins, Leland Stanford, and Collis Huntington invest in the proposed Central Pacific Railroad, an investment that will make them California's Big Four.

1864 MAY 26: Montana is organized as a territory.

OCTOBER 31: Nevada is admitted to the Union.

Colorado cavalry volunteers slay 133 Cheyennes and Arapahos at Sand Creek.

Kit Carson accepts the surrender of 8,000 Navajos.

1865 APRIL 9: Lee surrenders at Appomattox, effectively ending the Civil War.

The Union Pacific begins building a transcontinental railroad at Omaha.

1866 Indians massacre William J. Fetterman and eighty troops near Fort Kearney, Wyoming.

1867 MARCH 1: Nebraska is admitted to the Union.

1868 The Sioux sign a treaty with the United States at Fort Laramie, Wyoming.

1869 MAY 10: The Central Pacific and Union Pacific join at Promontory Point, Utah, creating the first transcontinental railroad.

MAY 19: Utah and Wyoming are organized as territories; Wyoming gives women the right to vote.

1871 APRIL 30: More than 100 Apaches are killed in the Camp Grant Massacre in Arizona.

1872 Apache chief Cochise surrenders to General O. O. Howard and is sent to a reservation.

Yellowstone becomes the first U.S. national park.

1873 The railroad arrives in South Dakota.

1874 Gold is discovered in the Black Hills of South Dakota.

1876 JUNE 25: Custer and his troops are slain at the Little Bighorn.

AUGUST 1: Colorado is admitted to the Union.

1877 The United States violates its treaty with Dakota Sioux by seizing the Black Hills.

Chief Joseph of the Nez Percé surrenders after the Bear Paw battle in Montana.

Crazy Horse is captured, then assassinated while in custody at Fort Robinson, Nebraska.

1878 Billy the Kid makes a name for himself as a killer in the Lincoln County War.

Wild Bill Hickok is shot to death in Deadwood, South Dakota.

1880 The Atchison, Topeka & Santa Fe Railroad reaches Santa Fe.

1881 JULY 14: Sheriff Pat Garrett shoots and kills Billy the Kid.

OCTOBER 26: Gunfight at the O.K. Corral.

Sitting Bull surrenders.

1882 Jesse James is killed by Bob Ford in St. Joseph, Missouri.

Stagecoach bandit Black Bart is captured in California.

Adolph Bandelier begins his exploration of Anasazi ruins in New Mexico.

Judge Roy Bean opens the Jersey Lily saloon in Langtry, Texas.

Free Chinese immigration ends.

1883 Theodore Roosevelt arrives in North Dakota to hunt buffalo, and buys a ranch.

Swiss artist Karl Bodmer tours the West.

Willa Cather and family move to Red Cloud, Nebraska.

The first Buffalo Bill Wild West Show is staged.

1886 Butch Cassidy robs his first bank, in Telluride, Colorado.

Geronimo surrenders to General George Crook.

1887 Silver is discovered in Leadville, Colorado.

1889 APRIL 22: Fifty thousand homesteaders swarm into Oklahoma on the first day of the land rush.

NOVEMBER 2: North and South Dakota are admitted to the Union.

NOVEMBER 8: Montana is admitted to the Union.

NOVEMBER 11: Washington State is admitted to the Union.

1890   MAY 2: Oklahoma is organized as a territory; part remains as the Indian Territory.
JULY 3: Idaho is admitted to the Union.
JULY 10: Wyoming is admitted to the Union.
DECEMBER 29: The massacre at Wounded Knee, South Dakota, ends the Indian Wars.

1892   The Dalton Gang raids Coffeyville, Kansas.

1896   JANUARY 4: Utah is admitted to the Union.

1906   APRIL 18: San Francisco earthquake and fire.

1907   NOVEMBER 16: Oklahoma is admitted to the Union.

1912   JANUARY 6: New Mexico is admitted to the Union.
FEBRUARY 14: Arizona is admitted to the Union.

2

Where the Western States Got Their Names

Arizona. From the Papago *Arizonac,* "place of the small spring." Also called the Grand Canyon State.

California. From the name for "earthly paradise" in Spanish lore. Previously called Alta California, as opposed to Baja California. Also called the Golden State.

Colorado. From the Spanish word for the color red, literally "red land, red earth." Previously the Colorado Territory; also called the Centennial State because it was admitted to the Union in 1876.

Idaho. From a Shoshone term meaning "light on the mountain." Also called the Gem State.

Kansas. From the Sioux word for "land of the south wind people," via the French *Kansas* and the Spanish *Escansque.* Previously the Kansas Territory; also called the Sunflower State.

Montana. From the Spanish for "mountainous." Previously the Montana Territory; also called the Treasure State.

Nebraska. From the Omaha *ni-bthaska,* meaning "river in the flatness," referring to the Platte River. Previously the Nebraska Territory; also called the Cornhusker State.

Nevada. From the Spanish for "snowy," or "snowed upon." Previously part of Washoe Territory; also called the Sagebrush State, the Silver State.

New Mexico. Named by Spanish explorers from Mexico in 1562. Previously Nuevo Mexico and the New Mexico Territory; also called the Land of Enchantment.

North Dakota. From the Sioux name for themselves, *Lakota,* meaning "friend," or "ally." Previously part of the Dakota Territory; also called the Flickertail State, the Sioux State.

Oklahoma. From the Choctaw word for "red people." Previously the Indian Territory; also called the Sooner State.

Oregon. From an Indian word for the Columbia River (in Algonquian, *Wauregan* is "beautiful water"). Also called the Beaver State.

South Dakota. See North Dakota, above. Previously part of the Dakota Territory; also called the Coyote State, the Sunshine State.

Texas. Via Spanish *tejas,* "allies," from a local Indian word, *texia,* for "friend" or "ally," applied to the numerous tribes allied against the Apache. Previously the Republic of Texas; also called the Lone Star State.

Utah. From the Navajo for "higher up" or "the upper land," but probably meant "land of the Ute." Previously the Utah Territory; also called the Beehive State, from the Mormon symbol of communal cooperation.

Washington. Named for George Washington. Previously the Washington Territory; also called the Evergreen State.

Wyoming. From the Algonquian *mache-weaming,* "at the big flats." Also called the Equality State.

PART II
THE NORTHERN GREAT PLAINS

Explorers called the vast, treeless plain stretching to the Rockies the Great American Desert, and wrote it off as unfit for white settlement. However, settlement began after the Civil War, spurred by the Homestead Act, the coming of the railroad, and land promoters. But not until the turn of the century would the Great Plains blossom like the rose with the introduction of dry-farming techniques, farm machinery, and hardy new crops such as winter wheat.

Badlands National Park, South Dakota.

Great Plains

0   150 miles
0   225 km

CANADA

MONTANA

Kenmare
Bottineau
5
Williston
Devils
Lake
New
Town   FORT
BERTHOLD   Minot
INDIAN
RES.   Garrison
Lake
Sakakawea   NORTH
DAKOTA
23
52
2
Grand
Forks
29
200
Medora
85   83   94   Fargo
Mandan ★ Bismarck   Jamestown
21   Wahpeton
13
281

STANDING ROCK
INDIAN RES.   SISSETON
INDIAN
85   RES.   Sisseton
CHEYENNE   Mobridge
RIVER   Aberdeen
INDIAN RES.   83
212   Watertown
Belle
Fourche   Lake   SOUTH   Redfield
Oahe   DAKOTA
Spearfish   281
Sturgis   Brookings
Deadwood   34   Madison
Lead   Rapid City   Pierre ★   Huron
BLACK HILLS   29
NAT'L. FOR.   Hill City Wall   Chamberlain
Keystone   90   Sioux
BADLANDS   Missouri River Mitchell Falls
Custer   NAT'L. PARK
PINE RIDGE   ROSEBUD   18
WYOMING   INDIAN RES. INDIAN 18 Winner   Sheldo
Pine   RES. Mission
Ridge   20   Yankton
Chadron   Vermillion
MINNESOTA
81   Sioux
City
29
NEBRASKA
71
Bridgeport
61   2
91   Fremont
Lake   80
McConaughy   North Platte   Omaha
80   Lincoln   Co
Ogallala   Kearney Grand   Bl
25   Island   Nebraska
76   6   Missi

3

North Dakota

BISMARCK

On the east bank of the Missouri River, this area was visited by Lewis and Clark in 1804. A settlement grew up here known as "The Crossing," doing a brisk business as a steamboat port. It grew rapidly after it became the eastern terminus of the Northern Pacific Railway. To help attract German investment in the transcontinental railroad, Bismarck was named for the chancellor of Germany. George Armstrong Custer came to take command of nearby Fort Abraham Lincoln, and in 1876 rode out from the fort to his fate at the Little Bighorn. The capital of the Dakota Territory, Bismarck became the capital of the new state in 1876.

Capitol (North 6th St.; 701/224-2480). Completed in 1934, this building, called the "Skyscraper of the Prairies," is eighteen stories tall, topped with an observation tower. Tours. Nearby is the famous statue "The Pioneer Family" by Avard Fairbanks. Open daily.

North Dakota State Museum (Capitol grounds in North Dakota Heritage Center; 701/224-2666). Has exhibits on the military occupation of the Northern Plains, and Native American and white uses of the buffalo. Open daily.

Camp Hancock Historic Site (Main and 1st streets; 701/224-2666). The fort was established in 1872 to protect Northern Pacific work gangs from the Indians. On site are the headquarters building, a vintage locomotive, and one of the city's oldest churches, moved here and restored. Open Wednesday through Sunday, mid-May to mid-September.

Double Ditch Indian Village State Historic Site (10 miles northwest via ND 1894; 701/224-2669). Contains the ruins of a large Mandan earth-lodge village that stood

here from 1675 to 1780, surrounding fortifications and refuse mounds. Open daily.

Riverboat Excursions (I-94, exit 235, on river; 701/223-3315). The steamboat *Far West* makes scenic trips on the Missouri. Open daily, Memorial Day to Labor Day.

BOTTINEAU

International Peace Garden (18 miles east on ND 5 to Dunseith, then 13 miles north on U.S. 281/ND 3; 701/263-4390, or 204/534-2510 in Canada). Astride the border, these formal gardens commemorate the lasting friendship between the United States and Canada. Peace chapel, bell tower, pavilion, Masonic Auditorium, Peace Tower. Open daily, weather permitting.

Monument to the Four Chaplains (downtown). Honors the chaplains (two Protestant, one Catholic, and one Jewish) who gave their life jackets to servicemen who had none when the transport *Dorchester* was torpedoed off Greenland in 1943.

DEVILS LAKE

This town started to grow when a Federal Land Office opened here in 1883.

Fort Totten State Historic Site (13 miles southwest on ND 57; 701/766-4411). Built in 1867 to protect travelers bound for Montana, the last fort before 300 wilderness miles, Fort Totten, with sixteen original buildings, is one of the best-preserved outposts of the Indian Wars. The *Pioneers' Daughters Museum* has vintage clothing

Mr. Wells and Mr. Fargo

Henry Wells worked at odd jobs until he got the bright idea of competing with the post office. He carried letters between Albany and Buffalo, New York, for six cents when the post office was charging two to four times as much. In 1844, Wells and William G. Fargo formed Wells & Company, the first freight company to operate west of Buffalo. Eight years later he set up Wells, Fargo & Company to enter the express and banking business in California, and soon had a virtual monopoly. The company expanded throughout the West and ultimately to the East Coast. Fargo, a grocery clerk before he went into the freight business, ran the field operation while Wells ran the business. Fargo was president of the company in the 1870s. The company's outfitting headquarters on the Great Plains grew up to be Fargo, North Dakota. Ironically, Wells, whose name is synonymous with the West, never lived west of Buffalo.

"They were a rugged set of men, these pioneers, well qualified for their self-assumed task. In the pursuit of wealth a few succeeded and the majority failed, as in all other spheres of activity ... the range cattle industry has seen its inception, zenith, and partial extinction all within a half-century."

—Conrad Kohrs, 1913

and artifacts. Interpretive center has a videotape on the fort's history and commissary display. The *Fort Totten Little Theatre* performs musicals Thursday, Saturday, and Sunday from early July to early August. Grounds open daily; museum open daily, Memorial Day to Labor Day.

FARGO

Named for native son William G. Fargo of the Wells-Fargo express service company, the state's largest city is now the commercial center of the rich Red River Valley. Fargo is also the hometown of Roger Maris, baseball's home-run champion, and a museum filled with personal memorabilia is in the West Acres Mall.

Bonanzaville, USA (4½ miles west of I-29 on Main Ave. or I-94, exit 85; 701/282-2822). Has more than forty-five buildings reconstructing the nineteenth-century farm era in the state. Hemp Antique Vehicle Museum. Plains Indians Museum. Train depot, 1884 locomotive, model railroad. Pioneer farm homes, church, general store, school, log cabins, sod house. Open daily, late May to late October; museums open Tuesday through Thursday the rest of the year.

GARRISON

Garrison came into being when the Army Corps of Engineers built the $300-million Garrison Dam on the Missouri, one of the largest rolled earth-fill dams in the world. A highway, ND 200, goes across the two-mile dam, which rises 210 feet above the river. Behind the dam, Lake Sakakawea stretches for 178 miles.

Knife River Indian Villages National Historic Site (16 miles south via ND 200, 701/745-3300). The visible remnants of Mandan, Hidatsa, and Arikara earth-lodge villages are an archaeological treasure of the Plains Indians. Among the early visitors to this area were Lewis and Clark, George Catlin, Karl Bodmer, Prince Maximilian, and John James Audubon. Summer programs include museum exhibits, slide shows, tours, Indian art and culture programs, guest speakers. Open daily.

GRAND FORKS

Originally a French fur-trading post where the Red River of the North meets the Red Lake River to form a fork, Grand Forks grew up as a frontier river town. When the railroad arrived, it began to develop as a modern city.

Campbell House (2405 Belmont Rd.; 701/775-2216). This was the 1879 log-cabin home of Tom Campbell, an agricultural innovator. Also on site are an 1870 log post office, a one-room schoolhouse, and the Myra carriage house, which has a collection of pioneer artifacts from the area. Open daily, May through October.

River Cruises (depart from 67 South Riverboat Rd.; 701/775-5656). The steamboat *Dakota Queen* gives afternoon and evening dinner cruises on the Red River. Sights include Alligator Alley, Boot Hill, and an Indian village. Open daily except Mondays, Memorial Day to Labor Day.

JAMESTOWN

After the soldiers and rail workers left, Jamestown became a transportation center under the watchful eye of Fort Seward. The town is on the James River, one of the longest nonnavigable rivers in the world.

Frontier Village (on I-94 at the southeast edge of town; 701/252-6307). A restored log cabin, school, church, railroad depot, land office, and jail. Large statue of bison. Theater is presented in the summer. Open daily in the summer

Whitestone Hill Battlefield State Historic Site (37 miles south on US 281, then 15 miles west on ND 13 to Kulm, then 15 miles south on ND 56, then east on unimproved road; 701/396-7731). This was the scene of one of the most significant battles between the U.S. Army and the Indians, a battle that marked the beginning of the twenty-year war with the Sioux. Following the 1862 Indian revolt in Minnesota, Gen. Alfred Sully moved to attack the Sioux in this area. After surrounding Sully's advance guard, 4,000 warriors under Chief Inkpaduta paused to apply warpaint. Sully used the time to bring up his main body of troops. Some 300 braves died in the battle, and the troops captured 250 women and children. Army casualties were twenty-two dead, fifty wounded.

The terrain here, rolling hills covered with prairie grass, is little changed today. Around a monument in the center of the battlefield are the grave markers of the twenty-two soldiers killed in the battle. Small museum with Indian artifacts and historical data. Open

This log cabin is one of forty-five reconstructed buildings at Bonanzaville, USA in Fargo, North Dakota. Other attractions include antique vehicles, an operating farmstead, a train depot with a vintage steam locomotive, and a museum of the Plains Indians.

Thursday through Monday, mid-May to mid-September. Limited wheelchair access.

Fort Seward Wagon Train. A week-long trip in late June, in wagons pulled by draft horses or mules, stopping at historic sites along the way. Everyone dresses and camps in the manner of the pioneers. For information, write Registrar, Box 244, Jamestown, ND 58401.

◆━I━◆

"If we make peace, you will not hold it."

—GALL, HUNKPAPA

Bonanza Farms

The Northern Pacific Railroad, its bonds practically worthless after the Panic of 1873, used land to pay off some of its stockholders. Two of them pooled their land to form a 12,000-acre farm near Fargo, North Dakota, in 1875, the first of the "bonanza farms." Soon there were about 300 of them in the Red River Valley, some as large as 65,000 acres. Bonanza farms made sense wherever there was flat land and rich soil that could be worked by modern machinery, and they spread to Oregon, Washington, Idaho, and California. They were geared to a single crop, usually wheat, and when other crops were introduced, they were gradually broken up. By 1915, nearly all were gone.

"The West did not provide what they needed. Make-believe fandangos, transvestite laundresses, hydrophobic wolves, ant-fights, crazed foreigners, pretty sunsets—this was not enough. The West was not dull, it was stupendously dull, and when it was not dull it was murderous. A man could get killed without realizing it. There were unbelievable flash floods, weird snakes, and God Himself did not know what else, along with Indians descending as swiftly as the funnel of a tornado."

—EVAN S. CONNELL,
　Son of the
　Morning Star

⊷Ⲓ⊶

Sent to North Dakota for his health, Theodore Roosevelt fell in love with the West. The future president wrote a book on his Western experiences, Ranch Life and the Hunting Trail, *which was illustrated by the artist Frederic Remington.*

KENMARE

Old Danish Mill (Central Ave. and South 2nd St. in city park; 701/385-4411). Built in 1902 and restored, the grain mill has hand-hewn wooden gears and millstones that weigh nearly a ton. Open daily.

Lake County Historical Society Pioneer Village (northeast on US 52; 701/385-4368). Includes a home, windmill, school, church, post office, barber and dress shop, mill, and meat market. Museum has regional pioneer artifacts. Open daily, June through September.

MANDAN

Named for the Mandan Indians who farmed here, this city once was an important railroad center, and now serves the surrounding farming and mining area.

Fort Abraham Lincoln State Park (4 miles south on ND 1806; 701/663-9571). Miners pouring into the Black Hills gold fields had inflamed the Sioux, and Lt. Col.

George Custer, in command of the fort and the Seventh Cavalry, set out from here with Gen. Alfred H. Terry's column in 1876 on their ill-fated expedition to the Little Bighorn. After the massacre, Terry and his troopers returned here on the steamer *Far West.* During 1877, soldiers from the fort participated in the Montana campaign against the Nez Percé. By the end of the 1880s, the railroad had been completed, most of the Indians had been confined to reservations, and the area was becoming heavily settled. The army abandoned the fort in 1891.

Some of the fort's buildings and an early Indian earth-lodge village have been restored. A museum explains the fort's history. Interpretive program in the summer. Open daily.

MEDORA

California Joe, a white guide with an 1875 expedition, said of this area, "There's gold from the grass roots down, but there's more

gold from the grass roots up. No matter how rich the gold placers in the Black Hills may prove to be, the great business in this region in the future will be stockraising."

In 1883, two colorful men came here to the center of one of the last great natural pastures to be opened to cattlemen: Theodore Roosevelt and the legendary Marquis de Mores. The future President, aged twenty-five, came to hunt buffalo and soon owned two ranches. Later he organized and served as first president of the Little Missouri Stockmen's Association. The disastrous winter of 1886–87 wiped out most of his herd, but he later wrote, "I never would have been President if it had not been for my experience in North Dakota." His ranches, sold in 1897, are now part of the nearby Theodore Roosevelt National Park. Antoine de Vallombrosa, the Marquis de Mores, a visionary wealthy Frenchman, established the town and named it for his wife, the daughter of a New York City banker. The marquis had a number of interests: a stage-coach line, a beef-packing plant, and a plan to ship beef to Eastern markets in refrigerated railroad cars. The current population of Medora is about one hundred.

Theodore Roosevelt National Park (701/623-4466). Gen. Alfred Sully, campaigning against the Sioux here in 1864, said it was "hell with the fires out . . . grand, dismal and majestic." The description still fits the 70,374 acres of spectacular badlands in the park, the state's foremost tourist attraction. Roosevelt came to the badlands in 1883 and purchased the Maltese Cross Ranch near Medora, returning the next year to establish another ranch, the Elkhorn, about thirty-five miles to the north.

The park preserves the land as Roosevelt knew it. Eons of wind and water have carved out odd rock formations, buttes and tablelands, canyons and rugged hills. Many forms of wildlife are here. Elk and a small herd of buffalo have been reintroduced in the park, which is divided into three units. *South Unit*

Laugh Kills Lonesome

Much of life in the Old West was unending toil, sheer boredom, and nagging doubts about the future. Anything that brought temporary relief was welcome, particularly if it involved competition. Bull-and-bear fights were popular in California. They reminded Horace Greeley, a visiting New York editor, of the scrappy traders on Wall Street. Dogfighting was transferred from England to the West, complete with pits, handlers, and elaborate rules. Cockfighting and impromptu horse races were common. All attracted bettors. When men got together there was usually a marksmanship contest. Tall tales were told, and elaborate practical jokes were played. Artist Charles M. Russell summed it up: "Laugh kills lonesome."

Many sports were simply hard work in disguise. Farmers held plowing and team-pulling contests. Farm families held "bees"—haying bees, threshing bees, flax-scutching bees, husking bees; there were quilting bees for the women; and spelling bees for the children. There were house-raisings and barn-raisings, always climaxed by a party with food, whiskey, and dancing. Logging camp entertainment included sawing, chopping, and birling contests. Miners showed off their skills with rock drilling and single- and double-jacking, driving a steel drill into solid rock with an eight-pound hammer. Heavy snows in the California mining camps made a sport (and a necessity) of "snow skates," as the primitive ten-foot skis were called.

With the coming of towns, political rallies and religious camp meetings became forms of entertainment. Every town had its champion foot racer, wrestler, and rough-and-tumble fighter. On the Great Plains, community rabbit drives were popular events. Many early sports faded with the frontier. The notable exception, the one truly Western sport, is the rodeo, a celebration of the brief heyday of the cowboy.

is accessible from I-94 at Medora, where there is a visitor center open daily, and Roosevelt's Maltese Cross cabin. *Elkhorn Ranch Site,* on the Little Missouri River, is reached by unimproved roads. *North Unit* is accessible from U.S. 85 near Watford City. Another visitor center is at the Painted Canyon Scenic Overlook on I-94, open daily

"We took away their country and their means of support, broke up their mode of living, their habits of life, introduced disease and decay among them, and it was for this and against this that they made war. Could anyone expect less?"

—GENERAL PHILIP
SHERIDAN, 1878

from May through September. Evening campfire programs from June to mid-September in both North and South units. Park open daily.

Chateau de Mores State Historic Site (1 mile west, off U.S. 10, I-94; 701/623-4355). A twenty-six-room, two-story farm mansion filled with French antiques. Library, servants' quarters, and relic room with de Mores's guns, books, saddles, clothing, and other possessions. Interpretive center. Tours in summer. Open daily.

Several historic buildings are nearby: *St. Mary's Catholic Church* was built in 1884 by the Marquis; *Joe Ferris Store,* built in 1885 by Roosevelt's partner, has been restored. Open daily in the summer.

Accommodations: *Rough Riders Hotel* (two blocks north of I-94 business; 701/623-4422). Built in 1884, the hotel has been restored and welcomes guests. Teddy

Roosevelt's unit in the Spanish-American War was named after this hotel.

MINOT

Once the big business here was buffalo hunting, and "plainscombers" stacked buffalo bones where this modern city now stands. There are coal and oil fields and ranches and farms nearby. Minot is the shopping center for a large area that extends into Canada.

Ward County Historical Society and Museum (state fairgrounds; 701/839-0785). Memorabilia from the area are displayed here. The village has the first county courthouse, a schoolhouse, a pioneer home, a church, a dental parlor, and a barbershop. Open daily, May through October.

NEW TOWN

Fort Berthold Indian Reservation (six miles west on ND 23, just after the Lake Sakakawea Bridge; tribal office, 701/627-4781). The home of the three affiliated Plains tribes—Arikara, Hidatsa, and Mandan—which had highly developed farming cultures on the Upper Missouri. Their heritage is presented here through a gift by Helen Gough, an Arikara, who left her oil money for a museum and college scholarships. *Three Affiliated Tribes Museum* (701/627-4477) has buckskin clothing, Indian farming tools, traditional foods, and paintings. An arts and crafts shop offers moccasins, beadwork, star quilts, shawls, princess powwow crowns, and men's staffs, all made on the reservation. Museum and shop open daily in the summer, weekends the rest of the year.

WAHPETON

Wahpeton is the Sioux word for "village of the leaves," and the trees grow thickly here,

Indian children wear full regalia at a tribal festival. Despite their acres of reservation land, the future is dim. Reservation life is hard. Family income is barely above poverty level, health standards are low, and educational opportunities are few.

where the Bois de Sioux and Otter Tail rivers converge to become the Red River of the North.

Fort Abercrombie State Historic Site (20 miles north, then east in Abercrombie; 701/224-2666). Built on the west bank of the Red River in 1857, this was the first federal post in what is now North Dakota, named for its builder, Lt. Col. John J. Abercrombie. The fort regulated the fur trade and became the logical gateway to the unexplored plains of the Northwest. In the Sioux uprising of 1862, some 2,000 white settlers were killed and more than 300 women and children taken captive. Fort Abercrombie was under siege until reinforcements arrived from Fort Snelling. In 1870 the fort was the scene of the treaty between the Chippewa and the Sioux that ended the conflict in eastern Dakota Territory. Settlers in covered wagons were soon rolling westward, and the fort was abandoned in 1877.

The fort has been rebuilt with blockhouses, stockade, and a guardhouse. A museum interprets the fort's history and has military artifacts and possessions of the early settlers. Open daily, mid-May to mid-September.

Richland County Historical Museum (2nd St. and 7th Ave. North; 701/642-3075). Displays of pioneer artifacts. Open weekends, April to May and October to November, also Fridays during the summer.

WILLISTON

Fort Union Trading Post National Historic Site (7 miles west on U.S. 2, then southwest on ND 1804W; 701/572-9083). Established in 1828 by the American Fur Company on the north bank of the Missouri, about three miles above the mouth of the Yellowstone, it was Fort Floyd until it was renamed in 1830. A formidable structure, the fort was one of the most important fur-trading centers and

a rendezvous for travelers. The first steamboats arrived in 1831, bringing, among other things, smallpox. The resulting plague lasted for six years and ravaged Indian tribes for hundreds of miles around. John James Audubon visited here in 1843 and wrote a detailed description of the 200-foot-square structure. When Gen. Alfred Sully moved a company of infantry into the fort in 1864, it was "an old dilapidated affair, almost falling to pieces." In 1867 the government bought the fort, dismantled it, and used the material to build Fort Buford, two miles away. Today much of the fort has been reconstructed. There is a visitor center in the Bugeois House. Tours and interpretive programs in the summer. Open daily.

Fort Buford State Historic Site (7 miles west on U.S. 2/85, then seventeen miles southwest on ND 1804; 701/224-2666). Fort Buford served primarily as the distribution center for government supplies and payments to peaceful Indians in the area. During the war with the Sioux, the fort became a major supply depot for military field operations, but it is best remembered as the site of the surrender of Sitting Bull in 1881. Among the original features existing on the site are a stone powder magazine, the cemetery, and the officers' quarters, which houses a museum. Open daily, mid-May through mid-September.

Buffalo Trails Museum (9 miles north on U.S. 2, then 13 miles east on County Rd. 8 in Epping; 701/859-4361). A complex of seven buildings. Dioramas of Indian and pioneer life, interior of a homesteader's shack. Historical artifacts. Open daily, June through August; Sundays in September and October.

Lewis and Clark Trail Museum (19 miles south on U.S. 85 in Alexandria; 701/828-3595). A diorama of Fort Mandan; furnished pioneer rooms, post office, country store, blacksmith shops, and farm machinery. Open daily, Memorial Day to Labor Day.

"Dun-colored sandhills crowded upon each other far into the horizon, wind singing in the red bunch grass or howling over the snow-whipped knobs of December, and the heat of July dancing over the hard land west of the hills. No Indian wars, few gun fights with bad men or wild animals—mostly it was just standing off the cold and scratching for grub. And lonesome! Dog owls, a few nesters in dugouts or soddies, dusty cow waddies loping over the hills, and time dragging at the heels—every day Monday."

—JULES SANDOZ, *Old Jules*

4

South Dakota

ABERDEEN

Two writers grew up in Aberdeen: L. Frank Baum, author of *The Wonderful Wizard of Oz,* and Hamlin Garland, author of *Son of the Middle Border.*

Dascotah Prairie Museum (21 South Main St.; 605/622-7117). Period rooms and pioneer and Indian artifacts. Open Tuesday through Saturday.

BELLE FOURCHE

Steers pass through here on their way to market, and the town has a real western flavor. In the early days, cattle ranchers and sheepherders fought a range war.

Johnny Spaulding Cabin (801 State St., opposite the post office). A two-story 1876 cabin, which now houses a tourist information office. Open daily except Sundays, June through August.

Tri-State Museum (831 State St.; 605/892-3705 or 892-3654). Regional historical exhibits and collections of fossils and animal heads. Open daily, mid-May to mid-September.

BROOKINGS

Agricultural Heritage Museum (Medary Ave. and 11th St.; 605/688-6226). Traces the development of farming in the state with changing exhibits. Open daily.

South Dakota Art Museum (Medary Ave. at Harvey Dunn St.; 605/688-5423). Important collections, including paintings of pioneers by Harvey Dunn and Indian art. Open daily.

Accommodations: *Spindel Bottom Farm* (Rte. 4, just off and parallel to I-29 south of town; 605/693-4375). A bed-and-breakfast on a little farm with sheep and horses near the Big Sioux River.

CHAMBERLAIN

Old West Museum (3 miles west via I-90, exit 260; 605/734-6157). An old-time Main Street and collections of pioneer and Indian artifacts, guns, antique automobiles. Buffalo and longhorn cattle. Open daily, May through October.

CUSTER

A member of Col. George A. Custer's 1874 expedition discovered gold, the gold rush of 1875-76 brought prospectors flocking to the area, and the prospectors touched off an Indian uprising.

Crazy Horse Memorial (5 miles north of Custer off U.S. 16, SD 385; 605/673-4681, museum: 673-2828). Crazy Horse, the Sioux chief who destroyed Custer and the Seventh Cavalry at the Little Bighorn, is to be remembered by what will be the largest statue in the world, carved from the granite top of Thunderhead Mountain. The statue, depicting the chief on horseback, will be 641 feet long and 563 feet high, eight feet taller than the Washington Monument. It was the life work of the late Korczak Ziolkowski, assistant to Gutzon Borglum, who carved the heads on Mount Rushmore. The sculpture was only roughly outlined at the time of Ziolkowski's death, although about eighteen times

The army on the move. Long columns of cavalry, artillery, and supply wagons, commanded by Gen. George A. Custer, cross the plains of the Dakota Territory. This 1874 expedition discovered gold in the Black Hills, sacred dwelling place of the Sioux gods.

as much rock has been blasted from the mountains as was removed from Mount Rushmore. The forty-year work of the sculptor is being carried on by his widow, Ruth, and seven of their ten children. Ziolkowski wanted the statue to be part of an Indian center with a museum, university, and medical center at the base of the mountain. The sculptor's eighty-two-room studio home, museum, and workshop contains a scale model of the Crazy Horse statue, antiques, and other sculpture. On the premises, unusual gates, fifty feet wide and twenty-four feet high, are set with brass silhouettes of more than 270 birds, animals, trees, and plants native to the Black Hills. Also here is the Indian Museum of North America. A slide presentation reviews the work on the mountain and Ziolkowski's life and works. Open daily.

Custer State Park (4 miles east on U.S. 16A; 605/255-4515). The site of the Gordon Stockade, built by the first gold rush party in 1874. The stockade represented the first successful penetration of the Black Hills, and the first result of Colonel Custer's deliberate violation of the 1868 treaty that guaranteed to the Sioux possession of their *Paha Sapa*, or Sacred Hills. On August 2, 1874, William

T. McKay and Horatio N. Ross, civilian prospectors with Custer's expedition, struck gold. News of the strike spread, and the John Gordon party, twenty-six men, a woman, and a child, left Sioux City in early October, arriving here December 23. They erected the stockade and started to mine, despite the

A gold strike in the 1870s in Deadwood Gulch, South Dakota, attracted people such as Wild Bill Hickok and Calamity Jane. Soon 25,000 people were digging in the hillsides.

Calamity Jane

Some say that Martha Canary's parents were killed while the family was moving to Utah, hence the nickname. The records, however, show that she grew up in the mining camp of Virginia City, Montana. A tall, big-boned girl who dressed like a man and could ride and shoot like a man, she lived with a succession of men, turning to prostitution when she needed the money.

Calamity Jane had a taste for the theatrical, boasted of wild exploits (she did once ride a bull down the main street of Rapid City, South Dakota), frequented saloons, and went on awesome sprees. By 1896 she was appearing on stage, peddling a wildly inaccurate biography of herself on the side. Some say she was married to Wild Bill Hickok for a while. The records, however, show that she married a Texan named Burke who worked as a hack driver in the Black Hills. Her tombstone in Deadwood has the name MRS. M. E. BURKE carved beneath CALAMITY JANE.

hard winter. The army changed its mind and escorted the Gordon party out of the Black Hills, but the cat was out of the bag. Thousands of prospectors came to the Black Hills the next year. The town of Custer was staked out in 1875 and had a population of 5,000 within a year. The Sioux had lost the *Paha Sapa,* but they would settle their score with Custer at the Little Bighorn.

Living-history demonstrations are given at the replica of the Gordon Stockade. The park has one of the largest publicly owned herds of bison in the country. *Black Hills Playhouse* presents theatrical productions six nights a week from mid-June to late August. The Peter Norbeck Visitor Center is open daily in the summer.

Custer County Courthouse Museum (411 Mt. Rushmore Rd.; 605/673-2443).

Contains memorabilia of the county. In nearby Way Park is an 1875 log cabin, the oldest in the Black Hills, which is furnished as a pioneer home. Both open daily, June through August.

National Museum of Woodcarving (2 miles west on U.S. 16; 605/673-4404, or 800/992-9818 outside of the state). Created by professional woodcarvers, including a Disney animator. Wooden Nickel Theater. Open daily, May through mid-October.

Wild Bill Hickok met his untimely demise during an 1876 poker game in Deadwood. He is buried at the top of Mount Moriah next to Calamity Jane, who carried a torch for him for many years.

DEADWOOD

When gold was discovered in Deadwood Gulch, people abandoned the town of Custer and swarmed here. At one time, some 25,000 were prospecting in Deadwood, but when a new strike was made at nearby Lead, Deadwood was abandoned. *Sic transit gloria mundi.* Today, Deadwood attracts visitors with memories of Wild Bill Hickok and Calamity Jane. A bust of Hickok by Korczak Ziolkowski is on Sherman Street. The main street of Deadwood runs through Deadwood Gulch; the rest of the town is on the sides of the steep canyon.

Adams Memorial Museum (Sherman and Deadwood streets; 605/578-1714). Exhibits recalling the town's rip-roarin' past. Open daily, May through September.

Mount Moriah Cemetery. Deadwood's "boot hill." Graves of Calamity Jane, Wild Bill Hickok, Preacher Smith, Sam Bullock, and others.

Old Style Saloon #10 (657 Main St.; 605/578-3346). Famous as the place where Wild Bill Hickok was shot and killed during a poker game. Collection of gold rush artifacts, guns, and photographs. Entertainment Open daily.

Ghosts of Deadwood Gulch Wax Museum (in Old Town Hall, Lee and Sheran streets; 605/578-3583 in season, 578-2510 off-season). Nineteen historical episodes in the Dakota Territory are depicted, featuring more than seventy life-sized wax figures. Open daily.

Broken Boot Gold Mine (south edge of town on U.S. 14). Guided tours of the historic underground mine. Daily, mid-May through September.

Bobtail Placer Mine (2 miles southwest on U.S. 14). For a fee, visitors may pan for gold here. Open daily except Sunday.

Accommodations: *Queen Anne Victorian* (22 Van Buren; 605/578-3877). A bed-and-breakfast in an 1892 house with period furnishings. Four guest rooms.

HILL CITY

This handsome town in the heart of the Black Hills was settled in 1876 during the gold rush.

Call of the Wild Museum (320 Main St.; 605/574-2039). Mounted specimens of hundreds of animals of North America. Open daily, May through October.

Dianne's Hillyo Museum (3 miles east via U.S. 16/SD 385; 605/574-2216). Pioneer, Indian and mining memorabilia. Clothing collection. Open daily, May through October.

1880 Train (Hill City Depot; 605/574-2222). Vintage railway equipment makes two-hour tours on original gold rush tracks to Keystone through Nail Forest. Daily, mid-June through Labor Day.

Wade's Gold Mine (3/4 mile northwest on Deerfield Rd.; 605/574-2279). Visitors may pan for gold; demonstrations of early methods of recovering gold. Tours. Open daily, May through September.

Whoop it up during Deadwood's "Days of '76" the first weekend in August, a three-day wingding with parades, rodeos (featuring the stagecoach holdup pictured here), and other festivities.

Wild Bill Hickok

James Butler Hickok looked like a legend—tall, handsome, with long flowing hair, all dressed in buckskin—and with the help of a dime novel he became one. As a young man he quarreled with his employer and shot him dead. A dime novel dubbed him "Wild Bill" and had him bravely killing thirty desperadoes. A Union soldier in the Civil War, he was a scout for General Sheridan. He was the marshal of Abilene, Kansas, when it was a rip-roarin' cow town, and was a performer for several years in Buffalo Bill's Wild West Show. In 1878 he married a woman who owned a circus, but left her after two weeks for the gold rush in the Black Hills. There, at Deadwood in 1876, playing poker in a saloon, he was shot from behind and killed. The hand he allegedly held, aces and eights, became known as the "dead man's hand."

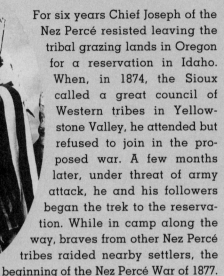

Chief Joseph

For six years Chief Joseph of the Nez Percé resisted leaving the tribal grazing lands in Oregon for a reservation in Idaho. When, in 1874, the Sioux called a great council of Western tribes in Yellowstone Valley, he attended but refused to join in the proposed war. A few months later, under threat of army attack, he and his followers began the trek to the reservation. While in camp along the way, braves from other Nez Percé tribes raided nearby settlers, the beginning of the Nez Percé War of 1877. Although Chief Joseph had no influence on the other Nez Percé tribes, the army insisted he had planned the attack. Chief Joseph was the only chief still alive to surrender the last of the Nez Percé at the Bear Paw battlefield in northern Montana. His reputation grew after the war. To his people he was a brave warrior and a statesman; to the whites he was a noble Indian, an uncorrupted child of nature.

HURON

Dakotaland Museum (on state fairgrounds, 8 blocks west on U.S. 14l; 605/352-4626). Has a log cabin and pioneer artifacts. Open daily, Memorial Day to Labor Day.

Hubert H. Humphrey Drug Store (233 Dakota St.; 605/352-4626). The vice-president owned this drug store until his death. The atmosphere is mid-1930s. Open daily.

Gladys Pyle Historic Home (376 Idaho Ave. Southeast; 605/352-2528). An 1894 Queen Anne, this was the home of the first woman to be elected a U.S. senator. Original furnishings, stained glass, ornate woodwork. Open daily, April through December; weekends the rest of the year.

Laura Ingalls Wilder Memorial (in De Smet, 33 miles east off U.S. 14; 605/854-3383 or 854-3181). *Little House on the Prairie* was based on the author's childhood experiences here. Among the buildings associated with Wilder are the family's original 1887 home, a house where they next lived (1879–80), and a replica of a period schoolhouse. Tours from late May to mid-September.

KEYSTONE

Once a mining town supplying miners for the Hugo, Holy Terror, and Peerless mines, Keystone is now the gateway to Mount Rushmore and Custer State Park.

Mount Rushmore National Memorial (3 miles southwest off U.S. 16A; 605/673-2250). Carved out of the granite of the mountain are the faces of four American presidents, together symbolizing the ideals on which the country is based: George Washington stands for independence; Thomas Jefferson for the democratic process; Abraham Lincoln for equality; and Theodore Roosevelt for prominence in world affairs. Gutzon Borglum, a sculptor of Danish descent, supervised the transformation of this 6,000-foot-high mountain into one of the most famous works of art in the world. The faces measure sixty feet from crown to chin; each nose is twenty feet long; the eyes are eleven feet across; the mouths are eighteen feet long. If the faces had bodies, they would stand taller than the Washington Monument. Borglum worked here from 1927 until his death in 1941. More than 360 people, laboring in thirty-man crews, did the actual sculpture. The cost: $990,000.

The Visitor Center has an audiovisual presentation on the history of the site. A museum displays tools and techniques used in construction. The main-view terrace has an audio presentation. A variety of wildlife, including a family of Rocky Mountain goats, is in the park. Open daily.

Rushmore-Borglum Store and Gallery (in town on U.S. 16A; 605/666-4449). Old newsreel footage of the carving of Mount Rushmore is shown here. Original models and tools of Borglum are on display, as is a collection of his paintings. Historic photographs and documents. Monument-sized replica of Lincoln's eye. Open daily, May to mid-October.

Rushmore Aerial Tramway (on U.S. 16A; 605/666-4478). A fifteen-minute ride giving a view of Mount Rushmore and the Black Hills across the valley. Open daily, mid-April through September.

Rushmore Helicopter Sightseeing Tours (1½ miles south on U.S. 16A; 605/666-4461). Helicopter rides over Mount Rushmore and other nearby points of interest. Daily, late May to late September.

Big Thunder Gold Mine (5 blocks east of stoplight; 605/666-4847 or 800/843-1300, ext. 774). For a fee, visitors can pan for gold in this authentic old gold mine. Historic film. Open daily, May through September.

Parade of Presidents Wax Museum (on U.S. 16A at east entrance to Mount Rushmore; 605/666-4455). Scenes from American history with nearly a hundred life-sized wax figures. Open daily, May through September.

Cosmos of the Black Hills (4 miles northeast, ½ mile off U.S. 16; 605/343-7278 or 343-9802). Odd optical and gravitational effects. Mystery house. Guided tours. Open daily, April through October.

LEAD

After gold was discovered in Custer, a chain of mines spread through the Black Hills to Deadwood and finally to Lead (pronounced *Leed*), where the Homestake Mine became one of the largest gold producers in the Western Hemisphere.

Homestake Gold Mine (Main and Mill streets; 605/584-3110). A ninety-minute tour of the surface workings of the 8,000-foot-deep mine, and explanation of gold production. Open weekdays, May through September.

Black Hills Mining Museum (323 West

Tall Bull and Roman Nose

No braver men rode the plains than the Dog Soldiers, the Cheyenne warriors. When they first tangled with the army in 1860, Tall Bull had been their chief for twenty years. Indians led by Tall Bull and Roman Nose mauled a detachment of cavalry in the Battle of Beecher's Island in Colorado in 1868. His Dog Soldiers fought General Sheridan in his winter campaign against the Indians of the Southern Plains. Refusing to surrender after the Battle of the Washita, Tall Bull went north. When the army destroyed a large Cheyenne encampment, he retaliated by raiding along the Kansas frontier. General Carr surprised and destroyed Tall Bull's camp in 1869 at Summit Springs, Colorado. Tall Bull was killed in the battle, and the Dog Soldiers were never again an effective fighting force.

Embittered by the massacre of the Cheyenne at Sand Creek, and trusting in the strong medicine of his war bonnet, Roman Nose became a leader in the Cheyenne-Arapaho War of 1864–65. His mistrust and belligerence aborted the peace talks. He was one of the chiefs of a force of Cheyennes and Kiowas that destroyed a cavalry unit near Prairie Dog Creek in Kansas in 1867 and the following year besieged General Forsyth's command at Beecher's Island. Roman Nose accidentally broke the medicine of his war bonnet before the battle and was mortally wounded.

"You come here
to tell us lies.
Go home where
you came from."
—CRAZY HORSE TO
GENERAL TERRY

❖-I-❖

"This is a good day
to die!"
—SIOUX BATTLE CRY

❖-I-❖

*A bust of Sitting Bull,
the great Sioux chief,
stands at his grave
site on a hill near the
Missouri River, on the
outskirts of Mobridge,
South Dakota. Sitting
Bull was trying to
leave the reservation
when he was killed by
an Indian policeman.
His death marked the
end of the Indian
Wars.*

Main St.; 605/584-1605). Exhibits tracing the development of mines in the area. Gold panning. Tours of an underground mine. Open daily, May to mid-October.

Accommodations: *Cheyenne Crossing* (605/584-3510). A bed-and-breakfast at a country store in the canyon.

MADISON

Prairie Village (2 miles west on SD 34; 605/256-3644). A replica of a pioneer town, with forty restored buildings, an 1893 steam merry-go-round, a steam train, antique tractors and automobiles. Open daily, Memorial Day to Labor Day.

Smith-Zimmermann State Museum (Dakota State University campus, Egan Ave. and 8th St. Northeast; 605-256-5308). Local history memorabilia. University also has the archives of Karl E. Mundt, the South Dakota senator.

MISSION

Rosebud Sioux Tribal Council (in Rosebud Indian Reservation, 5 miles west on U.S. 18, then 8 miles southwest on Bureau of Indian Affairs Road; 605/747-2361). The tribes here have included Loafer (Waglukhe), Minneconjou, Oglala, Two Kettle (Oohenonpa), and Upper Brulé and Wahzhazhe Sioux. Open daily.

Buechel Memorial Lakota Museum (5 miles west on U.S. 18, then 16 miles southwest on Bureau of Indian Affairs Road in St. Francis; 605/747-9997). A collection of Lakota Sioux artifacts. Open daily, late May through September.

MITCHELL

Oscar Howe Art Center (119 West 3rd St.; 605/996-7311). Housed in the 1902 former Carnegie Library Building, this gallery has a permanent exhibit of the oil paintings of the famed Sioux artist Oscar Howe. Exhibits of Indian art and culture. Open Tuesday through Saturday.

Prehistoric Indian Village Site (2 miles north via SD 37, exit 23rd Ave. to Indian Village Rd., then north; 605/996-5473). On this National Historic Landmark Archaeological Site, there is an ongoing study of a thousand-year-old Indian village. *Boehnem Memorial Museum* has Indian artifacts and exhibits, tours, and a visitor center. Open daily, June through August..

Friends of the Middle Border Museum (1311 South Duff; 605/996-2122). This seven-building complex features a restored 1886 home, a territorial school, a railroad depot, a country church, Native American and pioneer life exhibits, and antique automobiles and other vehicles. Open daily, June through August.

Enchanted World Doll Museum (615 North Main; 605/996-9896). More than 3,000 antique and modern dolls are displayed in scenes from fairy tales and storybooks. Doll houses. Open daily, April through October.

Corn Palace (604 Main; 605/996-7311). A huge building with turrets and towers, flamboyantly Byzantine, it has been rebuilt twice since it was constructed in 1892. Open daily, Memorial Day to Labor Day; weekdays the rest of the year.

MOBRIDGE

Once, Sioux and Arikara villages were here. When the Milwaukee Railroad built a bridge across the Missouri here in 1906, a telegrapher used the contraction "Mobridge" to indicate the location, and the name stuck. There are still many Native Americans in the area.

Sitting Bull Monument (3 miles west on U.S. 12, then 4 miles south on SD 1806) was sculpted by Korczak Ziolkowski. The burial ground of the great Sioux chief affords a beautiful view of the Missouri River.

Klein Museum (2 miles east on U.S. 12;

Sitting Bull and Gall

Sitting Bull

Sitting Bull. The most famous Indian in the West, Sitting Bull always impressed his warriors with his bravery. They attributed his success in battle to the strength of his visions; he believed his power came from a perfect accord with the universe. A Hunkpapa Sioux, his first battle honors came at age fourteen, fighting the Crow. In the 1850s he led his tribe against the Shoshoni, Assiniboin, and Crow to extend Sioux hunting grounds. He began to fight the whites when the army moved against him.

After the southern Sioux, including Red Cloud, made peace in exchange for a reservation in the Black Hills, they broke with tradition and made Sitting Bull chief of all the Sioux. When prospectors started arriving in the Black Hills, Sitting Bull ignored an order to move the Sioux to another area. He assembled some 11,000 Sioux, Cheyenne, and Arapaho near the Rosebud and Little Bighorn rivers to discuss the new threat. Sitting Bull fasted, and a vision came to him of dead soldiers falling like rain into their camp. Five days after Crazy Horse's victory at the Rosebud, Custer arrived, attacked the great encampment, and was massacred. Although he took part in neither battle, Sitting Bull, fearing massive retaliation, fled with his Sioux to Canada. Facing starvation, they returned and surrendered. Years later, he toured briefly with Buffalo Bill's Wild West Show. When Indian discontent flared during the Ghost Dance movement in 1890, Indian police attempted to arrest him at his cabin. After a sharp fight, Sitting Bull, his son, six of his bodyguards, and six policemen were dead.

Gall. There are two explanations of how Gall got his name: either because as a hungry boy he ate the gall bladder of an animal, or because he had a mean, bitter disposition. He certainly had the temperament to be a great warrior. When Sitting Bull became the holy man and political leader of the "hostile" Sioux, he made Gall, a Hunkpapa Sioux, his military chief. One of the chief architects of the Custer massacre, he followed Sitting Bull into exile in Canada, but quarreled with him and returned in 1880. He surrendered his braves the next year at the Poplar River in Montana, and was sent to a reservation. Gall was cooperative and became a judge of the Court of Indian Offices.

Gall

Red Cloud and Crazy Horse

As a young man, the Oglala Sioux Red Cloud gained a reputation for cunning and cruelty in wars against the Pawnee and Crow. After the opening of the Bozeman Trail through Sioux hunting grounds, he was a leader in the 1865–66 Powder River War, personally setting the trap that resulted in the Fetterman Massacre. The army assumed that Red Cloud was the foremost Sioux chief, arranged with him to send the Sioux to a reservation, and sent him on a celebrated trip to Washington. Angry at his assumption of leadership, most of the Sioux would not follow him to the reservation. He spent the rest of his life unhappily trying to mediate between the Sioux and the army.

The bold spirit and military skill Crazy Horse displayed fighting with Red Cloud made him a leader of the Oglala Sioux and Northern Cheyenne. Refusing to be confined to a reservation, he led raids on both whites and the rival Crow. In the Black Hills gold rush, Crazy Horse's village became the rallying point for tribes opposing white encroachment on their hunting grounds. In 1876, General Crook's 1,300 troops attacked Crazy Horse's forces on the Rosebud River. Crook withdrew with severe losses. Crazy Horse moved north and joined Sitting Bull at the Little Bighorn. In the battle, Crazy Horse attacked Custer from the north and west, while Gall and his Hunkpapa Sioux attacked from the south and east. After Sitting Bull fled to Canada, Crazy Horse waged a brilliant campaign against General Miles. He surrendered in 1877 and later was killed by soldiers attempting to arrest him for leaving the reservation without permission to visit his ailing wife.

605/845-7243). Sioux and Arikara artifacts, pioneer memorabilia, antiques, restored schoolhouse, farm machinery, art exhibits. Open daily, April through October.

Scherr Howe Arena (Main St.; 605/845-3700). Murals by Oscar Howe, a Dakota Sioux artist and professor at the University of South Dakota, depict the history and ceremonies of the Sioux. Open daily except Sunday.

PIERRE

Pierre (pronounced *Peer*) was built by cattlemen from the West and farmers from the East, and its central location made it a logical choice for the state capital.

State Capitol (Capitol Ave. East; 605/773-3765). Built of limestone, local granite, and marble. Tours on weekdays by appointment. Open daily.

Cultural Heritage Museum (900 Governors Dr., near State Capitol; 605/773-3458). Ethnographic, historic, and mining exhibits. On display is the Vérendrye Plate, a lead plate buried at Fort Pierre in 1743 by French explorers, the first known white men in South Dakota. Open daily.

State National Guard Museum (303 East Dakota; 605/773-3458). Displays of historic national guard artifacts. Open Mondays, Wednesdays, and Fridays.

Teton Sioux race their horses in front of Fort Pierre, South Dakota, in an 1833-44 painting by Karl Bodmer. Artists regularly accompanied western explorations, and their work gave the fascinated East its first look at the wonders of the West.

PINE RIDGE

This is a Sioux Indian community and the administrative center of the large Pine Ridge Reservation, where Brulé, Oglala, and Northern Cheyenne live.

Wounded Knee Battlefield (8 miles east on U.S. 18, then 7 miles north on unnumbered road). The slaughter that occurred here on December 29, 1890, had its origins in a vision. It came the year before to Wovoka, a quiet, peaceful Paiute, and was a curious mixture of Indian and Christian beliefs. Wovoka said of his vision: "The good days of the plentiful buffalo herds are coming back again. The son of God has come to earth again, and this time He has come to the Indian alone. The white people will all be destroyed because long ago they killed Him!" Within months a "Messiah Craze" swept from tribe to tribe in the West. The Sioux, desperate with hunger, seized on the belief and added a twist of their own. To their ritual of the Ghost Dance, which put participants into a trance, was appended the sacred Ghost Shirt, which they believed could not be pierced by a bullet.

Sitting Bull, the Sioux chief, embraced the Ghost Dance, and one was held at his camp on October 9, 1890. News of the Ghost Dance terrified the white community, and James McLaughlin, the Indian agent, received the telegraphed order "Arrest Sitting Bull." When the authorities came for him on December 15, Sitting Bull hesitated, a fight broke out, shots were fired, and Sitting Bull, his son, and six other Sioux were killed. Two weeks after the death of Sitting Bull, some 300 Hunkpapa and Minneconjou Sioux, two-thirds of them women and children, surrendered to the Seventh Cavalry and were taken to a camp on Wounded Knee Creek. The Indian camp was under the white flag of truce and ringed by 450 soldiers and four Hotchkiss machine guns. The soldiers ordered the Indians to turn in their guns. The decision was unwise. The Indians had shown no resistance, and they regarded their guns as their means of livelihood.

The body of the Sioux chief Big Foot lies frozen on the snow-covered battlefield where he died on December 29, 1890. Big Foot was captured at the battle of Wounded Knee, South Dakota, but did not survive the bitter cold.

—I—

"I shall not rest quiet in Montparnasse. . . . I shall not be there. I shall rise and pass. Bury my heart at Wounded Knee."

—Stephen Vincent Benét, *American Names*

Black Elk and Wovoka

The great holy man of the Oglala Sioux, Black Elk, a cousin of Crazy Horse, had a powerful mystical vision while still a boy. He interpreted it as a command to preserve the tribal heritage and help the Sioux regain their spiritual well-being. In the 1880s he became a noted healer and spiritual guide. After the suppression of the Sioux at Wounded Knee, he spent the rest of his life quietly on the reservation, preserving Sioux traditions and practices. In 1930, the poet John G. Neihardt took down Black Elk's oral biography, which was published as *Black Elk Speaks*. Later, Black Elk shared his knowledge of the Sioux religion with the anthropologist Joseph E. Brown, whose book, *The Sacred Pipe*, resulted from their conversations.

The last great Indian uprising began with a vision. The Hunkpapa chief Wovoka saw the Sioux triumphant over the white man, their spirits cleansed by performing the Ghost Dance, their bodies protected in battle by Ghost Shirts (buckskin shirts decorated with paintings of buffalo and thunderbirds). The army moved to arrest Wovoka in 1890, many Sioux left the reservation, and the uprising ended when the Seventh Cavalry massacred more than 200 Sioux men, women, and children at Wounded Knee.

The Ghost Dance, performed by Arapahos in this 1900 drawing, was believed to herald victory over the whites and the return of the great buffalo herds. The prophesies of the visionary Wovoka sent thousands of Indians into battle believing they were invincible.

Suddenly there was a defiant gesture, then an Indian fired his gun. The soldiers began firing point-blank at the Sioux camp, and many were killed in the first few minutes. However, enough Indians attacked the firing soldiers to kill twenty-five of them. Soon tepees were burning and the field was littered with Indian dead and wounded. Survivors scrambled in panic to the nearby ravines, pursued by the cavalry and raked with machine-gun fire. The bodies of men, women, and children were found scattered for two miles from the first encounter. The frozen dead were gathered up in wagons and buried together in a communal pit. The battle, the last major encounter between the army and the Indians, marked the end of the Sioux Nation, their leaders finally realizing that obedience to the white man's laws was the price of survival.

The battlefield is on the Pine Ridge Reservation, fragmented by a road system and other modern intrusions. On the site of the troop positions are the Wounded Knee store, post office, and a privately operated museum displaying battlefield relics. The modern Sacred Heart Mission is on a low hill near the site of the machine-gun battery. In the cemetery behind the church is the mass grave of the Indians who died in the battle. On the site of the Indian camp where the main fighting took place are a series of markers placed by the Sioux and the state historical society. Most of the sites and the surrounding lands, including the ravines that figured in the pursuit, are privately or tribally owned. Limited wheelchair access.

Red Cloud Indian School Heritage Art Museum (Holy Rosary Mission, 4 miles west on U.S. 18; 605/867-5491). Artworks by members of various tribes. Open daily.

RAPID CITY

Founded in the gold rush era, Rapid City was a boom town that came to stay. Not till

◆━I━◆

"The white men were frightened and called for soldiers. We have begged for life, and the white men thought we wanted theirs. We heard that soldiers were coming. We did not fear. We hoped that we could tell them our troubles and get help. A white man said the soldiers meant to kill us. We did not believe it. . . ."

—RED CLOUD, AFTER WOUNDED KNEE

well after World War II did tourism pass mining as the city's leading industry. This is an excellent place from which to explore the many sights in the area. A two-day driving tour covering some 300 miles could include the Black Hills National Forest, the old mining towns of Deadwood and Lead, Custer, Crazy Horse Memorial, Hill City, Keystone, and the Mount Rushmore National Memorial.

Sioux Indian Museum and Crafts Center (Halley Park, West Blvd.; 605/348-0557) has changing exhibits of arts. Craft shop with authentic goods. Administered by Indian Arts & Crafts Board of the U.S. Department of the Interior. Accessible to the handicapped. Open daily June through September, every day except Monday the rest of the year.

Minnilusa Pioneer Museum (Halley Park, West Blvd.; 605/394-6099) displays artifacts of the Black Hills and western South Dakota. Animal and bird collection. Open daily June through September, every day except Monday the rest of the year. Closed January.

Dahl Fine Arts Center (713 7th St.; 605/394-4101) has three galleries: Mural Gallery, with a 200-foot cyclorama depicting 200 years of American history, and two galleries of regional art. Accessible to the handicapped. Open daily except major holidays,

Thunderhead Underground Falls (ten miles west via SD-44; 605/343-0081) has one of the oldest gold-mining tunnels in the Black Hills area. Falls are inside mine. Open daily May through October.

Geological Sites. Visitors with an interest in natural history have a rich selection in and around the city: Museum of Geology (O'Harra Memorial Bldg., South Dakota School of Mines and Technology, St. Joseph St.; 605/394-2467); Stage Barn Crystal Cave (11 miles north, then two miles west of I-90, Stage Barn Canyon Rd., exit 48; 605/787-4505); Black Hills Petrified Forest (11 miles northwest, one mile off I-90, on Elk Creek Rd. near Piedmont); Crystal Cave Park (three miles west via SD-44; 605/342-8008); Sitting Bull Cave (nine miles south on US-16; 605/342-2777); Black Hills Caverns (four miles west on SD-44; 605/343-0542 or 348-9637); Dinosaur Park (west on Quincy

St. to Skyline Dr.; 605/343-8667); and Bear County USA (eight miles south via US-16; 605/342-2290).

Circle B (15 miles west via SD-44, then a mile north on US-385; 605/348-7358). Chuckwagon and western show. Wagon rides. Shoot-outs. Accessible to the handicapped. Reservations required.Open daily early June to Labor Day.

Flying T Chuckwagon (six miles south on US 16; 605/342-1905) offers supper and a western show. Accessible to the handicapped. Reservations suggested. Open daily May through September.

Stagecoach West (Box 264, Rapid City, SD 57709; 605/343-3113) offers lecture tours to Mount Rushmore, Black Hills, Custer State Park, and Crazy Horse Memorial.

Black Hills Heritage Festival is in early July. Central States Fair, with a rodeo, is in early August. For further information: Convention and Visitors Bureau, 444 Mt. Rushmore Rd., PO 747, Rapid City, SD 57709; or phone 605/343-1744.

The city has an excellent selection of motels, motor hotels and hotels. Audrie's Cranbury Corner (west on SD-44; Mrs. Audry Kuhnhauser, RR 8, PO 2400, Rapid City, SD, 57702; 605/342-7788) is a bed-and-breakfast with fireplaces and hot tubs in most of the antique-filled guest rooms. No smoking. Moderate. Sylvan Room (Hilton Hill Hotel, 445 Mt. Rushmore Rd.; 605/348-8300) is a pleasant alternative to western supper shows.

REDFIELD

Spink County Historical Memorial Museum (southeast corner of Courthouse Square; 605/472-0758) has vintage furniture and other household items, tools and farm machinery. Accessible to the handicapped. Open daily June through September.

There is a motel with a café in town, more accommodations in Aberdeen.

SIOUX FALLS

In 1839 Jean Nicolet probably was the first

Trouble erupted when prospectors of gold poured into the Black Hills, the sacred homeland of the Sioux. Tribal relics and mementos are preserved in exhibits at the Sioux Indian Museum & Crafts Center in Rapid City, South Dakota.

white man to see the falls here. In the 1850s the Dakota Land Company of Minnesota and the Western Town Company of Dubuque worked together to develop the area. The thirty-odd residents elected members of a territorial legislature in 1858, and the next year a newspaper, the Democrat, began publication. The settlement was abandoned after threats of an Indian attack in 1862, but was reestablished three years later. Now Sioux Falls is the state's largest city.

Siouxland Heritage Museum has museums at two different sites in the city. Pettigrew Home and Museum (8th St. and Duluth Ave.; 605/339-7097) is the restored 1889 Queen Anne home of the state's first senator. Indian and natural history galleries. Accessible to the handicapped. Open daily except Mondays and holidays. Old Courthouse Museum (200 West 6th St.; 605-335-4210) is a restored three-story Romanesque 1890 courthouse. Permanent exhibits of area history. Special exhibits on local culture. Accessible to the handicapped. Open daily except Mondays and holidays.

Center for Western Studies (Augustana College, 29th St. and Summit Ave.; 605/336-5516 or 336-4007) has a museum and archival center on western heritage. Art exhibits. Tours. Open daily except Sunday.

Sioux Falls College (22nd and Prairie Ave.; 605/331-5000). Lorene B. Burns Indian Collection. Historic Yankton Trail crossed this area and marker indicates the site. Accessible to the handicapped. Open weekdays except during college vacations.

Indian Mounds (22nd St. and Kiwanis Ave.). Site of a thousand-year-old burial ground. Scenic overlook.

Civic Fine Arts Center/Museum (235 West 10th St.; 605/336-1167) has good collection of Western art. Permanent and changing exhibits. Open daily.

USS *South Dakota* **Battleship Memorial** (West 12 and Kiwanis Ave.; 605/339-7060) has the same dimensions as the battleship and is bordered by the ship's lifeline stan-

---

Sacajawea

The thirteen-year-old daughter of a Shoshone chief was the guide for Lewis and Clark on their great expedition to the Pacific. When Sacajawea was ten, she was taken captive by a party of Hidatsa and sold as a wife to Toussaint Charbonneau, a French Canadian who lived with the tribe. Lewis and Clark met Charbonneau at Fort Mandan, and hired him and Sacajawea as their interpreters. At one Shoshone camp along the way, she was reunited with her brother, Cameahwait, who was now a chief. Carrying her infant son on a cradle board, she dutifully continued with the expedition. On the way back, she and Charbonneau left the expedition at the Hidatsa village at the mouth of the Knife River—and Sacajawea then fades from history.

---

chions. Museum of World War II artifacts. Open Memorial Day to Labor Day.

Sioux Empire Fair is at the Lyons Fairgrounds in late August. For further information: Chamber of Commerce, Box 1426, Sioux Falls, SD; 605/336-1620.

The city has a wide selection of motels and motor hotels. Magnolia's (805 West Ave. North; 605/338-6040), a bit of New Orleans in Sioux Falls, serves up Cajun specialties. Inexpensive.

SISSETON

Fort Sisseton State Park (20 miles west on SD-10, then south on SD-25; 605/448-5701) once quartered 400 soldiers in some forty-five buildings. Abandoned in 1889, the post was used as a transient camp by the Works Progress Administration during the Depression, which restored fourteen of its brick and stone buildings. Visitor Center has historical exhibits. Camping. Open Memorial Day to Labor Day.

Fort Sisseton Historic Festival, including a muzzle-loading rifle competition, cavalry and infantry drills, and crafts, is at the park the first weekend in June. Antique Auto Festival is held the first weekend in June.

"I believe that when Crazy Horse was killed, something more than a man's life was snuffed out. Once, America's size in the imagination was limitless. After Europeans settled and changed it, working from the coasts inland, its size in the imagination shrank. Like the center of a dying fire, the Great Plains held that original vision longest. Just as people finally came to the Great Plains and changed them, so they came to where Crazy Horse lived and killed him. Crazy Horse had the misfortune to live in a place which existed both in reality and in the dreams of people far away; he managed to leave both the real and the imaginary place unbetrayed."

—IAN FRAZIER,
Great Plains

SPEARFISH

Classic Auto Museum (two miles east on US-85, junction of Heritage Dr. and Service Rd., I-90 exit 14; 605/642-7340) has excellent collection of more than a hundred antique and classic automobiles. Some motorcycles. Dolls. Accessible to the handicapped. Open daily May to mid-September.

D.C. Booth Historic Fish Hatchery (321 Canyon St.; 605/642-7730) offers tour of restored 1898 Booth home and buildings of one of the first fish hatcheries in the west. Visitors may feed fish. Visitors Center. Open daily during the summer.

Star Aviation Air Tours (town airport; 605/642-4112 or 800/742-8914 in South Dakota, or 800/843-8010 outside of state) give flights over the Badlands, Mount Rushmore, Devils Tower, and the gold rush country in the summer.

Black Hills Sawdust Day, testing such lumberjack skills as tree felling, chain-saw throwing, and saw bucking, is in City Park in September. Black Hills Passion Play is presented at the Amphitheater (400 St. Joe St.; box office: 605/642-2646) Tuesday, Thursday and Saturday, June through August. For further information: Chamber of Commerce, 140 West Jackson, Box 550, Spearfish, SD 57262; or phone 605/642-4112.

There are several motels in town. Sluice (Heritage Dr., a mile and a half east at I-90 exit 14; 605/642-5500) serves up prime ribs and Gulf shrimp in an old-time mining decor. Inexpensive.

STURGIS

Now a Black Hills trading center, Sturgis was known as "Scooptown" when it was a wagon stop on the way to Fort Meade. Soldiers who came to town were "scooped" of their pay by the likes of Poker Alice, a noted cigar-smoking card shark.

Old Fort Meade Cavalry Museum (one mile east on SD-34, SD-39; 605/347-2818 or 347-9822) is on the site of the original fort where the surviving members of the 7th Cavalry came after the Battle of the Little Bighorn. Old cavalry quarters. Cemetery. Museum displays fort memorabilia. Videos of fort history. Open daily mid-May to late September.

Bear Butte State Park (six miles northeast of SD-79; 605/347-5240) has displays of Indian history and culture at the Visitor Center. Open daily May through mid-September.

Spring Festival, featuring hot-air balloon rally and antique automobile show, is on Mother's Day weekend. For further information: Chamber of Commerce, 606 Anna St., Box 504, Sturgis, SD 57785; 605/347-2556.

Sturgis has a motel with a café next door.

VERMILLION

Settled in 1859 below the bluffs of the Missouri River, the town had to move to higher ground after the flood of 1881 changed the river's course. This area was claimed twice by France and once by Spain before being sold to the United States as part of the Louisiana Purchase.

University of South Dakota (Dakota Street on SD-50 Bypass; 605/677-5236) has a collection of Western art in the Warren M. Lee Center for the Fine Arts. Accessible to the handicapped. Open daily. Also on the campus (Clark and Yale sts.; 605/677-5326) is the Shrine to Music Museum with more the 4,000 antique instruments from around the world. Oscar Howe Gallery with paintings by the Sioux Indian Artist. Open daily.

W. H. Over State Museum (1110 Ratingen St.; 605/677-5228) has exhibits including a life-sized diorama of a Teton Dakota Indian village. Stanley J. Morrow collection of historical photographs. Accessible to the handicapped. Open daily.

There are two motels and a café in town.

WALL

The town, settled in 1907, grew up as a stop on the Chicago & North Western Railroad, and now is a trading center and the gateway to Badlands National Park.

Wall Drug Store (on US-14, I-90; 605/279-2175) has an animated cowboy orchestra and chuckwagon quartet. Art gallery and twenty-three western shops. Traveler's chapel. Open daily, except Sunday in the winter.

Western Dakota Ranch Vacations (nine miles east off I-90; 605/279-2158) is a bed-and-breakfast in a ranch home, offering private baths, wagon rides, and excellent hunting. Dinner is also available with advance notice. Inexpensive.

There are two motels and a café in Wall.

WATERTOWN

This town got off to a rocky start. Right after it was settled in 1874 there was as grasshopper invasion, and four years later a prairie fire burned it down. Now it is the county seat and a recreation center.

Kempeska Heritage Museum (27 1st Ave. Southeast; 605/886-5404) has displays of military and Indian artifacts and pioneer history. Open daily in the summer, daily except Sunday the rest of the year.

Mellette House (421 5th Ave, Northwest; 605/886-4730) was the home of Arthur C. Mellette, the last territorial and the first state governor. Original furnishings. Heirlooms and family portraits. Open daily except Monday from May through September.

There are a number of motels in town, most with restaurants or cafés.

WINNER

Tripp County Museum (one mile east on US-18; 605/842-1556) has pioneer buildings including a house, church, school, general store, law office, and railroad depot. Indian artifacts. Fire trucks. Antique organs. Open daily June through September.

Elks Rodeo is at the fairgrounds the last weekend in July.

Winner has two motels and a café.

YANKTON

From 1861 to 1863 this was the first capital of the Dakota Territory, and a number of restored buildings date from territorial days. Jack McCall was hanged here for murdering Wild Bill Hickok.

Dakota Territorial Museum (610 Summit Ave. in Westside Park; 605/665-3896). Restored Dakota Territorial Legislative Council Building. Restored schoolhouse, railroad depot, blacksmith shop, saloon. Military display. Accessible to the handicapped. Open daily except Tuesday from Memorial Day to Labor Day, by appointment the rest of the year.

Cramer-Kenyon Heritage House (509 Pine St.; 605/665-7470) is an 1890s Queen Anne home with vintage furnishings. Guided tour. Open Memorial Day to Labor Day, the rest of the year by appointment.

Heritage Days with pioneer displays and cowboy and miner music is at nearby Lewis & Clark Lake in July. Riverboat Days is at Riverside Park in mid-August. South Dakota and Open Fiddling Contest is in mid-September. The Lewis and Clark Playhouse (Lewis & Clark Lake; box office: 605/665-4711) presents productions from mid-June to mid-August. For further information: Chamber of Commerce, 219 West 4th St., Box 588, Yankton, SD 57058; or phone 605/665-3636.

There are several motels in town. Black Steer (3rd and Pine Sts.; 605/665-5771) charcoal-broils steals and barbecues baby pork ribs on an open-hearth grill.

"Beyond the railroad tracks are nothing but the brown plains, with their lonely sights—now a solitary horseman at a traveling amble, then a party of Indians in paint and feathers . . . then a drove of ridgy-spined long-horned cattle, which have been several months eating their way from Texas, with their escort of four or five much-spurred horsemen, in peaked hats, blue-hooded coats, and high boots, heavily armed with revolvers and repeating rifles, and riding small wiry horses."

—ISABELLA L. BIRD, IN A LETTER FROM CHEYENNE, 1873

5

Nebraska

AUBURN

Brownville (9 miles east on U.S. 136; 402/274-3203). A restored 19th-century riverboat town of more than thirty buildings, many of which are open to the public, including the Captain Baily Museum, the Land Office, which contains a tourist center, the Carson House, the Depot Museum, the Old Dental Office, the Agriculture Museum, and the Schoolhouse Art Gallery. Open daily, June through September, weekends in May and September–October.

Museum of Missouri River History (402/825-3341). A former Corps of Engineers dredge, *Captain Meriwether*, drydocked and restored, is now a museum with river artifacts and memorabilia. *The Spirit of Brownville* gives two-hour cruises on the Missouri River, Thursday through Sunday from Memorial Day to Labor Day.

Nemaha Valley Museum (1423 19th St.; 402/274-3203). Exhibits of area history, period rooms, farm equipment. Open Wednesday through Sunday, May to early December.

Indian Cave State Park (8 miles south on U.S. 73, then 15 miles east on NE 62). Located on the oak-covered Missouri River bluffs. Partly restored buildings on Old St. Deroin town site. Indian petroglyphs in cave. Scenic overlooks. Open daily mid-April through October.

BEATRICE

Beatrice (pronounced *be-AT-riss*) was named for the daughter of Judge John Kinner, a member of the Nebraska Associa-tion, which founded this settlement on the Blue River in 1857. Beatrice visited a few times but never lived here. Two hometown boys made good in Hollywood, Harold Lloyd and Robert Taylor.

Homestead National Monument (4 miles northwest, just off NE 4; 402/233-3514). Marking the site of one of the first claims staked under the great land giveaway of 1862, this site commemorates the pioneers who settled the American frontier. In this grassy corner of southeastern Nebraska, Daniel Freeman and his wife Agnes claimed their free 160 acres under the Homestead Act. They broke the sod, cultivated the land, and built the brick schoolhouse that was used until 1967 and still stands today. The 160-acre site also includes the Palmer-Epard cabin, a typical frontier log home. It was built on a nearby homestead in 1867. In places where no wood was available, pioneers cut blocks of the densely packed sod out of the ground and built structures known as "soddies." The Visitor Center displays photographs of sod homes, the tools used to make them, and chronicles of the stalwart people who plowed the prairies. From the center, a short trail leads to the Palmer-Epard cabin, into the forest surrounding Cub Creek, through the restored prairie, and by the Freeman gravesite. Open daily.

Gage County Historical Museum (2nd and Court streets; 402/228-1679) is in the former 1908 Burlington Depot and the adjoining building. Rotating displays of historic artifacts of the county. Open daily except Monday, May through September; Tuesday through Friday and Sunday the rest of the year.

BLAIR

Tower of the Four Winds (campus of Dana College, 2848 College Dr.; 402/426-7215). On a hill overlooking

A family of prospective homesteaders pose by the covered wagon containing their worldly goods in the Loup Valley of Nebraska in 1886. The Homestead Act opened up the Great Plains to settlement. This land, once considered worthless, became "the breadbasket of the nation."

The Homestead Act

Free land was the great attraction of the West, although for a long time the land was free only in the imagination of the pioneers. Until the Civil War, pioneers were charged $1.25 an acre for government land in the West. Settlers felt they had earned title to the once worthless land by clearing it, tilling it, building houses and roads and schools, and paying taxes. To have to pay for the land when they needed the money for seed, livestock, farm implements, and food would simply have sent them into debt.

Eastern factory workers and many politicians supported free land, but it was voted down by Southern congressmen who wanted to slow the growth of the West. After the South seceded, President Lincoln signed a free land measure in 1862. The Homestead Act allowed any citizen (or anyone who intended to become a citizen) to select any surveyed but unclaimed tract up to 160 acres and gain title to it after living on the land for five years and making certain improvements. The act included millions of acres in the upper Mississippi and Missouri valleys, although vast acreage farther west had been granted to railroads or bought up by speculators. Despite this, the Homestead Act enabled 1,623,691 settlers to acquire farms.

the town, this forty-four-foot tower displays a mosaic interpretation of a vision seen by the Oglala Sioux prophet Black Elk. Open daily.

Fort Atkinson State Historical Park (1 mile east of U.S. 75 and Fort Calhoun; 402/426-4175). Established in 1819 as Camp Missouri, this was the winter encampment of the Yellowstone Expeditionary Force under Col. Henry Atkinson. The next year, floodwaters destroyed the settlement, which was moved from the river's edge to the top of the bluff and renamed Fort Atkinson. Fort Atkinson prospered. Teamsters, laborers, traders, hunters and trappers, Indians, and the "Fighting Sixth" Infantry gave Nebraska's first settlement a population of about a thousand. The complex included eight ten-room log houses, a council house, a brickyard, a lime kiln, a sawmill, a gristmill, rock quarries, a bakery, a school, and a library with 500 books. The first steamboat, *Western Engineer*, came in 1819. The Indians responded: "White man, bad man. Keep Great Spirit chained, build fire under him to make him paddle their boat." Some of the old barracks have been rebuilt. Museum. Park open daily. Museum open daily, late May to early September.

BRIDGEPORT

Chimney Rock National Historic Site (13 miles west off U.S. 26/NE 92; 308/436-4340). In the 19th century, this was one of the major landmarks for travelers on the Oregon Trail, a welcome break in the endless monotony of the prairie, and a good camping spot just south of the North Platte River, which was a dependable water supply. When they saw the 500-foot column of sandstone, they knew they were near the Rockies. Chimney Rock has eroded considerably since it was first sighted in 1813 by Robert Stuart and a band of traders returning from the Oregon country, but it is still impressive.

From Memorial Day to Labor Day, the State Historical Society maintains a trailer with exhibits about the history and geology of the site. Open daily.

Oregon Trail Wagon Train (12 miles west via U.S. 26/NE 92; reservations: 402/586-1850). One-to-six-day trips from May to October on a re-creation of an 1840s wagon train with authentic covered wagons.

CHADRON

In 1893, nine horsemen left here on a 1,000-mile race to Chicago for a $1,000 purse. A former outlaw, Doc Middleton, was one of the starters, but John Berry beat him to the door of Buffalo Bill's Wild West Show in thirteen days, sixteen hours.

Museum of the Fur Trade (3½ miles east on U.S. 20; 308/432-3843). Displays depicting the history of the fur trade in America, 1500–1900. Gun collection, Native American exhibits, garden of primitive crops, restored trading post and storehouse used by James Bordeau, a French fur trader. Open daily, June through Labor Day.

30 miles to water
20 miles to wood
10 miles to hell and
I gone there for
good

—Carved on a
   deserted shack
   near Chadron,
   Nebraska

Rising nearly 500 feet above the south bank of the North Platte River, Chimney Rock, now a National Historic Site, marked the end of the prairies for early settlers, many of whom described it in their journals. A mobile museum is on the site in the summer.

Captured Alive by Indians!

Nothing was more terrifying to the Western pioneer than the thought of being captured by Indians. "Save the last bullet for yourself," husbands advised their wives. Yet from the earliest day on, many were captured and lived to tell about it—and write about it, creating a curious subcategory of American literature. The first account, *La Relación* of Alvar Núñez Cabeza de Vaca, describes his shipwreck, his capture by Indians in 1528, and his wanderings through the Southwest. Readers thrilled to Captain John Smith's tale of his capture by the Powhatan Indians and salvation by the intervention of Pocahontas. By the middle of the 18th century, captivity narratives were a mainstay of the printer's trade, and hack writers were churning them out with little concern for accuracy. Books like *The Affecting History of the Dreadful Distresses of Frederic Mandheim's Family* were the dime novels of their day, and were used to build support for the extermination of the Indians. The tales from the West tended to be more factual and less sensational, and included Nelson Lee's *Three Years Among the Comanches* and Fanny Kelly's *Narrative of My Captivity Among the Sioux Indians.* Recently there has been a resurgence of captivity narratives, but with a twist. Novels and movies such as *A Man Called Horse, Little Big Man,* and *Dances With Wolves* have used the theme of Indian captivity to suggest that Indian life, by its very simplicity, was more meaningful than that of contemporary whites.

COZAD

Robert Henri Museum (218 East 8th St.; 308/784-4154). The childhood home of the influential artist, member of the Ashcan School of American painters. Open daily, Memorial Day to Labor Day.

CRAWFORD

Fort Robinson State Park (3 miles west on U.S. 20; 308/665-2660). Established in 1877 as the military arm of the Red Cloud Agency of the Sioux, a garrison of some 950 soldiers set up Camp Robinson in 1874, later moving the post about a mile west to a beautiful valley protected on the north by a wall of cliffs rising an almost sheer 1,000 feet. The camp became a fort in 1878 as the Sioux War was drawing to a close. Crazy Horse and his band of 217 men, 672 women and children, and some 2,000 ponies came here to surrender. Four months later, Crazy Horse, the first to break Custer's line and the last to surrender, was bayoneted to death by a soldier who was attempting to take the Sioux chief to the guardhouse under circumstances that are not clear to this day.

In the park, the *Fort Robinson Museum,* in the former 1905 headquarters building, has Indians and soldiers' weapons, costumes and uniforms, and other artifacts. The exhibit buildings include the 1874 guardhouse, a 1904 harness repair shop, a 1906 blacksmith shop, a 1900 wheelwright shop, an 1887 adobe officer quarters, and the 1908 veterinary hospital. *Trailside Museum* has natural history exhibits and offers day and overnight natural history tours. Open daily, April through mid-November, weekdays the rest of the year.

Crazy Horse Museum (end of West Main St. in city park; 308/665-1462) Indian and pioneer artifacts. Open summer weekends.

Accommodations: *Fort Robinson Lodge*

(in Fort Robinson Park; 308/665-2660). Twenty-four two-to-five-bedroom kitchen cabins and seven larger units. Open Memorial Day to Labor Day.

FAIRBURY

Rock Creek Station State Historic Park (6 miles southeast via NE 8 and county road; 402/729-5777). A legend began at this Pony Express station and Oregon Trail stop in 1861. The station was opened two years before by Dave McCanles, who built a log cabin and a toll bridge across Rock Creek. Business was good, and he hired a young man named James Butler Hickok as a stable-hand. Returning from a trip to Texas with his son, McCanles got into a gunfight with Hickok and was killed. Hickok pleaded self-defense. Acquitted, Hickok was dubbed "Wild Bill." A story in *Harper's Magazine* had Hickok singlehandedly killing ten "reckless, blood-thirsty devils" of "The M'Kandlas's Gang" with a pistol and a bowie knife, emerging triumphant although carrying eleven buckshot and thirteen knife wounds. Ned Buntline and other writers of Westerns continued to build the legend of Wild Bill Hickok.

Today, Rock Street Station encompasses some 350 acres of prairie hilltops, creek bottoms, and rugged ravines. Deep ruts, carved by the wagons that traveled the Oregon Trail, are clearly visible. The post office and ranch houses have been restored. Covered wagon rides. Visitor center with interpretive slide presentation and exhibits. Open daily. Limited wheelchair access.

FREMONT

Founded in 1856 and named for John C. Frémont, explorer, Union general, and presidential candidate, the town got off to a slow

start. Crops failed, and lots in town sold for 75 cents each. It began to grow when travelers on the Overland Trail brought trade.

Louis E. May Historical Museum (1643 North Nye Ave.; 402/721-4515). The twenty-five-room 1874 home of the city's first mayor, furnished in vintage style. Open Wednesday to Sunday, April through December.

Fremont and Elkhorn Valley Railroad (depot; 402/727-0615). A steam locomotive with vintage cars makes trips to Nickerson and Hooper and back. Daily except Mondays, June through August; weekends in April–May and September–October.

GERING

Scotts Bluff National Monument (3 miles west on NE 92; 308/436-4340). This 800-foot bluff in western Nebraska was a welcome landmark and a favorite camping site for wagon trains traveling on the Oregon Trail. Fur traders, Mormons, gold seekers, and later Pony Express riders and the first transcontinental telegraph all went through

Scotts Bluff, an 800-foot bluff in the valley of Nebraska's North Platte River, was a landmark for fur traders, gold seekers, pioneers on the Oregon Trail, and Pony Express riders. The transcontinental telegraph also went through nearby Mitchell Pass.

OPPOSITE: A view of Crow Butte from the grounds of Fort Robinson.

The Indian Fighters

William Tecumseh Sherman. The general who marched through Georgia was not the sort who would go easy on the Indians. Sherman believed Indians should be punished for their atrocities, put on reservations, and forced to stay there. He put his philosophy into action on the Red River, and continued to influence military policy in the West after he was made commander-in-chief of the army in 1869.

Philip Sheridan. During Reconstruction, Sheridan ruled Texas and Louisiana with an iron hand. Southerners hated him, and President Andrew Johnson called him an "absolute tyrant" and relieved him of command, sending the Union's greatest cavalry hero west to fight Indians. He soon launched an unexpected winter campaign, which resulted in temporary peace with the Comanche, Cheyenne, and Kiowa. In 1869 he was given command of the Division of the Missouri, which included the entire Plains region. He directed large-scale campaigns against the Southern Plains tribes in 1874–75 and the Sioux in 1876–77. In 1883 he was made commander-in-chief of the army. Like Sherman, he believed that military control of the reservations was essential, and that Indians should be punished for misdeeds. He is remembered for saying, "The only good Indian is a dead Indian."

George Armstrong Custer. His classmates would have laughed at the idea that Custer would be a general two years after graduating from West Point. He almost didn't graduate, but the Civil War had begun and junior officers were in short supply. His reckless daring soon caught the eye of the generals, and, in a cavalry shakeup, he was made a brigadier general. He commanded the cavalry at Gettysburg that turned back Jeb Stuart. At war's end, Custer was the Union army's youngest major general, but he was a lieutenant colonel when he was given command of the new Seventh Cavalry. Court-martialed for mistreating his troops, he was suspended for a year. In 1874, gold was discovered in Sioux territory in the Black Hills. The Sioux went on the warpath, and the army moved against them. At the Battle of the Little Bighorn, Custer apparently disobeyed orders and attacked a large Indian camp. He and most of his command lost their lives. The news of the disaster created a public outcry and the legend of Custer's Last Stand.

Mitchell Pass to skirt this dry, dusty bluff. There are no buffalo here now, but in 1843 one party noted that "it took the herd two entire days to pass, even at quite a rapid gait." At the Visitor Center, the *Oregon Trail Museum* depicts the story of westward migration on the trail. Exhibit of the work of artist and photographer William Henry Jackson. Toll road to the summit and spectacular vistas. Visitors may walk part of the Oregon Trail.

North Platte Valley Museum (11th and J streets; 308/436-5411). An 1887 sod house and an 1889 log house. Local history artifacts and memorabilia. Open daily, May through August.

GOTHENBURG

Pony Express Station (Ehman Park; 308/537-2680). The building was used as a Pony Express station in 1860–61, later as a stop for the Overland Stage. Memorabilia, artifacts. Open daily, May through September.

GRAND ISLAND

French trappers named the settlement for a large island in the Platte River. The Union Pacific had the town moved five miles north to its present location on the railroad.

Stuhr Museum of the Prairie Pioneer (3133 West U.S. 34, junction of U.S. 281, 4 miles north of I-80 Grand Island exit; 308/381-531 6). Designed by Edward Durell Stone, the museum is on an island in a man-made lake. Grounds but not all buildings are open daily. Also at the museum are the following:

Railroad Town, containing sixty original buildings, among which are three homes, the cottage where Henry Fonda was born, a schoolhouse, a newspaper office, a bank, a post office, a hotel, a church, a depot, and blacksmith, shoemaker, and barbershops. An 1890 steam train. Open daily, May through September.

Gus Fonner Memorial Rotunda displays the Indian and Old West collections of Gus Fonner. Open daily.

Antique Auto and Farm Machinery Exhibit has more than 200 vehicles on display. Open daily, May through September.

Heritage Zoo has more than 200 domestic and exotic animals, and a petting zoo. Pony and train rides. Open daily, April through October.

Sandhill Crane Migration. Each spring, thousands of sandhill cranes as well as ducks, geese, hawks, and eagles stop at the Mormon Island Preserve on the Platte River before flying north to Canada and Alaska. Free guided tours take visitors to a concealed blind where they can observe birds. For information, phone 308/382-9210.

HASTINGS

Hastings came into being practically overnight in 1872 when two railroad lines intersected, and within eight years its population was more than 3,000.

Hastings Museum (1300 North Burlington Ave., U.S. 281 at 14th St.; 402/461-2399). Indian and pioneer artifacts, antique automobiles, and horse-drawn vehicles. A sod house and a country store. J. M. McDonald Planetarium has sky shows daily, at 2:30 and 4:30 P.M. Museum open 9 A.M. to 5 P.M. daily; 1 to 5 P.M. on Sunday.

Willa Cather Historical Center (38 miles south via U.S. 281 on Webster St. in Red Cloud; 402/746-3285). Letters of the author, first editions, photos, Cather family memorabilia, and a research library. Open daily except Monday, May through September. Other interesting buildings include Red Cloud Depot, St. Juliana Falconieri Catholic Church, Grace Church. *My Antonia Farmhouse* is open by appointment only.

Alfred Terry. A Connecticut lawyer, Terry became a general in the Civil War, went on to lead the campaign against the Sioux, and became embroiled in the aftermath of the Little Bighorn. Although he had no love for Custer, he reinstated him so that he could lead his regiment against the Sioux. After the massacre, Terry accepted unmerited criticism rather than tarnish Custer's reputation. He ordered the court-martial of Maj. Marcus Reno, Custer's second-in-command. Terry never fought again, serving on numerous army Indian commissions and commanding the Department of the Missouri.

George Crook. Sherman said the greatest Indian fighter of them all was this Ohio farm boy who finished near the bottom of his West Point class. In the field, Crook reputedly could probe "the little secrets of the inner Indian," yet he was known for protecting Indians from the excesses of the army and the government. As a young officer he fought Indians in the Rouge River and the Yakima wars. He served with distinction in the Civil War, then fought the Paiute in the rugged desert of eastern Oregon, pacifying the region within a year. When President Grant sent him to Arizona to fight the Apache, he reorganized his command, employed Indian scouts, and put constant pressure on the roving war parties. In two years most of the Apache were on reservations. As commander of the Department of the Platte, Crook led the Powder River and Yellowstone expeditions against the Sioux. Defeated by Crazy Horse at the Rosebud, he failed to link up with Terry, a circumstance that may have played a part in the massacre at the Little Bighorn. Crook was returned to Arizona in 1881 when the Apache rose again. After eight months of hard campaigning, Crook had the Apache back on reservations. The Apache went on the warpath two years later, and Crook's last campaign ended in the surrender of Geronimo. After leaving the army, he worked for better treatment of the Indians. At Crook's death, his old adversary, Red Cloud, said, "He never lied to us. His words gave my people hope."

General George Crook

Some citizens hoped the town that grew up around Fort Kearney would be the capital of Nebraska because of its central location. Originally located where Nebraska City now stands, the fort was moved here in 1848 to protect travelers on the Oregon Trail.

✦—I—✦

"In God we trusted In Nebraska we busted"

—SIGN ON WAGON OF
HOMESTEADER
LEAVING NEBRASKA

KEARNEY

Named for the nearby frontier outpost, Kearney (pronounced *CAR-nee*) once hoped to be the state capital because of its central location.

Fort Kearney State Historical Park (8 miles southeast on NE 10; 308/234-9513). The starting point of the "trunk line" of the Oregon Trail was Fort Kearney on the Platte River. All the feeder routes led here, then followed the Platte, North Platte, and Sweetwater rivers to South Pass in southwestern Wyoming. The fort was established in 1848 to protect travelers on the Oregon Trail from the Indians and serve as an important source of supplies and services. The coming of the Union Pacific ended the use of wagon trains, and Fort Kearney was abandoned in 1871. The stockade wall and several buildings have been reconstructed, including the stockade and the sod blacksmith-carpenter shop. Museum and interpretive center. Open daily, Memorial Day to Labor Day.

Fort Kearney Museum (131 South Central Ave.; 308/234-5200). Displays of historical items. Open daily, June through Labor Day.

George W. Frank Home (Kearney State College campus, 900 West 25th St.; 308/234-8559). A 1905 three-story mansion with Tiffany windows and vintage furnishings, this was once the social center of the town. Open daily, June through August.

Museum of Nebraska Art (24th and Central; 308/234-8559). Paintings, drawings, prints, and sculpture by Nebraskans or depicting Nebraska subjects. Open daily, June through August.

Trails and Rails Museum (710 West 11th St.; 308/234-3041). A restored 1898 depot, 1880s freighters' hotel, and 1871 schoolhouse. Steam locomotive, flatcar, and caboose. Open daily, April through October.

Harold Warp Pioneer Village (12 miles south via NE 10 in Minden; 308/832-1181 or 800/445-4447). With the theme "How America Grew Since 1830," the village includes three town blocks and twenty-six buildings, including an original sod house, a Pony Express station, and a schoolhouse, representing the country's pioneer heritage. More than 50,000 artifacts are on display, including farm implements, vintage tractors, steam locomotives, some 350 antique automobiles, and twenty-two vintage airplanes. Open daily.

LEXINGTON

Originally this was Plum Creek, a stop on the Oregon Trail. It changed its name to Lexington when the Union Pacific came to town.

Dawson County Historical Society Museum (805 North Taft St.; 308/324-5340). Displays include prehistoric Indian artifacts, a history gallery with a general store, an 1888 rural schoolhouse, an 1885 railroad depot, a locomotive and caboose, farm equipment, and a 1917 experimental biplane.

Open daily, March through November; daily except Sundays the rest of the year.

LINCOLN

In 1867, Lincoln and Omaha both wanted to be the state capital, and when Lincoln was chosen, the paraphernalia of government was moved here by wagon train at night to avoid an armed band of Omaha boosters. At that time the population of Lincoln was thirty. William Jennings Bryan went to Congress from here in 1896; John J. Pershing, who would lead the American Expeditionary Forces in World War I, taught military science here at the University of Nebraska. In 1934, Nebraska became the only state to have a unicameral legislature.

Capitol (1445 K St.; 402/471-0448). Built in the 1920s, this building is the state's third capitol, its central tower rising 400 feet and topped by a 32-foot bronze statue of "The Sower." Guided tours daily except holidays. Nearby is a statue of Abraham Lincoln by Daniel Chester French, who created the statue in Washington's Lincoln Memorial.

Executive Mansion (1425 H St.; 402/471-3466). The 1957 neo-Georgian home of the governor is open to visitors Thursday afternoons.

Christlieb Collection of Western Art (Love Library, 13th and R streets; 402/472-6220). On exhibit are 400 works by Western artists, including Russell and Remington. The collection also includes 4,000 books on the West. Open daily.

State Museum of History (15th and P streets; 402/471-4754). Exhibits of artifacts from prehistoric times until the 1950s. Indian Gallery, period rooms. Open daily except holidays.

Fairview (4900 Sumner, near 48th St., south of U.S. 34; 402/471-4764). Built by William Jennings Bryan in 1902, this was his home until 1917. Original furnishings and memorabilia. Open daily.

The Younger Brothers

Few outlaws were as resourceful or ruthless as the four Younger brothers, Coleman, John, James, and Robert. After their father was slain by Union agitators in Kansas, Coleman, the oldest, known as Cole, rode with Quantrill's Raiders, participating in the raid on Lawrence, Kansas, a flagrant atrocity of the Civil War. Later he hunted down Texas farmers who were trading with the Union, pausing to marry Myra Belle Shirley, who became notorious as Belle Starr. Returning home, he learned he was wanted for a few prewar murders, so he moved on and met Jesse James. It was the beginning of a fateful relationship. The Youngers and the Jameses went on a bank-robbing spree. The Pinkerton Detective Agency was hired to track them down, and they killed a Pinkerton and a sheriff in an 1874 gunfight in which John Younger was fatally wounded. In Northfield, Minnesota, in 1876, the Cole-Younger gang rode into a death trap. The survivors escaped and split up. Jim, Bob, and Cole Younger were captured and sentenced to life in prison. Cole and Jim were pardoned in 1901. Jim became a recluse and was killed. Cole and Frank James organized and toured in a Wild West show.

Statehood Memorial (1627 H St.; 402/471-4764). The restored 1869 home of Thomas P. Kennard, Nebraska's first secretary of state. Open daily.

Ferguson Mansion (16th and H streets; 402/471-4765). A 1910 restored Renaissance Revival mansion with period furniture. Open daily.

Robber's Cave (3245 South 10th St.; 402/423-3370). Pawnee Indians once inhabited this natural cave, later used by desperadoes, gamblers, and horse traders. Open daily except Saturdays.

McCOOK

This town began in 1882 as Fairview, but the Burlington & Missouri Railroad changed its name and its economic future.

George W. Norris Home (706 Norris

Buffalo Bill's 18-room ranch house, outbuildings, and a buffalo display attract visitors to North Platte, Nebraska, hometown of the Pony Express rider, Indian fighter, buffalo hunter, and showman. The town is the railroad and agricultural hub of the area.

"I love to roam the wide prairie, and when I do it, I feel free and happy, but when we settle down, we grow pale and die."

—SATANTA, KIOWA CHIEF

Ave.; 308/345-5293). Built in 1886, the house has its original furnishings. A museum traces the life and achievements of the famous senator. Open daily, June through August; weekends in September and October.

Museum of the High Plains (421 Norris Ave.; 308/345-3661). Indian and pioneer artifacts. Apothecary shop, flour mill. Paintings by World War II POWs. Open Tuesday through Saturday.

Heritage Days are in May. The *Red Willow County Fair and Rodeo* are in mid-July.

NEBRASKA CITY

This town was settled in 1855, and was a trading post on the Missouri River.

Arbor Lodge State Historical Park (1 mile northwest on U.S. 75; 402/873-7222). The park contains the fifty-two-room mansion of J. Sterling Morton, originator of Arbor Day in 1874 and later Grover Cleveland's secretary of agriculture. The mansion is open daily, April through October.

John Brown's Cave (on NE 2 near 20th St.; 402/873-3115). This was a station on the Underground Railroad for runaway slaves on the way from Missouri to Canada, run for a time by the famous abolitionist. Museum. Open daily, April through October.

Wildwood Period House (Steinhart Park Rd. in Wildwood Park, ½ mile west on NE 2, then north; 402/873-6340). An 1869 house with Victorian furnishings. Open daily except Mondays, mid-April through October.

NORTH PLATTE

Buffalo Bill Ranch State Historical Park (1 mile north on Buffalo Bill Ave.; 308/532-4795). The former Indian scout and buffalo hunter owned this ranch, and his wife Louisa stayed here while he traveled with his Wild West Show. Cody's eighteen-room house, barn, and outbuildings are open to visitors. Interpretive film. Buffalo. Open daily, Memorial Day to Labor Day.

Lincoln County Historical Museum (2403 North Buffalo Bill Ave., 308/532-4795). Exhibits and vintage rooms relating to the early history of the county. Railroad village with depot, house, church, schoolhouse, log house, and barn. Open daily, Memorial Day through Labor Day.

Fort McPherson National Cemetery (14 miles east on I-80 to Maxwell, then 3 miles south on county road). Graves of soldiers and scouts who fought in the Indian wars.

OGALLALA

Great cattle herds once came to this shipping center on the Union Pacific Railroad.

Front Street (519 East First St.; 308/284-4601). A reminder of the days of the cattle drives. Cowboy museum, general store, and saloon. Nightly shows in the summer in the Crystal Palace. Open daily.

Boot Hill (between 11th and 12th sts.). The last resting place of many cowboys who rode day and night to reach Ogallala, their "eyelids pasted open with tobacco." There have been no burials here since the 1880s.

Mansion on the Hill (1004 North Spruce St.). An 1890s Victorian home with period furniture. Open daily except Thursday.

Ash Hollow State Historical Park (29 miles northwest on U.S. 26). This thousand-acre park is on the Oregon Trail, and the cave and spring have been used from prehistoric times to the present day. Interpretive center, restored school. Open daily.

OMAHA

After the Omaha Indians signed a treaty with the government in 1854, they left here, leaving only their name. Those waiting for the new territory to open came across the Missouri from Council Bluffs, Iowa, to stake their claims, and the town soon boomed. Ponca chief Standing Bear was put on trial here, the first time a court held that Indians were human beings and entitled to the rights and protection guaranteed by the Constitution. Pioneers heading west came to Omaha by steamboat to join wagon trains. When Omaha was named the eastern terminus of the Union Pacific and the first rails laid in 1865, the city prospered.

Joslyn Art Museum (2200 Dodge St.; 402/342-3300). A 1931 art deco building with important collections, including art of the western frontier, Indian artifacts, and archaeological displays. Open daily except Mondays.

The frontier was about gone in 1898 as the citizens of Omaha turned out to enjoy the Indian Day parade. Founded in 1854, the city endured tornadoes, grasshopper plagues, flood, and drought to prosper as a river port and the eastern terminus of the Union Pacific Railroad.

"The face of the country was dotted far and wide with countless hundreds of buffalo. They trooped along in files and columns, bulls, cows, and calves, on the green faces of the declivities in front. They scrambled away over the hills to the right and left; and far off, the pale blue swells in the extreme distance were dotted with innumerable specks. . . . The prairie teemed with life. Again and again I looked toward the crowded hillsides, and was sure I saw horsemen; and riding near . . . I found them transformed into a group of buffalo. There was nothing in human shape amid this vast congregation of brute forms."

—FRANCIS PARKMAN, *The Oregon Trail*, 1859

Great Plains Black Museum (2213 Lake St.; 402/345-2212). Artifacts and memorabilia relating to the contribution of African-Americans to the area since territorial days. Rare photographs. Open weekdays.

Union Pacific Historical Museum (1416 Dodge St., in Union Pacific Headquarters Building; 402/271-3530). A large collection of artifacts of the railroad's history. A Lincoln display includes a small replica of his funeral car. Open daily except Sundays.

Western Heritage Museum/Omaha History Museum (Union Station, 801 South 10th St.; 402/444-5071). Exhibits relating to the city's history from 1880 to 1954. Byron Reed Coin Collection. Open daily except Mondays.

General Crook House (30th and Fort streets; 402/455-9990). Originally called Quarters I, Fort Omaha, this Italianate house was first occupied by Gen. George Crook, commander of the Department of the Platte. Antiques. Open daily except Saturdays.

Gerald Ford Birth Site (32nd and State streets). A model of the former President's childhood home, with memorabilia. Betty Ford Rose Garden. Open daily.

Mormon Pioneer Cemetery (32nd and State streets; 402/453-9372). Some 600 Mormons camped near the city died during the cruel winter of 1846–47. A monument here commemorates their suffering.

Boys Town (136 and West Dodge Rd.; 402/498-1140). In 1917, Father Edward J. Flanagan founded this community for orphaned, abandoned, and handicapped children. Father Flanagan Museum, Hall of History, tours, Visitor Center. Open daily.

Trolley (402/551-0710). Trackless *Ollie the Trolley* runs weekdays along Douglas and Farnam streets to the Old Market, Central Park Mall, and 16th Street Mall.

Strategic Air Command Museum (2510 Clay St., 12 miles south via U.S. 75 in Bellevue; 402/292-2001). SAC aircraft and missiles of the past and present are on display here. Open daily.

Historic Bellevue (9 miles southeast via NE 73; 402/293-3080). A town whose restored buildings include Old Church (1856), the first church in the Nebraska territory; Old Depot (1869); Settlers' Log Cabin (circa 1830s); and Fontenelle Bank (1856); all with period furnishings. The *Sarpy County Historical Museum* (24th and Clay streets; 402/292-1880) has exhibits of area history. Tours of museum and other historic sites. The *Belle of Brownville* (departs from Hawarth Park; 402/292-6165 or 292-BOAT) is a vintage riverboat giving afternoon and dinner cruises on the Missouri. Daily except Mondays, Memorial Day to Labor Day.

SIDNEY

Sidney was established as a division point on the Union Pacific Railroad, and Fort Sidney was built nearby to provide military protection for railroad workers.

Fort Sidney Post Commander's House (1108 6th Ave.). Restored building of old Fort Sidney. Open daily, Memorial Day to Labor Day . Other structures include *Double Set Officer's Quarters Museum* (544 Jackson St.), which housed married officers, also open daily, Memorial Day to Labor Day; and *Powder Post* (1003 5th Ave.), which is not open to the public.

WINNEBAGO

Winnebago Reservation (Tribal Council, 402/878-2272). In the northeast part of the state, on the Missouri River. There is an annual powwow, usually in late July. Call the tribal office for exact dates and times. The town of Winnebago is on the reservation. Adjoining the reservation to the south is the *Omaha Reservation* (Tribal Council, 402/837-5391).

6

Kansas

ABILENE

A famous cow town, Abilene in 1867 was where the Chisholm Trail met the Kansas Pacific Railroad. More than a half-million cattle were shipped east from Abilene between 1867 and 1871. With as many as 500 cowboys being paid off at one time at this trail end, it took U.S. marshals like Wild Bill Hickok and Tom Smith to keep the peace. Abilene was the boyhood home of Dwight D. Eisenhower.

Eisenhower Center (201 Southeast 4th St., east of KS 15; 913/263-4751). This was the Eisenhower family home, on land plowed by Dwight and his five brothers. Exhibits of mementos, souvenirs, and gifts received during his career. Orientation film in Visitor Center, where murals depict Eisenhower's life. Library with presidential papers. Eisenhower and his wife, Mamie, are buried in the Meditation Chapel. Open daily.

Hall of Generals (100 Southeast 5th St.; 913/263-4194). Wax figures of famous generals who served under Eisenhower during World War II. Open daily.

Dickinson County Historical Museum (412 South Campbell St.; 913/263-2881). Artifacts of Indian and pioneer days, antique toys, displays on cowboys and cattle trails, carousel, Heritage Center. Open daily, early April through late October; weekends the rest of the year. Next door is the *Museum of Independent Telephony,* with a collection of telephones from 1876 to the present. Same schedule as museum.

Old Abilene Town (201 Southeast 6th at Kuney St.; 913/263-4612). A replica of the old cattle town. Original buildings. Stagecoach rides from May through August. Open daily.

Accommodations: *Victorian Reflections* (303 North Cedar St.; 913/263-7774). A bed-and-breakfast in a century-old Victorian house with period furnishings.

ARKANSAS CITY

In this town near the Oklahoma border, some 45,000 homesteaders started the dash for the Cherokee Strip on September 16, 1893, in a race held by the government to give away land for settlement in what was then the Oklahoma Territory.

Cherokee Strip Museum (1 mile south on U.S. 77; 316/442-6750). Artifacts of the land rush days. Open daily except Monday.

Accommodations: *Schumann Gast Haus* (615 South B St.; 316/442-8220). A refurbished early-20th-century home with distinct Germanic overtones, now a working guest house. Breakfast is included in the rates.

ATCHISON

French explorers, Lewis and Clark, and the Yellowstone Expedition all camped on this landing site on the Missouri River. Later, steamboat and wagon traffic kept the town bustling. Mail coaches left daily on the seventeen-day run to Denver. In 1859 an Atchison bond issue helped build a railroad from here to St. Joseph, Missouri. Another bond issue built the Atchison, Topeka & Santa Fe Railroad.

Cray Historical Home Museum (805 North 5th St.; 913/367-3046 or 367-6110). A 19th-century house with

Where the Buffalo Roamed

About 25,000 years ago, the ice sheet that covered the upper Mississippi valley melted, and the Southwest became a desert. Large grass-eating mammals moved northward, but some species didn't make it, including several species of bison and the horse. The only survivors were the deer, the antelope, and the smallest of the bison (though the term is relative: the American buffalo stood about seven feet tall at the shoulder and weighed up to a ton). The buffalo gradually filled the Great Plains and spilled over into other areas, reaching their peak population of some 40 million by the 17th century. They roamed from the Gulf of Mexico to the Canadian woods, and from the Rockies to the timbered belt along the Mississippi. Some made it as far east as Virginia and the Carolinas.

When the ancestors of the Indians came, they found the buffalo too large and tough to be attacked in the open with crude spears. They learned that fire could stampede a herd into running off a cliff or into a swamp, and crippled bison were easy prey. Later, better weapons were developed; the dart and throwing stick and the bow and arrow were capable of wounding a buffalo from ambush. Buffalo became the main food supply of the Plains Indians, but hunting was still hit-or-miss until they acquired the horse from the Spanish. A hunter on a fast, well-trained horse could kill enough buffalo to feed an entire camp.

The Plains Indians grew in number as they became better buffalo hunters. They became nomads, following the herds year-round. Explorers and fur traders also found the buffalo to be a dependable meat supply, and a market developed for tanned buffalo hides. The Oregon Trail divided buffalo country into northern and southern segments, and no longer did the herds roam freely. The Indians fought unsuccessfully to keep from being driven off their hunting grounds.

When the railroad reached Kansas, eastern tanners began buying buffalo hides by the millions. Thousands of buffalo hunters swarmed over the plains to meet the demand. All but a few herds had vanished by 1883, leaving only piles of weathered bones to be shipped east and turned into fertilizer and bone china. Once the buffalo had effectively kept cattlemen and farmers off the Plains; nothing could stand in the way of the trampling herds. After 1883, cattle grazed on the grasslands and farmers plowed the valleys. Near the end of the century, the only buffalo left were a herd in the woods of northern Alberta and a few kept by ranchers. The government now preserves small herds, among which are one on the National Bison Range in western Montana and another in Yellowstone Park.

period furniture and a children's display. Open Sundays, Memorial Day to Labor Day.

BELLEVILLE

Pawnee Indian Village Museum (13 miles west on U.S. 36, then 8 miles north on KS 266; 913/361-2255). The museum is next to a Pawnee village of the early 1800s. Partly excavated earth-lodge floor, displays of Pawnee culture. Open daily except Mondays.

COFFEYVILLE

Colonel James A. Coffey, who built a house and store near the Verdigris River in 1869, gave the town its name, but the Dalton Gang made it famous. On October 5, 1892, the three Dalton brothers and two accomplices tried to rob two banks at the same time, and a running gun battle with the local citizens broke out. Of the robbers, only Emmett Dalton survived. Several defenders were killed or wounded. Wendell Willkie, the Republican presidential candidate in 1940, once taught school here.

Dalton Museum (113 East 8th St.). Artifacts of the Dalton raid, and mementos of Wendell Willkie and baseball great Walter Johnson. Open daily.

Brown Mansion (2019 Walnut St.; 316/251-0431). Designed by protégés of Stanford White, this turn-of-the-century house has original furniture, a Tiffany chandelier, and hand-painted canvas wall coverings. Open daily.

COUNCIL GROVE

The town grew up around an Indian campground in a grove of oak trees near the Neosho River and became the last stopping place on the Santa Fe Trail between the Missouri River and Santa Fe. Many turn-of-the-century buildings still stand.

Prairie French

French explorers, trappers, and traders gave the great American grassland its name, *prairie*, French for "large meadow." Other French words were used for things on the prairie: *boise de vache* ("cow wood") for buffalo chips, which were used for campfires; *butte* for "hill"; "cache" from *cacher*, "to hide"; and "gopher" from *gaufre*, for "honeycomb," from the animal's complex burrows. Even the word *pioneer* is from the Old French *peonier*, which first meant "foot soldier" and later "explorer" and "settler."

Pioneer Jail (502 East Main St., on U.S. 56). Built in 1849, this was for a long time the only jail on the Santa Fe Trail. Open daily.

Council Oak Shrine (210 East Main St.). Here, U.S. commissioners signed a treaty with the Osage Indians in 1825, an event that gave the town its name.

The Madonna of the Trail Monument (Union and Liberty streets). A statue of a pioneer woman with a musket and her children commemorates the National Old Trails Road.

Post Office Oak (East Main St. between Union and Liberty streets). A cache at the base of this huge oak tree served as an unofficial post office for pack trains on the Santa Fe Trail from 1825 to 1847.

Custer's Elm Shrine (Neosho St., 6 blocks south of Main St.). A hundred-foot-tall elm tree is said to have sheltered the camp of General Custer when he was leading an expedition in the area.

Kaw Methodist Mission and Museum (500 North Mission St.; 316/767-5410). In this 1851 stone building, Methodist missionaries taught Indians, and later it was the first school in Kansas for the children of settlers. Open daily except Mondays.

Accommodations: *Cottage House Hotel* (23 North Neosho St.; 316/767-6828). An 1876 Victorian mansion with twenty-six guest rooms, listed on the National Register of Historic Places. Breakfast is included in the rates.

"The unshorn fields, boundless and beautiful, For which the speech of England has no name— The Prairies."

—WILLIAM CULLEN BRYANT, "THE PRAIRIES"

Troublemakers in Dodge City, in 1890, answered to these Peace Commissioners. From left to right are Charles Bassett, W. H. Harris, Wyatt Earp, Luke Short, L. McLean, Bat Masterson, and Neal

DODGE CITY

Santa Fe Railroad construction crews laid out Dodge City, and the town was named after nearby Fort Dodge. This was buffalo country, with vast herds estimated at more than twenty-four million. The buffalo had been hunted for years, but the coming of the railroad provided the transportation that made the hides commercially profitable. A skilled hunter could make $100 a week. By 1875 the herds were almost gone. In a few years, however, cattle drives made Dodge City the cowboy capital of the West. Bat Masterson and Wyatt Earp were peace officers here, helping to fill Boot Hill.

Historic Front Street (316/227-8188). Two blocks of the main street of the 1870s have been reconstructed, including the Long Branch Saloon, which offers entertainment from late May to late August; Saratoga Saloon, blacksmith and gunsmith, saddle shop, drugstore, and many others. The *Beeson Gallery* has exhibits and Dodge City artifacts. The *Hardesty House*, home of a cattle baron, has been restored and furnished with period pieces. Open daily.

Boot Hill Museum (Front St.; 316/227-8188). Both the Front Street Museum and cemetery are on the site of the original Boot Hill Cemetery. Depot and locomotive *Boot Hill Special,* Old Fort Dodge jail, gun collection, stagecoach rides in the summer. Open daily.

Home of Stone (112 East Vine St.; 316/227-6791). An 1870 home preserved with original furnishings. Tours. Open daily, June through August.

Accommodations: *Lora Locke* (Central and Gunsmoke; 316/225-4161). A historic 1920s hotel with a good dining room.

EMPORIA

William Allen White, one of the country's most famous editors, and his nationally quoted *Emporia Gazette* made this town famous.

Red Rocks (927 Exchange St.). The William Allen White residence, an unusual three-story Victorian Gothic home, is private but worth a drive by.

Emporia Gazette Building (517 Merchant St.; 316/342-4805). A one-room museum of newspaper machinery used in White's time. Open daily except Sundays.

Front Street in Dodge City has been reconstructed to show what it looked like when the town was the cowboy capital of the West. The coming of the railroad made Dodge City the terminus of the great Texas cattle drives.

As white hunters slaughtered buffalo on the Great Plains, the hides, estimated at 40,000, piled up as shown here in 1878 at the Rath & Wright hide yard in Dodge City, Kansas. Buffalo hunting was considered great sport and many wealthy Europeans made the long trip overseas to join the fun.

FORT SCOTT

Located only five miles from the Missouri border, Fort Scott became a center for pre–Civil War agitation by proslavery and antislavery forces. Rival groups had headquarters in the Free State Hotel and Western Hotel.

John Brown and James Montgomery were among the antislavery leaders who met here.

Fort Scott National Historic Site (Old Fort Blvd. at the junction of U.S. 69 and U.S. 54; 316/223-0310). Established in 1842 as a military post between Fort Leavenworth and land designated for the displaced Cher-

William Barclay "Bat" Masterson

Like his friend Wyatt Earp, Bat Masterson made the mistake of outliving the Old West. He worked on the railroad and was a buffalo hunter by age twenty. He fought at Adobe Walls, when Comanche and Kiowa attacked hunters operating in their hunting grounds. After working as an army scout in the Red River War, he went to Texas, where he was badly wounded in a fight over a dance-hall girl. In Dodge City, Kansas, Masterson became a lawman, then was elected sheriff, making friends with Wyatt Earp and Doc Holliday. After a time gambling in Leadville, Colorado, he went to Tombstone, Arizona, but left before the shootout at the O.K. Corral. He became a serious gambler, first at respectable houses, then in dives. Asked to leave Denver in 1902, he went to New York, never to return to the West. He was nearly broke when Theodore Roosevelt appointed him a deputy U.S. marshal. A boxing expert, he refereed the match between John L. Sullivan and "Gentleman Jim" Corbett, and was a sportswriter on the New York *Morning Telegraph*, where, in 1921, he died at his desk of a heart attack.

"People went West with such high hopes that often they were destroyed before they really had time to become disappointed. Perhaps the idea of opportunity was just too potent. While the land was open, certainly, that idea was virtually self-sustaining. Bust here, boom there. Drought in Texas, try Nebraska. Too hot in Kansas, try Colorado. Grazed out in Wyoming, try the Dakotas.

—LARRY MCMURTRY

okee and named for Gen. Winfield Scott, the hero of the Mexican War, Fort Scott was home to the dragoons, the mounted infantrymen who kept peace among the Indians and escorted settlers through the wilderness. The fort's eighteen buildings were built by the infantry. The original bakery, hospital, officers' quarters, and quartermaster's storehouse have been restored to look as they did in the 1840s. The enlisted men's barracks, stables, post headquarters, and guardhouse have been historically re-created. An army base at different periods until the 1870s, Fort Scott played an important role in the development of the West. In the summer, park rangers lead tours of the sixteen-acre site. Weekend lectures cover garrison life, the Mexican and Civil wars, and Indians. A five-acre plot of specially cultivated tall-grass prairie surrounds the fort, a reminder of the almost extinct vegetation that once covered much of the Great Plains. Open daily.

HAYS

Fort Hayes (Frontier Historical Park, southwest edge of town; 913/625-6812). This fort guarded the Smoky Hill Trail and the workers on the Kansas Pacific Railroad. Because of flooding, it was moved in 1867 from its original site, fifteen miles west on Big Creek. Indians periodically burned nearby stage stations, Custer's Seventh Cavalry was headquartered here for several summers in the late 1860s. Nearby Hays City, as it was called then, was a wild frontier town. There are two well-preserved structures, the limestone blockhouse and guardhouse, and the rebuilt officers' quarters. Army and Indian artifacts are displayed in the guardhouse museum. There is a small buffalo herd. Open daily.

Ellis County Historical Society and Museum (100 West 7th St.; 913/628-2624). Pioneer and ranch artifacts, antique photo-

graphic equipment, restored church. Open weekdays.

Cathedral of the Plains (St. Fidelis Church, 900 Catherine Ave., 9 miles east on I-70, then 1½ miles south in Victoria; 913/735-9218). A 141-foot-high, twin-towered building built by parishioners in 1911, with hand carvings and Munich art glass. Open daily.

HORTON

Kickapoo Indian Reservation (7 miles west of town; 5 miles east of junction of U.S. 75 and KS 20; 913/486-2121). The Kickapoo hold a powwow the third weekend in July at the powwow ground, with both traditional and powwow dancing. The Kickapoo Green Corn Dance is also performed. Arts and crafts are sold, including leatherwork, beadwork, wood carvings, and jewelry. Indian food is on sale, including corn soup. Open daily.

INDEPENDENCE

In 1869 the Independent Town Company obtained 640 acres of the Osage Indian Reservation from the tribe to found a town, and when the tribe moved to Oklahoma the next year, a treaty opened the reservation to settlement. Natural gas was discovered here in 1881 and oil in 1903, spurring the town's growth. Among the citizens of Independence were Alfred M. Landon, Republican presidential candidate in 1936, author Laura Ingalls Wilder, playwright William Inge, and oilman Harry F. Sinclair.

Independence Museum (8th and Myrtle streets; 316/331-3515). Indian and pioneer artifacts, period rooms. Open Thursday through Saturday.

Little House on the Prairie (13 miles southwest on U.S. 75; 316/331-1890). A

Pioneer Life

The pioneers were hardy souls, forced to rely on their own resources. They hunted for their food. Their cabins and furniture were fashioned from materials at hand. Their clothing was homemade, their medicines came from native herbs. Death was often sudden, and could come in the form of a storm, an accident, or an Indian attack.

Life in a settlement was as crude as on a backwoods farm. Goods were severely limited. A family often lived in one room, where they cooked, ate, slept, entertained, and carried on such fireside industries as spinning, weaving, shoemaking, and woodworking. Cabins were often smelly and bug-ridden. Little attention was paid to personal hygiene, and disease took a heavy toll, particularly malaria, typhoid, smallpox, and cholera. Doctors were few, and families had to rely on folk remedies, mineral curatives, and superstitions. Babies were delivered by their fathers or by midwives. Frontier life was particularly hard on women; they aged quickly and many died at an early age.

Pioneers were hospitable, partly because they craved company and news. They peppered guests with questions, never thinking that they were being rude. The father loved to brag of his accomplishments, his land, his strength, his marksmanship, his wife and children. Visitors were rare; isolation was the norm, and it stunted intellectual growth and coarsened manners and speech.

Religion was simple. Most of the ministers were laymen, and their interpretations of scripture were literal. The revival meeting was as important socially as religiously. Elections, stump speeches, and political debates were always well attended.

Mythology aside, there were few loners among the pioneers. Settling an area was a cooperative affair. Neighbors helped one another to raise their cabins, clear their land, and harvest their crops. The frontier and its rigors and hardships, its manners and mores, left a lasting imprint on the national character.

reproduction of the log cabin where the family of Laura Ingalls Wilder lived in 1869–70. One-room schoolhouse and old post office. Open mid-May to early September.

Elk City State Park (7 miles northwest, off U.S. 160). Near this 857-acre park is Table Mound, site of one of the last Osage villages. Visitors still find arrowheads and other artifacts. Open daily.

Accommodations: *Auntie Em's* (316/331-8937, after 6 P.M. weekdays). A bed-and-breakfast in a 1903 Queen Anne home.

IOLA

Allen County Historical Museum (207 North Jefferson; 316/365-3081). Indian and pioneer artifacts and memorabilia. Open Tuesday through Sunday, May through September.

Old Jail Museum (205 North Jefferson). A re-creation of a sheriff's office and living quarters and, in the basement, an 1869 solitary confinement cell and an 1891 cage cell. Open Tuesday through Sunday, May through September.

Westward Ho, the Wagons

The "prairie schooner" that took the early settlers to the West was developed by the Pennsylvania Dutch in the Conestoga River valley in the early 19th century, and was first used to haul furs from Lancaster to Philadelphia. The design was distinctive, with a long, deep wagon bed, forty-two inches wide, and bowed in the middle like a boat. The wheels had wide tire irons for negotiating dirt roads, and the back wheels were larger in diameter than the front. Depending upon the load, a Conestoga wagon was pulled by four or six horses or oxen. The wagon was not designed for passengers, and the teamster or driver walked along beside the wagon or rode the left wheelhorse. Use of the original Conestoga wagon was at its peak between 1820 and 1850, and the name was used as well for the wagons on the Santa Fe, Oregon, and California trails, though they differed from the true Conestoga wagon somewhat in size and design.

KANSAS CITY

The town of Wyandot City was settled in 1843 by the Wyandot, an educated tribe from Ohio, who bought land from the Delaware. The Wyandot brought government, schools, churches, business, and agriculture. When the area was flooded with people on their way to the gold fields of California, the Indians sold their property to the whites. Soon the town, renamed Wyandotte, was booming. Other towns grew up nearby, and Wyandotte and seven others merged to form Kansas City.

Huron Indian Cemetery (Huron Park, Center City Plaza, between 6th and 7th streets). The Wyandot tribal burial ground, containing some 400 graves. Open daily.

Wyandotte County Historical Society and Museum (15 miles west, northeast of I-70, Bonner Springs exit, at 631 North 126th St. in Bonner Springs; 913/721-1078). Wyandot relics, pioneer artifacts, and horse-drawn fire engine. Open daily, Tuesday through Sunday.

Agricultural Hall of Fame and National Center (630 North 126th St.; 913/721-1075). Exhibits here trace the history and development of agriculture in America. Collections of farm machinery, butter churns, antique automobiles. Period shops, seasonal outdoor demonstrations. Open daily, April through November.

Old Shawnee Town (12 miles southwest on I-35 to Johnson Dr., then west; 913/268-8772). A re-creation of a typical pioneer town of the 1800s. Buildings, both originals and replicas, have vintage furnishings. Open daily.

Shawnee Methodist Mission (3403 West 53rd St. at Mission Rd., 1 block north of U.S. 56 in Shawnee Mission; 913/268-8772). Established in 1839 as an Indian mission and school, the site has three original buildings. Open daily.

Grinter House (1420 South 78th St., west on KS 32 in Muncie). The circa-1857 home of Moses Grinter, first permanent white settler in Wyandotte County. Period furnishings. Open daily.

LARNED

Fort Larned National Historic Site (6 miles west on KS 156; 316/285-6916). Established in 1860, this fort played an important role in the taming of the West, providing armed escorts for mail stages and wagon trains, distributing government food and supplies to the Plains Indians, and defending the construction of the railroad that eventually made the fort obsolete. Ironically, the fort was both an Indian agency and the host to such Indian fighters as Kit Carson, George Armstrong Custer, and Buffalo Bill Cody. The fort was all but abandoned in 1878, by which time most of the Indians in the area had been removed to the Indian Territory.

A quadrangle of nine original stone buildings surround the old five-acre parade ground with its 100-foot flagstaff. A tenth building, the six-sided defensive blockhouse, was reconstructed in 1988. The Visitor Center has a museum with Indian artifacts, including a human scalp and a buffalo-tooth necklace embellished with a coin of President James Monroe. Tours. In the summer there are weekend living-history programs. Nearby is a portion of the old Santa Fe Trail, rutted by the wheels of countless wagons. The fort has a restored prairie with mixed native grasses and wildflowers, which is the home to colonies of prairie dogs, coyotes, owls, hawks, and eagles. Open daily. Limited wheelchair access.

Santa Fe Trail Center (2 miles west; 316/285-2054). Exhibits here depict the history of the trail and the settlements along it. Open Tuesday through Sunday.

LAWRENCE

This town was founded in 1854 by the New England Emigrant Aid Company, one of the organizations financing the emigration of Northerners to Kansas to prevent it from entering the Union as a slave state. The center of Free State activities, Lawrence was close to a state of war from 1855 until the Free Staters triumphed in 1859. In 1863, William Quantrill, the Confederate guerrilla leader, led a raid on Lawrence, killing some 150 citizens.

University of Kansas (Mount Oread, overlooking the Kansas River; 913/864-3506). On campus, the *Spencer Museum of Art* has a good selection of Western art in its collections. Open daily except Mondays. The *Museum of Anthropology* in Spooner Hall has displays of the Indian culture. Open daily.

Haskell Indian Junior College (23rd and Barker streets; 913/749-8450). More than 120 tribes from thirty-seven states are represented in the student body. Founded in 1884, the campus is a registered historic landmark. Tours. The *American Indian Athletic Hall of Fame* is open weekdays.

Watkins Community Museum (1047 Massachusetts St.; 913/841-4109). Housed in an 1800s bank, the museum has exhibits and artifacts relating to the county's history.

"The more [Indians] we can kill this year, the less will have to be killed the next year, for the more I see of these Indians, the more convinced I am that they all have to be killed or be maintained as a species of paupers."

—Gen. William T. Sherman

The Civil War in the West

Compared to the great battles of the East, fighting west of the Mississippi was limited mostly to skirmishes fought over a vast area, amounting to little more than a sideshow. With the exception of the Battle of Pea Ridge in Arkansas, which kept Missouri in the Union, most battles are forgotten today, although Union forces denied the mineral wealth of the Southwest to the Confederacy by winning the Battle of Glorieta Pass.

Guerrilla fighting was intense on the Kansas-Missouri border, a continuation of the proslavery and free-state clashes of the 1850s. The climax was the massacre at Lawrence, Kansas, in which William Quantrill's Confederate raiders killed 183 civilians and burned 185 buildings. Kansas Unionist guerrillas then ravaged northern Missouri so fiercely that it became known as "the Burnt District."

Among the tragic victims of the war were the Five Civilized Tribes in Indian Territory. Forced to choose sides, they suffered hunger, house burning, and exile. After the war, the government took half of the land of the Indians who had joined the South, but also took as much from those who were loyal to the North. Ironically, the Cherokee leader Stand Watie became the only Indian general in the Civil War, and was the last Confederate general to surrender.

Kansas All-Sports Hall of Fame. Open daily except Mondays.

Accommodations: *Halcyon House* (1000 Ohio St.; 913/841-0314). A bed-and-breakfast in a circa-1886 Victorian near the University of Kansas. Eight guest rooms.

LEAVENWORTH

The first incorporated town in the Kansas Territory in 1854, Leavenworth was proslavery but loyal to the Union in the Civil War . In the years prior to the war, it was the headquarters of an overland supply and transportation operation, sending wagons northwest to the Oregon Trail and southwest to the Santa Fe Trail. On the outskirts of the city is Fort Leavenworth, founded in 1827, the oldest military post west of the Mississippi in continuous operation. A federal penitentiary is adjacent to the fort.

Fort Leavenworth (3 miles north on U.S. 73; 913/684-5604). From its founding in 1827, this has been an important military installation. Centrally located on the main westward travel routes in the 19th century, it figured prominently in the Plains campaigns against the Indians, as well as in the Mexican War and Civil War, and now is a modern training center. Replacing Fort Atkinson, Nebraska, on the Permanent Indian Frontier, it was the base of the First Dragoons, an experimental regiment of ten companies. During the Mexican war, it was the base for Gen. Stephen Kearny's Army of the West, which occupied New Mexico and California, and after the war it was the chief supply depot for Western army posts. In 1854, Andrew H. Reeder, the first territorial governor of Kansas, was inaugurated here. When the Civil War ended, the frontier had advanced well beyond here, but the fort continued as a quartermaster depot and ordnance arsenal. In 1881 it became a school for infantry and cavalry officers, and in 1901 the General Service and Staff School. Today it is the headquarters of the Command and General Staff College. Also here is the U.S. Disciplinary Barracks, a military prison founded in 1874, and a National Cemetery. The fort's museum has artifacts of the Army of the West and the fort's history. Fort and museum are open daily.

Leavenworth County Historical Museum (334 5th Ave.; 913/682-7759). A Vic-

Established in 1827, Fort Leavenworth in Kansas is the oldest military post in continuous operation west of the Mississippi. The town once was the headquarters for a huge supply operation. Wagons from here traveled both the Oregon and the Santa Fe trails.

torian home with period furnishings and local mementos. Schoolroom, barbershop, and general store. Open daily except Mondays.

LINDSBORG

A band of Swedish immigrants founded the town in 1869 and pioneered cooperative farming in the area. Their heritage is evident in the Old World motifs in the business district.

McPherson County Old Mill Museum (120 Mill St.; 913/227-3595). Exhibits relating to Swedish, Indian, and pioneer culture. Natural history collections and exhibits. The park has the restored 1904 Swedish Pavilion and the old Smoky Valley Roller Mill. Museum open daily except Mondays.

Accommodations: *Swedish Country Inn* (112 West Lincoln; 913/227-2985). A bed-and-breakfast a half-block from the historic district. Swedish pine furniture and handmade quilts. Bicycles available for the use of guests.

MANHATTAN

Fort Riley (9 miles southwest off I-70; 913/239-3911). Activated in 1853 at the Smoky Hill and Republican forks of the Kansas River to help guard the Smoky Hill Trail to Denver, this fort was the base of several expeditions against the Indians as far west as Santa Fe. Here in 1866 Custer organized the Seventh Cavalry Regiment. The Cavalry School was here from 1891 to 1946. On the fort grounds is the first Kansas territorial capitol, built in 1855, a two-story limestone building furnished in the period. Two other historic structures are an officers' quarters, a stone building once occupied by Custer, and the post chapel. The state's first native limestone church, St. Mary's Chapel, built in 1855, is still in use. A marker commemorates the Battle of Wounded Knee, the final major engagement involving Seventh Cavalry troops from Fort Riley. Marked tour. The U.S. Cavalry Museum contains army memorabilia and artifacts. Open daily.

Goodnow House Museum (2301 Clafin Rd.; 913/539-2731). The 1860 stone home of pioneer educator Isaac Goodnow. Open daily except Mondays.

Hartford House (2309 Clafin Rd. in Pioneer Park; 913/537-2210). An unusual prefabricated house, one of ten brought here by Free-Soilers in 1855, it houses the *Riley County Historical Museum,* which has exhibits of the pioneer days. Open daily except Mondays.

Accommodations: *Kimble Cliff Bed and Breakfast* (6782 Anderson Dr.; 913/539-3816). A farmhouse furnished with antiques.

MARYSVILLE

Heading west out of St. Joseph, Missouri, this was the first home station on the Pony Express route. Among the emigrant parties that camped near here was the ill-fated Donner party.

Koester House Museum (919 Broadway; 913/562-3101). A restored 1876 Victorian home with original furnishings. Open daily.

Pony Express Barn Museum (106 South 8th St.; 913/562-9874). Pony Express memorabilia and Indian artifacts are on display in the circa-1859 building. Doll collection. Displays of harness equipment and old tools. Open daily, late May to early September.

MEADE

Meade County Historical Society (200 East Carthage; 316/873-2359). Exhibits of furnished rooms chronicle the history of the county. Open daily except Mondays, from September through May.

The Daltons

It began, perhaps, when Lewis Dalton, a saloonkeeper, abandoned his wife and fifteen offspring. Three died young, three became farmers, the eldest stayed home with his mother, and one became a lawman killed in the line of duty. The rest of the boys robbbed and shot their way into Western folklore. Grattan, Robert, and Emmett were the core of the Dalton Gang. When Frank Dalton, a deputy sheriff in what is now Oklahoma, was killed, Grat took his place, appointed Bob to his posse, and let Emmett tag along. They worked both sides of the legal fence, stealing horses and killing a man who had taken up with Bob's girfriend. Discredited as lawmen, they formed a gang and robbed a gambling house in New Mexico. Emmett was wounded in the robbery, and the Daltons went into hiding. They went to California, where brother Bill was a prospering politician, and robbed a train. Grat and Bill were arrested; Grat was convicted, and Bill was acquitted but ruined politically. Grat escaped and rejoined the gang in Oklahoma. They robbed and murdered for a year, staying one step ahead of the law. In 1892 the Daltons decided to rob the two banks in Coffeyville, Kansas, but the town was waiting when they rode in. Grat and Bob and two other gang members were killed, and Emmett was badly wounded and captured. Sentenced to life imprisonment, Emmett was paroled after fourteen years, formed a gang, and was badly wounded again robbing a bank in Longview, Texas. He made it as far as Ardmore, Oklahoma, where he was killed by lawmen.

The Dalton Gang Hideout (502 South Pearlette; 316/873-2731). In 1887, Eva Dalton arrived in town, established a millinery shop, and married J. N. Whipple, described as a "half-hearted merchant and a whole-hearted poker player." Whipple owned a tiny house south of town atop a hill that sloped gently to a creek. Eva's brother, Emmett Dalton, attended the wedding and more brothers soon arrived. The Dalton Gang became a phantom presence in the area, stealing horses and robbing trains. Questions about Eva's involvement in her brother's peccadilloes finally forced her and her husband to move away in 1893. The house was sold for taxes, and the new owners were startled to find strangers arriving, expecting a friendly welcome. The owner investigated and found a wash covered with boards and soil leading from a secret entrance under the stairway in the house to the barn some distance away—the Dalton Gang's secret hideout.

Today the Whipple home and the tunnel have been restored. At the south end of the ninety-five-foot tunnel, the reconstructed barn houses a museum of artifacts and memorabilia, including the W. S. Dingess collection of antique guns. Open daily. Limited wheelchair access.

MEDICINE LODGE

Before the coming of the white man, various tribes of Plains Indians used a medicine lodge on a spot on the Medicine River that they considered sacred. When the government planned a peace council in 1867, the tribes chose as a site the location of the present town. A treaty opened the area to settlement. Medicine Lodge was the hometown of the hatchet-wielding prohibitionist Carry Nation.

Medicine Lodge Stockade (junction of U.S. 160 and U.S. 281; 316/886-9982). A replica of the 1874 log house with authentic furnishings, and a house built of gypsum. Museum with pioneer relics. Open daily, April through November.

Carry A. Nation Home Memorial (211 West Fowler Ave. at Oak St.; 316/886-3553). A museum of the temperance crusader's memorabilia. Original furnishings. Open daily, April through November.

NEWTON

The Santa Fe Railroad extended its line to this point in the 1870s, and Newton took over from Abilene as the northern terminus of the Chisholm Trail. Russian Mennonites settled in this area in the 1870s, bringing with them the Turkey Red hard winter wheat they had developed on the steppes. This revolutionized the state's agriculture and made it one of the world's great wheat producers.

Kauffmann Museum (1 mile north via KS 15 in North Newton, on the campus of Bethel College; 316/283-1612). The museum contains exhibits on the Cheyenne and the Mennonites, as well as a log cabin, an 1880s farmhouse, and a barn and windmill. Open daily except Sundays.

Accommodations: *Hawk House Bed & Breakfast Inn* (307 West Broadway; 316/283-2045). Guest rooms in a house on a working grain farm.

OBERLIN

Last Indian Raid Museum (258 South Penn Ave.; 913/475-2712). This museum honors those killed here in the Northern Cheyenne raid of 1878. Garments and tools, church, school, doctor's office, depot, jail, and Indian artifacts. Open daily except Mondays.

OSAWATOMIE

In 1856 the militant abolitionist John Brown attacked proslavery settlers here. Five of Brown's followers were killed in the battle.

John Brown Memorial Park (10th and Main streets; 913/755-4384). The park has a life-sized statue of the abolitionist and a log cabin he once used, containing period furnishings. Picnicking permitted. Park open daily; cabin open daily except Sundays.

OTTAWA

The Ottawa Indians were given land here in 1832 in exchange for their lands in Ohio.

The Reverend Jotham Meeker established the Ottawa Indian Baptist Mission in 1837. During the border warfare, Ottawa was the headquarters for Free State supporters, including John Brown.

Ottawa Indian Burial Grounds (northeast of town). The last resting place of Jotham Meeker.

Old Depot Museum (Tecumseh St.; 913/242-3536). The museum houses area relics, a model railroad room, period rooms, and a general store. Open Sundays, from May to September.

Dietrich Cabin Museum (City Park, Main and 5th streets; 913/242-3536). A restored 1859 log cabin with period furnishings. Open Sundays, May through September.

SALINA

A New York newspaper correspondent chose this site to establish a store to trade with Indian hunting parties. Gold miners stopped by in the 1860s to stock up on their way to Pike's Peak. The Smoky Hill River flooded in 1904, destroying most of the town.

Prehistoric Indian Burial (4 miles east on KS 140). On this site are the skeletons of 146 Indians, many of whom were over six feet tall, believed to be prehistoric. Indian artifacts. Open daily.

Smoky Hill Historical Museum (211 West Iron St.; 913/827-3958). Indian and pioneer relics, an old general store, fossils. Open daily except Mondays.

Central Kansas Flywheels Museum (1100 West Diamond Dr.; 913/825-8473). Antique farm machinery and area artifacts. Open daily, May through August.

TOPEKA

A young Pennsylvanian, Col. Cyrus K. Holiday, wanted to build a railroad and chose a town site on the Kansas River in

1854. The town became the county seat in 1857 and the state capital four years later. In 1878, during the building westward of Holiday's railroad—the Atchison, Topeka & Santa Fe—begun in Topeka in 1869, the railroad's offices and machine shops were established. They are still important to the city. This is the hometown of former vice-president Charles Curtis, part Kaw Indian and a descendent of one of Topeka's earliest settlers.

State Capitol (on a 20-acre square in the center of the city; 913/296-3966). This building resembles the Capitol in Washington. There are murals on the first floor by David H. Overmeyer, on the second floor by John Steuart Curry and Lumin Martin Winter. Tours are available. Open weekdays.

On the grounds are statues of Lincoln and the Pioneer Woman by Topeka-born sculptor Merrell Gage.

Kansas State Historical Society (120 West 10th St. at Jackson St.; 913/296-3251). Artifacts of Indian and Western history. Large newspaper collection. Open daily except Sunday.

Kansas Museum of History (6425 Southwest 6th St.; 913/272-8681). Material and displays relating to the history of the state and the Great Plains. Art gallery. Open daily.

Accommodations: *Heritage House* (3535 Southwest 6th St.; 913/233-3800). A historic inn with fifteen guest rooms. Breakfast.

Jesse had a wife,
    she's a mourner
    all her life;
His children, they
    were brave.
But that dirty little
    coward who shot
    Mr. Howard
Has laid poor Jesse
    in his grave.

—"JESSE JAMES,"
FOLK SONG

Jesse and Frank James

Jesse James was a lad who killed many a man.
    He robbed the Glendale train.
He took from the rich and gave to the poor.
    He'd a hand and a heart and a brain.

Jesse James

Or so the old song goes. In truth, Jesse and his brother Frank were thieves and murderers. Born to a Missouri minister, Jesse rode with "Bloody Bill" Anderson during the Civil War, participating in the massacre of twenty-four unarmed Union soldiers; Frank rode with Quantrill's notorious guerrillas. The James brothers robbed the first of many banks in 1869. Amid a crowd of thousands, they robbed the box office at a Kansas City fair. In 1874 a Pinkerton detective tossed a bomb into a house in which he thought they were hiding, killing their mother and injuring a half-brother. In 1876, Jesse and Frank joined with the Younger brothers to rob the bank in Northfield, Minnesota. It was a death trap. Three were killed, the Youngers were captured, and Jesse and Frank barely escaped. They lived quietly under assumed names for three years before venturing to rob a train in Missouri. With $10,000 on their heads, one of the gang made a deal. On April 3, 1882, while Jesse (alias Mr. Howard) was allegedly standing on a chair straightening a picture, he was shot to death by "that dirty little coward" Robert Ford. The Kansas City *Journal* headlined: GOODBYE JESSE. Frank surrendered, was acquitted of robbery and murder, and lived quietly until his death in 1915.

Eastern Kansas, where this pioneer log home was built, is fertile and hilly, with lakes and streams, but Western Kansas is part of the Great Plains. There Turkey Red winter wheat seed, introduced in 1864 by Mennonite immigrants from Russia, helped make Kansas the "bread basket of the nation."

WICHITA

The Wichita Indians built a village of grass lodges here in 1864. The next year James R. Mead set up a trading post and sent his assistant, Jesse Chisholm, on a trading expedition to the Southwest. His route became famous as the Chisholm Trail, over which longhorn cattle were driven through Wichita to the Union Pacific yards at Abilene. When the railroad reached here in the early 1870s , this became the "cow capital." By 1880, however, farmers had run their fences across the trail, and the cattle drives were shifted west to Dodge City.

Wichita-Sedgwick County Historical Museum (204 South Main St.; 316/265-4717). Indian and local artifacts, period rooms, and a costume collection. Open daily except Mondays.

Indian Center Museum (650 North Seneca; 316/262-5221). Exhibits of Indian art. Open daily, May through September, daily except Mondays the rest of the year.

Wichita Art Museum (619 Stackman Dr.; 316/268-4921). The museum's collection of American art includes paintings and sculpture by Charles M . Russell. Open daily except Mondays.

Fellow-Reeve Museum of History and Science (Friends University campus, University and Hiram streets; 316/261-5800). Indian and pioneer relics. Open Tuesday through Friday during the school year.

Edwin A. Ulrich Museum of Art (Wichita State University campus, Hillside and 17th streets; 316/689-3456). A 3,000-piece collection of American art.

Old Cowtown Museum (1871 Sim Park Dr.; 316/264-0671). A forty-building village depicting life here from 1865 to 1880. Open daily.

Accommodations: *Max Paul* (3910 East Kellogg; 316/689-8101). An inn with individually decorated rooms, some with fireplaces, in three Tudor-style cottages. Formal gardens.

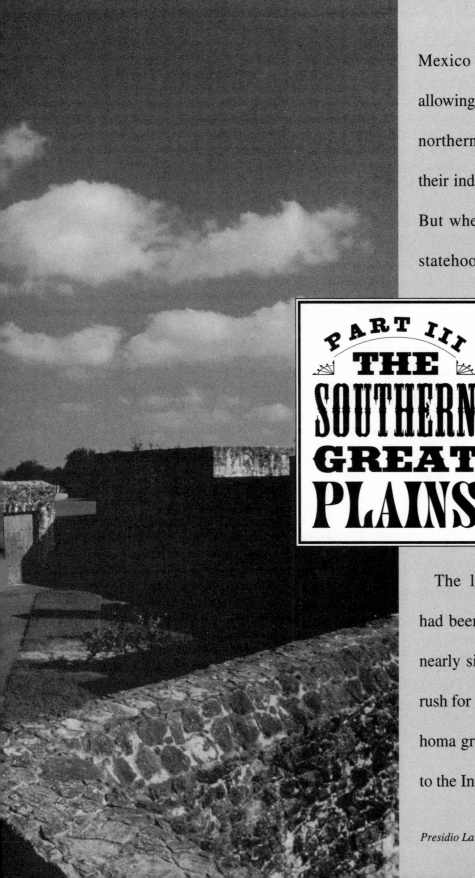

Mexico made the mistake of allowing American settlers into its northern provinces. Texans won their independence 15 years later. But when the republic achieved statehood, Mexico objected and war broke out again. During the Civil War, Texas cast its lot with the Confederacy and suffered through Reconstruction.

The land northeast of Texas had been the Indian Territory for nearly sixty years when the great rush for free land began. As Oklahoma grew, government promises to the Indian were trampled.

Presidio La Bahia, in Goliad, Texas.

PART III
THE SOUTHERN GREAT PLAINS

7

Oklahoma

ANADARKO

This town began in 1859 as the Wichita Indian Agency. The Bureau of Indian Affairs is headquartered here today.

Indian-USA (2½ miles southeast on OK 8; 405/247-5661). A reconstruction of the villages of seven Plains tribes: Apache, Caddo, Kiowa, Navajo, Pawnee, Pueblo, and Wichita. Tours led by Indian guides, dance ceremonies, arts and crafts shop. Open daily.

Southern Plains Indian Museum and Crafts Center (east on U.S. 62; 405/247-6221). Historic and contemporary arts of the Southern Plains region are displayed here. The museum is run by the Indian Arts and Crafts Board of the U.S. Department of the Interior, the gallery by the Oklahoma Indian Arts and Crafts Cooperative. Open daily.

National Hall of Fame for Famous American Indians (east on U.S. 62; 405/247-5555). Outdoor bronze busts of noted Indians. Visitor Center. Open daily.

Anadarko Philomathic Museum (Rock Island Depot, 311 East Main St.; 405/247-6118). Indian doll collection, paintings, military uniforms and equipment, and photographic collection. Old physician's office, country store. Open daily except Sundays.

BARTLESVILLE

Woolaroc (13 miles southwest on OK 123, Woolaroc exit; 918/336-0307). A preserve for bison, elk, deer, and other wildlife. A museum on the grounds has paintings by Remington, Russell, and other Western artists, and

The promise of free land in the Indian Territory lured crowds to sign up for an Oklahoma land run. Some 36,000 prospective settlers registered in these tents in September 1893. Between 1889 and 1901, 17 million acres were settled this way, turning unsettled tracts into cities overnight.

Performing rope tricks at rodeos, Will Rogers developed and refined the unique humorous commentary on current events that would make him one of the biggest and most beloved stars of the 1920s and 1930s. He often said, "I never met a man I didn't like."

Fort Washita played an unusual role in the Indian Wars, protecting the Five Civilized Tribes from their enemies, the Plains Indians. Still visible are ruins of forty-eight buildings.

Indian, pioneer, and cowboy artifacts. Collection of Colt handguns. The Lodge, built in 1927 as a private home, has paintings, Indian blankets, and bark-covered furnishings. The National Y-Indian Guide Center has displays of Indian arts and crafts. Nature trail. Open daily except Mondays.

Frank Phillips Mansion (1107 South Cherokee Ave.; 918/336-2491). Built in 1908 by the founder of Phillips Petroleum, this Greek Revival house has original furnishings. Open daily except Mondays.

Nellie Johnstone Oil Well (Johnstone Park, 300 block of North Cherokee; 918/337-5267). A replica of the first commercial oil well in the state. Open daily, late May to Labor Day.

Tom Mix Museum (6 miles north on OK 123, at junction of Delaware and Don Tyler avenues in Dewey; 918/534-1555). Memorabilia of the first "King of the Cowboys," including stills from his films. Open daily except Mondays.

CLAREMORE

The humorist Will Rogers was born halfway between here and Oologah, but claimed Claremore as his hometown because, he said, "nobody but an Indian could pronounce Oologah." Claremore is the county seat of

Rogers County, named for Will's father, Clem. It is also the home of Lynn Riggs, whose play *Green Grow the Lilacs* became the Rodgers and Hammerstein musical *Oklahoma!*

Will Rogers Memorial (1 mile west on Will Rogers Blvd.; 918/341-0719). On twenty acres once owned by the humorist, the memorial has Rogers mementoes; the library has films and tapes. Jo Davidson's statue of Rogers is in the foyer. Rogers's tomb is in the garden. Open daily except major holidays.

Will Rogers Birthplace (12 miles northwest on OK 88, then 2 miles north off U.S. 169; 918/341-2818). The house where Oklahoma's favorite son was born. Open daily.

Lynn Riggs Memorial (Thunderbird Library, Rogers State College; 918/341-7510). Has author's personal effects, original manuscripts, original "surrey with the fringe on top." Open daily except Sunday.

J. M. Davis Gun Museum (333 North Lynn Riggs Blvd.; 918/341-5707). More than 20,000 firearms, as well as arrowheads, saddles, posters, and other artifacts are on display. Collection of John Rogers sculptures. Open daily.

DURANT

Fort Washita (16 miles northwest via OK 78-199, on the east shore of Lake Texoma; 405/924-6502). Built in 1842 to protect the Five Civilized Tribes from the Plains Indians, the fort served as a Confederate supply depot during the Civil War. Remains of forty-eight buildings. Open daily.

Chickasaw Council House (Lake Texoma, 14 miles west on US 70). At the northern end of the lake, on the courthouse grounds in Tishomingo, is the log cabin that was the first seat of government of the Chickasaw Nation in the Indian Territory. The cabin, enclosed in a larger building, has Chickasaw history displays. Open daily.

Three Valley Museum (16th and Locust; 405/920-1907). In the Choctaw Nation Headquarters, the museum displays Indian art and beadwork, old dolls. Open weekdays.

EL RENO

Fort Reno (3 miles west on Old U.S. 66, then a mile north; 405/262-5291). This fort guarded the Darlington Agency during and after the Cheyenne uprising of 1874. In 1877, after Custer's defeat at the Little Bighorn, Dull Knife and more than 900 Cheyennes arrived under escort at the agency. The next year Dull Knife and many braves escaped and headed for their northern homelands. Troops from Fort Reno and other posts pursued and captured them in Nebraska and brought them back. In 1889 the garrison guarded the border against the "Sooners," so named because they rushed in before the official opening of the Land Run. The only surviving building has been restored and refurnished. Open daily.

Canadian County Historical Society Museum (Wade and Grand streets; 405/262-5121). Housed in a 1907 Rock Island Depot, the museum has pioneer and Indian exhibits. On the grounds is an agriculture exhibit barn, a historic hotel and railroad exhibit, a log cabin and an old schoolhouse. Open Tuesday through Friday and Sundays.

ENID

Museum of the Cherokee Strip (507 South 4th St.; 405/237-4433). Materials relating to the Plains Indians, the 1893 rush for land, and the early settlement of the area are on display. Open daily.

Homesteader's Sod House (30 miles west on U.S. 60, then 6 miles north of Cleo Springs on OK 8; 405/463-2441). Built in 1894 by Marshall McCully, this is reputedly

the only house of this type still standing in the state. Period furnishings. Open daily except Mondays.

GUTHRIE

On the eve of the great land rush, there was a small frame railroad station and a partly completed land registration office here. Hours later there was a tent city of 20,000. Guthrie was the territorial capital and the first state capital. Today it has one of the outstanding collections of Victorian buildings in the country. Outstanding are the old opera house and the Guthrie Railroad Hotel.

Oklahoma Territorial Museum (402 East Oklahoma Ave.; 405/282-1889). Exhibits relating to life in the territory are on display. Next door is the Carnegie Library, the site of the inaugurations of the last territorial and the first state governor. Open Tuesday through Sunday.

State Capital Publishing Museum (301 West Harrison; 405/282-4123). In the 1902 State Capital Publishing Company building, the museum has vintage printing equipment and original furnishings of the first newspaper published in the territory. Open daily except Monday.

Accommodations: *Harrison House* (124

Territory Days at Fort Reno celebrates the time when this old fort in Wyoming's Canadian River valley protected settlers during the Cheyenne uprising of 1874. A military cemetery is on the grounds. In 1948 the fort was made into a livestock research laboratory.

The Five Civilized Tribes

As America grew, the Indians were forced to give way or face extermination. At first it just happened, then Indian relocation became government policy. After the Louisiana Purchase, President Jefferson suggested moving the five major tribes of the Southeast (Cherokee, Creek, Choctaw, Chickasaw, and Seminole) west of the Mississippi. They posed no threat; they were peaceful and had adopted some of the white culture. They were simply in the way.

Jefferson's suggestion became policy under President Jackson. First a number of Cherokees were relocated. Under pressure, the Chickasaw began moving in the 1820s. The Choctaw were ousted in 1830; the Creek during the winter of 1834–35, many of them dying on the journey. The removal of the remaining Cherokees went to the Supreme Court, which ruled that the Cherokee Nation was a distinct community occupying its own territory. President Jackson ignored the decision and began parceling out Cherokee land to white settlers. In 1839, troops rounded up the Cherokee and marched them west with heavy loss of life along the "Trail of Tears." The Seminole moved only after the longest and costliest war fought by the United States against Indians. (Some Cherokees and Seminoles hid out and are the ancestors of those still living in the East.)

The five tribes were placed in what now is Oklahoma. Repeatedly attacked by the Cheyenne and the Kaw, they banded together in 1843 to form the Five Civilized Tribes, a common front against the "wild tribes" of the buffalo country. The tribes owned slaves, and the Civil War brought new problems. The Chickasaw, Choctaw, and Seminole promptly sided with the Confederacy. The Cherokee tried to remain neutral, but soon entered into a treaty with the Confederate government. The Creek divided into Confederate and Union parties. Military action in Indian country brought suffering, especially to the Cherokee and the Creek.

After the war, large tracts of land were taken from the tribes in retribution for their Southern sympathies. In 1901, Congress granted citizenship to every Indian in the Indian Territory, then revoked their land grants. In 1905, Congress denied a petition to create a separate state for the tribes, making the Indian Territory part of the Oklahoma Territory. When Oklahoma became a state in 1907, the Five Civilized Tribes were moved to reservations.

Delegates from thirty-four tribes pose in 1880 in front of Creek Council House in Indian Territory. Forced to migrate from the East, the Five Civilized Tribes adopted white ways but still lost their lands to whites when the Oklahoma Territory was opened to settlement.

West Harrison; 405/282-1000). In what was the first bank in town, this hotel has twenty-three guest rooms named after famous Guthrie residents such as O. Henry, Lon Chaney, and Tom Mix, who once tended bar in town. Breakfast is included in the rates.

LAWTON

Fort Sill Military Reservation (4 miles north on U.S. 277; 405/351-5123). Founded in 1869 by Gen. Philip Sheridan, this was the site of an ill-fated experiment in Indian management. President Grant, stung by criticism of corruption on the reservations, decided to appoint churchmen as Indian agents. The Quakers responded enthusiastically, and were sent here to convert some of the fiercest tribes in the West into peaceful farmers. Under the "Quaker Policy," the army could be involved only at the request of the Quaker Indian agents. The Indians soon were raiding settlements in Texas, returning to safety here, and defying the army to do anything about it. Finally the Quaker agent asked the army to punish the Indians, then resigned when he was criticized by his superiors. The Red River War of 1874–75 was the result. In 1894, Geronimo and his Apaches were settled here after their exile in Florida.

Fort Sill is an artillery training and command center. Nearly all the old stone buildings have survived, and forty-three of them constitute the Old Post National Historic Landmark. Of note are the *Sherman House*, where, in 1871, Gen. William Tecumseh Sherman was nearly killed on the front porch by Kiowas; *Old Post Headquarters*, from which post generals conducted their Indian campaigns; and *Old Post Chapel*, one of the oldest houses of worship still in use in Oklahoma. The *U.S. Army Field Artillery and Fort Sill Museum* has Indian and cavalry artifacts. Open daily.

Museum of the Great Plains (Elmer Thomas Park, 601 Ferris Blvd.; 405/355-3541). Displays relating to Indians, exploration, the fur trade, settlement, and ranching. Period rooms depict a street of a frontier town. Outdoors is a railroad depot, a 300-ton locomotive, a trading post, and a trader's cabin. Open daily.

MUSKOGEE

Muskogee was once a trading post in Indian country on the old Texas Road near the confluence of the Verdigris, Grand, and Arkansas rivers. After it became a town, the U.S. Union agency for the Five Civilized Tribes was located here.

Five Civilized Tribes Museum (Agency Hill, in Honor Heights Park; 918/683-1701). Artifacts and art of the Cherokees, Chickasaws, Choctaws, Creeks, and Seminoles. Open daily.

Cherokee Courthouse-Tahlonteeskee (24 miles south via OK 10 in Gore). A replica of the council house and courthouse of the Cherokee Nation West. In 1809, Chief Tahlonteeskee, a leader of the original Cherokee Nation, led a band of 300 and settled in what is now Arkansas. Twenty years later the expansion of the Arkansas territory forced these Western Cherokees to move farther west, and they established their council ground here. After Tahlonteeskee died, his brother, John Jolly, became chief and welcomed Sam Houston to the area, where he lived from 1829 to 1833 (Houston's Cherokee wife, Talihina, is buried at the Fort Gibson National Cemetery). The Eastern Cherokees arrived here in 1839, won control of the nation, and moved the capital to Tahlequah in 1843. This was the courthouse for the Canadian District of the Cherokee Nation until statehood in 1907. Open daily.

Fort Gibson Military Park (6 miles east on U.S. 62 to Fort Gibson, then a mile north on OK 80; 918/478/2669). Established in

"If a man loses anything and goes back and looks carefully for it he will find it, and that is what the Indians are doing now when they ask you to give them the things that were promised in the past; and I do not consider that they should be treated like beasts, and that is the reason I have grown up with the feelings I have."

—SITTING BULL, SIOUX

Education went west with the homesteaders. A young teacher (center) and her pupils pose in front of their one-room, sod school-house in the Oklahoma Territory around 1895. Children were let out of school to work on family farms during planting and harvesting.

1824, Fort Gibson was one of the most important posts on the "Permanent Indian Frontier." During the Civil War it was occupied briefly by Confederate forces. Later it was a stronghold in the Indian Territory. Today the original log stockade and eleven outlying log buildings have been reconstructed. Period rooms depict early army life. Open daily in the summer. Nearby is the Fort Gibson National Cemetery.

OKLAHOMA CITY

On the morning of April 22, 1889, when the Oklahoma Land Run began, this was barren prairie; by nightfall it was a tent city of 10,000. In 1928 the city learned it was atop one of the country's largest oil fields. Now there are oil wells even on the lawn of the Capitol building.

State Capitol (Northeast 23rd St. and Lincoln Blvd.; 405/521-3356). Daily tours. Opposite the Capitol, the *State Museum of History* (405/521-2491) has an extensive collection of Indian artifacts and exhibits on the state's history. Open daily except Sundays.

Oklahoma Art Center (fairgrounds at junction of I-40 and I-44; 405/946-4477). The collection includes a selection of Western paintings. Open daily except Mondays.

American Indian Center (Kirkpatrick Center, 2100 Northeast 52nd St.; 405/427-5461). A museum complex with a special gallery for Indian art exhibits. Open daily.

Harn Homestead and 1889er Museum (312 Northeast 18th St.; 405/235-4058). A

Mustangs

A mustang is a wild, unclaimed horse of Spanish blood, and millions of them once roamed the West. Ranchers treated them as either range pests to be exterminated, or as a cheap, unwanted commodity to be exploited. Inhumane methods were used to capture wild horses , and the pet-food industry provided a ready market for them. When mustangs were in danger of extinction, they found a friend in Mrs. Velma "Wild Horse Annie" Johnston of Reno, Nevada, who was almost singlehandedly responsible for the "Wild Horse Annie" Act, passed by Congress in the 1970s. The act prohibits the use of airborne and mechanized vehicles in rounding up mustangs. Later legislation set aside two areas for them, the Pryor Mountain Wild Horse Range near the Montana-Wyoming border, and the old bombing range at Nellis Air Force Base in Nevada. When placed under federal protection, the number of mustangs had dwindled to 17,000.

homestead claimed in the 1889 Land Run. A 1904 farmhouse is furnished with vintage objects. Three-story stone and wood barn. One-room schoolhouse. Open Tuesday through Saturday.

National Cowboy Hall of Fame and Western Heritage Center (1700 Northeast 63rd St., off I-44 near I-35, between Martin Luther King and Kelley avenues; 405/478-2250). The West of Yesterday Gallery has life-sized re-creations of early Indian and pioneer life. Its art collection includes Remington's "Coming Through the Rye" and J. E. Fraser's "End of the Trail," as well as the John Wayne collection of guns, knives, Hopi kachina dolls, and paintings. Portrait gallery of Western movie stars. Open daily.

Oklahoma National Stock Yards (2500 Exchange Ave.; 405/235-8675). One of the largest stockyards in the world. Auctions of cattle, hogs and sheep in the Exchange Building.

Accommodations: *The Grandison* (1841 Northwest 15th St.; 405/521-0011). This three-story Victorian, with a pond and gazebo, has five guest rooms with private baths. The bridal suite has a working fireplace, lace curtains, and a claw-foot tub. Breakfast is included in the rates. *Flora's Bed & Breakfast* (2312 Northwest 46th St.; 495/840-3157). An antiques-filled home overlooking the city.

PAWHUSKA

This is the capital of the Osage Indian Nation, and the Osage Agency conducts all tribal business. The first Boy Scout troop in the country was organized here in 1909.

Osage Tribal Museum (Grandview Ave.; 918/287-2495). Memorabilia, costumes, and arts and crafts of the original inhabitants of the state. Finger-woven sashes are an Osage specialty. Open weekdays.

Osage County Historical Society Museum (700 North Lynn Ave.; 918/287-

9924). In the old Santa Fe depot, the museum has Western and Indian artifacts. Memorabilia of the first U.S. Boy Scout troop. Open daily.

Drummond Home (21 miles south on OK 99 in Hominy; 918/885-2374). The restored 1908 Victorian residence of Fred Drummond, a merchant and cattleman. Original furnishings. Open daily except Mondays.

PAWNEE

Pawnee Tribal Offices (Main St.; 918/762-3624). The Pawnee were Plains Indians who lived in earth-covered lodges, farmed, and were much more peaceful than the other Plains tribes. Pawnee is a corruption of the Indian word *pariki*, meaning "horn," which refers to the traditional dressing of the scalp lock, the hair stiffened with fat to make it stand erect and curved like a horn. The Pawnee Agency has several historic buildings, including the tribal offices. Open daily except Sundays.

Pawnee Bill Museum and Park (On U.S. 64; 918/762-2513). The fourteen-room 1910 home of Pawnee Bill, a star of Buffalo Bill's Wild West Show. Original furnishings.

Oh, bury me not on the lone prairie, Where wild coyotes will howl o'er me, Where the rattlers hiss, and the crow flies free. Oh, bury me not on the lone prairie.

—"THE LONE PRAIRIE," COWBOY SONG

Pawnee Bill led his own Wild West show before he joined forces with his rival, Buffalo Bill. Around the turn of the century, shows like this captured the imagination of the country and had a great influence on how Easterners perceived the Western experience.

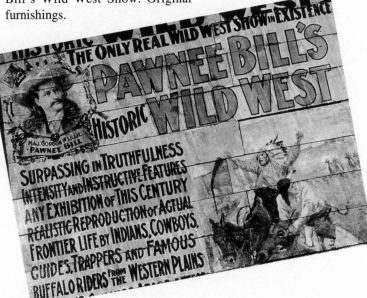

Belle Starr

Poor choices in men turned Myra Belle Shirley, a student of the classics as a girl, into Belle Starr, bandit queen. She was married briefly to the notorious Cole Younger, who fathered her first child. Then she took up with James Reed, a robber of banks and trains, had another child, and fled to California with him when the law closed in. By 1869 the Reeds were in Texas, rustling cattle. Belle rode with Reed, dressed in a velvet skirt and plumed hat. When Reed was killed, she left the children with her mother and went to the Indian Territory, moving in with a Cherokee named Sam Starr. In 1883, she and Starr went to prison for horse theft. After Starr was killed in a gunfight, Belle took up with Jim July, a young Creek bandit. He was arrested and taken to Fort Smith, Arkansas, for trial. Belle rode along, and on the way home she was shot in the back and killed.

"We do not take up the warpath without a just cause and honest purpose."

—PUSHMATAHA, CHOCTAW

◆–I–◆

Sequoyah, the famed Cherokee who created an eighty-six-character alphabet for the Cherokee language, built this one-room cabin and lived here for many years. The Cherokees were the first tribe with a constitution and a body of law written in their own language.

Wild West Show mementos. Longhorn cattle and buffalo graze in a pasture on the grounds. Open daily.

PONCA CITY

Pioneer Woman Museum (701 Monument Rd.; 405/765-6108). Pioneer home and ranch exhibits, costumes and memorabilia of family life. Bryant Baker statue memorializing the courage of the women who settled the West. Open daily except Mondays, June through August, Wednesday through Saturday the rest of the year.

Cultural Center (1000 East Grand Ave.; 405/765-5268). Housed in the Marland-Paris Historic House, the center includes the DAR Museum, the Indian Museum, the Bryant Baker studio, and the 101 Ranch Room. Open daily.

POTEAU

Kerr Museum (8 miles southwest on U.S. 271, then 1 mile east; 918/647-8221, ext. 116). The museum documents the develop-

ment of eastern Oklahoma, and has Choctaw artifacts. Open daily.

Spiro Mound Archaeological State Park (15 miles north and east on U.S. 59; 918/962-2062). Nine earthen mounds dating from A.D. 1200–1350. An interpretive center displays excavated artifacts. Open daily.

Peter Conser House (4 miles south, then 3½ miles west of Heavener; 918/653-2493). The restored home of a senator in the Choctaw legislature. Open daily except Mondays.

Heavener Runestone (northeast of Heavener, off U.S. 59). Eight runes, or Scandinavian cryptography, which, scholars believe, were inscribed by Vikings in A.D. 1012. Other runes, using the Scandinavian alphabet of the 3rd through 10th centuries A.D., were inscribed on several stones found in the area.

SALLISAW

Sequoyah's Home (11 miles northeast on OK 101; 918/775-2413). A one-room log

cabin built by Sequoyah, the Cherokee scholar who created an eighty-six-character alphabet for the Cherokee language, the first written Indian language. California's redwood trees, the majestic Sequoias, were named in his honor. Visitor center. Small museum. Open daily except Mondays.

SHAWNEE

Potawatomi Indian Nation Museum (8 Beard St.; 405/275-1480). The museum houses material relating to the history of the Citizen Band Potawatomi Tribe, which has its headquarters here. The gift shop has Potawatomi and other Indian arts and crafts. Open daily except Sundays.

Seminole Nation Museum (524 South Wewoka Ave., 30 miles southeast via OK 3, U.S. 270, OK 56 in Wewoka; 405/257-5580). The museum chronicles the forced migration of the Seminole Nation from Florida west over the infamous Trail of Tears, to establish their capital here. Displays include a Seminole house similar to those seen in Florida. Dioramas of a stickball game, the Whipping Tree, and the Old Wewoka Trading Post. The art gallery and craft shop have unusual work of the tribe's artisans. Open daily except Mondays.

Mabee-Gerrer Museum of Art (St. Gregory's College, 1900 West MacArthur Dr.; 405/273-9999). The collection includes work by Western artists and artifacts of North American Indians. Open daily except Mondays.

TAHLEQUAH

After being driven from the east, the Cherokee tribes met here in 1839 to form the Cherokee Nation. They signed a constitution written using the Cherokee alphabet created by Sequoyah. The Cherokee published the first newspaper published in Indian Terri-

tory. In 1885 they established the first commercial telephone line in Oklahoma. It was later sold to the Southwestern Bell Telephone Company, which established a monument to this remarkable enterprise in the Old Courthouse Square.

Cherokee National Capitol (U.S. 62S; 918/456-3742). Built in 1867, the building is open Monday through Friday.

Cherokee Heritage Center (3½ miles south on U.S. 62, then 1 mile east on Willis Rd.; 918/456-6007). Reconstructions of 1650 and 1890 Cherokee villages. Living-history demonstrations. A museum has a collection of Cherokee Nation artifacts and mementos. Open daily.

Murrell Home Museum (3 miles south on OK 82, then 1 mile east on Murrell Rd.;

"One does not sell the earth upon which the people walk."

—CRAZY HORSE, SIOUX

The Seminole-Negro Scouts

These brave men were descended from runaway slaves who lived with the Seminole in Florida. When the tribe was forcibly resettled in Oklahoma, many of them went to Mexico instead. The U.S. Army found them there and recruited many of the men, promising money, food, and land for them and their families.

The Seminole-Negroes dressed like Indians, had an uncanny ability to find and follow trails that were weeks old, and could live off the desert. They were made scouts, and in nine years compiled an enviable record: in twenty-six engagements, twelve of them major, no scout was killed or seriously wounded, although sometimes they were outnumbered eight to one.

In one engagement, their commanding officer and three scouts ambushed a party of some thirty Comanches. When the tide turned against them, the scouts mounted and started to ride away, but noticed that the officer was unable to reach his horse. Covered by two other scouts, Sergeant John Ward rode back and scooped him onto his horse, and the four escaped uninjured. All three scouts were awarded the Medal of Honor.

The story of the Seminole-Negro Scouts has a sad ending. The War Department refused to honor its promise, saying it was out of land. A few scouts deserted, but the rest stayed on to fight some more.

The Murrell Home, built in Tahlequah in Indian Territory (present-day Oklahoma) now is a museum. The national capital of the Cherokee Nation is nearby, and in the summer the Cherokee Heritage Center presents the "Trail of Tears," a musical drama of the tribe's tragic history.

the development of North America, and the Indian. Works by Frederic Remington, Charles Russell, George Catlin, and others. Indian artifacts. Library has 80,000 items. Bookstore and gift shop. Founded by Thomas Gilcrease, an oilman of Creek descent. Open daily.

Tulsa County Historical Society Museum (2501 West Newton St.; 918/585-5520). In the Gilcrease Mansion, the museum has memorabilia, rare books , and household goods. Open daily except Mondays.

Creek Nation Council Oak Tree (18th and Cheyenne). The "Council Oak" stands as a memorial to the Lochapokas Creek Indian tribe, which, in 1834, brought law and order to a near wilderness.

Discoveryland! Outdoor Theater (10 miles west via West 41st St.; 918/496-0190). *Oklahoma!,* Rodgers and Hammerstein's musical tribute to the state, has found a national home here. Performances Monday through Saturday, June through August.

918/456-2751). A pre–Civil War mansion with many original furnishings. Open daily except Mondays.

Trail of Tears. A professional cast presents James Vance's musical history of the Cherokee people in the Tsa-La-Gi amphitheater at the culture center. Performances nightly except Sundays, June through mid-August.

Accommodations: *Lodge of the Cherokees (Tsa-La-Gi)* (4 miles west-southwest on U.S. 62; 918/456-0511). This 100-room motel is owned and operated by the Cherokee Nation. Here the Restaurant of the Cherokees features fry bread and other Indian specialties. A gift shop has Cherokee arts and crafts.

TULSA

Thomas Gilcrease Institute of American History and Art (1400 Gilcrease Museum Rd.; 918/582-3122). An important collection of art concerning the westward movement,

WAURIKA

On a mesa here, early Chisholm Trail drovers made two piles of sandstone boulders, each about twelve feet high, that could be seen for ten to fifteen miles in either direction.

Chisholm Trail Historical Museum (2 miles southeast via U.S. 70; 405/228-2166). The Chisholm Gallery tells the story of the trail. Pioneer Gallery. Slide presentation. Open daily except Mondays.

WOODWARD

Plains Indians and Pioneers Museum (2009 Williams Ave.; 405/256-6136). The museum has exhibits on Indian culture and pioneer life. Personal effects of Temple Houston, son of Sam Houston. Vintage bank memorabilia, and a building from nearby Fort Supply. Open daily except Mondays.

8

Texas

ABILENE

Founded in 1881 as a railhead on the Texas and Pacific Railroad, Abilene cut short the long cattle drives to Dodge City. It was a tough town in the early days, but quieted down under the influence of religious fundamentalists.

Fort Phantom Hill Ruins (14 miles north on FM 600; 915/677-1309). A few buildings and chimneys are all that remain of the fort, built in 1851 to stop Indian raids. The infantry stationed here were ineffectual against the Comanche, and the fort was abandoned. Later it was an outpost of the Texas Rangers, and the army used it briefly during the Indian Wars of the 1870s. It is on private property, but may be visited. Open daily. Limited wheelchair access.

Buffalo Gap Historic Village (14 miles south on U.S. 89; 915/572-3365 or 572-3572). A small pioneer village restored by Dr. R. Lee Rode of Abilene. Buildings include courthouse, depot, church, and blacksmith shop. Open daily, April through October; weekends the rest of the year.

ALBANY

Fort Griffin State Historical Park (15 miles north on U.S. 283; 915/762-3592). From this fort, founded in 1867, soldiers took part in the campaigns against the Kiowa and Comanche. The fort was abandoned in 1881. A visitor center has material on the fort's history. On the grounds are replicas of some of the original buildings and the ruins of others. Home of the State Longhorn Herd. Open daily.

ALICE

Originally named Bandana, this town began in 1878 because a nearby town would not grant right-of-way to the Texas-Mexican Railroad. It was renamed Alice in honor of the daughter of Capt. Richard King, the founder of the nearby King Ranch. From 1888 to 1893, Alice probably was the largest cattle-shipping point in the world.

South Texas Museum (66 South Wright St.; 512/668-8891). The museum is in an early-20th-century ranch house built to resemble the Alamo, and has material on the area's ranching and oil industry. Open Tuesday through Friday.

ALPINE

Fort Davis National Historic Site (40 miles north via TX 114 to Fort Davis, then just out of town on TX 17; 915/426-3225). The San Antonio–El Paso Road attracted Kiowa, Comanche, and Mescalero Apache raiders. This was the largest and most important of the outposts built along the road. In the nearby desert in the 1850s, the army tested camels as replacements for mules. The western forts were evacuated when Texas seceded. Confederates took them over, but withdrew when they failed to conquer New Mexico. Wrecked by the Apaches, Fort Davis was deserted for years. In 1867 the army returned and rebuilt it. Some regiments stationed here, composed of ex-slaves, called "buffalo soldiers" by the Indians, fought against Victorio's Apaches. The routes of the Texas Pacific and Southern Pacific railroads bypassed Fort Davis, and it was closed down in 1891.

The remains here are the most extensive of any fort in the Southwest. The 460-acre site in the Davis Mountains encompasses some twenty-five original structures and the foundations and ruins of dozens of others. A restored barracks houses a visitor center and a museum that displays exhibits of fort life and the Indian War. Five buildings are restored and refurbished in the style of the 1880s. An audio re-creation of a Retreat Parade echoes over the parade grounds. Open daily.

Overland Trail Museum (2 blocks south of Fort Davis; 915/426-3808). Named after the trail that once passed this way, the museum has local history exhibits. Open by appointment.

Museum of the Big Bend (Sul Ross State University campus, U.S. 90E; 915/837-8143). The museum has historical mate-

rial of the Big Bend region, a reconstructed general store, a blacksmith shop, and a stagecoach. Open daily except Mondays.

AMARILLO

In 1887 the Fort Worth & Denver City Railroad and the Atchison, Topeka & Santa Fe met here in the Panhandle and by the early 1890s it was a great cattle shipping market. First it was a tent city called Ragtown, then Amarillo, which is Spanish for "yellow," the color of a nearby creek.

Lee and Mary E. Bivins Home (100 South Polk; 806/373-7800). A 1905 late Georgian Revival, this was the home of a rancher who owned some one million acres and 60,000 head of cattle. Open daily.

Kwahadi Indian Dancers (1615 Bellaire; 806/352-9003). A ninety-minute show of authentic dances presented by a Boy Scout Explorer Post in their own theater.

A Day in the Old West Tours (806/374-1497, or 800/692-1338 in Texas). Various tours in the Palo Duro Canyon area, including Cowboy Morning with a chuckwagon breakfast, visits to the Figure 3 Ranch, and performances of *Texas* (see below) in season. Daily.

Alibates Flint Quarries National Monument (32 miles northeast on TX 136 to entrance, 6 miles south of Fritch; 806/857-3151). For nearly 12,000 years, Indians came here to mine flint, which is as hard as fine steel, to make tools and weapons. Although Alibates flint comes from one ten-square-mile area in the Panhandle, archaeologists have found arrowheads and tools made of it in many places in the Southwest and the Great Plains. The quarries are no more than shallow depressions surrounded by rubble. Near the pits are several small prehistoric ruins. Petroglyphs are on a bluff nearby. Entry by guided tour only. Tours daily from Memorial Day to Labor Day. Limited wheelchair access.

Brand Names

Cattle branding was introduced to the West by Spanish ranchers. A permanent and distinctive mark burned into an animal's hide became the accepted legal proof of ownership. By 1848, Texas required the registration of each brand with the county clerk, and cattle associations in the northern cattle states maintained "brand books." On the range, unbranded cattle belonged to those industrious enough to rope and brand them. Calves were branded at the spring roundup, the brand placed on the left hindquarters where it could be seen easily by a right-handed roper.

Early brands used numerals, letters, symbols (for example, a spur or a pitchfork), or acronyms (XIT stood for "Ten in Texas"), but as the number of herds increased, variations were introduced. A quarter circle under a brand made it "rocking"; placed above the brand made it "flying"; rounding the sharp angles of a letter made it "running"; a diagonal mark before a letter made it a "slash." The letter could be placed in an unusual position: a tilted letter was "tumbling"; a letter lying on its side was "lazy"; and an upsidedown letter was "crazy." Ranchers still brand their cattle, but today most purebred stock is marked with a metal ear tag or a tattoo inside the ear.

Panhandle Plains Historical Museum (2401 4th Ave., 1 block east of U.S. 87 in Canyon, 16 miles south on U.S. 87; 806/656-2244). The museum has several exhibits of archaeological material from this region, and a model of what a Panhandle Pueblo structure might have looked like. Exceptional collection of Southern Plains Indian artifacts, gun collection, art gallery, gift shop. Open daily.

Boys Ranch and Old Tascosa (36 miles northwest on FM 1061 to U.S. 385, then north 2 miles to Spur 233; 806/372-2341). Tascosa flourished for about twenty years and then died around 1887 when the railroad passed it by. Billy the Kid and Pat Garrett were here briefly. All that remains is the old courthouse (now a museum) and Boot Hill. Nearby 10,000-acre Boys Ranch was founded in 1939 for homeless or delinquent boys. Open daily in summer.

Texas, a Musical Drama (Palo Duro Canyon State Park, 12 miles east on TX 217 to Park Rd. 5; reservations, 806/655-2185). This presentation tells of pioneer life in the Panhandle, with a cast of eighty. Nightly except Sundays, late June through late August.

Accommodations: *Hudspeth House* (in Canyon, at 1905 4th Ave.; 806/655-9800). A bed-and-breakfast built from the lumber of an old cotton gin in 1909, this lodging has seven guest rooms decorated with antiques.

AUSTIN

In 1838 a party of buffalo hunters, including Mirabeau B. Lamar, vice-president of the Republic of Texas, camped on the Colorado River here. When Lamar became president of the republic in 1839, he suggested the spot as the site of a permanent capital. It was named for Stephen F. Austin, son of Moses Austin, leader of the first American colony in Texas. When Texas became a state, Austin remained the capital.

State Capitol (north end of Congress

Stephen Austin

The American colony in Texas was founded and led to independence by Stephen Austin, a Yale man who grew up in Missouri. Austin's father was planning to start a colony in Texas when he died in 1821. Austin took over, negotiating a land grant from Mexico on the Colorado and Brazos rivers. After Mexico won its independence from Spain, he was able to get new laws favorable to the colony. By 1830, however, with some 8,000 Americans in Texas, Mexico cut off immigration. The Americans set up a separate government and framed a constitution that Austin took to Mexico City, where he was jailed on a charge of inciting insurrection. He was released, and returned to Texas to find the Americans on the verge of revolt. Austin commanded the troops that fought the Mexican army at San Antonio. Later he went to Washington, where he negotiated recognition of the Texas Republic.

Ave.; 512/463-0063). The largest state capitol in the country, it is built of pink granite from Burnet, which donated the granite in return for building a railroad to the town. Tours daily.

Texas State Library (1201 Brazos St.; 512/463-5455). This library has the Texas Declaration of Independence and other historic documents. A forty-five-foot mural depicts state history. Genealogy library. Open weekdays.

Texas Confederate Museum (112 East 11th St.; 512/472-2596). On the first floor of the 1857 Old Land Office, this museum has guns, uniforms, documents, and flags. Open weekdays. On the second floor, the *Daughters of the Republic of Texas Museum* (512/477-1812) has relics of the Texas Republic. Open Wednesday through Sunday.

Archer M. Huntington Art Gallery (Ransom Center, 23rd and Jacinto; 512/471-7324). Excellent Western art is in the permanent collection. Open daily.

O. Henry Home and Museum (409 East 5th St.; 512/472-1903). The Victorian cottage home, with original furnishings, of

The Black Frontier

Only recently have historians noted the role played by African-Americans in the Old West. Estevan, an "Arabian black," survived a shipwreck off the Texas coast in 1529, managed to find his way back to Mexico, and helped lead an expedition to the Southwest. A black man named York accompanied the Lewis and Clark expedition as Clark's body servant, and learned to be a skilled hunter and interpreter. A free black, Jacob Dodson, proved to be a valuable member of John Frémont's second and third expeditions. Blacks were active in the fur trade in various positions, including that of independent trader. One historian noted that "the old fur traders always got a black if possible to negotiate for them with the Indians . . . because they could manage them better than white men, with less friction."

Blacks were less racially arrogant and more apt than whites to marry Indian women and maintain lasting associations with Indians . Free black farmers, stockbreeders, and craftsmen, attracted to the Texas frontier by Mexico's racial tolerance, stayed despite the Texas Republic's racist laws. William Goyens, a free black with a white wife and several slaves, settled in 1821 at Nacogdoches, where he operated a large blacksmith shop, speculated in land, and served as an interpreter to the Cherokee. He enjoyed the confidence and respect of Sam Houston. The Ashworth clan of free blacks were by 1850 the largest cattle raisers in Jefferson County.

George Bush, a freeborn mulatto, went to Oregon in 1844 and settled on Puget Sound. A successful farmer, he helped build the first American-owned gristmill and sawmill, and introduced the first mower and reaper. His son, William Owen Bush, served during the first two terms of the Washington State legislature. Another black, George Washington, grew wealthy as a farmer and in 1872 founded the town of Centerville (now Centralia, Washington).

In colonial times, many runaway slaves made their way to Mexico, where they encountered comparatively little racial discrimination. In 1781, more than half of the original settlers of Los Angeles were of black ancestry. In 1849 a few hundred Seminole-, Creek-, and Cherokee-blacks, commanded by John Horse, left the Indian Territory, crossed Texas, and entered Mexico, where they received government land grants as military colonists. They help fight off Comanche and Apache raids, as well as slave-hunting raids by white Texans. Several hundred of their descendants are now Mexican farmers and stockbreeders.

author O. Henry (William Sydney Porter). While living here, he edited the short-lived weekly *Rolling Stone*. Open daily except Mondays.

French Legation Museum (802 San Marcos St.; 512/472-8180). The building housed the *chargé d'affaires* to the Republic of Texas. Creole architecture and furnishings. Open daily except Mondays.

Neill-Cochran House (2310 San Gabriel; 512/478-2335). A Greek Revival mansion built in 1853 for George Washington Hill, but never occupied by him. Restored and furnished with antiques. Tours. Open Wednesday through Sunday.

Historic Areas. There are two old sections of the city worth touring, Old Pecan Street, which is now 6th Street, with many restored Victorian buildings, and Congress Avenue, which is on the National Register of Historic Places.

Accommodations: *Southard House* (908 Blanco; 512/474-4731). This 1900 city landmark, convenient to the capitol and the University of Texas, has five guest rooms with private baths. Breakfast included. *The McCallum House* (113 West 32nd St.; 512/451-6744). An elegant late-Victorian bed-and-breakfast with antique furnishings. It has four guest rooms.

BEAUMONT

Spindletop, the first great Texas oil gusher, blew in here in 1901, oil spouting 200 feet into the air. In the oil boom, oil rigs were so thick in the Spindletop Field that a person could reportedly cross from platform to platform without touching the ground. Exxon, Gulf, Mobil, and Texaco all began here.

Gladys City Boom Town (Lamar University campus, University and Cardinal drives; 409/835-0823). A reconstruction of the boomtown that sprang up after Spindletop, its fifteen clapboard buildings include company offices, a saloon, and a general store.

The Lucas Gusher Monument, a fifty-eight-foot granite shaft, pays tribute to the Spindletop pioneers. Open daily except Mondays.

John J. French Museum (2995 French Rd.; 409/898-1906). A restored 1845 Greek Revival house, the oldest house in the city, the museum has a re-created tannery and frontier trading post. Open daily except Mondays.

McFaddin-Ward House (1906 McFaddin; 409/898-0348). A Beaux Arts colonial built in 1906 for a wealthy Texas rancher and oilman, the house is elegantly furnished. Tours. Open daily except Mondays.

BRACKETTVILLE

This town started as a supply village for nearby Fort Clark, which remained an active U.S. Army cavalry post until 1946. Descendants of the Black Seminole Indian scouts who served during the Indian campaigns still live here.

Fort Clark (U.S. 90, east edge of town; 512/563-2493). Founded in 1852, this fort guarded the San Antonio–El Paso road. Officers who served here included George C. Marshall, George S. Patton, and Jonathan Wainwright. Many fort buildings still stand. The Old Guardhouse has a small museum, open weekends. The fort is the grounds of a resort; phone before visiting.

Seminole Indian Scout Cemetery (3 miles south on FM 3348). After the Seminole War in Florida, the Black Seminoles were relocated to Oklahoma, but many migrated into Texas. The army hired about 150 as scouts assigned to Fort Clark, and they proved themselves brave and loyal. Many are buried here, including four who were awarded the Congressional Medal of Honor.

Alamo Village Movieland (Shahan HV Ranches, 7 miles north on RR 674 to entrance; 512/563-2580). A replica of the Alamo was built here in the 1950s for the

Nearly 1,000 blacks went to the California Gold Rush as slaves or free men. There were black mining companies, and their success was mirrored in the names of some of the early mining camps: Nigger Gulch, Nigger Hill, Nigger Creek, and Nigger Bar. Barney Ford , a runaway mulatto, worked his way from Chicago to Denver in the early 1860s to discover that territorial law prohibited blacks from filing mining claims. He became a barber and went on to operate restaurants and hotels, owning leading hotels in Denver and Cheyenne.

In the Civil War, blacks on the Western frontier were the first of their race to take up arms on behalf of the Union and their own freedom. In Kansas they were organized into Union regiments in which blacks served as equals. Long before the government authorized black enlistment, blacks were serving in Kansas volunteer regiments. These units, often working with Indian-black and white regiments, were engaged in savage border warfare.

After the war, many blacks joined Western regiments in fighting Indians. Charley Tyler and Britton Johnson were famed as Indian fighters. Four regiments were formed with black enlisted men and white officers. The Indians called them "buffalo soldiers" from the texture of their hair. During a quarter century, the buffalo soldiers fought nearly 200 engagements. The campaigns against the Apache chiefs Victorio and Nana were conducted almost entirely by black troopers. Between 1870 and 1890, fourteen black soldiers were awarded the Medal of Honor.

Black vaqueros had been active on the northern frontier of Mexico as early as the mid-16th century, but the heyday of blacks in the cattle country was the 1870s, when the great herds of Texas cattle were driven north. Black cowboys were numerous and often of outstanding ability. "Nigger Add," Matthew "Bones" Hooks, and "Bronco Sam" Stewart were among the legendary black horsebreakers. Bob Lemmons was famous for his ability to "walk down" a band of wild horses and eventually lead them into a corral by convincing them that he was really "one of them." Bill Picket was an outstanding rodeo performer. Some black cowboys, including "80 John" Wallace and Jess Pickett, both of Texas, saved their wages, bought little spreads, and eventually became prosperous ranchers.

Some blacks, individually or in groups, went to the Great Plains to be homestead farmers. They called themselves "Exodusters," out of the Egypt of the post-Reconstruction South to the Promised Land of Kansas.

John Wayne epic *The Alamo*. Nearby is an Old West town with a jail, a store, a stagecoach barn, a blacksmith, a bank, and other buildings. More than thirty feature films and television movies have been made here. Live entertainment in the summer. Cantina. Open daily.

BRENHAM

Washington-on-the-Brazos State Historical Park (14 miles northeast on TX 105, 5 miles northeast on FM 912; 409/878-2214). The site of the signing of the Texas Declaration of Independence in 1836, the 154-acre park contains *Independence Hall*, a replica of the building in which the declaration was signed; the *Anson Jones House*, the home of the last president of the Republic of Texas; and the *Star of the Republic Museum* (409/878-2214), which has exhibits on the Republic. All are open daily, March through August; Wednesday through Sunday the rest of the year.

Stephen F. Austin State Historical Park (23 miles southwest on TX 36; 409/830-1959). The site of the seat of Anglo-American colonies in Texas. Replica of the Austin home. Open daily.

Accommodations: *Country Life, Ltd.* (705 Clinton; 409/830-0477). A bed-and-breakfast with two guest rooms furnished with antiques.

BROWNSVILLE

Brownsville started as a fort, and the fort was the spark that ignited the Mexican War. In 1846, Gen. Zachary Taylor built here on the Rio Grande across from Matamoros. The Mexicans attacked the fort and the war was on. Among the first casualties was Major Jacob Brown; the fort and later the city were named after him. During the Civil War, Brownsville was the only unblocked port of the Confederacy. The last battle of the war was fought at Palmito Hill, about fourteen miles east of here, six weeks after Lee had surrendered at Appomattox.

Historic Brownsville Museum (641 East Madison; 512/548-1313). Housed in a 1928 Southern Pacific depot, the museum has historic documents, artifacts, and photographs. On the grounds are a small locomotive and two cabooses. Open Tuesday through Saturday.

Charles Stillman House (1305 East Washington at 13th). The restored 1850 home of Charles Stillman, a merchant from Connecticut, who founded Brownsville. Many original furnishings and memorabilia. Open daily except Saturdays.

Fort Brown (600 International, just east of Gateway Bridge; 512/542-3367). Now part of the Texas Southmost College, the old fort buildings include the post headquarters, guardhouse, hospital, medical laboratory, and morgue. Phone for schedule.

Mexican War Battlefields (marker commemorating the battles of Palo Alto and Resaca de la Palma, intersection of FM 1847 and FM 511). On May 8, 1846, Gen. Zachary Taylor and some 2,300 troops, on their way to relieve besieged Fort Brown, clashed with a Mexican force of 6,000 at Palo Alto, about ten miles from the fort. Deadly fire from Maj. Samuel Ringgold's light horse artillery helped overcome the heavy odds. Nine Americans, including Ringgold, and more than 300 Mexicans were killed in the battle. The next morning the Mexican army was waiting for Taylor, dug into a strong position in a dry streambed called Resaca de la Palma. The Americans once again drove off the Mexicans. Among the company commanders was Ulysses S. Grant, a young lieutenant. Some 120 Americans were killed or wounded. Mexican casualties were more than a thousand.

Palmito Hill Battlefield (marker on TX 4, about 14 miles east of Brownsville). Word of Lee's surrender had not reached the 300

Broadcast Days on the Range

The first real western drama series, "Death Valley Days," was broadcast in 1933, and it was on the air longer than any other. A year later came "The Lone Ranger," his horse Silver, and Tonto. The "Tom Mix Show" debuted the same year. Mix, a western movie star, was impersonated by an actor, and the program started the boxtop premium craze. The singing cowboys Gene Autry and Roy Rogers soon had programs. Other popular radio westerns of the 1930s included "The Range Rider," "Red Ryder," and "The Cisco Kid."

The first so-called adult western, "Gunsmoke," debuted on radio in 1952; in it Matt Dillon (played by William Conrad) was the marshal of Dodge City in the 1870s. Relying more on character and mood than on action, it became a top-rated program and spawned rivals such as "Death Valley Days" and "Fort Laramie."

Tom Mix

Gene Autry, who owned a number of radio stations, was the first western star to take advantage of television. His "Flying A" production company churned out low-budget serials: "The Range Rider," "Annie Oakley," "Buffalo Bill, Jr.," and "The Adventures of Champion" (featuring his own horse). Another star, Hopalong Cassidy, played by William Boyd, bought up the rights to his films, leasing them as reruns on television. He later produced and starred in a new series and became the favorite of millions of children. From radio came "The Lone Ranger," "Sky King," and the "Roy Rogers–Dale Evans Show," and these were joined by new westerns for children, including "Wild Bill Hickok" and "Kit Carson."

The first adult western on television was the excellent but short-lived "Frontier," and it was followed by "The Life and Legend of Wyatt Earp." They disappeared in a cloud of "Gunsmoke," which moved to television and recast movie actors in the key rolls. It was among the top programs for twenty years. Other successful adult westerns were "Have Gun, Will Travel" and "The Rifleman."

In 1955, "Cheyenne" became television's first hour-long western, and was followed by a number of others, including "Wagon Train" and "Rawhide." In 1959, "Bonanza," the first western in color, was a success.

Westerns peaked in the late 1950s, with as many as thirty-seven series in production. There were shows on Bat Masterson, Judge Roy Bean, and Custer; shows on the Texas Rangers, the Pony Express, and the building of the transcontinental railroad; shows featuring colorful locales: "The Dakotas," "The High Chaparral," and "The Big Valley." As late as 1967, there were still fifteen westerns on televison, but by 1970 there were six, by 1973 only "Gunsmoke," and by late 1975 none.

Confederate soldiers when they went out from Fort Brown to drive off some 1,600 Union troops trying to capture the cotton stored in the Brownsville warehouses.

DALLAS

John Neely Bryan came to the upper Trinity River in 1841 to trade with the Caddo Indians, and named the settlement after a former neighbor in Arkansas, Joe Dallas. The Houston & Texas Central Railroad arrived in 1872, and the Texas & Pacific came the next year. Over the ensuing years, Dallas became the business and cultural center of Texas.

Age of Steam Railroad Museum (Fair Park, 2 miles east via I-39; 214/239-1646). A collection of engines and rolling stock, circa 1900 to 1950, including the world's largest locomotive, a complete 1930s passenger train, and the city's oldest depot. Texas railroad memorabilia. Open Thursday through Sunday.

Hall of State (Fair Park; 214/421-5136). Exhibits, murals, and statuary depicting the history of Texas, and an exhibit on the cowboy from 1600 to the present. Open daily.

Dallas Museum of Art (1717 North Harwood; 214/922-0220). Its extensive collections include one of excellent Western art. Open daily except Mondays.

Old City Park (1717 Gano; 214/421-5141). A collection of thirty-seven early buildings, most moved from other locations in the city, including Millermore, the largest antebellum home in North Texas. Open daily except Mondays.

Dallas Public Library (1515 Young; 214/670-1700). The world's largest display of Navajo blankets is housed here, as are copies of the Texas and U.S. declarations of independence, and a Dallas Police exhibit. Open daily.

Dallas County Historical Plaza (bounded by Commerce, Elm, Houston, and Market streets). In the area where Dallas began are John Neely Bryan's log cabin, Old Red (the 1891 county courthouse), and the John F. Kennedy Memorial, designed by Philip Johnson. One block west on Elm is Dealey Plaza, site of Kennedy's assassination.

Historical Districts. There are several districts worth exploring: the downtown Arts District, East End (Deep Ellum), Swiss Avenue, and the West End.

DEL RIO

Some 400 archaeological sites in the area give evidence of the presence of Indians here thousands of years ago. A Spanish expedition arrived in the early 1600s and named the area San Felipe del Rio. The springs here were an important watering spot on the old Chihuahua Road, later supplying water to stagecoaches on the San Antonio–San Diego route. A permanent settlement came when ranchers moved in after the Civil War.

Whitehead Memorial Museum (1306 South Main; 512/774-3611, ext. 244). Artifacts are on display in an old store. Other buildings on the grounds include a chapel, an office, a replica of Judge Roy Bean's store (the grave of the judge is nearby), a log cabin, and a barn. Exhibits of Indian, pioneer, and Seminole scouts. Open Tuesday through Saturday.

Judge Roy Bean Visitor Center (60 miles northwest on U.S. 90 in Langtry; 512/291-3340). Part-time judge and full-time saloonkeeper, Roy Bean called himself "The Law West of the Pecos," and ruled this town with a six-shooter, horse sense, and a sense of humor. His courtroom was his saloon, and he often fined the defendant a round of drinks for the house. Bean was infatuated with Lillie Langtry, the English music-hall performer known as "the Jersey Lily," and named the town and his saloon after her. He wrote to Langtry often, inviting her to visit her namesake town. She finally accepted, but before her 1904 visit, Judge Bean died. There is a visitor center exhibit on the Fitzsimmons-Mahar heavyweight title fight, which Bean staged here in 1896. Behind the center is the original saloon. Open daily.

Seminole Canyon State Historical Park (41 miles northwest via U.S. 90; 512/292-4464). Some of the oldest pictographs in North America are in Fate Bell Shelter in this 2,173-acre park. Guided tours twice daily. A visitor center has exhibits on pre-Columbian Indians that inhabited this area. Open daily. Limited wheelchair access.

DENISON

In the 1850s this was a stop on the Butterfield Stage Line that ran from St. Louis to San Francisco, the stage entering Texas on a raft poled across the Red River by slaves.

Eisenhower Birthplace State Historic Site (208 East Day at Lamar; 214/465-8908). Dwight David Eisenhower, future five-star general and two-term President, was born on October 14, 1890, in this two-story frame house next to the tracks of the railroad for which his father worked. The next spring the family moved to Abilene, Kansas. When Eisenhower entered West Point, he was unsure of his birthplace and listed it as Tyler, Texas. When he became famous in World War II, Jennie Jackson, principal of a Denison elementary school, wrote the general's mother, who confirmed that this house was his birthplace.

Grayson County Frontier Village (2 miles southwest via TX 75, Loy Lake exit; 214/465-4990). A collection of frontier homes and structures from the mid-1800s, with period furnishings and artifacts. Open Wednesday through Sunday, May through October.

EAGLE PASS

In 1850 the army built Fort Duncan to protect the Texas border, and the town of Eagle Pass grew up around it. The county was named for Samuel Maverick, a signer of the Texas Declaration of Independence. He refused to brand all his cattle, and as a result any unbranded animal found on the range was said to be one of his—a "maverick."

Fort Duncan Park (Bliss between Monroe and Adams; 512/773-2748). Occupied by Confederates during the Civil War, the fort was regarrisoned with Union troops in 1868 and remained active until 1900. It was reactivated in 1916 to protect the border during the Mexican Revolution, and was later used as a training base during World War II. Eleven old post buildings survive. A small museum is in the old headquarters building. Open daily.

EL PASO

In the mid-1600s, the mission of Nuestra Señora de Guadalupe was built here, in the heart of the village called El Paso del Norte,

John Wesley Hardin

The deadliest gunfighter was the son of a Methodist circuit rider, a hot-tempered drinker, gambler, and racist named John Wesley Hardin. In the first grade, he stabbed a school-mate, had a .44 at the age of eight, killed his first man, a former slave, at fifteen, and, from 1868 to 1878, killed more than twenty men. Many of his killings were politically or racially motivated, and he was a hero to unreconstructed Confederates. Hardin was proud of his reputation and scornful of rival gunfighters. Wild Bill Hickok, marshal of Abilene, Kansas, backed off after attempting to disarm Hardin. In 1874 he was wounded while killing a deputy sheriff in Comanche, Texas. Texas Rangers tracked him to Alabama and sent him to prison. Later he drifted to El Paso, fell on hard times, lived with a bar girl, and began to write his autobiography. While drinking in a saloon, he was shot and killed by John Selman, a professional gunman who apparently just wanted to be the man who killed John Wesley Hardin.

a way station between Chihuahua City and Santa Fe. Spanish colonists fleeing the Pueblo Revolution in northern New Mexico in 1861 settled here. After Texas won its independence, El Paso became the major border city, primarily because it was the key pass on the best all-weather route to the West Coast. During the California Gold Rush, the army moved in to protect travelers from the Apache. Fort Bliss was an important army post by 1861, but Apache raids continued as late as 1879. El Paso attracted bandits and gunmen. John Wesley Hardin, who claimed to have killed forty men, was killed here in 1895, and is buried in Concordia Cemetery.

Fort Bliss (east of U.S. 54, between Fred Wilson Rd. and Montana Ave.; 915/568-4158 or 568-2804). Once the army's largest cavalry post, this is now the home of the Air Defense Center. On Pleasanton Road, facing

Charles Goodnight

Millions of cattle were driven across Southwestern trails blazed by Charles Goodnight. He went to Texas with his family, became a scout, and by 1865 was a cattleman seeking a better market for his herd than Texas offered during Reconstruction. He and Oliver Loving decided to try New Mexico, and their route there became the Goodnight-Loving Trail, one of the most used in the Southwest. On their third trip, Loving was killed by Indians, but Goodnight continued to drive cattle to New Mexico. In 1875 he marked out the Goodnight Trail from Alamogordo Creek in New Mexico to Granada, Colorado, where he had a ranch. Goodnight also introduced Hereford bulls to the West, and developed the "cattalo" by breeding buffalo with polled Angus cattle.

the main parade ground, are three adobe buildings representing the fort as it appeared from 1854 to 1868. The Cavalry Museum traces the service's proud history through paintings, photographs , documents, and artifacts. Outside is a display of cavalry vehicles through the years. Open weekdays.

Americana/Southwestern Museum of Cultural History (Performing Arts Center, Civic Center Plaza, Santa Fe Street; 915/859-7913). Pre-Columbian, tribal, historic, and contemporary art of the Americas is displayed here. Pottery is used to symbolize the region's cultural history. Open Tuesday through Saturday.

El Paso Centennial Museum (University of Texas at El Paso, University and Wisconsin; 915/747-5565). The museum has displays ranging from geological and paleontological specimens to Indian pottery. There is a collection of 600 glass plate negatives of scenes from Santa Fe to Chihuahua taken from 1880 to 1897. On the grounds is Engine No. 1, an El Paso & Southwestern Railroad steam engine. Open daily except Mondays.

El Paso Museum of Art (1211 Montana; 915/541-4040). Pre-Columbian, American, and Mexican Colonial art. Changing exhibits. Open daily.

El Paso Museum of History (15 miles east on I-10E, at Americas Ave. exit; 915/858-1928). This was formerly the cavalry museum, and still contains guns, uniforms, and saddles. Dioramas now tell of local history. Gift shop. Open Tuesday through Saturday.

El Paso Valley Missions Drive. About a 26-mile trip; drive 12 miles southeast on I-10 to Zaragosa Rd., then two and a half miles southwest to *Ysleta*. Built in 1682 and the oldest mission in Texas. Take the crossroads from Ysleta Mission south about a half-mile, then south on FM 258 three miles to *Socorro*, the oldest parish church in Texas. Continue southeast about six miles to *San Elizario*. The Presidio Chapel here, circa 1777, was built to replace one established in 1682. This was the site of the Salt War, a bitter struggle over the rights to salt found in nearby flats.

Tigua Indian Reservation (14 miles east off Alameda at 108 South Old Pueblo Rd.; 915/859-7913). Time was not kind to the Tigua. A search was made in the 1950s to locate the remaining members of the tribe, and only some fifty were found. Three hundred years of neglect and intermarriage had taken its toll. However, efforts to revive the tribe have succeeded, and now there are more than 600 Tiguas connected with the small reservation. The main attraction is a living-history pueblo, where tribe members show what the daily life of their ancestors was like: weaving, making pottery and jewelry, baking Indian bread in adobe ovens, and dancing. Pottery and jewelry are sold in the arts-and-crafts center. Nearby is the Ysleta del Sur Mission, founded by the tribe in 1681. The present church was built in 1908 on the original foundation. At the *Ysleta Del Sur Pueblo Cultural Center*, a small museum depicts the cultural history of the Pueblo Indians, the ancestors of the Tiguas. Open daily.

Hueco Tanks State Historical Park (U.S. 62E to Montana St., then 24 miles east to Ranch Rd. 2775, then north to park; 915/857-1135). This waterhole was visited by man as early as 8,000 B.C. (*Hueco*, pronounced *WAY-co*, is the Spanish word for the hollowed-out rock basins that trap water in the desert.) On the nearby rocks are more than 2,000 pictographs painted by Apache and other tribes. In the 860-park are the ruins of a stagecoach station, picnic areas and campsites, and a playground. Guided tours in the summer. Self-guided tour maps are available. Open daily.

Accommodations: *Room With a View* (821 Rim Road; 915/524-4400). A bed-and-breakfast in a Spanish-style mansion built in the late 1920s, with a view of two countries and two states. *Indian Cliffs Ranch* (30 miles east on I-10 to the Fabens exit, then north 5 miles on FM 793; 915/544-3200). The ranch offers trail rides, hayrides, wagon-train rides, a zoo, and a playground. Visitors may stay overnight at Fort Misery, a replica of a frontier fort.

FORT STOCKTON

Indians used the nearby Comanche Springs for centuries before the white man arrived. A cavalry post was established near the springs in 1859 at the crossing of the San Antonio–El Paso Trail and the Comanche War Trail, but was closed after the railroad arrived in 1886. Later, Sheriff A. J. Royal terrorized the town, and in 1894 six leading citizens drew lots to decide who would shoot the sheriff. Royal was murdered at his desk, and his killer was never caught.

Annie Riggs Memorial Museum (301 South Main; 915/336-2167). Once a stagecoach stop, this adobe hotel, managed by Riggs from the early 1900s to her death in 1931, has an eclectic collection of artifacts: a 22,000-year-old mammoth tusk found nearby, a model of the old fort, and the desk at which Sheriff Royal was shot. Open daily.

Old Fort Stockton (4 blocks off U.S. 290 at Rooney St., between 2nd and 3rd at Water and 5th). The 1867 guardhouse and three buildings in Offices' Row are still standing. Sheriff Royal is buried here. Open daily.

White-Baker Ranch Headquarters (27 miles east off I-10, exit 188; 915/395-2436). One guest room with bath is available in this 1890s ranch house, and two that share a bath. Breakfast is included in the rates; other meals may be arranged.

FORT WORTH

In 1849, Maj. Ripley Arnold established an outpost overlooking the Trinity River to protect settlements to the east—Dallas and Lonesome Dove—from Indian raids. The major named the camp after his commander, William Worth. A settlement grew up around the fort, but by 1853 the frontier had moved west and the soldiers went west with it to Fort Belknap. After the Civil War the great cattle drives began. Longhorns selling for five dollars in Texas would bring thirty or more in Northern markets. Fort Worth was the last stop on the Chisholm Trail before the Indian Territory. Drovers stocked up here, and whooped it up in Hell's Half Acre, a wild section of town. The railroad arrived in 1876, and the city became "Cowtown," a major shipping point for cattle. Amos G. Carter, founder of the *Fort Worth Star-Telegram*, the "Colossus of Cowtown," was fond of saying, "Fort Worth is where the West begins; Dallas is where the East peters out."

Amos Carter Museum (3501 Camp Bowie Blvd. at Montgomery and West Lancaster; 817/738-1933). The museum has a magnificent collection of Western art and an important collection of American art, as well as an American photography collection of 250,000 prints. Open daily except Mondays.

Cattleman's Museum (1301 West 7th

Richard King

The largest ranch in the West was assembled by Richard King, a former steamboat captain and Confederate blockade runner. Born in New York to Irish immigrants, at thirteen he worked his way to Mobile, Alabama, as a cabin boy. Starting out as a deckhand on a steamboat, he rose to captain, and was a partner in a company building steamboats on the Rio Grande. In the Civil War he ran cotton to Mexico for the Confederacy. In 1853, King bought 15,000 acres of the Santa Gertrudis land grant in south Texas, eventually accumulating 1,270,000 acres on which he had 40,000 cattle and 6,600 horses. His descendants, the Klebergs, developed the first American breed of beef cattle, the Santa Gertrudis, a mixture of Shorthorn and Brahma.

at Collier; 817/332-7064). Displays in the headquarters of the Texas and Southwestern Cattle Raisers Foundation recount the development of ranching and the cattle industry and such early cattle barons as Charles Goodnight, Richard King, and A. H. "Shanghai" Pierce. Open weekdays.

Fort Worth Museum of Science and History (11501 Montgomery; 817/732-1631). Exhibits on Texas history, anthropology, geology, natural sciences, and medical science. Open daily.

Log Cabin Village (2200 block of University Dr. at Rogers Rd.; 817/926-5881). Seven mid-1800s log cabins have been moved here, restored, and furnished with period antiques. Working gristmill. Craft demonstrations. Open daily.

Sid Richardson Collection of Western Art (Sundance Square, 309 Main St.; 817/332-6554). The collection, owned by the Sid Richardson Foundation, which operates the museum, includes fifty-two Remingtons and Russells collected by the late oilman and philanthropist. Open daily except Monday.

Stockyards National Historical District (North Main and Exchange; 817/625-5082). Once the stockyards here were the largest in the world, and 70 million head of cattle passed through them. The stockyards are located in a one-square-mile area known as Niles City, a tax haven created to lure the big meatpackers to locate here. After a court fight, Fort Worth annexed Niles City in 1922. Open daily.

Thistle Hill (1509 Pennsylvania, south end of Summit; 817/336-1212). This house was a 1903 wedding present from cattle baron W. T. Waggoner to his daughter Electra and her husband, A. B. Wharton. Electra became a local legend, spending $20,000 in one day at Neiman-Marcus, getting a butterfly tattoo in Europe, and spending three hours a day in a milk bath. Tours. Open Sunday through Friday.

Accommodations: *Stockyards* (109 East Exchange; 817/625-6427). This restored early-20th-century hotel with Western decor in the stockyards district has fifty-two rooms, a café, and entertainment. *Medford House* (2344 Medford Court East; 817/924-2765). This 1926 Tudor home, built for oilman J. C. Maxwell, has a one-bedroom suite in its carriage house.

FREDERICKSBURG

In 1846, 120 Germans, led by Baron Ottfried Hans von Meusebach, settled here in Comanche territory under the auspices of the Society for the Protection of German Immigrants in Texas. They named their town Fredericksburg after Prince Frederick of Prussia, and the baron changed his name to John O. Meusebach. He also negotiated a peace treaty with the Comanche that was generally respected by both parties. During the Civil War, the Germans, opposed to slavery, hid out in the hills or fled to Mexico to avoid service in the Confederate Army. In 1912 they built their own railroad to connect with the nearest line, and it was in service until 1941.

Admiral Nimitz State Historical Park (340 East Main; 512/997-4379). Chester

Nimitz, commander-in-chief of the U.S. Pacific fleet during World War II, grew up in town, and this museum is housed in the restored Steamboat Hotel once owned by his grandfather. Exhibits and an audiovisual program focus on the Pacific war. The Japanese Garden of Peace, containing a replica of the study and teahouse of Japanese Admiral Togo, was a gift of the people of Japan. On Austin Street is the Pacific History Museum, with military planes, tanks, and other weapons. Open daily.

Pioneer Museum Complex (309 West Main; 512/997-2835). Buildings here include the 1849 Kammiah House, the 1870s Fassel House, a barn and smokehouse, a Sunday House (farmers came to town for Saturday market day, and rather than go home and return for church Sunday, they built small houses in town), and the 1855 First Methodist Church. Small firefighting museum. Open daily, May through Labor Day; weekends the rest of the year.

Bauer Antique Toy Museum (233 East Main; 512/997-9394). A collection of toys dating from 1875 to 1950, including a hand-carved circus train. Open daily except Tuesdays.

Vereins Kirche Museum (Market Square; 512/997-3832). Pioneer artifacts and local memorabilia housed in a replica of the original octagonal community church. Open weekdays.

Accommodations: *Country Cottage Inn* (405 East Main; 512/977-8549). An 1850 limestone Sunday house, furnished with German antiques and Texas primitives. Five guest rooms. Breakfast is included in the rates.

GALVESTON

Spanish soldiers stationed on this island in the mid-1700s named it after Count Bernardo de Gálvez, viceroy of Mexico. When they left, pirate Jean Lafitte took over from 1817 to 1821. He built a house and a fort and seized and looted at least a hundred Spanish ships until he was ordered out by the American navy. During the Texas Revolution, the four ships of the Texas navy were stationed here, and the town was briefly the Texas capital. A Union force held Galveston briefly during the Civil War. It became the third-largest port in the country, but it was devastated by a hurricane in 1900 that killed more than 6,000, the greatest natural disaster in American history.

The Strand National Historical Landmark District (between 19th and 25th streets). Restored to its mid-1800s appearance, this site contains one of the great concentrations of 19th-century commercial buildings in the country. The Strand was once known as "the Wall Street of the Southwest." Today the area is full of shops and restaurants.

Galveston County Historical Museum (2219 Market; 409/766-2340). Housed in an 1906 bank building, the museum tells the story of the city from the time of the Karankawa Indians to the hurricane. There are several reconstructed buildings, including a railroad depot and general store. Open

Once known as the "Wall Street of the Southwest," Galveston's Strand District contains one of the finest concentrations of Victorian commercial buildings in the country, despite the damage suffered in the 1900 hurricane, which flooded the city and killed 6,000 people.

daily in the summer, daily except Mondays the rest of the year.

Railroad Museum (123 Rosenberg; 409/765-5700). The museum houses thirty life-sized sculptures of travelers in an old Santa Fe railroad station, and has an outdoor display of vintage trains and a working model of the Port of Galveston. Steam train excursions on some summer weekends. Open daily.

Elissa: A Tall Ship for Texas (Pier 19 off Water St.; 409/763-1877 or 763-0027). A restored century-old, 150-foot-long, square-rigged, iron-hulled barque that called at Galveston several times in the 1880s. Open daily.

Bishop's Palace (1402 Broadway; 409/762-2475). This four-story 1886 mansion, once the residence of the bishop and a triumph of Galveston architect Nicholas Clayton, is beautifully detailed and decorated, and is considered one of the most architecturally significant buildings in the country. Tours. Open daily during the summer, daily except Tuesdays the rest of the year.

Ashton Villa (2338 Broadway; 409/762-3933). This 1859 Gothic Revival mansion has a cast-iron veranda and other period details. A film on the 1900 hurricane is shown here, and there is an archaeology exhibit. Tours. Open daily.

Islander Trolley Sightseeing Tour (21st and Seawall Blvd.; 409/763-0864). Hour-long narrated tours of the Strand and other historic sites. Daily.

Lone Star Historical Drama Association (2016 The Strand; reservations: 409/737-3440). This theater company presents *The Lone Star*, the official state play of Texas, in the summer, alternating with performances of *Oklahoma!*

Accommodations: *Dickens Loft* (2021 The Strand; 409/762-1653). Five guest rooms furnished with antiques in a former 1856 warehouse. Breakfast and afternoon tea.

GOLIAD

This is one of most historic towns in Texas. In 1749 the Spanish built a mission and fort and taught the Indians to raise cattle. Bernardo de Gálvez purchased beef here when he and his troops went to the aid of American revolutionists in the South. At the beginning of the Texas Revolution in 1835, American colonists seized the fort here. In March 1836 the Mexican army defeated Col. James Walker Fannin's force at the nearby Battle of Coleto. Fannin and his men were brought here as prisoners. On Palm Sunday, Fannin and more than 300 Texas soldiers were executed in what became known as the Goliad Massacre.

Fannin Battleground State Historic Site (1 mile south on U.S. 183 to Park Rd. 6; 512/645-3405). On the site is a replica of the 1749 Missión Espiritu Santo de Zuñiga. The mission displays artifacts of colonial days. Open daily.

Presidio La Bahia (2 miles south on U.S. 183). This was the site of the first signing of the Texas Declaration of Independence, and later the Goliad Massacre. The complex includes a chapel, a quadrangle compound, and a museum with artifacts and

The Presidio La Bahia is the site of the Goliad Massacre, the 1836 execution of Col. James Walker Fannin and his men by orders of Santa Anna. This is the most fought-over fort in Texas history. The first Texas Declaration of Independence was signed here.

displays of the Texas Revolution. Open daily.

Accommodations: *White House Inn* (203 North Commercial; 512/645-2701). A bed-and-breakfast in an old home in the historic district.

GONZALES

The first shot of the Texas Revolution was fired here on October 2, 1835. Mexico gave the town a cannon to defend itself against the Indians. When the American settlers became dissatisfied with Mexican rule, they refused to give up the cannon. When troops came to take it by force, Gonzales unfurled the first Texas battle flag, which bore a single star and the words "Come and Take It," and the Mexicans withdrew.

Gonzales Memorial Museum (414 Smith St.; 512/672-6350). The "come and take it" cannon is here, as well as other artifacts and memorabilia. Open daily.

Pioneer Village (one mile north on U.S. 183; 512/672-2157). Six reconstructed 19th-century buildings, including a log cabin and a blacksmith shop. Open Wednesday through Sunday, except January.

Gonzales County Jail (414 St. Lawrence; 512/672-6350). Restored cells and a gallows. Open daily.

GRAHAM

This was an Indian reservation in the 1850s until the Comanche were moved to Oklahoma. Eight miles north is the site of the Warren Wagon Train Massacre, in which seven teamsters were killed, an incident that prompted the army to move against the Indians in Texas.

Fort Richardson State Historic Park (30 miles northeast via U.S. 380; 817/567-3506). This, the most northerly frontier fort in Texas, was active from 1867 to 1878.

Quanah Parker

The son of a white captive and a Comanche chief, Quanah Parker spent most of his life trying to please both the Indians and the whites. On the reservation at Fort Sill, he was a favorite of the Texans who grazed their cattle there, and his willingness to adapt to the white man's ways helped make him a chief and a property owner. Many Comanches denounced Parker as a half-breed in the pay of the cattlemen, but he was able to negotiate favorable terms for the tribe. In his old age, he was a local celebrity and his home near Cache, Oklahoma, was a showplace for visiting dignitaries.

Seven restored buildings and two replicas. Museum and library. Open daily.

Fort Belknap (11 miles west on TX 61; 817/846-3222). This fort was the anchor of a chain of forts stretching from the Red River to the Rio Grande. Founded in 1851, it was abandoned in 1876. Six restored buildings include the magazine, the commissary store, and two barracks. The fort is open daily, the museum daily except Wednesdays and Sundays.

GROESBECK

Old Fort Parker State Historic Site (4 miles north via TX 14 and Park Rd. 35; 817/729-5253). The fort was built in 1834 by the Parker family. In 1836, Comanches overran the fort and captured five, including nine-year-old Cynthia Ann Parker. She grew up in captivity, married a Comanche chief, and lived with the Indians until recaptured with her two-year-old daughter years later. She was the mother of Quanah Parker, the last great Comanche chief. Log blockhouse and stockade. Memorabilia. Open Wednesday through Sunday.

Limestone County Historical Museum (210 West Navasota St.). Artifacts of the town and Fort Parker. Open Mondays, and Wednesday through Friday.

HOUSTON

Houston was founded in 1836, the same year as the Republic of Texas, by Augustus and John Allen, brothers and promoters from New York, and it became the the republic's first capital.

San Jacinto Battleground (6 miles southeast on I-43 to I-610, then 1½ miles east to TX 225, then 10 miles east to TX 134 an d 3 miles west to battleground; 713/ 479-2421). A 570-foot concrete shaft faced with Texas limestone (Washington Monument is 555 feet high) and bearing a lone star on top marks the site of the Battle of San Jacinto. On April 21, 1836, General Sam Houston suddenly attacked the superior forces of Santa Anna, routed them, and took the Mexican general prisoner. The victory here ended the Texas War of Independence, avenged the massacre at the Alamo six weeks earlier, and led to the founding of the Republic of Texas. Museum. Open daily.

Museum of Fine Arts (1001 Bissonnet; 713/526-1351). A permanent collection including pre-Columbian and Indian works, as well as paintings by Remington and other Western artists. The museum has the Lillie and Hugh Roy Cullen Sculpture Garden. Tours. Open daily except Mondays.

Museum of Art of the American West (1221 McKinney in One Houston Center; 713/650-3933). The museum has both 19th-century and contemporary works in changing exhibitions. Open weekdays.

Houston Police Academy Museum (17000 Aldine-Westfield Rd.; 713/230-2300). A 5,000-item collection of weapons, uniforms, and vehicles from frontier days to the present. Tours. Open weekdays.

Fire Museum (2403 Milam; 713/524-2536). In an 1898 fire station, this museum

A 570-foot shaft with a lone star on top marks the site, near Houston, of the Battle of San Jacinto. Here on April 21, 1836, General Sam Houston routed the superior Mexican forces, taking Santa Anna prisoner, avenging the Alamo, and ending the Texas Revolution.

has a rare "watertower" truck and other vintage equipment, including hats, axes, and uniforms. Open daily except Mondays.

Museum of Printing History (1324 West Clay; 713/522-4652). Located in the Graphic Arts Conference Center, this museum has early printed documents, printing equipment, and historic newspapers. Open weekdays.

Bayou Bend (1 Westcott St.; 713/529-8773). The twenty-eight-room antebellum mansion of the late Ima Hogg and her two brothers now houses her important collection of American decorative arts, furniture, paints, metals, ceramics, and other artifacts. Tours by reservation, Tuesday through Saturday, except August.

Accommodations: *Sara's Bed & Breakfast Inn* (941 Heights Blvd.; 713/868-1130). A bed-and-breakfast in a 1900 gingerbread Victorian in Houston Heights, four miles from downtown. Twelve guest rooms are filled with antiques and named after Texas cities.

HUNTSVILLE

Founded as an Indian trading post in the 1830s, Huntsville was the home of Sam Houston, father of Texas independence.

Sam Houston Memorial Museum (1836 Sam Houston Ave.; 409/295-7824). In a fifteen-acre park that was once part of Sam Houston's homestead, seven buildings include the museum, his law office, the War and Peace exhibit hall, his home (Woodland), and the Steamboat House, where he died in 1863. Houston memorabilia in the museum include a silver service made from the silver dollars he received as a pension for his services with Andrew Jackson in the War of 1812 and many relics of the Texas Revolution, including Santa Anna's saddle. Tours. Open daily except Mondays.

Sam Houston Grave and Monument (Oakwood Cemetery, Ave. I and 9th St.).

Sam Houston

Texas and Sam Houston were inseparable until the Civil War presented him with a moral dilemma. He grew up in Tennessee, where he learned to speak Cherokee. Serving in the War of 1812, he made friends with Andrew Jackson, then became a lawyer and a U.S. congressman. He was elected governor in 1826, but resigned after his wife left him in 1829, and went to live with the Cherokee in Arkansas, becoming their spokesman. He made several trips to Texas on their behalf, and decided to settle there.

When Texas sought its freedom from Mexico, Houston was commander-in-chief of the Texas army, and fashioned the victory over Santa Anna's superior forces at San Jacinto. Elected president of the republic in 1836, he obtained United States recognition of Texas. After Texas became a state, Houston served as a U.S. senator for fourteen years. He gradually split from Southern ideology, voting for antislavery measures that made him unpopular with his constituents. After Texas seceded in 1861, he refused to swear allegiance to the Confederacy, and returned to private life.

Houston's headstone bears Andrew Jackson's tribute: "The world will take care of Houston's fame."

JOHNSON CITY

Lyndon B. Johnson National Historic Park. This park interprets the life of Lyndon Baines Johnson, thirty-sixth President of the United States. He grew up here and retired here after forty years of public service. The Texas hill-country site represents all phases of his life from his birth to his burial on the banks of the Pedernales.

In 1952, Johnson bought 2,000 acres here, remodeled the eight-bedroom ranch house, and added outbuildings and an airstrip. The house later became known as "the Texas White House." At this retreat he often worked as President, vacationed, and received foreign dignitaries.

The park has two units. The unit in Johnson City consists of the Boyhood Home, the Visitor Center, and the 1860s Johnson Settlement. The LBJ Ranch Unit consists of the President's birthplace, the family cemetery, the Texas White House, and the ranch. The *Boyhood Home* (one block off Main St.) is a 1901 Victorian frame house with period furnishings and family heirlooms. Johnson lived here from 1913 to 1934. A short walk away is the *Johnson Settlement,* a restoration of the cabin owned by the President's grandfather, a longhorn cattle driver in the mid-1800s.

At the LBJ Ranch unit (13 miles west via U.S. 290, Park Rd. 49) is the *Birthplace,* a reconstructed two-bedroom farmhouse, typical of the late 19th century, with a "dogtrot," as the open hallway was called. The Johnson family lived here from 1907 to 1913 and from 1920 to 1922. Nearby is the family cemetery where Johnson is buried. The *LBJ Ranch House,* built of limestone and wood, may only be visited on a bus tour from the Visitor Center. Open daily.

Lyndon B. Johnson State Historical Park (directly across Park Rd. 52 from LBJ Ranch; 512/644-2252). The park occupies 710 acres on the Pedernales River. The Visitor Center has Johnson family memorabilia. Nearby is the 1840 Behrens Cabin, with period furnishings. The Sauer-Beckmann homestead is the site of a living-history program. Tour buses leave from the Visitor Center. Open daily.

KERRVILLE

Charles A. Shreiner came from France to Texas with his parents, and served with the Texas Rangers and the Confederate army before opening a country store. By 1900 the Charles Shreiner Company owned 60,000 acres, and the hair of the goats it raised made Kerrville the mohair center of the world.

Cowboy Artists of America Museum (1550 Bandera Hwy.; 512/896-2553). The museum houses permanent collections of works of members and rotating displays, as well as a Western art library. Open daily, June through August; daily except Mondays the rest of the year.

Hill Country Museum (226 Earl Garrett St.; 512/896-8633). The turreted mansion, built in 1879 by Charles Shreiner, displays family memorabilia and historic artifacts of the area.

Accommodations: *Y.O. Ranch* (I-10 west to TX 41 at Mountain Home, then 18 miles south to ranch; 512/640-3222). Half-day tours are available of this working ranch founded in 1880 by Charles Shreiner, the home of more than a thousand longhorns. Several historic buildings have been moved here and restored. There are guest rooms in the lodge or in old cabins. Restaurant. Reservations required.

KINGSVILLE

Richard King, a riverboat captain, bought part of a Spanish land grand here, called the Santa Gertrudis, in the early 1850s, and started what was to become one of the largest and best-known ranches in the world. After King died, his widow helped finance the St. Louis, Brownsville & Mexico Railroad on the provision that Kingsville would be its headquarters. The new railroad made its first trip to the new town on July 4, 1904.

King Ranch (2½ miles west on TX 141; 512/592-8516). When Richard King first purchased this land, the area was so sparsely settled he had to go to Mexico to buy cattle and find men to work the ranch. During the Civil War, the King Ranch was a way station on the Cotton Road, over which cotton was shipped south to Mexico to trade for war matériel. Later, herds carrying his famous "Running W" brand were taken up the cattle trails to northern markets. King bought more land at every opportunity. Prior to his death in 1885, he owned some 600,000 acres. Later purchases by his widow, Henrietta, and son-in-law, Robert Kleberg, increased the size of the ranch to 1,250,000 acres. Among the achievements of the King Ranch was the development of a new breed of cattle called the Santa Gertrudis, and the breeding of thoroughbred racehorses, including Assault, the 1946 Triple Crown winner, and several winners of the Kentucky Derby. Now the stable breeds championship quarter horses. Only the twelve-mile loop drive is open to the public. A map and a guide cassette are available at the gatehouse. The drive includes views of feeding pens and show pens. Pastures contain cattle and quarter horses. Drive open daily.

John E. Connor Museum (Texas A&I campus, 820 Santa Gertrudis at Armstrong; 512/595-2819). This museum, which depicts the bicultural heritage of South Texas, contains a large collection of cattle brands and branding irons. Open daily except Saturdays.

LA GRANGE

La Grange was founded by Col. John H. Moore, an Indian fighter from Tennessee, who settled here in the late 1820s and later became a hero in the Texas Revolution. More recently, the city became notorious as the home of the Chicken Ranch, immortalized in the motion picture *The Best Little Whorehouse in Texas.*

Monument Hill State Historic Site (2 miles south off U.S. 77, west on Loop Rd. 92; 409/968-5658). Here a 48-foot-tall monument marks the common grave of the men killed in the massacre of Dawson's company in 1842, and those of the Mier Expedition

executed in 1843 in the Black Bean episode. Nicholas Mosby Dawson was leading fifty-three volunteers to San Antonio to help fight a Mexican force at San Antonio when they were surrounded by 400 Mexican troops with cannon. Thirty-six of Dawson's men were killed. All but three of the rest were captured. Later, 700 Texas militia went to repel the Mexicans, but when they reached the Rio Grande, many were disgruntled and the commander ordered a return to San Antonio. Some 300 refused and attacked the Mexican town of Mier. Believing they were outnumbered, they surrendered and were marched off to Mexico City. On the way, 188 escaped, but all but twelve were recaptured. Santa Anna ordered that one in ten of the prisoners be executed, and 159 white beans and seventeen black beans were placed in a pot. Those drawing black beans were shot. Later their bodies were retrieved, brought here, and buried with military honors. Another state historic site in the park is the *Kreische House and Brewery*, one of the first commercial breweries in the state when it opened in the 1850s. Park open daily. Tours of the brewery are conducted on weekends.

Faison House Museum (822 South Jefferson; 409/986-5532). This was the home

The King Ranch, the world's largest privately owned ranch and one of the most scientifically run, is the home, shown above, of the Klebergs, the descendants of Richard King, an enterprising steamboat captain who came here in 1853 and built an 823,400-acre empire.

Ride 'Em, Cowboy!

The sport of the West is the rodeo, a legacy of the early Spanish vaqueros. In 1847, a Captain Main Reid described a Santa Fe "roundup" as "a Donnybrook fair" with prizes for "the best roping and throwing" along with "horse races and whiskey and wine" and "much dancing in the street." Things haven't changed much since. Pecos, Texas, is credited with having hosted the first rodeo on July 4, 1883, and the "oldest consecutive annual rodeo" began in Payson, Arizona, the next year.

A rodeo cowboy has no salary, no sponsors, no guarantee. He answers to no one. His ability to win prize money keeps him in competition. When he loses, the rodeo announcer always says, "He came a long distance, paid his own way, and all that he will take home is your appreciation."

The rodeo is the only major American sport to emerge from an industry, the range-cattle industry, and most events are tests of basic range skills, mainly riding and roping. Bronc riding is the equivalent of breaking a horse, but riding Brahma bulls has no purpose other than to provide excitement. Bull riding requires a bullfighter to pull the bull away from the rider after he has fallen. The bullfighter evolved into the rodeo clown, providing humor as well as protection.

Steer wrestling was introduced by Bill Picket (one *t—ad is wrong*), a Texas cowboy of black and Indian descent. After roping a steer, he would dis-

THE NORMAN FILM MFG. CO.
PRESENTS

BILL PICKETT
WORLD'S COLORED CHAMPION...in
'THE BULL-DOGGER'
Featuring The Colored Hero of the Mexican Bull Ring
in Death Defying Feats of Courage and Skill.
THRILLS! LAUGHS TOO!
Produced by NORMAN MFG. CO.
JACKSONVILLE, FLA.

mount, throw the steer, then bite its upper lip, which enabled him to control the steer. Bulldogs, sometimes used as cattle dogs, would bite the lip to subdue cattle, so Picket's method was called "bulldogging." Will Rogers was a trick-riding and fancy-roping star before he became famous as a humorist. He could throw three ropes at one time and catch a horse and rider as they galloped by—one loop catching the rider, one the horse's neck, the third the horse's front legs.

Rodeo jargon includes such terms as *hazer*, a cowboy who rides alongside and guides a steer that is to be wrestled; *piggin' string*, the short rope used to tie three legs of a roped calf; *day-money*, the money won from each complete go-round of contestants in an event; *hooey*, the half-hitch used to secure a rope around a calf's legs; *twister*, a cowboy who competes in riding events; and *rank*, an adjective describing an animal that is tough and hard to handle.

Rodeo cowboys are superstitious. Accidents happen in threes, they believe. A hat tossed on a bed in the presence of a rider who is competing that day will bring him bad luck. A yellow shirt is bad luck. If a cowboy drops a glove in the ring, he must dismount and pick it up. If someone hands it to him, he will have an accident.

A rodeo is good fun, and a key to the character of the Old West. And it's *ROW-dee-oh*. Only dudes pronounce it *row-DAY-oh*.

of N. W. Faison, who escaped the fate of the Dawson company, only to be captured by the Mexicans. After his release, he bought the house in 1866. It contains some original furniture and Faison family memorabilia. Open Sundays, April through October.

LAREDO

Thomas Sanchez founded a town here in 1775, starting a ferry service across the Rio Grande, for which the Spanish authorities gave him some 110 square miles of land. A dispute over the boundary here left Laredo in a no-man's-land, and the Independent Republic of the Rio Grande was formed in 1840 and lasted 283 days. The dispute was settled by the Mexican War, after which most of the Hispanic residents moved across the Rio Grande and formed Nuevo Laredo, now the larger of the two cities. Two railroads came in the 1880s—the Texas Mexican from Corpus Christi and the Great Northern from San Antonio—to link up with the National Lines from Mexico. Since then, Laredo has been the major Texas gateway to Mexico.

Museum of the Republic of the Rio Grande (San Agustin Plaza, 1000 Zaragoza; 512/727-3480). The records and memorabilia of the short-lived republic are displayed in the former capitol building. The original three-room structure was built in 1834. The republic gave Laredo a seventh flag, one more than the six normally considered to have flown over most of Texas. Open daily except Mondays.

Nuevo Santander Museum (Laredo Junior College, west end of Washington St.; 512/722-8351, ext. 321). Named after the original Spanish province in which the town was founded in 1755, the museum is housed in several restored buildings of old Fort McIntosh. Displays in the old Fort Chapel interpret the cultural history of the area. Guided tours are available of the other buildings: the Guardhouse, with material on the military history of the fort, and the Commissary and the Commissary Warehouse, which house a small art museum and a science collection. Open daily except Saturdays.

LIVINGSTON

Alabama-Coushatta Indian Reservation (16 miles east on U.S. 190; 409/563-4391, or 800/392-4794 in Texas). The Alabama gave that state their name, but were driven west to the Big Thicket area of Texas with the Coushatta about 150 years ago. Both tribes were members of the Creek Confederacy, their languages practically identical. Some of these Indians helped Sam Houston in the Texas War for Independence, and others fought for the Confederacy in the Civil War. Houston was influential in getting a reservation for them in the 1850s, but they later were mistreated by the whites and lived in poverty. Today the reservation has a reconstructed Indian village, the Museum of Alabama and Coushatta Culture and History, the Indian Chief Railroad, the Inn of the Twelve Clans restaurant, and an arts-and-crafts shop. Guided tours of the Big Thicket. Reservation open daily.

Polk County Memorial Museum (601 West Church at Drew; 409/563-4391). This museum has Alabama-Coushatta exhibits, a country store, a log cabin, and a steam locomotive. Open weekdays.

MARSHALL

For a time during the Civil War, this was the working Confederate capital in exile of Missouri, which was under Union control. Confederate arms were stored in the basements of the Methodist Church and the Odd Fellows hall.

Harrison County Historical Museum (Old Courthouse, Peter Whetstone Square; 214/935-7868). This museum has an eclectic array of exhibits: Caddo Indian and pioneer artifacts, Victorian needlecraft and pressed glass, old toys; there are transportation, communications, and business exhibits, and an Ethnic Group Heritage Room. Open daily except Mondays.

Josey's Ranch (5 miles north on TX 42; 214/935-5358). The home of the Josey Championship School of Calf Roping and Barrel Racing. Visitors welcome. Tours. Open daily.

Bored in the Saddle

The cowboy was underpaid, overworked, poorly fed, often tired, and usually bored and lonely. Most became cowboys because they were looking for a new beginning, a second chance. After the Civil War, many cowboys were Confederate veterans. Union veterans, particularly from New England, were also drawn to the range.

One in seven cowboys was black; some had been slaves in Texas, while others were fleeing the hardships of Reconstruction. Another one in seven was Mexican, and there was a sprinkling of Indians. The range had its share of prejudice, but usually one cowboy would acknowledge, if sometimes grudgingly, the skills of another, whatever his race or background. A handful of blacks were trail bosses, and a few became well-known rodeo performers. There were British cowboys, some seeking adventure, others exiled by their families in the hope that the outdoor life would change their dissolute ways.

Whatever their backgrounds, cowboys lived in a heavily Spanish culture: the roundup, branding, western saddle, roping, and cowboy clothing—all were adopted from Mexican vaqueros, who had taught the first Texas cowboys their trade. Words like *cincha* (cinch), *catallerango* (wrangler), and *reata* (lariat) reveal the origins of the cowboy's trade.

Life revolved around the long drive to market and the spring and fall roundups. Each cowboy drove back scattered cattle to the roundup site. The foreman would select the calves to be branded, then the cowboy would chase a calf toward the branding fire, rope it, bring it down, and call for the branding iron. Roping was dangerous work; a steer suddenly pulling a rope taut could topple horse and rider, or the rope could cut off fingers misplaced on the saddle horn.

On the drive, which could take three or four months and cover more than a thousand miles, the cowboy had to keep the line of cattle moving along the course set by the trail boss. Cowboys flanked the column, which stretched for several miles. Another cowboy, the *wrangler*, oversaw the *remuda*, or *cavvy*, a group of fresh saddle horses; on the trail a cowboy could easily wear out two horses a day. The cowboy myth romanticizes the relationship between the cowboy and his horse, but most cowboys rode horses owned by their employer.

T. C. Lindsey & Co. General Store (U.S. 80E to FM 1998, then east on FM 1998 to FM 134, then south two miles to store in Jonesville; 214/687-3382). The store opened in 1847 and is still going strong. It also sells antiques and collectibles, and has been a setting in two Disney movies.

MASON

Fort Mason was one of a chain of army posts built in the early 1850s, a day's ride apart, from the Red River to the Rio Grande, intended to protect early settlements from the Indians. When the frontier pushed westward after the Civil War, Fort Mason was abandoned but the settlement around it lived on. The Mason County War broke out in the mid-1870s, a violent feud between German and Anglo settlers, triggered by cattle rustling. Hired guns were brought in and a dozen men were killed before Texas Rangers restored order.

Fort Mason Officers Quarters (Rainey and Post Hill; 915/347-5758). This was at various times the home of some of the great Civil War leaders: George Armstrong Custer, Albert Sidney Johnston, and Robert E. Lee, who was the fort commander in 1861. The building is a reproduction. When the fort was abandoned, the townspeople stripped the buildings down to the foundations to use the materials for new buildings in town. Open daily.

MIDLAND

Halfway between Dallas and Fort Worth, Midland was the junction of many trails, including the Comanche War Trail, and was the site of the last Comanche raid into Texas. It was a small town until oil was discovered in the vast Permian Basin in the 1920s.

Midland County Museum (in the public library, 301 West Missouri; 915/683-2708).

A working day on the trail could last fourteen hours, almost all of it in the saddle. Part of every night was spent watching the cattle in case they might be "spooked" into stampeding by lightning, noise, or a sudden movement. The only relaxation was around the campfire, gossiping or spinning yarns. The chuck wagon was more than a traveling kitchen; it was "home," and the cook was doctor, barber, seamstress, blacksmith, and keeper of the peace.

At the end of the trail, the cowboy let off steam, perhaps squandering the hundred or so dollars he made on the drive on clothes, liquor, gambling, and prostitutes. A certain amount of hell was raised, but violence was comparatively rare.

On the ranch in the summer, cowboys kept busy tending cattle and treating them for diseases, repairing fences, and doing farm chores. The bunkhouse was one single large room that offered little privacy. Meals were better and more varied than on the trail, although bacon and beans were staples. One dish was "sonofabitch stew," made of beef heart, liver, testicles, and other organ meats.

Most cowboys were let go after the fall roundup, working in town at what jobs they could find or "grub-line riding," going from one ranch to another for an odd job or free meal. Those who were kept on performed repairs and maintenance on the ranch. Some were given the loneliest job of all, "line riding," patrolling the boundaries of the ranch, living in a primitive hut, riding out every day to track down stray cattle, killing wolves and other predators, and rarely seeing another living soul.

Come spring, the cycle would start again, and ranchers would begin hiring for the roundup. Most cowboys were young, generally in their early twenties. On average, a cowboy would spend about seven years on the range before looking for a more human and settled life doing something else.

A hodgepodge collection that includes the death masks of Butch Cassidy, Jesse James, and Bob Ford, who killed Jesse, and the skull of Midland Man, found near here, proving that man lived in the area some 20,000 years ago. Open daily except Fridays and Sundays.

Museum of the Southwest (1705 West Missouri; 915/683-2882). An extensive collection of contemporary Southwestern art. Open daily except Mondays.

Permian Basin Petroleum Museum (1500 I-20WE at TX 349 exit; 915/683-4403). The largest oil industry museum in the country, it includes an audiovisual program on oil exploration, hands-on exhibits, and a large collection of antique drilling equipment outside in the Oil Patch. Open daily.

NACOGDOCHES

One of the five original Spanish missions in Texas was here, but it was abandoned until Captain Antonio Gil y Barbo returned in 1779 with a group of Spanish settlers. In 1832, East Texas settlers, ordered to surrender their firearms, banded together and defeated the Mexican garrison at the Battle of Nacogdoches. Mexican troops were never again stationed in East Texas.

Old Stone Fort Museum (Clark and Griffith blvds.; 409/568-2408). Rebuilt from an original 1779 structure, this museum has exhibits on East Texas history, Indian artifacts, a gun collection, and pioneer relics. Open daily.

Sterne-Hoya Home (211 South Lanana: 409/560-5426). The house was built by Adolphus Sterne in 1828 for his bride. Sam Houston was baptized a Roman Catholic here in 1833, to comply with the Mexican law that landholders must be Catholic. In the house is the Hoya Memorial Library, which displays early area memorabilia. Open daily except Sundays.

Indian Mound (500 block of Mound St.). The last remaining Caddo burial mound of several in the area. Items recovered from here are displayed at the Old Fort Museum.

Millard's Crossing (4 miles northeast on U.S. 59; 409/569-6969). A 19th-century village of restored homes, including a Victorian mansion and farmhouse, with period furnishings and antiques. Guided tours. Open daily except Wednesdays.

Accommodations: *Tol Barret House* (409/569-1249). This bed-and-breakfast, on a tree farm on Route 4 south of town, has a guest room in the old kitchen house behind the 1848 house, and several others in nearby houses.

NEW BRAUNFELS

The Republic of Texas captured the imagination of Germany, then a loose confederation of small states and principalities. The Germans saw Texas as an Eden. Several noblemen, hoping to make money in Texas, formed a *Mainzer Adelsverein* (League of Nobles) to sponsor Germans emigrating there. Prince Carl von Solms-Braunfels, commissioner-general of the Society for the

Millard's Crossing, near Nacogdoches, has many East Texas pioneer homes furnished with period antiques. In 1826, Hayden Edwards of Nacogdoches declared this area free of Mexico and named it the Republic of Fredonia. When Edwards's neighbors ignored him, he fled.

Protection of German Immigrants in Texas, and 200 immigrants arrived in Galveston in 1844 and, for $1,111, purchased 1,265 acres on the Guadalupe River and founded this town, named after the town in Germany where the prince had his castle. Within months, several thousand Germans arrived, only to find that war had broken out with Mexico and there was no transport to New Braunfels. An epidemic killed several hundred. The rest went to New Braunfels, taking the epidemic with them. As many as 3,000 may have died. During all this, the prince went home to Germany. Despite all this, by 1850 Braunfels was the fourth-largest city in Texas.

Sophienburg Museum (401 West Coll at Academy; 512/629-1572). Formerly the prince's administration building, this museum has exhibits telling the story of the German immigrants from their departure through their hardships to their success. Archives, guided tours, gift shop. Open daily.

Lindheimer House (491 Comal; 512/625-8766). The restored 1852 home of Ferdinand Lindheimer, educator, guide and botanist. Original furnishings and memorabilia. Tours. Open daily, May through August; daily except Wednesdays the rest of the year.

Accommodations: *Gruene Mansion Inn* (I-35 to Canyon Rd. exit, left on Hunter Rd., then left at Gruene Hall to 1275 Gruene Rd.; 512/629-2641). Guest quarters in the outbuildings of a Victorian mansion on a bluff overlooking the Guadalupe River. In season, minimum stay is two nights.

PORT ARTHUR

Oil made Port Arthur, and its slogan is "We Oil the World." Two interlocking events in the late 1890s made it a city and a port: the arrival of Arthur Stillwell's Kansas City, Pittsburgh & Gulf Railroad, and the dredging of a canal from Lake Sabine to the Gulf. But Stillwell made two mistakes: he went

---

John Ringo

Conflicting stories surround John ("Johnny") Ringo. Was he a gentleman bandit or a cold-blooded killer? Was he a college graduate or an eighth-grade dropout? An erratic loner, a heavy drinker, apparently an intellectual by frontier standards, Ringo was deadly with a gun, once shooting a man in the throat for refusing to drink with him. Involved in the "Hoodoo War," one of the many feuds in Texas in the 1870s, he killed two men, escaped from jail, and vanished. He turned up in the Clanton gang in Tombstone in 1882, although he steered clear of the O.K. Corral. He challenged Doc Holliday to a shootout, but both were arrested before anything happened. Wyatt Earp suspected his brother was murdered by Ringo. Ringo became despondent and was found shot to death. Earp claimed he killed Ringo, some say he was killed by a drinking companion, others that he was a suicide.

---

broke and sought help from John "Bet-a-Million" Gates. Gates got the benefit of Stillwell's foresight when the Spindletop oil well blew in just ten miles to the north. The only reminder of Stillwell was his first name, with which he christened the city.

Port Arthur Historical Museum (Gates Memorial Library, 317 Stillwell at Proctor; 409/983-4921). This museum tells the story of the city in a hodgepodge of material ranging from Jim Bowie's 1831 contract to pay a dowry, to a photograph of the 1923 queen of the city. Open weekdays.

Sabine Pass Battleground State Historical Park (14 miles south on TX 87 to Sabine Pass, then south 1½ miles on FM 3322; 409/971-2559). This is the site of one of the most unusual battles of the Civil War. On September 8, 1863, a Union fleet of twenty vessels and several thousand men tried to invade Texas through Sabine Pass. Facing this force was Company F of the Texas Heavy Artillery: six cannon, forty Irish dockworkers, and Lt. Dick Dowling, a young barkeep from Houston. In the battle, which lasted less than an hour, the Union lost two gunboats and sustained 65 casual-

The Goodnight-Loving cattle trail, the Chidester Stage Line, and the California Trail passed near Fort Concho, Texas, now a National Historic Landmark. The largest fort of the Indian Wars still standing, it offers visitors twenty restored buildings.

ties and 315 men captured; its forces returned to New Orleans. Dowling and his men suffered no casualties. Open daily.

RUSK

Texas State Railroad State Historical Park (3½ miles west on U.S. 84; 214/683-2561, or 800/442-8951 in Texas). The park celebrates the era when the railroad was king. Visitors ride beautifully restored coaches pulled by steam engines from Rusk to Palestine and back, a total of fifty-one miles, through pine and hardwood forests and pasturelands, and across thirty bridges. Both depots are set in parks, and there is a layover for lunch. There are campsites, and a depot theater shows a film on railroad history. Trains run weekends, mid-March through late May; Thursday through Monday, late May until mid-August; and weekends again from mid-August through early November. Reservations recommended.

SAN ANGELO

The town grew up along the California Trail and the Goodnight-Loving stage line. When

Fort Concho was built across the Concho River, it was a cluster of saloons, gambling houses, brothels, and a trading post. The soldiers referred to it simply as "Over the River."

Fort Concho National Historic Landmark (213 East Ave. D near Concho River; 915/657-4441). One of a number established shortly after the Civil War, the fort succeeded because of its ample supply of water. German craftsmen from Fredericksburg built the walls of sandstone and limestone, and it is one of the best preserved forts in the West. Around the parade grounds are barracks, officers' quarters, headquarters, a commissary store, and a school. Exhibits tell of the fort's role in the opening of the West. The fort is owned by San Angelo, and the people of the city have a special relationship with it. Members of the Fort Concho Infantry give demonstrations at the fort, and all the schoolchildren in the county spend a day in the old schoolhouse, wrestling with *McGuffey's Reader.* Tours. Open daily.

San Angelo Fine Arts Museum (Fort Concho Quartermaster Bldg.; 915/658-4084). Changing exhibits, usually of regional artists. Open daily except Mondays.

Miss Hattie's Museum (18½ East Concho; 915/655-2158). A house of ill repute from 1896 until it was closed by the Texas Rangers in 1946, it has been faithfully restored, and has reproductions of the clothes worn by the "soiled doves." Open Tuesday through Sunday.

SAN ANTONIO

Fray Antonio de San Buenaventura Olivares founded the Mission San Antonio near the tree-lined river here in 1718. Four more missions were built along the river in the next thirteen years. While the first mission was being built, Don Martín de Alarcón, captain general and governor of the Province of Texas, established a military post here, and

San Antonio has been a military center ever since. At the Alamo, from February 23 to March 6, 1836, a small band of Texans fought off the 5,000 troops of Santa Anna. All the 185 defenders were killed, including Davy Crockett, Col. James Bowie, and Col. William Travis. Their heroic stand inspired the battle cry "Remember the Alamo." Three months after the Alamo fell, San Antonio was almost deserted, but in the 1840s a number of German immigrants gave new life to the city. In the 1870s this was a tough cow town filled with gamblers, adventurers, and new settlers. Over the years, six flags have flown over San Antonio: those of France, Spain, Mexico, the Republic of Texas, the Confederate States of America, and the United States.

The Alamo (Alamo Plaza, Alamo and Houston; 512/225-1693). By 1761, seven stone houses and the church tower were finished, and an aqueduct brought water from the river. The Alamo was secularized in 1793 and joined with the nearby settlements to become San Antonio de Bexar, the capital of the province. The mission building was a dilapidated ruin in 1835 when it was surrendered to Texas revolutionaries. Col. William B. Travis took over the walled mission grounds, but could make only a few defensive repairs before he was confronted by another Mexican army, commanded by Gen. Antonio López de Santa Anna. Travis refused to surrender, and Santa Anna laid siege to the Alamo. On March 1, thirty-two reinforcements managed to get inside, but the siege ended at dawn on March 6, with all the defenders dead. Today the Alamo is administered by the Daughters of the Republic of Texas, who give tours of the chapel and the Long Barrack Museum. Open daily.

San Antonio Missions National Historical Park. Conquistadors crossing the Rio Grande in search of riches were harassed by the Tejas Indians, for whom Texas was named, and New Spain decided to colonize its northern areas. Bringing the Indians into the Spanish society required that

The engraving, above, shows Texas troops arriving to help defend the Alamo. The spiritual heart of Texas is the Alamo, the mission church where in 1836 Davy Crockett, Jim Bowie, William Travis, and 185 other Texans stood off General Santa Anna and his 5,000 troops. All the defenders were slain, but their gallantry led to Texas's freedom. The entrance to the Alamo is shown in the photograph, below left.

Jim Bowie

Jim Bowie was a legend before he arrived at the Alamo. Like another Alamo defender, Davy Crockett, he was born and raised in Tennessee. Moving to Louisiana, he reputedly rode alligators and helped pirate Jean Lafitte smuggle slaves. He was famous for designing the knife that bore his name. Its long blade with a curved tip was lethal in a fight. Bowie moved to Texas in 1828 and fitted right in. He married the daughter of the Mexican vice-governor, learned Spanish, and became a Catholic. He fought with the Mexicans against the Indians, then sided with the Americans in the revolt. He was commanding a volunteer force in San Antonio when William Travis arrived with his troops. They shared the defense of the Alamo, but clashed when Bowie's men would not accept Travis's leadership. Bowie was bedridden with pneumonia the last eleven days of the siege, but before he was killed, according to legend, he slew a number of Mexicans from his bed with his famous knife.

they be converted to Catholicism, at that time a nationalistic religion controlled and subsidized by the Spanish crown. To accomplish this, a chain of missions was established along the San Antonio River, the greatest concentration of Catholic missions in North America. Six Franciscan missions were established in East Texas, and formed the foundation of the city of San Antonio. The architecture of the missions is basically Spanish, which includes many styles and motifs. The mission builders, skilled craftsmen from Mexico, modified the basic Spanish model to meet the requirements imposed by the frontier. Four of the five make up the San Antonio Missions National Historic Park (the fifth is the Alamo). Tours of the missions leave from the Alamo, and one can also visit them by car, by following the Mission Trails beginning downtown and going south on South Alamo Street.

Mission Concepcion (807 Mission Rd. at Felisa; 512/229-5732). The oldest unrestored stone Catholic church still in use in the country, it has changed little in 200 years. Colorful geometric designs originally covered the walls, but the patterns have faded. Indians continued to practice the Catholic faith after Texas independence, and today some members of this parish are probably descendants of those early converts.

Mission San Jose (6539 San Jose at Mission Rd.; 512/229-4770). A major social and cultural center, the mission was referred to by a visitor in 1777 as "the queen of the missions." The rich mission attracted Apache and Comanche raiders. Troops were stationed here, and taught the resident Indians how to defend themselves with guns and lances. The ornate carving on the outside is largely original. Of particular interest are Rosa's Window, the large granary with its flying buttresses, and the living quarters and arches of the former convent.

Mission San Juan Capistrano (9101 Graf at Ashley; 512/229-5734). By the mid-1700s, San Juan was a large regional supplier of agricultural produce, with 6,000 sheep and cattle on the nearby Rancho Pataguilla. Indian artisans produced iron, wood, cloth, and leather goods. A trading network extended east to Louisiana and south to Coahuila, Mexico. Though in the city now, San Juan is pastoral and charming. A museum has exhibits on mission life. Nearby, on the way to Misión Espada, is the *Espada Aqueduct*. It is part of the original irrigation system built in the 1730s and is reputedly the only Spanish one left standing.

Mission San Francisco de la Espada (10040 Espada Rd.; 512/627-2021). This mission seems as remote today as it must have two centuries ago. As mission buildings became more elaborate, Indians became masons and carpenters, and their influence is evident today. The interior of the church is decorated simply, allowing the carvings of the saints to stand out.

All missions are open daily. Some parts of some missions are not accessible to wheelchairs.

Paseo del Rio (512/299-8610). The city's famous twenty-one-block River Walk is lined with shops, hotels, and sidewalk cafés. Open daily.

San Antonio Museum of Art (200 West Jones; 512/226-5544). In a restored old brewery, the museum has pre-Columbian, Spanish colonial, and Mexican folk art collections. Admission includes a ride on the 1913 trolley outside. Open daily.

McNay Art Museum (6000 North New Braunfels at U.S. 81B; 512/824-5368). The museum has a collection of Western art of the past century among its treasures. Open Tuesday through Sunday.

Institute of Texas Cultures (HemisFair Plaza; 512/226-7651). Displayed here are imaginative exhibits on the many ethnic groups that have helped make Texas. Film and slide shows. Open Tuesday through Sunday.

Texas Rangers Museum (Breckenridge Park, 3805 Broadway; 512/822-9011). Guns, badges, saddles, and pictures of the 160 years of ranger history are on display. Open Tuesday through Sunday, May through August; Wednesday through Sunday the rest of the year.

Hertzberg Circus Collection (210 West Market; 512/299-7810). On exhibit here are Tom Thumb's carriage, a model circus, posters, costumes, and photographs. Open daily in the summer, daily except Sundays the rest of the year.

Hall of Texas History and Buckhorn Hall of Horns (Lone Star Brewery, 600 Lone Star Blvd.; 512/226-8301 weekdays, 226-8303 weekends). Dioramas of memorable periods in the state from 1534 to 1898. Also, collections of animal trophies and horns and memorabilia dating from 1881. Open daily.

Fort Sam Houston (North New Braunfels at Grayson; 512/221-4886). Still an active base, the fort has a number of historic buildings around the quadrangle, including a military museum with guns and uniforms. A medical museum displays an early army surgeon's equipment. Open daily.

La Villita (bounded by South Alamo, Nueva, South Presa, and the river; 512/299-8610). A restored 250-year-old Spanish settlement with galleries, shops, and cafés. Open daily.

Spanish Governor's Palace (105 Military Plaza; 512/224-0601). Built in 1749, this was the home and office of Spanish colonial administrators. Open daily.

José Antonio Navarro State Historic Site (228-232 South Laredo; 512/226-4801). A complex of three adobe houses built around 1850, with period furnishings, documents, and pictures. Tours. Open daily.

Brackenridge Eagle (3810 North St. Mary's; 512/735-8641). Visitors are taken

"A Texas Ranger must ride like a Mexican, track like a Comanche, shoot like a Kentuckian, and fight like the devil."

—OLD TEXAS SAYING

The Texas Rangers

A few good men can make a difference and become a legend. The Texas Rangers were created by American settlers in 1826, when Texas was still part of Mexico. The settlers agreed to keep "twenty to thirty rangers in service all the time." The Constitution of the Texas Republic created a permanent corps of Texas Rangers to be stationed on the Indian frontier. They supplied their own horses and weapons and had no uniforms.

From the beginning, their record was exceptional. Rangers defeated the Comanche in the battles of Council House and Plum Creek. A Ranger regiment served with distinction in the Mexican War. After statehood, the Rangers were inactive, but were back in action after the Civil War, restoring law and order during Reconstruction.

From 1874 to 1890 they fought Indian raiders, cattle thieves, stagecoach and train robbers, and other outlaws. Sam Bass and John Wesley Hardin were slain by Rangers. Today the Texas Rangers, still under 100 in number, maintain their tradition of swift law enforcement. They use modern technology, but still go into the bush on horseback in pursuit of criminals.

around Brackenridge Park on a replica of an 1865 steam train, with stops at attractions. Operates daily.

VIA San Antonio Streetcar (512/227-2020). A reproduction of a 1920s city streetcar, its route includes downtown, St. Paul's Square, the King William District, and El Mercado. Operates daily.

The Texan (Amtrak Station, 1174 East Commerce; 512/377-2900). Dinner is served in the diner of a restored train on a three-hour evening round trip to the Pleasanton vicinity. Thursday through Sunday. Reservations required.

Roosevelt Bar (Menger Hotel, 204 Alamo Plaza; 512/223-4361). This is where Teddy Roosevelt reputedly recruited many of his Rough Riders. The long wooden bar is a touch of the Old West. Closed Sundays.

UVALDE

Settlement began here after the army established Fort Inge nearby, but the garrison was moved and Indians began raiding the defenseless village, then called Encina. The settlers hung on; Encina became the county seat in 1856, and changed its name to Uvalde. Pat Garrett lived here for a while after he killed Billy the Kid in 1881. Uvalde's most famous son was John Nance Garner, vice-president of the United States from 1933 to 1941.

Garner Museum (333 North Park; 512/278-5081). The museum is housed in Garner's former home, which he gave to the city as a memorial to his wife after her death in 1948. He moved to the small cottage behind the house, where he died in 1967, weeks before his ninety-ninth birthday. Memorabilia include a hundred gavels sent to him by friends when he broke his gavel during his first day as the Speaker of the House of Representatives. "Cactus Jack" Garner went to Congress in 1903 and served there until he became Roosevelt's first vice-president. He has been quoted as saying the office "isn't worth a bucket of warm spit." Open daily except Sundays.

WACO

In 1837 a company of Texas Rangers set up a frontier outpost near the Brazos River, where the Hueco (*WAY-co*) Indians had lived for centuries. The outpost was abandoned, and in 1845 Neill McLennan established the first permanent settlement. An early settler, Shapley P. Ross, a Texas Ranger captain, operated a ferry. A number of cotton plantations flourished nearby, but did not survive the Civil War. The coming of the cattle drives rescued Waco's economy.

Texas Ranger Hall of Fame and Museum (I-35 and Brazos River; 817/754-1433). Memorabilia of the elite force are on display here. There is a twenty-minute film on ranger history, and a collection of firearms. Present-day Company F of the Texas Rangers is stationed in this replica of the original 1837 fort. Gift shop. Picnicking. Open daily except Mondays.

John Nance Garner, FDR's first vice-president, and a colorful Texan, is remembered at the Garner Memorial Museum, shown below, in his hometown of Uvalde, and by the Cactus Jack Festival, which is held in October.

Historic Houses. There are five restored mid-1880s houses that may be visited. A tour brochure is available at the Tourist Information Center at the Texas Ranger Hall of Fame.

WICHITA FALLS

In 1837 in a New Orleans poker game, John C. Scott won land certificates for 12,000 acres in what now is Wichita County. The certificates lay in a trunk for seventeen years, until his heirs heard a railroad would be coming through their land, so they came here and laid out the town. The railroad didn't come, but the town was surveyed. A railroad did come in 1882, and the town prospered. In 1910, oil was discovered, and a few years later Wichita Falls became a boomtown.

Wichita Falls Museum (2 Eureka Circle; 817/692-0923). A collection of American art and exhibits on the history of the area. Open daily except Mondays.

Wichita Falls Area Fire and Police Museum (Ave. H and Giddings; 817/692-0923). In a 1925 fire station are displays of vehicles, weapons, uniforms, badges, and other police and fire artifacts dating from the 1880s. Tours. Open Sundays.

Kell House (900 Bluff; 817/723-0623). Built in 1909 by one of the city founders, the house has been restored and refurnished with family furniture. Period clothing. Tours. Open Tuesday through Friday and Sundays.

WIMBERLEY

Pioneer Town (1 mile west on River Rd.; 512/847-2517). A reconstructed 1880s Western town with a half-scale replica of an 1873 steam engine that pulls a train on a mile-long ride, a Victorian Opera House where melodramas are presented, and an

Sam Bass

"A kinder-hearted fellow you'd scarcely ever see," goes the song, and Sam Bass is remembered as a Western Robin Hood. The truth is that he was a moderately successful bandit with no known philanthropies. Born in Indiana, he was a hired hand in Texas at age eighteen, keeping company with a small-time crook named Joel Collins. They went to the Black Hills in the gold rush and robbed stages, then robbed a train in Nebraska of $60,000 in gold coins. Returning to Texas, they robbed more trains, and soon the Rangers were in hot pursuit. Newspapers called the four-month chase the "Bass War." Betrayed by a crony, Bass was fatally wounded while robbing a bank, dying, according to the song, with "the world bobbing all around."

old-time Medicine Show at the Wagon Camp area. The Museum of Western Art in the Opera House (open by appointment) has a large collection of Remington bronzes. Café. Gift shop. Open daily, Memorial Day through Labor Day; weekends in the fall and spring. Closed December through February.

WOODVILLE

Heritage Village Museum (2 miles west on U.S. 190; 409/283-2272). The museum includes a number of restored and reconstructed early buildings: an 1866 log cabin, an 1850s general store, a blacksmith shop, a barbershop, an 1888 newspaper plant, and a 1906 school, now the Pickett House Restaurant. Gift shop. Open daily.

Alan Shivers Museum and Library (302 North Charlton; 409/283-3709). An 1881 Victorian house that Governor and Mrs. Shivers saved from demolition, restored, and gave to his hometown. Shivers memorabilia. African Safari Room. Freedom Shrine. Shivers's collection of Texiana and rare books. Open Monday through Saturday.

PART IV

THE ROCKY MOUNTAINS

At first, only Indians and trappers loved the mountains. To others they were a great wall, something to get through on the way to somewhere else. To explorers seeking passes, they were a puzzle to be solved. To the pioneers in wagon trains, they were the supreme test of strength and endurance. To railroad builders, they were the supreme engineering problem. Then came the greatest mining boom the world has ever known.

Lake Mills and Longs Peak, in Rocky Mountain National Park, Colorado.

CANADA

WATERTON-GLACIER INT'L PEACE PARK

BLACKFEET INDIAN RES.

Browning

Chinook

Milk River

Havre

Malta

FORT PECK INDIAN RES.

Sandpoint

Coeur d'Alene

Wallace

COEUR D'ALENE INDIAN RES.

St. Maries

Flathead Lake

Polson

FLATHEAD INDIAN RES.

Fort Benton

Great Falls

Missouri River

FORT BELKNAP INDIAN RES.

Fort Peck Lake

Sidney

NORTH DAKOTA

Moscow

Dworshak Res.

Missoula

Drummond

Lewistown

MONTANA

Lewiston

NEZ PERCE INDIAN RES.

Helena

Deer Lodge

Boulder

White Sulphur Springs

Yellowstone R.

Miles City

Grangeville

Hamilton

Anaconda

Butte

Bozeman

Billings

Hardin

Livingston

CROW INDIAN RES.

N. CHEYENNE INDIAN RES.

SOUTH DAKOTA

IDAHO

Salmon

Virginia City

Dillon

BIGHORN CANYON NAT'L REC. AREA

Sheridan

Devil's Tower

Challis

Stanley

SAWTOOTH NAT'L REC AREA

St. Anthony

YELLOWSTONE NAT'L PARK

Cody

Buffalo

Newcastle

Rapid City

Weiser

Idaho City

GRAND TETON NAT'L PARK

WYOMING

Boise

Butte City

Jackson

Dubois

WIND RIVER INDIAN RESERVATION

Snake River

Shoshone

Blackfoot

Riverton

Casper

Pocatello

Lava Hot Springs

Lander

Douglas

Jerome

Twin Falls

Burley

LaBarge

Farson

Fort Laramie

NEBRASKA

Rawlins

Evanston

Green River

FLAMING GORGE NAT'L REC. AREA

Continental Divide

Laramie

Cheyenne

Great Salt Lake

DINOSAUR NAT'L MON

Fort Collins

Sterling

NEVADA

Salt Lake City

Craig

Estes Park

Boulder

Greeley

Colorado River

Central City

Denver

Burlington

UTAH

Glenwood Springs

Georgetown

Idaho Springs

Golden

Aspen

Leadville

Breckenridge

Fairplay

Manitou Springs

Colorado Springs

Grand Junction

Gunnison

Cripple Creek

Montrose

Salida

COLORADO

Ouray

Cañon City

Pueblo

Telluride

Arkansas River

La Junta

Silverton

Pagosa Springs

Cortez

Durango

Aldamosa

Trinidad

UTE MTN. INDIAN RES.

S. UTE INDIAN RES.

ARIZONA

NEW MEXICO

N

150 miles

225 km

9

Montana

ANACONDA

"Copper king" Marcus Daly built a smelter here, and the town of Copperopolis grew up around it. Renamed Anaconda in 1894, it figured in the War of the Copper Kings, fought between Daly and W. A. Clark over the location of the state capital. Clark's Helena won.

Visitor Center (306 East Park St.; 406/563-2400). Smelter artifacts, an outdoor railroad exhibit, and a video presentation on the attractions of the area can be found here. Open daily except Sundays in the summer; weekdays the rest of the year.

Copper Village Museum and Arts Center (401 East Commercial; 406/563-2422). Area history, a copper smelter display. Art exhibits, theater, music, films, classes. Open daily except Mondays, closed holidays.

Sapphire Mines and Ghost Towns (near Georgetown Lake, 15 miles west on Pinter Scenic Route MT 1). Inquire at the Visitor Center for exact locations.

Hearst Free Library (Main and 4th; 406/563-2400). This classic period building was completed in 1889 and donated to the city by George and Phoebe Hearst. Hearst, one of Daly's partners in Butte's Anaconda Mine, made his fortune in mining; his son, William Randolph Hearst, became a prominent publisher. Open daily except Sundays.

National Ghost Town Hall of Fame Museum (Fairmont Hot Springs Resort, 1500 Fairmont Rd., east of I-90; 406/797-3241). This museum is dedicated to the preservation of ghost towns of the West. Exhibits. Open daily.

Big Hole National Battlefield (22 miles southwest on MT 274, then 40 miles southwest on MT 43; 406/689-3155). The homeland of the Nez Percé Indians was the area where Oregon, Washington, and Idaho now meet. They were peaceful people who grazed horses on the valley grasslands, gathered edible roots and bulbs on the prairies, fished the streams, and hunted buffalo east of the mountains. Gold miners, settlers, and stockmen began moving into Nez Percé lands in the mid-1880s. Seeking peace, the Indians signed a treaty in 1855 at Wallowa Lake, Oregon, which confined them to a reservation that included much of their ancestral land.

The treaty allowed whites to live on the reservation with the consent of the Nez Percé. Increased demand for land forced a new treaty in 1863, which reduced the reservation to a quarter of its original size. A third of the tribe lived off the reservation, and refused to sign the new treaty. These were known as the "nontreaty" Nez Percés. In 1877 the Bureau of Indian Affairs ordered the nontreaty Nez Percés to move onto the reservation. General O. O. Howard ordered them to be on the reservation within thirty days. Chief Joseph, a nontreaty Nez Percé spokesman, responded, "My people have always been friends of white men. Why are you in such a hurry? I cannot get ready to move in thirty days. Our stock is scattered and Snake River is very high. Let us wait until fall, then the river will be low." Howard threatened to use force if the deadline was not met.

A small party of Nez Percés attacked a group of white settlers, killing four who reportedly had cheated the Indians. Fearing retaliation, most of the nontreaty Indians fled to White Bird Canyon. Encamped in tepees here along the east bank of the Big Hole River, some 800 Nez Percé Indians, including 125 warriors, were awakened by gunfire just before dawn on August 9, 1877. Troops fired point-blank as the Indians stumbled out of their tepees. Men, women, and children were shot

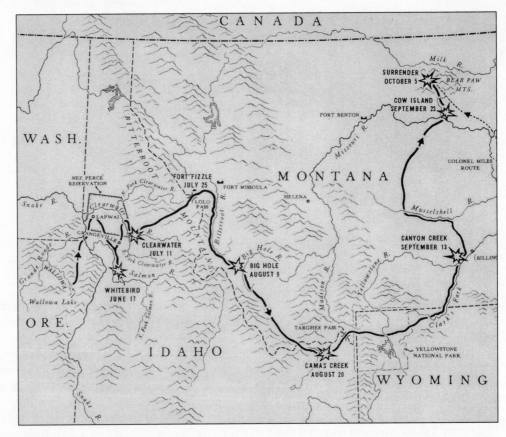

indiscriminately. The stunned Nez Percé warriors rallied, forcing the troops to retreat. The troops were pinned down and the main body of the Nez Percés broke camp and moved off to the south.

Chief Joseph later recalled, "I said in my heart that, rather than have war, I would give up my country. . . . I would give up everything rather than have the blood of white men upon the hands of my people. . . . I blame my young men and I blame the white man. My friends among the white men have blamed me for the war. I am not to blame. When my young began the killing, my heart was hurt. Although I did not justify them, I remembered all the insults I had endured, and my blood was on fire. Still I would have taken my people to the buffalo country without fighting, if possible. I could see no other way to avoid war. We moved over to White

Bird Creek . . . and there encamped, intending to collect our stock before leaving; but the soldiers attacked us and the first battle was fought."

General Howard sent a force to quell the uprising, but it was repulsed with heavy losses. For a month, the nontreaty Nez Percés moved east, engaging in only minor skirmishes with army troops. Meanwhile, Howard, under increasing criticism and pressure, summoned troops from the West Coast to begin an encircling movement. His force caught up with the Indians on July 11 near the Clearwater River. They fought inconclusively for two days, then the Nez Percés withdrew.

The nontreaty Nez Percés realized they now had to leave the Idaho Territory. They set out to join the Crow in buffalo country, which their hunters had used for generations.

Chief Joseph was to shepherd the Nez Percés dependents along the trail. By August, the Nez Percés had crossed the mountains and reached the Bitterroot Valley in Montana. They did not know that a second pursuing force, commanded by Col. John Gibbon, was nearby. On August 7, the Nez Percés reached the Big Hole River. Believing they were out of danger, they set up their tipis for the first time since leaving Clearwater. They relaxed, sang, and danced, but they were spotted and a surprise attack was mounted at dawn. The troopers entered the camp, but warriors forced them back and pinned them down for more than a day. Chief Joseph used this respite to gather his people together and lead them southward.

The cost of the battle to the Indians was high. Some thirty braves and forty women, children, and old people had been killed. The army suffered heavy casualties, but considered the Battle of Big Hole a victory, partial revenge for the massacre at the Little Bighorn the year before. Realizing the army would continue to harass them, the nontreaty Nez Percés decided to join Sitting Bull in Canada.

The *Visitor Center* has exhibits pertaining to the Nez Percé Indian War period and an audiovisual program to orient visitors to the park. Trails beginning at the lower parking area lead to several points of interest: the *Nez Percé Camp,* where the battle began; the *Siege Area,* where the soldiers were pinned down for thirty-six hours; the *Howitzer Site*; and the *Capture Site*, a twenty-minute walk away. Open daily. Limited wheelchair access.

The 1,170-mile *Nez Percé National Historic Trail* follows the route of the Nez Percé War from Joseph, Oregon, to the Bearpaw Battlefield in Montana. The Big Hole Battlefield Trail follows this route for about twenty-two miles, usually a two-day hike.

Accommodations: *Coppertown Gallery Bar & Inn* (23 Main St.; 406/563-2372). A bed-and-breakfast with ten guest rooms with private baths.

BILLINGS

In the beginning, the Northern Pacific Railway built the town and named it after its president, Frederick K. Billings. Today it attracts tourists, serves the area's strip mines, and is the headquarters of the Custer National Forest.

Peter Yegan, Jr., Museum (Logan Field Airport on Mt 3; 406/256-6811). An interesting mélange of Indian artifacts, a steam locomotive, and vintage guns, saddles, and horse-drawn vehicles. Excellent view of the mountains and Yellowstone Valley. Open daily except Saturdays.

Western Heritage Center (2822 Montana Ave.; 406/256-6809). Changing exhibits tell the history of the Yellowstone Valley. Open daily except Mondays.

Oscar's Dreamland (7 miles southwest via I-90 to King Ave. exit and South Frontage to Shiloh underpass; 406/245-4598). The dream of Oscar O. Cooke, this is reputedly the world's largest private collection of farm impedimenta: fifteen acres of tractors, threshers, plows, steam engines, vintage cars, covered wagons and draft horses. Railroad ride. Open daily, May through mid-October.

Range Rider of the Yellowstone (off Chief Black Otter Trail, near airport). Silent screen cowboy star William S. Hart posed for this life-sized bronze statue of a cowboy and his horse.

Boothill Cemetery (east end of Chief Black Otter Trail). Many lawmen and outlaws found their last resting place here.

Indian Caves (5 miles southeast off U.S. 87/212). Pictographs on the walls remind visitors that these caves were inhabited 4,500 years ago. Picnicking. Open daily.

Pompey's Pillar (28 miles east off I-94; 406/259-8426). This prominent rock formation was once used by Indians for smoke signals. Captain Clark of the Lewis and Clark expedition named it and carved his name into it. Open daily, Memorial Day to Labor Day.

Accommodations: *Feather Cove Inn*

"Tell General Howard I know his heart. What he told me before, in Idaho, I have in my heart. I am tired of fighting. . . . My people ask me for food, and I have none to give. It is cold, and we have no blankets, no wood. My people are starving to death. Where is my little daughter? I do not know. Perhaps, even now, she is freezing to death. Hear me, my chiefs. I have fought; but from where the sun now stands, Joseph will fight no more forever."

—CHIEF JOSEPH, NEZ PERCÉ

(5530 Vermillion Rd.; 406/373-5679). A bed-and-breakfast with four guest rooms with private baths. *PJ's Bed and Breakfast* (722 North 29th St.; 406/259-3300). Ten guest rooms with private baths in a historic house.

BOULDER

Elkhorn Ghost Town (7 miles south of town on MT 69, then 11 miles north on county road; 406/994-4042). Outstanding examples of frontier architecture of Montana's 1880s silver boom.

BOZEMAN

John M. Bozeman led immigrants here and they named the town for him. In the beginning the area was agricultural, then mining took over, and now it's agricultural again. Bozeman is the entrance to the huge Gallatin National Forest and is convenient to Yellowstone.

Museum of the Rockies (south 7th Ave. and Kagy Blvd. South; 406/994-2251). Several interesting Indian exhibits, dinosaurs, and art and science displays. Open daily.

Red Cloud, an Oglala Sioux chief, led attacks on wagon trains using the Bozeman Trail, which linked the North Platte River with the Montana mines. He poses (center) with his delegation and a white interpreter at a Fort Bridger peace parlay in the early 1870s.

BROWNING

This town revolves around the Blackfeet Indian Reservation, which is one of the outstanding recreation areas in the country, 1.5 million acres of natural beauty adjacent to Glacier National Park and an easy drive from Yellowstone National Park. There are eight major lakes and 175 miles of rivers and streams on the reservation, the home of 5,000 Blackfeet. The land historically was the hunting grounds of the Blackfeet, once among the most powerful tribes of the Northwest Plains, their territory extending west of the Rocky Mountains from the North Saskatchewan River to the headwaters of the Missouri.

Museum of the Plains Indian and Crafts Center (west at junction of U.S. 2 and 89, 13 miles from Glacier National Park; 406/338-2230). The Department of the Interior and the Indian Arts and Crafts Board administer this excellent collection of tribal artifacts of Northern Plains and Blackfeet Indians. The crafts shops sell moccasins, basketry, bead and featherwork, tanned hides, and other Indian handwork, much of it made at the nearby Blackfeet Reservation. Open daily, June through September; weekdays the rest of the year.

BUTTE

This city began as a silver boomtown, and when the silver started to run out, the miners discovered copper. Fortunes were made and lost fighting for control of the ore, culminating in the War of the Copper Kings. The mesa on which the city sits is called "the richest hill on earth."

Butte Historic District. Much of

Accommodations: *Voss* (319 South Wilson; 406/587-0982). This 1883 inn has Victorian decor and is furnished with antiques. Breakfast is included in the rates.

Indians traditionally killed only what they needed to provide food and clothing for their tribe. They were appalled by the wholesale slaughter of buffalo by white hunters. In this 1865–1875 painting by John M. Stanley, Blackfoot hunters chase buffalo near Three Buttes, Montana.

Montana's history was written in mineral-rich Butte. A two-hour walking tour includes historic mansions, churches, union halls, the courthouse, the fire hall, and an original copper mine. Phone 406/494-5595 for a self-guiding tour brochure.

Arts Chateau (321 West Broadway; 406/723-7600). The handsome 1898 home of Charles Clark is now an art museum with some excellent examples of Western art. Open daily except Mondays.

Copper King Mansion (219 West Granite St.; 406/782-7580). This is the restored thirty-two-room home of Senator W. A. Clark, one of the early Copper Kings. Frescoed ceilings and walls. Hand-carved fireplaces. Stained-glass windows. Pipe organ. Silver and crystal collection. Open daily.

Mineral Museum (on West Park St. campus of the Montana College of Mineral Science and Technology; 406/496-4266). The museum has a collection of 15,000 mineral specimens, with emphasis on Montana minerals. Open daily during the summer.

World Museum of Mining and Hell Roarin' Gulch (1 mile west on West Park St. at Orphan Girl Mine; 406/723-7600). A re-creation of Hell Roarin' Gulch, an 1899 mining camp. Displays of mining equipment. Open daily except Mondays, late March through November.

Neversweat & Washoe Railroad (leaves from museum). A renovated railcar carries passengers to and from the Kelly Mine, the last operating underground mine in Butte. Runs daily, Memorial Day to Labor Day.

Old No. 1 (departs from Chamber of Commerce office, 2950 Harrison Ave.). A replica of a vintage streetcar that tours the city from June through Labor Day.

CHINOOK

The town is named after the warm winds that come in January and February and melt the snow and expose the grass for cattle to graze.

Chief Joseph Battleground State Monument (16 miles south on MT 240). Fleeing from Big Hole, the Nez Percé had a few skirmishes with the army as they headed north to what is now Yellowstone National Park. They hoped to obtain warriors and assistance along the way from the Shoshone and the Crow Nation. Both refused, not wanting to risk trouble with the army. On September 30, 1887, here in the Bear Paw Mountains of Montana near the Canadian border, the Nez Percé were surprised by army troops commanded by Col. Nelson A. Miles. After five days of fighting and intermittent negotia-

"Several now-forgotten Army officers did a better job fighting Indians on the plains, but Custer's fame is the victory of fun and myth over complicated history. Pursuing his boy's dream of a life on the Great Plains, a land which was itself a dream in many people's minds, Custer finally ran into the largest off-reservation concentration of Indians ever in one place on the continent, and gave them what was possibly the last really good time they ever had."

—Ian Frazier, *Great Plains*

The Return of the Horse

The Old West is unimaginable without horses, yet for ages there were none there. Herds of small wild horses once roamed the West, but for some unknown reason they became extinct about 7,000 years ago. The Spanish brought domesticated horses with them, and when they colonized the Southwest they developed the open-range method of pasturing cattle and horses, which is still in use today. The stock was supervised by riders who visited the herds every few weeks. Twice a year, all the cattle and horses were rounded up separately. In the spring the horses were branded, and the older horses were kept to be broken and trained. In the fall, mature horses were cut from the herd to be taken to market.

Pueblo Indians helped the Spanish ranchers care for their horses, and some Indians ran off, taking horses with them, to join the tribes of buffalo hunters on the Great Plains. Their skills in breaking, handling, and using horses were passed on to others. The horse spread rapidly through the Plains, reaching all the tribes between 1650 and 1770.

West of the Rockies, the horse moved northward to the Navaho, Ute, and Shoshone, reaching southern Montana about 1690. Shoshone herds supplied horses to the Crow and the tribes of the Columbia Basin, where the Nez Percé soon became famous for their fine mounts. Explorers and fur traders found a plentiful supply of Indian horses at reasonable prices for their ventures. As early as 1793, traders were buying horses from tribes in northern Texas and taking them to New Orleans and Natchez for use on plantations.

When the Santa Fe Trail opened in 1821, traders swapped cloth and hardware for silver and horses. The demand grew so great that large herds of horses from Mexico and California were brought to Santa Fe. When the wagons rolled west on the Oregon Trail, the Rockies and the desert took a heavy toll on horses. They were replaced by horses bought from the Nez Percé and Cayuse, and later all Western horses were called cayuses. The army, frustrated by the ease with which mounted Indians eluded pursuit, slaughtered their horses at every opportunity. Custer killed about 800 horses captured from a Cheyenne village.

Until the coming of the railroad, all mail, express, and passenger service was handled by stagecoaches; a change of horses was needed for each fifteen miles a coach traveled. In the settled areas, horses were the the local transportation, carrying riders, pulling buggies, carts, buckboards, wagons. The West raised sufficient horses for all its needs and every year shipped many thousands to the East. When times were hard in the East, the market for Western horses suffered. Many breeders would have gone under if it hadn't been for the Boer War. British agents bought thousands of horses in Colorado, Montana, and Wyoming, and shipped them to South Africa.

Two breeds are associated with the West: the Appaloosa, introduced into Mexico by the Spanish, and the quarter horse, developed as a sprint racer in the American colonies and later raised in large numbers in Texas. The quarter horse, ideal for handling cattle, is today the most numerous registered breed in the world.

tions, they surrendered, probably more exhausted than defeated, ending Montana's Indian wars.

Custer Battlefield National Monument (2 miles south of Crow Agency, 1 mile east of U.S. 87/I-90 on U.S. 212; 406/638-2621). It was a small battle as battles go, lasting less than an hour. The Seventh Cavalry lost some 225 men; the Indians, about a hundred. But the Battle of the Little Bighorn, "Custer's Last Stand," was the stuff of legend, and it captured the imagination of generations of Americans.

In 1868 a treaty was signed at Fort Laramie, Wyoming, that gave the Sioux, Cheyenne, and other Great Plains tribes a large part of eastern Wyoming as a permanent reservation. The United States promised to protect the Indians "against the commission of all depredations by people of the United States." But in 1874 gold was discovered in the Black Hills, the heart of the new reservation, and thousands of prospectors swarmed into the area in violation of the treaty. The army tried to keep the prospectors out, but failed. Unsuccessful efforts were made to buy the Black Hills from the Indians. The Indians left the reservation and attacked travelers and raided nearby settlements. In December 1875, the Commissioner of Indian Affairs ordered the Indians to return to the reservation before January 31, 1876, or be treated as hostiles. The Indians failed to comply, and the army was called in.

At the beginning, George Armstrong Custer was a minor player, a lieutenant colonel in command of a regiment, the Seventh Cavalry. Three separate army expeditions were launched: one under Gen. George Crook from Fort Fetterman in the Wyoming Territory; another under Col. John Gibbon from Fort Ellis in the Montana Territory; the third under Gen. Alfred Terry from Fort Abraham Lincoln in the Dakota Territory. Their forces were to converge and attack the Indians concentrated in southeastern Montana under the leadership of Sitting

Custer (center) hunted more than Indians on his Black Hills expedition. He titled this 1874 photograph "Our First Grizzly." The Black Hills were sacred to the Sioux. The discovery of gold there began the series of events that culminated at the Little Bighorn.

Bull, Crazy Horse, and other chiefs. Crook's troops clashed with a large Sioux-Cheyenne force along the Rosebud River and were forced to withdraw. The Indians moved west toward the Little Bighorn River. Terry and Gibbon, meanwhile, met on the Yellowstone River near the mouth of the Rosebud.

Believing the Indians were in the Little Bighorn Valley, Terry ordered Custer up the Rosebud to approach the Little Bighorn from the south. Terry and Gibbon's force went back up the Yellowstone and Bighorn rivers to approach from the north.

At dawn on June 25, the Seventh Cavalry located the Indian camp. Custer decided to attack, ignoring warnings that the camp stretched for eight miles along the river and contained as many as 40,000 Indians. He divided his regiment into three battalions, retaining five companies and assigning three companies each to Maj. Marcus Reno and Capt. Frederick Benteen. A twelfth company stayed behind to guard the pack train. Benteen was sent to scout the bluffs to the south; Custer and Reno headed toward the Indian camp. Custer galloped north near the river and was last seen heading for the lower end of the camp. Reno led his companies

Curley, a Crow scout for Custer at the Little Bighorn, was the sole survivor in Custer's immediate command. Before the fighting began, Curley was dispatched with a message to General Terry; then he apparently returned and watched the battle rage from a safe distance.

When Custer and his Seventh Cavalry first spotted the Sioux encampment at the Little Bighorn, it must have looked something like this 1891 photograph. Shown is the "Villa of Brule," the great hostile Indian camp on the river Brule near Pine Ridge, South Dakota.

down the valley to attack the upper end of the camp. A large force of Sioux rode out to intercept Reno. He formed a line of battle and attempted to make a stand, but was nearly overwhelmed. The troops retreated in disorder to the river bluffs, where Reno was met by Benteen, who had been sent by Custer with a curt written order: "Come on. Big village. Be quick, bring packs."

Reno and Benteen distributed ammunition to their troops and led them north, where they could hear heavy gunfire. An advance company under Capt. Thomas Weir went about a mile downstream and up a high hill, from which the area where Custer was believed to be was visible. The gunfire had stopped, and Weir could see no trace of Custer or his troops. When the rest of Reno and Benteen's troops arrived, they were attacked by a large force of Indians. Reno ordered the troops back to the river bluffs, where they held their defensive positions the rest of the hot day and most of the next. The Indians withdrew when Terry and Gibbon's columns approached. Reno and Benteen had

lost forty-seven men and sustained fifty-two wounded.

Meanwhile, Custer and his five companies, about 225 men, had been surrounded and slain in fierce fighting. Custer's precise movements have never been determined, but the battle was described by Two Moons, a Northern Cheyenne: "The shooting was quick, quick. Pop-pop-pop, very fast. Some of the soldiers were down on their knees, some standing. . . . The smoke was like a great cloud, and everywhere the Sioux went, the dust rose like smoke. We circled all around him—swirling like water around a stone. We shoot, we ride fast, we shoot again. Soldiers drop, and horses fall on them."

The Indians removed most of their dead from the battlefield when they broke camp. The tribes scattered, and most of them returned to the reservation and surrendered during the next few years. Major Reno was criticized sharply for his retreat from the valley. A court of inquiry in 1879 exonerated him, but the controversy lingers to this day.

A sign of the times came late in 1989, when Barbara Booher, a full-blooded Ute and Cherokee Indian, was appointed superintendent of the Custer Battlefield National Monument. She vowed to cut through the Custer myth and tell the Indian side of the battle. Among her plans were a permanent exhibit of Native American culture at the Visitor Center and monuments to Indians who died in the battle. "The story is out of balance," Ms. Booher says. "It doesn't take much to look at the exhibits and see that everything is tilted toward who was the loser in that battle."

The tour begins at the *Reno-Benteen Battlefield*, four and one-half miles from the Visitor Center. Here Major Reno, leading three companies of Custer's divided command, met the first attack on the afternoon of June 25. Forced to retreat, his troops took positions on these bluffs and were soon joined by Captain Benteen's men. Until the Indians left late the next day, Reno and Benteen were confined to defensive action (in the vicinity of the Seventh Cavalry Memorial).

Captain Weir moved forward to the hill now known as *Weir Point* in an attempt to locate Custer, but by the time he arrived here, the firing had stopped. An Indian attack forced Weir off the hill.

Along the crest of *Calhoun Ridge*, men of Company L fell in battle, as indicated by interpretive signs. Marble markers between this ridge and Custer Hill show where the men of Companies F and I perished.

Most of the battlefield and the valley where the Indian camp was located can be seen from *Custer Hill*. On the west side of the hill, just below the monument, are 52 markers showing as nearly as possible where the remnant of Custer's battalion made its "last stand." The bodies of Custer, his brothers Tom and Boston, and his nephew "Autie" were all found in this group. West of the monument, on a knoll between the hill and the river, markers indicate where companies

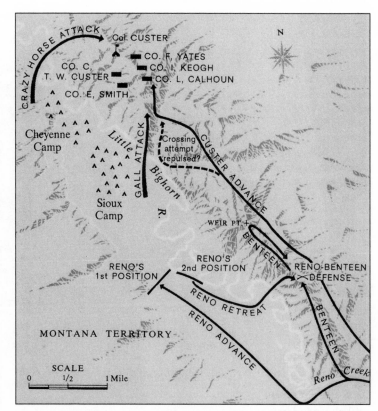

C and E were overwhelmed. The first graves were dug hastily where the soldiers had fallen. In 1881 the bodies were reinterred in a common grave around the memorial shaft bearing the names of all the fallen. The bodies of eleven officers and two civilians were exhumed for reburial elsewhere at the request of relatives. Custer's remains were reburied at the U.S. Military Academy, West Point, New York, on October 10, 1877.

A short walk from the Visitor Center is the *Custer Battlefield National Cemetery*. Of the battle dead, only a few unidentified remains and the body of Lt. John Crittenden are here, along with soldiers killed in other Indian engagements on the Northern Plains and in other wars. The brown stone lodge was used as the quarters of the cemetery superintendents, who were known to the Indians as the "Ghost Herders."

A museum in the *Visitor Center* displays Seventh Cavalry and Indian artifacts. Park

The Battle of Little Bighorn

◆━Ι━◆

"We will go down and make a crossing and capture the village."

—GEORGE ARMSTRONG CUSTER, ON ARRIVING AT THE LITTLE BIGHORN

Buried at the Little Bighorn are several members of Custer's family who fought with him. The body of the general was removed and reburied at West Point. The photograph shows the little hill where the battle was fought and the flatness of the land.

✠

"The West became show business almost immediately. Within a year of taking the famous First Scalp for Custer (a scalp still shrouded in controversy), Buffalo Bill had his Wild West Show going, and only a decade later he was racing eight European kings around Earl's Court in a stagecoach at Queen Victoria's Jubilee, while Indians, resting between mock battles, played pingpong behind the tents."

—LARRY MCMURTRY

rangers lecture on the battle hourly during the summer months. The nearest place for food and overnight accommodations is Hardin, fifteen miles north on I-90. Open daily. Limited wheelchair access.

DEER LODGE

The discovery of gold here touched off a gold rush, and the town became a stagecoach station linking the early mining camps. Traces of old mining camps are nearby.

Grant-Kohrs Ranch National Historic Site (north edge of town, off I-90; 406/846-2070). Once the headquarters of a ranch of more than a million acres, the site is preserved in its original state. The house, called the "finest home in the Montana Territory," has original furnishings. Also preserved are the bunkhouses and barns. Ranch hands and blacksmiths are at work in the summer. Animals. Visitor Center. Tours. Open daily.

Powell County Museum (north edge of town, off I-90; 406/848-3111). The museum has artifacts and displays depicting the history of the county and southwestern Montana. Open daily, June through Labor Day.

Montana Territorial Prison (1106 Main St.; 406/846-3111). This castlelike structure, the first territorial prison in the West, held prisoners from 1871 to 1979. A sandstone wall, built in 1893, surrounds the five-acre compound. The 1912 cellblocks are intact. Open daily. The prison complex includes the *Montana Law Enforcement Museum*. Open Wednesday through Sunday, June to Labor Day.

DILLON

This town began as a Union Pacific Railroad stop, but the surrounding area is rich in gold-rush lore.

Beaverhead County Museum (15 South Montana St.; 406/683-5027). Artifacts and vintage photographs from the nearby old mining camps. Open daily.

Bannack State Historic Park (off MT 278 west of Dillon; 406/834-3413). The site of the first territorial capital and the first major gold strike. A tour includes Sheriff Henry Plummer's gallows, the jailhouse, and Hotel Meade. Visitor center. Open daily during the summer.

DRUMMOND

Bearmouth Ghost Town (14 miles west on U.S. 10/12, I-90). In 1896 the mines here produced a million dollars' worth of gold and silver. Bearmouth was once considered as a location for the state capital. According to legend, a fortune is buried in a baking-powder can on the slopes above the town. Visitors may try to find it.

Pintler Scenic Route (62 miles of MT 1, off I-90 beginning at Drummond). A loop through the heart of Gold West Country through high mountain passes, to mining and ghost towns, through Philipsburg and Anaconda, and along the shores of scenic Georgetown Lake. The magnificent peaks of the Anaconda-Pintler Wilderness form the backdrop.

FORT BENTON

Old Fort Benton Ruins (on the riverfront, near Main St.; 406/622-3278). Originally built by the American Fur Company at the head of the Missouri River in 1848, the fort was rebuilt of adobe four years later and named after Senator Thomas H. Benton of Missouri. After the beaver in the area nearly became extinct, the fort languished until gold was discovered in Bannack in 1862, then became an important steamboat port. Just before the Civil War, a military route was built from here to Walla Walla, Washington, the first wagon road over the northern Rockies. It took forty-seven days for loaded wagons to travel the 624 miles. Later the Whoopup Trail to Canada began here. After the American Fur Company closed down operations, the fort was leased to the government, and the Seventh Infantry was stationed here. Today the fort is a picturesque ruin.

Museum of the Upper Missouri (1800 Front St.; 406/622-5185). Artifacts from the days of trappers, steamboats, and stage-coaches. Open daily, mid-May to mid-September.

GREAT FALLS

Charles M. Russell Museum (400 13th St. North; 406/727-8787). The studio of the great artist of the American West contains paintings, bronzes, and the important Trigg collection, as well as an exhibit of Russell's contemporaries and a collection of Browning firearms. Open daily except Mondays during the winter.

Accommodations: *Three Pheasant Inn* (626 5th Ave. North; 406/453-0519). This 1910 Victorian home offers four rooms and breakfast. The gardens have a century-old fountain and a gazebo.

HAMILTON

Fort Owen State Monument and St. Mary's Mission (20 miles north off U.S. 93 in Stevensville; 406/542-5500). More a trading post than a fort, this was Montana's first white settlement. St. Mary's, the first Catholic mission in the Northwest, was established by Father Pierre-Jean Owen in 1850. Nearby are an 1868 pharmacy, Chief Victor's house, and an Indian cemetery. The mission's history is depicted in stained glass at the church. Tours. Open daily, May through September.

Daly Mansion (2 miles northeast on County 269; 406/363-6004). Built in 1890 by Irish immigrant Marcus Daly, one of Montana's "copper kings," the mansion contains forty-two rooms, seven Italian marble fireplaces, original furniture, and a "doll house" built for the Daly children. Fifty landscaped acres. Tours, June through early September.

Ravalli County Museum (Main and 5th sts.; 406/363-3338). A collection of local historical artifacts is housed in the handsome Ravalli County Courthouse. Open daily.

HARDIN

Now the trading center for Indians from the nearby Crow Reservation, Hardin was settled after the area was opened to white settlers in 1906.

Crow Agency (on I-90 south of Hardin; 406/638-2601). This large reservation surrounds much of the Bighorn Canyon Recreation Area and encompasses the Custer Battlefield. One of the nation's best-known Indian powwows, the *Crow Fair*, is held here in August, when the Crow Agency becomes the "Tipi Capital of the World." On sale during the fair is the fabulous beadwork, usually in floral design, for which the Crow are known.

On the west side of the reservation, *Chief Plenty Coups State Historical Park* contains the home and burial site of the last chief of the Crow. His log home and store remain as evidence of his efforts to adopt the lifestyle of the white man. A visitor center and interpretive displays explain the Crow culture. Open daily.

HAVRE

Havre (*HAV-er*) serves the cattle and wheat-producing area of northern Montana, and is an important division point on the Great Northern (now the Burlington Northern) Railway.

Wahkpa Chu'gn Archaeology Site (on U.S. 2 near town; 406/265-5152 or 265-9913). The largest and best-preserved bison kill site in this part of the Great Plains, this site contains the Wahkpa Chu'gn Buffalo Jump area, where Plains Indians once stampeded buffalo off a cliff to harvest them. Tours on summer evenings.

H. Earl Clack Memorial Museum (on Hill County Fairgrounds, one half mile west on U.S. 2; 406/265-9913). Archeological material from the Wahkpa Chu'gn site and artifacts of area history are displayed here.

Summer lecture and tour program. Open daily, mid-May through mid-September.

Fort Assinniboine (8 miles southwest off U.S. 87; 406/265-9913). When constructed in 1880, this was the largest military fort west of the Mississippi. It was used as a fort until 1911. Some original buildings still stand. Tours on summer Sundays.

Rocky Boys Indian Reservation (15 miles southwest on U.S. 87 in Box Elder; 406/395-4478). The home of the Chippewa and Cree is in the foothills of the Bearpaw Mountains. Fine fishing and camping; visitors need both a state license and a tribal permit to fish. Tipis for rent for camping. Open daily.

HELENA

In 1864 a party of hapless prospectors decided to take a last chance and dig in a gulch here (now Main Street). They hit a vein containing more than $20 million worth of gold. The mining camp, known as Last Chance, was renamed Helena, after a town in Minnesota. The city is known as "the Queen City of the Rockies."

State Capitol (bounded by Lockey and Roberts streets, 6th and Montana avenues; 406/444-4789). The sandsone-faced building, topped with a copper dome, contains murals by Charles M. Russell, E. S. Paxton, and other Western artists. Open daily, mid-June through Labor Day.

Montana Historical Society Museum (225 North Roberts St.; 406/444-2694). The Montana Homeland exhibit depicts the history of the state. There is an important Charles M. Russell collection, the Haynes Gallery of Montana Photography, a military history room, and a historical library. Open daily, Memorial Day to Labor Day; daily except Sundays the rest of the year.

Last Chance Tour Train (departs from museum). A covered train tours the city's major points of interest, including Last

Chance Gulch. Daily in the summer.

Original Governor's Mansion (304 North Ewing St.; 406/444-2694). Built in 1898, this restored twenty-two-room brick house was used as the residence of nine governors from 1913 to 1959. Tours. Open daily except Mondays, June through August.

Gold Collection (Northwest Bank; 406/447-6400). A display includes nuggets, gold leaf, gold dust, and coins. Open weekdays.

Pioneer Cabin (280 South Park Ave.). Built in 1864, the cabin contains authentic furnishings. Open daily, Memorial Day to Labor Day.

Reeder's Alley (on South Park, near the east end of Last Chance Gulch). A restored area of early Helena that once housed miners, Chinese laundry workers, and muleskinners. Visitor center. Open daily.

Frontier Town (15 miles west on U.S. 12, atop the Continental Divide; 406/442-4560). An authentic-style village built of hand-hewn logs. Dining room, unique Western bar, museum, chapel, and gift shop. Spectacular view of the Continental Divide. Open daily, April through October.

Marysville (northwest off Secondary 279). Once a gold camp, this is now a small community with several buildings on the National Register of Historic Places.

Sapphires (northeast of the city on the Missouri River; 406/442-4120). Visitors dig for sapphires and other gems, or sift through "pay dirt" at Castles Sapphire Mine, French Bar Mine, Cleatus Mine, El Dorado Mine, Spokane Bar Mine, or the Love Stone Mine.

LEWISTOWN

Once a small trading post on the Carroll Trail, Lewistown boomed during the gold rush and now is the center of wheat farms and cattle ranches.

Fort Maginnis (15 miles east on U.S. 87). The ruins of an 1880 frontier post.

Ghost towns. There are several abandoned gold camps nearby: *Maiden* (10 miles north on U.S. 191, then 6 miles east), *Kendell* (16 miles north on U.S. 191, then 6 miles west on a gravel road), and *Giltedge* (14 miles east on U.S. 87, then 6 miles northeast).

LIVINGSTON

Emigrant Gulch (37 miles south off U.S. 89). After the discovery of gold here in 1862, two camps, Chico and Yellowstone, flourished, but the Crow Indians were troublesome and the gold ran out. The ghost towns are worth a visit.

Park County Museum (118 West Chinook; 406/222-3506). Called "The House of Memories," this museum has Indian and archaeological exhibits, material on Yellow-

Jim Bridger

Mountain man Jim Bridger knew the West like the back of his hand, and was justly famous as a trapper, guide, and scout. Orphaned in St. Louis at fourteen, he became a blacksmith's apprentice, quitting in 1822 to make an expedition to the Rockies. Three years later he was the first white man to see the Great Salt Lake. Bridger worked for trappers and became a partner in a fur-trading company. In a battle with the Gros Ventre in 1832, part of an arrow was embedded in his back, where it remained for years. He worked for the American Fur Company until the fur trade declined, then, with Louis Vasquez, built Fort Bridger in Wyoming, which became an important way station for emigrants to Oregon and California. The fort was sold to Mormons after ten years. Bridger was in constant demand as a guide. In 1850 he led an expedition in search of a pass through the Rocky and Wasatch mountains, discovering Bridger's and the Cheyenne passes. He guided an expedition to Yellowstone and the Berthoud party in an attempt to find a short route from Denver to Salt Lake. Although troubled by failing eyesight, he surveyed the length of the Bozeman Trail for the Union Pacific.

stone Park pioneers, a Northern Pacific Railroad Room, a library, a stagecoach, and other historical artifacts. Open daily, June to Labor Day.

Depot Center (Park and 2nd streets; 406/222-2300). The center houses Yellowstone Days, a major art and history exhibit from the Buffalo Bill Historical Center in Cody, Wyoming. Open daily, mid-May to mid-October.

Downtown Livingston. The historic district includes 436 buildings, most within walking distance of one another.

Accommodations: *Talcott House Bed & Breakfast* (405 West Lewis; 406/222-7699). Five guest rooms with shared baths in a historic house.

MALTA

Little Rocky Mountains (40 miles southwest on U.S. 191; 406/654-1240). An island of mountains on the plains, the area is rich in Old West lore. According to legend, Butch Cassidy and Kid Curry hid out here. Gold mining arrived in 1884, and by World War II the Little Rockies had yielded $25 million in gold. Tour a modern gold-mining operation at Pegasus Gold's *Zortman Mine* (406/673-3252).

MILES CITY

Range Riders Museum (on U.S. 10/12 at the west end of town; 406/232-6146). The complex includes the Fort Keogh officers' quarters, the Pioneer Memorial Hall, Old Milestown Main Street, a heritage center, Indian artifacts, and the 400-piece Bert Clark Gun Collection. Open daily, April through October.

Fort Keogh (2 miles southeast). Several original buildings and the parade ground remain of what was the largest army post in Montana from 1877 to 1908.

Coffrin's Old West Gallery (1600 Main St.; 406/232-3076). Featured here is the work of early photographer L. A. Huffman, who captured the era of the Indian Wars, buffalo herds, frontier towns, life on the range, and the arrival of the railroads.

O'Fallon Museum (80 miles east via U.S. 12 in Baker; 406/778-3265). Housed in the old town jail, the museum has a collection of period clothing and military uniforms. A separate building houses vintage machinery and local memorabilia. Open daily except Saturdays.

Montana Agates (along the Yellowstone River, from Custer to Sidney). The river is renowned for the quality and abundance of agates found on its shores. Sometimes called "plume" or "moss" agates, Montana agates are famous for the variety of scenic designs sealed in their interiors. Inquire locally for guide service. Petrified wood, colored jaspers, and fossils are also common in the area.

MISSOULA

An important crossroads since the time of Lewis and Clark, Missoula has attracted explorers, hunters, traders, Indians, farmers, and merchants.

Historical Museum at Fort Missoula (5 miles south from I-90 via Reserve St. to South Ave., then 1 mile west; 406/728-3476). The museum contains exhibits on forest management and timber production in western Montana, and ten historic structures, four of which are restored. From 1877 to 1947 this was Fort Missoula, of which seven buildings remain. Other exhibits relate to railroad and military history. Open daily except Mondays.

Missoula County Courthouse (220 West Broadway; 406/721-5700). Built in 1908, the courthouse occupies a full city block and contains eight murals of Montana history by E. S. Paxton, noted Western artist. Open daily except Sundays.

A lonely farmer turns over the first sod on his homestead in Sun River, Montana, in 1908. His four horses indicate he was better off than most. He probably was preparing to plant wheat. Within a few years, tawny oceans of wheat would stretch to the horizon.

Accommodations: *Goldsmith's Inn* (809 East Front; 406/721-6732). A bed-and-breakfast with six guest rooms.

POLSON

According to legend, Paul Bunyan dug the channel from Flathead Lake to the Flathead River near here.

Flathead Indian Reservation (7 miles south on U.S. 93 in Pablo; 406/675-2700). Although called Flathead, the Indians here are the Salish and Kootenai. Before the buffalo vanished, the two tribes used to hunt together. Of special interest are the lower Flathead Lake and Wildhorse Island, the National Bison Range (a 19-mile self-guided tour), the Ninepipe and Pablo wildlife refuges, the Mission Mountains Tribal Wilderness, and the St. Ignatius Mission. Open daily.

Polson-Flathead Museum (8th Ave. and Main St.; 406/883-3409). The museum has Indian artifacts dating from the opening of the Flathead reservation in 1910, as well as an old stagecoach and a wildlife display. Open daily, July and August.

Garden of the Rockies Museum (15 miles southwest via U.S. 93 to Ronan, then to Round Butte Rd., turning at stoplight; 406/676-5210). The museum features displays on Indian culture, homestead life, and the logging industry. Open daily except Sundays, May through September.

SIDNEY

MonDak Heritage Center (120 3rd Ave. Southeast; 406/482-3500). A seventeen-unit street scene of the early 1900s. Area history, art exhibits, and a research library. Open daily except Mondays.

Fort Union Trading Post National Historical Site (22 miles north via MT 200 to Fairview, then north 18 miles on Williams County 58, on the Montana–North Dakota border; 701/572-9083). The preeminent fur-trading post on the Missouri River from 1829 to 1867, Fort Union was a colorful mix of riverboaters, fur traders, Plains Indians, and frontier capitalists. The *Bourgoise House*, once the setting of elegant dinners for distinguished travelers, is now the Visitor Center, which interprets one of the most colorful eras of the westward expansion. Tours. Tipi display. Open daily.

VIRGINIA CITY

After escaping from Indians, six men discovered the world's largest placer gold deposit in Alder Creek here, and within a month, 10,000 miners had arrived. Then came bands of desperadoes, and the camp had 190 murders in seven months. Vigilantes hunted down twenty-one road agents, only to learn that their leader was the sheriff. Nearly $300 million worth of gold was taken from Alder Creek, but the gold ran out and Virginia City and Nevada City became ghost towns. A restoration program has brought back much of the atmosphere of the early mining towns.

Thompson-Huckman Memorial Museum (Wallace St.). Relics of the gold camps. Open daily, May through September.

Virginia City–Madison County Historical Museum (Wallace St.). The museum traces the history of western Montana. Open daily, early June through September.

St. Paul's Episcopal Church (Elling Memorial). Built in 1902 on the site of an 1867 church, this is the oldest Protestant congregation in the state. Tiffany windows.

Boot Hill. This cemetery contains the graves of five road agents hanged by vigilantes.

Restored buildings. These include a dressmaker's shop, a Wells Fargo Express office, a livery stable, a barbershop, a blacksmith shop, a general store, and the offices of the *Montana Post*, the first newspaper in the state, as well as *Gilbert's Brewery* (East Cover St.), built in 1864. The original brewery machinery is intact. During the summer, musical shows are presented here nightly.

Old Opera House (foot of Wallace St.; reservations: 406/843-5377). From mid-June to Labor Day, the Virginia City Players present 19th-century melodramas here daily.

Nevada City (1½ miles west on MT 287). Original buildings, including early mining camp stores, houses, a school, and offices. The Music Hall has a collection of mechanical bands. Open daily.

Robbers' Roost (15 miles west on MT 287). An old stage station often used by outlaws. Open daily.

Accommodations: *Fairweather* (On U.S. 287; 406/843-5377). This hotel, which has six rooms with bath, nine with shared baths, has Old West decor and a balcony overlooking Virginia City. Open January through Labor Day. *Nevada City* (one-half mile west on U.S. 287; 406/843-5377). An inn with fifteen rooms, plus twelve in cabins. The atmosphere is determinedly gold rush era. The inn serves as the information center for Nevada City. Open June through August.

WHITE SULPHUR SPRINGS

The Castle (on U.S. 12; 406/547-3965). Built in 1892, this a chateau-type, gray stone Victorian mansion furnished with period furniture and antiques. The Meagher County Museum, displaying local artifacts, is housed here. Open daily, May to mid-September.

Castle Ghost Town (6 miles east on U.S. 12, then south over unpaved road through part of the Lewis and Clark National Forest). Some buildings remain of this silver camp, where Calamity Jane once lived. Some 1,600 claims were staked here before a decline in silver prices led to the panic of 1892–93.

10

Idaho

BLACKFOOT

Fort Hall Indian Reservation (South on I-15 to the Simplot Road Exit, then 2 miles west; 208/238-3700 or 785-2965). This 528,000-acre reservation north of Pocatello opened in 1869 and is home to 2,700 Shoshone and Bannock Indians. The Bannock roamed throughout the Western mountains, and Lewis and Clark mistook them for Shoshone; the Bannock speak Shoshone but physically resemble the Nez Percé. Suffering from hunger, the Bannock left the reservation in 1878 and killed several settlers at Camas Prairie. Some 1,000 were recaptured after a battle at Clark's ford, in which many Bannock women and children were slain.

At the reservation, arts and crafts are sold, including excellent leatherwork and distinctive floral-design beadwork. Small museum. Open daily.

BOISE

French trappers called this wooded area *les boises* (the woods), and the name became anglicized to Boise (*BOY-zee*). Settled during Gold Rush days, Boise was overshadowed by Idaho Falls until it was named the territorial capital in 1864. Now it is Idaho's capital and, with some 100,000 people, its largest city.

State Capitol (8th and Jefferson streets). The Corinthian-design building, built between 1905 and 1920 and faced with Boise sandstone, has changing exhibits of state history. Facing the capitol grounds is a monument to Frank Steunenberg, the Idaho governor killed in 1905 in the aftermath of labor strife in the mines. Open daily.

Idaho State Historical Society Museum (610 North Julia Davis Dr.; 208/334-2120). Ten historic interiors, including a print shop, a bank, a saloon, and a Chinese temple, are on display, along with historical exhibits. Open daily. Next to the museum, the *Boise Tour Train* (208/342-4799), an 1890 steam train, makes a one-hour narrated tour of the city and its historical areas. Daily, June through Labor Day weekend; weekends in May and from Labor Day through October.

Old Idaho Penitentiary (2½ miles east on ID 21; 208/334-2844). Displays depict prison methods, lawmen, and famous inmates. Slide show on prison history. Self-guided tour through the cells and other areas. Admission includes "Electricity in Idaho" and "Idaho Transportation" exhibits. Open daily.

Accommodations: *Sunrise Inn Bed & Breakfast* (2730 Sunrise Rim Rd.; 208/362-0507). Two guest rooms with a shared bath. *Sulphur Creek Ranch* (7153 West Emerald; 208/377-1188). Near the Middle Fork of the Salmon River, this lodging has five guest units.

BURLEY

A vast irrigation project turned a near-desert into a thriving agricultural area, and created Burley, which has one of the largest potato-processing plants in the world.

Sawtooth National Forest (9 miles east via U.S. 30 to Decio, then 15 miles south on ID 77). This vast recreational area includes Howell Canyon, Lake Cleveland, and four other glacial lakes. Of historical interest is the *City of Rocks National Reserve* (22 miles south of Burley on ID 27 to Oakley, then inquire for best route), which resembles a city carved in stone. Early westward-bound travelers carved their names and messages into the rock.

Mountain Men

Some of the freest men who ever lived were mountain men, trappers who would spend precarious months menaced by Indians, grizzly bears, storms, and the other hazards of a lonely wilderness life.

A mountain man starting out on a hunt was described by George Frederick Ruxton in his 1849 book, *Adventures in Mexico and the Rocky Mountains:*

> Two or three horses or mules—one for saddle, the others for packs— and six traps which are carried in a bag of leather called a *trap-sack.* Ammunition, a few pounds of tobacco, dressed deer-skins for moccasins, etc., are carried in a wallet of dressed buffalo-skin, called a *possible-sack.* . . . Round the [trapper's] waist is a belt, in which is stuck a large butcher-knife in a sheath of buffalo-hide, made fast to the belt by a chain or guard of steel; which also supports a little buckskin case containing a whetstone. A tomahawk is also often added; and, of course, a long heavy rifle is part and parcel of his equipment.

Leaving his cabin, he went to the mountains, following streams, looking for signs of beaver. He set traps baited with "medicine," a substance obtained from the beaver's scrotum, and made his camp nearby. In the morning he checked the traps, skinning the captured beavers. The skins were stretched over a frame to dry, then scraped, folded, and bundled. The run would be trapped out in a day or two, and the trapper would move on. In a three-month hunt, a trapper could cover more than a thousand miles, and at every stop he had to pitch camp, find food, cut firewood, and care for his horses.

In the summer, the mountain man went to a rendezvous to mingle with traders, other trappers, and Indians to sell some furs and trade others for supplies. In a good year, a mountain man might make $130, much of which went for liquor and gambling. Then he was off again, hunting until the weather forced him into winter quarters.

The era of the mountain man was brief; by 1840, overtrapping had made the beaver scarce. Some mountain men never settled down; a few became expedition guides. The first wagon train to cross the Sierras was led by a former mountain man, eighty-one-year-old Caleb Greenwood.

Stagecoach bandits allegedly buried their loot here. For further information, write the Supervisor, 2647 Kimberly Road East, Twin Falls, ID 83301, or phone 208/737-3200.

Cassia County Historical Museum (East Main St. and Hiland Ave.; 208/678-7172). Pioneer cabins and artifacts, a collection of wagons, and a restored private railroad car. Open daily.

CHALLIS

This small town is at the entrance to the **Challis National Forest**, a vast recreation area containing the Frank Church–River of No Return Wilderness and 12,665-foot Mount Borah, the highest mountain in the state. Fishermen flock here to try their luck on the Middle Fork of the Salmon River. There are several ghost towns in the area. The most accessible is *Bayrose* (8 miles south of Challis on U.S. 93, then 4 miles west on an unimproved road).

COEUR D'ALENE

Beautifully situated among lakes and rivers, Coeur d'Alene (*core-da-LANE*) is the center of the state's lumbering industry and the gateway to the recreational facilities of the Idaho Panhandle.

Fort Sherman Museum (North Idaho College campus; 208/664-3448). The museum is housed in the powder house of what was, circa 1880, Fort Coeur d'Alene. Among the exhibits are a log cabin used by forest firefighters and artifacts of pioneers, loggers, and miners. Open Tuesday through Saturday, May through September.

Park Museum (near the waterfront next to City Park; 208/664-3448). Exhibits relating to Indian history, steamboating, lumbering, and big-game hunting. Open Tuesday through Saturday, April through October.

Lake Coeur d'Alene Cruises (City Dock, east of City Park; 208/765-4000). Six-hour boat trips up Lake Coeur d'Alene into the St. Joe River, reputedly the world's highest navigable river.

Accommodations: *Greenbriar Inn Bed & Breakfast* (315 Wallace St.; 208/667-9660). Seven guest rooms, some with private baths. *Loon Cottage Inn* (north in Spirit Lake; 208/623-5400). Two guest rooms with a shared bath. Continental breakfast.

GRANGEVILLE

The discovery of gold in the Florence Basin made Grangeville a gold-rush town in the 1890s. It was also a focal point in the Nez Percé War; White Bird Hill (5 miles south of town on U.S. 95) was the site of the famous White Bird Battle.

IDAHO CITY

The population of this city is now only 300, but it was world-famous during the gold rush; the eighteen-square-mile Boise Basin here is said to have produced more gold than all of Alaska. Flecks of gold can still be found in the gravel beneath the town.

Boise Basin Museum (Montgomery St.; 208/392-4550). In a restored 1867 building, artifacts of the gold-rush era are on display. Open daily, Memorial Day to Labor Day; weekends in May and September.

Boot Hill (Main St.). This restored forty-acre cemetery contains the graves of many gunfight victims.

Gold Hill (1 mile north on Main St.). This was the location of the rich Boise Basin placer mine.

JEROME

Jerome County Historical Museum (Pioneer Hall, 220 North Lincoln; 208/324-

> "After all, the supplying of drink to the Indians will be a means of gaining their goodwill, discovering their secrets, calming them so that they will think less often of . . . executing their hostilities, and creating for them a new necessity which will oblige them to recognize their dependence upon us more directly."
>
> —BERNARDO GÁLVEZ, 1786

Dime Novels

The dime novel and the West were made for each other, and their relationship flourished for more than thirty years. The man who brought them together was Erastus Beadle, who moved to New York in 1858, intending to become a publisher of inexpensive books for a mass audience. After success with handbooks and songbooks, he launched his Dime Novel series, fictional adventures published once a week with a distinctive orange cover. From 1860 to 1865, Beadle sold a total of five million dime novels, an astounding number for its day. (An early success was *Seth Jones; or, The Captives of the Frontier.*)

Beadle quickly learned that a standardized product attracted a mass audience, and perfected a series of formulas for adventure fiction. Many of his writers could grind out a 35,000-word story in less than a week. Fictional characters such as Deadwood Dick and Hurricane Nell appeared in a number of books. Writers also turned real Westerners into dime-novel characters. William F. Cody was transformed into Buffalo Bill in *Buffalo Bill, the King of Border Men,* by Ned Buntline, which appeared in 1869. It was an overnight sensation. When Buffalo Bill became a showman, he hired writers to produce dime novels about him, and more than 600 appeared in his lifetime. Wild Bill Hickok and Calamity Jane also became myths in dime novels.

2711). Guided tours and changing displays relating to local history. Open daily except Sundays.

LAVA HOT SPRINGS

Lava Hot Springs Museum (City Park, Main St.; 208/776-5254). Photographs and memorabilia relating to the town's history from the Indians through the fur trappers to its present-day resort community. Guided walking tour by appointment. Slide show. Open daily.

LEWISTON

The Clearwater and Snake rivers meet here, and the Bitterroot Mountains surround the town, making it one of the prettiest in the state.

Nez Percé National Historical Park (12 miles east via U.S. 95 in Spalding; 208/843-2363). Made up of twenty-four separate sites, all related to the culture and history of the Nez Percé, the park spreads over more than 12,000 square miles of north-central Idaho. Visitor center and museum. Self-guided walks. Interpretive exhibits. Culture demonstrations in the summer. Open daily.

Castle Museum (23 miles north on ID 3 in Juliaetta; 208/278-3081). A three-story handmade *faux* Scottish castle filled with antiques. Open daily, April through October.

Luna House Museum (3rd and C streets; 208/743-2535). Built in 1868, this was the first hotel in town; it contains pioneer and Nez Percé artifacts. Open Tuesday through Saturday.

Auto tours. U.S. 12 runs parallel to the Lewis and Clark Trail east to Montana, with interpretive signs along the way. The Chamber of Commerce (2207 East Main St.; 208/

743-3531) has maps for this and other tours.

Accommodations: *Sheep Creek Ranch* (717 3rd St.; 208/746-1393 or 800/952-5560). Ninety miles up the Snake River from Lewiston, the ranch has two guest rooms with baths. Horseback riding. Trail trips.

MOSCOW

Located in Paradise Valley in the Palouse Hills country, Moscow grew up around Fort Russell, where in 1877 settlers sought refuge from Chief Joseph and his Nez Percé. A monument at 810 B Street marks the site of the old fort.

Latah County Historical Society (McConnell Mansion, 110 South Adams St.; 208/882-1004). In this 1886 building are period furnishings and exhibits and artifacts relating to the town's early history, as well as a historical library. Open Tuesday through Saturday.

Appaloosa Horse Museum (Moscow-Pullman Hwy.; 208/882-5578). Photographs, paintings, and artifacts of the Appaloosa horse, vintage cowboy equipment, Nez Percé clothing, and a saddle collection. The building houses the national headquarters of the Appaloosa Horse Club. Open Monday through Friday.

Accommodations: *Twin Peaks Inn* (2455 West Twin Rd.; 208/882-3898). Three guest rooms. Breakfast.

POCATELLO

Once the site of an Indian reservation, the city was named after the chief who granted the railroad the right-of-way and building privileges.

Idaho Museum of Natural History (Idaho State University campus, southeast side of the city on U.S. 30N; 208/236-3166). The museum has fossils of large mammals of the Ice Age, the Fuji collection of Western rocks, Indian beadwork and basketry, and animated dinosaurs. Tours. Open daily except Sundays.

Bannock County Historical Museum (West Center St. and South Garfield Ave.; 208/233-0434). Artifacts of the early days of Pocatello and Bannock counties, and of the Shoshone and Bannock Indians. Open Tuesday through Saturday.

Standrod House (848 North Garfield Ave.; 208/234-6184). A restored Victorian mansion lavishly decorated and furnished with antiques. Open Monday through Friday.

ST. ANTHONY

Fort Henry Trading Post Site (7 miles west along Henry's Fork of the Snake River). Here, in 1810, was built the first fort on what the early voyageurs called the "accursed mad river."

A Nez Percé chief, Looking Glass, sits for a photographer in front of a tipi in 1887, a decade after the disastrous Nez Percé War. Like so many Western conflicts, it started when the Indians were forced from their homeland to make room for white settlers.

John Charles Frémont

Before he was forty, John Frémont explored the West, excited the East with narratives of his journeys, and helped free California. His first expedition was as Nicollet's mapmaker, charting the land between the Missouri and the upper Mississippi. Then he was sent to survey the Platte and Kansas rivers. His detailed reports were creating a sensation. With Kit Carson as his guide, he mapped the area from Missouri to the mouth of the Columbia River. Now a national hero, Frémont was called "the Pathfinder to the West." On his third expedition he explored the Arkansas and Red rivers and the Great Salt Lake, then entered California, joining forces with Robert Stockton, who was leading the revolt against the Mexicans. He settled in the California Republic, but lost his savings through poor investments. After statehood he was a U.S. senator. He made a final expedition in 1853–54, vainly seeking new mountain passes. He was a Civil War general and was twice nominated for president.

Sand Dunes (6 miles west on local road). Idaho's own wind-sculptured Sahara Desert is thirty miles long and a mile wide. Some of the dunes are a hundred feet high.

ST. MARIES

St. Joe Ghost Town Site (12 miles east on St. Joe River Rd.). Now only ruins remain of what was one of the wildest towns in the West, considered even tougher than the gold camps of the Yukon.

SALMON

Lemhi (29 miles south on ID 28). The Mormons started a colony here in 1855, naming the town after a figure in *The Book of Mormon*. They built a fort, but were driven out by Indians three years later. The walls of old Fort Lemhi are still standing in this historic ghost town. There are other ghost towns in the area. For information, contact the Chamber of Commerce, 200 Main St.; 208/756-4935.

SANDPOINT

Vintage Wheel Museum (218 Cedar St.; 208/263-7173). Horse-drawn vehicles, vintage autos, and logging equipment. Open daily.

Bonner County Historical Society Museum (Lakewood Park, Ontario and Ella streets; 208/263-2344). Material relating to the history of the county, including a newspaper collection dating from 1899. Open Tuesday through Saturday.

Accommodations: *River Birch Farm* (west on ID 2 in Laclede; 208/263-3705). A bed-and-breakfast with four rooms.

SHOSHONE

Shoshone Indian Ice Caves (17 miles north on ID 75; 208/886-2058). These caves are naturally refrigerated and thirty feet wide, forty feet high, and 1,000 feet long. A statue of Shoshone chief Washaki is nearby. Museum of Shoshone artifacts, minerals, and gems. Tour. Open daily, May through October.

STANLEY

Salmon River Expeditions. Along the Middle Fork of the Salmon River are Indian pictographs, caves, abandoned gold mines, and a variety of wildlife. Several outfitters offer float trips. For a list, write or phone the Idaho Outfitters and Guides Association, P.O. Box 95, Boise, ID 83701; 208/342-1438.

TWIN FALLS

Shoshone Falls (5 miles northwest on the Snake River). Called "the Niagara of the West," the falls drop 212 feet (52 more than Niagara). Best visited in the spring or fall. Excellent view from the lookout point or Shoshone Falls Park on the bank of the river. Park open daily, May through August.

Herrett Museum (315 Falls Ave.; 208/733-9554). Exhibits relating to the archaeology of the Americas. Open Tuesday through Saturday.

Twin Falls Historical Society Museum (2 miles east on U.S. 30/93; 208/734-5547). Early frontier shops, farm machinery, household items, and clothing. Open Monday through Friday, May through September.

WALLACE

Wallace District Mining Museum (509 Bank St.; 208/753-7151). Gold was discovered in Wallace in 1882, silver in 1884. Exhibits and a slide show tell the history of mining here. The museum has information on tours of mines and old mining towns in the area. Open daily during the summer; Monday through Friday, September through April.

Northern Pacific Depot Railroad Museum (219 6th St.; 208/752-0111). A re-creation of a 1910 railroad depot and material on the railroad history of the Coeur d'Alene mining district. Open daily, April through October; Tuesday through Saturday the rest of the year.

Sierra Silver Mine Tour (507 Bank St.; 208/752-5151). A one-hour guided walking tour through a depleted silver mine includes demonstrations of mining methods and the operation of modern equipment. Tours every twenty minutes. Open daily, mid-May through September.

Accommodations: *Jameson Bed &* *Breakfast* (304 Sixth St., 83873; 208/556-1554). Six guest rooms furnished with antiques.

WEISER

Intermountain Cultural Center and Museum (Hooker Hall, 2295 Paddock Ave.; 208/549-0450). The history of Washington County is depicted through artifacts and memorabilia. Open Wednesday through Sunday, April through November, except holidays.

Fiddlers Hall of Fame (10 East Idaho; 208/549-0450). Photographs of champion fiddlers and a collection of old-time fiddles. Open Monday through Friday.

Jet boat tours. These tours go into Hells Canyon, through rapids, and stop at an Indian site. For further information, write or phone the Chamber of Commerce, 8 East Idaho St., Weiser, ID 83642; 208/549-0452.

Ye say they all have
passed away.
That noble race
and brave;
That their light
canoes have
vanished
From off the crested
wave
That mid the forest
where they
roamed
There rings no
hunter's shout
But their name is
on your waters;
Ye may not wash
it out.

— LYDIA HUNTLY
SIGOURNEY,
"INDIAN NAMES"

Jedediah Smith

The explorations of mountain man Jedediah Smith helped open the West to settlement. Leading an expedition to the Black Hills, he was told by Indians of a pass through the Rockies. He followed their directions to South Pass, which became the wagon-train gateway to Oregon and California. In search of new trapping grounds, Smith set out in 1826 on his greatest expedition. From the Great Salt Lake he went to the Colorado Plateau and along the Colorado River to the Mojave Desert, crossing the Sierras into California to become the first American to go overland through the Southwest. He then went north through the San Joaquin Valley, crossed Ebbetts Pass, and crossed the Great Basin, another first. In 1830 he led expeditions through present-day Wyoming and Montana, reporting to Washington on British activities in the Northwest. Smith wanted to retire, but was persuaded to lead a supply train to Santa Fe in 1831. Riding ahead to look for water, he ran into a Comanche hunting party and was killed.

11

Wyoming

BUFFALO

Situated at the foot of the Bighorn Mountains, Buffalo began as a trading post at Fort McKinney, one of the last of the old military installations. In 1892 the Johnson County Cattle War erupted, and several people were killed before federal troops intervened.

Fort Phil Kearny State Historical Site (13 miles north on U.S. 87; 307/684-9331). This fort was involved in one of the most tragic chapters in the history of the Indian Wars. Sioux opposition to prospectors using the Bozeman Trail across their hunting grounds to reach the Montana gold fields led to bloody warfare in 1866–68. The Sioux forced the army to abandon forts in this region, and the army was ordered to establish a new line of forts along the trail. Red Cloud, leader of the combined Sioux, Arapaho, and Cheyenne warriors, was unable to prevent the building of this fort, but kept it under continual siege. On December 21, 1866, Lt. Col. William J. Fetterman, a greenhorn, led his 18th Infantry to rescue a supply train. Disobeying his superior, Col. Henry B. Carrington, he charged over a hill in pursuit of a band of Sioux under Crazy Horse, and met the main body of warriors. Fetterman and his entire command, seventy-nine soldiers and two civilians, were wiped out in minutes. Two more battles, the Hayfield and Box Canyon fights, were waged near the fort before the region was made safe. The Visitor Center has exhibits depicting the fort's history. Open daily.

Johnson County–Jim Gatchell Memorial Museum (10 Fort St.; 307/684-9331). The museum has dioramas of the Wagon Box Fight, the Johnson County Cattle War, and the town's main street in the 1880s, as well as Indian material and artifacts of local history. Open daily, June through Labor Day.

Occidental Hotel (10 Main St.). This establishment was made famous by Owen Wister's classic Western novel *The Virginian*.

Accommodations: *V Bar F Cattle Ranch* (18 miles east of I-90, between Buffalo and Gillette, off the Red Hills exit; 307/758-4382). There is a guest room in the ranch house, as well as a guest house that can accommodate up to six people. Family-styled meals in the ranch house. Prairie dog hunting, fishing, and birdwatching.

CASPER

A railroad terminus in cattle country until oil was discovered in 1890 in the Salt Creek Field, Casper was later the site of the Teapot Dome naval oil reserve, which was the subject of a Washington scandal in the 1920s.

Fort Caspar Museum (4001 Fort Caspar Road; 307/235-8462). In this restored fort are exhibits relating to Fort Caspar, the Oregon and Mormon trails, the Pony Express, and local and area history. Museum open daily except winter Saturdays. Fort buildings closed in the winter.

Natrona County Pioneer Museum (Central Wyoming Fairgrounds; 307/235-5775). Settlers' artifacts are displayed in the first church built in Casper, in 1887. Open daily except Tuesdays, mid-May to mid-September.

Accommodations: *Hotel Higgins* (18 miles east on I-25, then 1 mile north in Glenrock at 416 West Birch; 307/438-9212). Built in 1916, the hotel has been restored to original condition and furnished with period antiques.

CHEYENNE

Named for a tribe in the area, Cheyenne became a town when the Union Pacific Railroad arrived in 1867. Among the 4,000 newcomers were promoters, gamblers, confidence men, and professional gunfighters who gave the town the reputation of "Hell on Wheels." Still the center of a large, productive region, Cheyenne is the state's capital and largest city.

State Capitol (head of Capital Avenue). Tours of this 1887 building are available Monday through Friday in June and August.

Governors' Mansion (300 East 21st St.; 307/777-7878). Built in 1904, this was the residence of the state's governors from 1905 to 1976, and the first in the country to be occupied by a woman governor, Nellie Tayloe Ross, from 1924 to 1927. Open Tuesday through Saturday.

State Museum (Barrett Bldg., 24th St. and Central Avenue; 307/777-7024). Ethnological, archaeological, and historical exhibits of early Wyoming and the West are on display. In the building is the Wyoming State Art Gallery. Open daily in the summer; weekdays the rest of the year.

National First Day Cover Museum (702 Randall Blvd.; 307/634-5911). An excellent collection of American stamps dating from 1840, in addition to first-day covers. Open weekdays.

Cheyenne Frontier Days Old West Museum (near Frontier Park Arena; 307/778-7290). A collection of weapons, carriages, and clothing from frontier days. Open weekdays.

Accommodations: *Bear Mountain Back Trails* (56 miles northeast on U.S. 85; 307/834-2281). A working ranch with two guest rooms. Fishing, hiking, camping, fossil hunting, and jeep tours available.

A rodeo crowd cheers as an intrepid cowboy tries to stay aboard a bucking bronco. Rodeo events were originally developed to test the skills of a cowboy.

FAR LEFT: A statue of a cowboy breaking a wild horse stands in front of the capitol in Cheyenne, Wyoming.

BELOW: Cheyenne, Wyoming's capital and largest city, once was called "Hell-on-Wheels," attracting professional gunmen, gamblers, and confidence men in search of a fast buck. Cheyenne Frontier Days, an annual event since 1897, is a rip-roarin' reminder of those days.

Buffalo Bill

Buffalo Bill symbolized the Old West to more people in more parts of the world than anyone else ever did, and he was a real part of the frontier he later so successfully romanticized.

William F. Cody rode for the Pony Express and served in a Union cavalry regiment in the Civil War; then, after marrying and failing as a hotel keeper, he was a guide and scout. In the late 1860s he was a buffalo hunter, supplying meat to railroad construction workers, who started calling him "Buffalo Bill."

General Sheridan hired Cody as his chief of scouts. In four years he took part in sixteen Indian skirmishes. He was also a guide for hunting parties of notables, including Grand Duke Alexis of Russia and a writer who used the pen name Ned Buntline. Buntline made Buffalo Bill the hero of a popular dime novel, the book became a play, and Cody starred in it for a year. He continued to appear on the stage for eleven years.

In 1883 he organized his own showcase, Buffalo Bill's Wild West Show, which was an immediate success. The stars included Buck Taylor ("King of the Cowboys"), Annie Oakley ("Little Miss Sure Shot"), and, for one season, Sitting Bull. The acts included a Pony Express relay race, an attack on the Deadwood Stage, Custer's Last Stand, and the roping, bronco riding, and cowboy fun that later became the rodeo. The show toured Europe and was performed at Queen Victoria's Diamond Jubilee. Buffalo Bill and his show remained on the road for thirty years.

CODY

Buffalo Bill Cody founded this town and devoted time and money to its development. He arranged for a railroad spur from Montana, built a hotel and named it after his daughter Irma, and talked his friend Theodore Roosevelt into building what then was the world's tallest dam, just west of town.

Buffalo Bill Historical Center (720 Sheridan Ave.; 307/587-4771). A four-museum complex. The *Buffalo Bill Museum* has personal and historical memorabilia of the Indian scout and showman, including guns, saddles, trophies, posters, and clothing. The *Winchester Arms Museum* displays some 5,000 rifles and pistols, a collection begun in 1860 by Oliver Winchester. The *Whitney Gallery of Western Art* has an important and comprehensive collection of Western paintings and sculpture from the early 1800s until the present. The *Plains Indians Museum* displays artifacts of the Indians of the Plains tribes, including art, clothing, weapons, tools, and ceremonial paraphernalia. Open daily, May through September; daily except Mondays the rest of the year.

Old Trail Town and the Museum of the Old West (1 mile west on Yellowstone Highway). Twenty-five reconstructed buildings, dating from 1879 to 1901, and a cemetery are on the site of what was Old Cody City. A cabin here was once used as a rendezvous by Butch Cassidy and the Sundance Kid, and another by Curley, the Crow Indian scout who was the only member of Custer's command to escape from the Little Bighorn. In the cemetery is the grave of Jeremiah "Liver Eatin'" Johnson. Open daily, mid-May through mid-September.

Accommodations: *Irma Hotel* (1192 Sheridan; 307/587-4221). Built by Cody for his daughter Irma in 1902, the hotel is still going strong. Ornate furnishings and antiques. *The Lockhart* (109 West Yellowstone; 307/587-6074). A six-room bed-and-

Old Trail Town, a pseudo–ghost town near Cody, Wyoming, was assembled from reconstructed buildings, including a cabin once used as a rendezvous by Butch Cassidy and the Sundance Kid. Jeremiah "Liver Eatin'" Johnson is buried in the nearby cemetery.

breakfast, furnished with antiques, is the 1899 home of writer Carolyn Lockhart.

DOUGLAS

Plentiful water and good grass here attracted first cattlemen, then homesteaders. The town was named for Stephen A. Douglas, the Little Giant.

Wyoming Pioneer Memorial Museum (State Fairgrounds, west end of Center St.; 307/358-9288). Large collections of Indian and pioneer artifacts, antiques, and classic automobiles are on display. Open Monday through Friday.

Fort Fetterman State Museum (10 miles northwest on WY 93; 307/358-2864 or 777-7014). Founded in 1867 on the Bozeman Trail, on a plateau above the valley of the LaPrele Creek and the North Platte River, the fort figured in the campaigns in the late 1860s and 1870s against the Northern Plains tribes. This was the base for General Crook's three expeditions in 1876 into the Powder River area, which included the battles of Powder River and the Rosebud, and the defeat of Dull Knife's Cheyennes. The last expedition in 1876–77 ended the major phase of the Army-Indian conflict on the Northern Plains. Fort Fetterman was abandoned in 1882, but Fetterman City, the prototype for "Drybone" in Owen Wister's western novels, became an outfitting point for wagon trains. Museum, restored officers' quarters, ordnance warehouse. Open daily, mid-May through Labor Day.

Accommodations: *Akers Ranch Bed & Breakfast* (1 mile off I-25, Inez exit; 307/ 358-3741). A working ranch with five rooms in a cabin and bunkhouse. Breakfast included.

"Down to the smallest detail the Show is genuine. It brought back vividly the breezy wild life of the Plains and the Rocky Mountains. It is wholly free from sham and insincerity and the effects it produced upon me by its spectacles were identical with those wrought upon me a long time ago on the frontier. Your pony expressman was as tremendous an interest to me as he was twenty-three years ago when he used to come whizzing by from over the desert with his war news; and your bucking horses were even painfully real to me as I rode one of those outrages for nearly a quarter of a minute."

—MARK TWAIN, IN A LETTER TO BUFFALO BILL, 1886

The Iron Horse

The Old West rode in on the horse and out on the Iron Horse. The first railroad to reach the Mississippi was the Chicago & Rock Island in 1854, and two years later it bridged the great river. Thirteen years later, on May 10, 1869, at Promontory Point, Utah, tracks of the Central Pacific and the Union Pacific met and were joined, completing the first transcontinental railroad. The railroad slowly but surely changed the character of the West. Soon it would no longer be the frontier.

Congress wanted a transcontinental railroad and, during the 1850s, authorized five surveys along the forty-fifth, forty-second, thirty-seventh, and thirty-second parallels, all of which would become the transcontinental routes. In 1862 the forty-second parallel was chosen as the initial route. Congress gave huge grants of public lands to the builders, and promised loan subsidies. By the time it was completed in 1869, four Midwestern railroads were ready to link it to the East.

Within twenty years, railroads were built on the other routes. In 1881 the Atlantic & Pacific Railroad joined with the Southern Pacific at Deming, New Mexico. Two years later, Jay Cook and Henry Villard completed the Northern Pacific between Minneapolis–St. Paul and Seattle. California's Big Four won the race to build the southernmost transcontinental railroad and by 1885 controlled the line from New Orleans to Los Angeles. From 1887 to 1909, the Milwaukee railroad completed its West Coast extension.

James J. Hill took over a decrepit railroad that ran between Minneapolis and Winnipeg, extended it to the Pacific, and renamed it the Great Northern. By the turn of the century, Hill had merged the Great Northern, the Northern Pacific, and the Burlington into one of the most efficient and profitable transportation systems in the world.

It was one thing to build a railroad, however, and another to make it profitable. Railroad agents were sent through the rural areas of the East, the British Isles, Germany, and Scandinavia, distributing handbills and making public addresses to attract farmers to the West to raise the grain and livestock to be shipped to market via the new rail lines. The railroads worked with the settlers to improve their lot and make their farms profitable.

There was a dark side. The railroads sold the land at high prices, keeping the settlers in debt. The railroads paid no local taxes, placing the financial burden of local government entirely on the settlers. Large areas of land went undeveloped, either because the railroads couldn't sell it or held it off the market in anticipation of higher profits in the future. Granges and the Populist Party were formed to combat unfair railroad practices.

DUBOIS

Wind River Reservation (west of town; 307/255-8265). Two famous Indians are buried here: Sacajawea, the Shoshone woman who led Lewis and Clark's expedition across the Rockies and down the Columbia River to the Pacific; and Chief Washakie, the great Shoshone leader. In nearby Ethete, St. Michael's Mission has a collection of Arapaho arts and crafts. The reservation operates day-long Singing Horse Tours, which give visitors the opportunity to experience the culture and history of the tribes. The stops include the *Riverton Museum* in Riverton; the *Mission Heritage Center*, the *Indian Heritage Center Gallery* in St. Stephens; the *Pioneer Museum* in Lander; *Sacajawea Site, Washakie Site, Robert's Mission,* and the *Living History Indian Village* in Fort Washakie.

Dubois Museum (west on U.S. 26/287 at 909 West Ramshorn; 307/455-2284). Displays and exhibits relating to early life here. Logging equipment and tools. Tieboat used in the drives down the Wind River. Indian artifacts. Open daily, May through September.

Accommodations: *Badlands Bed & Breakfast* (8 miles east on U.S. 26/287; 397/455-2161). A solar log home on the Wind River, with mountain views. Four-person guest room with private bath.

EVANSTON

Fort Bridger State Historic Site (36 miles east on I-80; 307/782-3842). When the fur trade declined, Jim Bridger, the scout and explorer, borrowed money and opened a small trading post and fort here on the Green River to supply travelers on the Oregon Trail. It soon became popular and prosperous. The first schoolhouse in Wyoming was here, and probably the first newspaper—which consisted of daily bulletins of Civil War news, prepared by the fort's telegrapher. Bridger was forced out of the operation by Mormons under Brigham Young in 1853, who later abandoned and burned the fort. The army took over Fort Bridger and rebuilt it, keeping it in service until 1890. A museum in the partially restored fort tells the history of Bridger's fort and trading post.

"Most famous gunmen were town people. They slept in boardinghouses, not under the stars. Wyatt Earp, who served as a lawman in Dodge City and other places, owned saloons, operated gambling halls, and died in Los Angeles. After a career on various sides of the law ... the gambler and gunman Bat Masterson spent his last years in New York as a sports columnist for the *Morning Telegraph,* where he died at his desk of a heart attack. Western gunfights were alcohol-related, or else involved battles over gambling, prostitution, or political preferment. They were closer in spirit to drug wars in the Bronx than to duels of honor."

—Ian Frazier, *Great Plains*

REPRESENTATION OF LIFE IN A COW CAMP.

Fort Laramie, the last outpost for settlers heading west, stood at the confluence of the Laramie and North Platte rivers in Wyoming. Built in 1834 and first used by fur traders, it protected wagon trains from thieves and other dangers after gold was discovered in California.

Open daily, Memorial Day to mid-October, weekends the rest of the year.

Accommodations: *Pine Gables Lodge* (1049 Center St.; 307/789-2096). A bed-and-breakfast in a restored 1883 mansion that is listed in the National Register of Historic Places. Guest rooms have private baths and are furnished with antiques.

FORT LARAMIE

Fort Laramie National Historic Site (southwest of town on WY 160 and 20 miles northwest of Torrington; 307/837-2221). Searching in 1834 for a site for a trading post, fur trapper William Sublett found one on the Laramie River, near its confluence with the Platte. After he and his party built Fort William, he sent runners to tell Sioux and Cheyenne chiefs that he was in business to buy buffalo robes, but not until the American Fur Company bought the post in 1838 was it an important fur-trading center. In the 1840s, Fort Laramie was a stopping place for emigrant parties following the Oregon Trail. Early relations with the Indians were peaceful, but later the Indians began to attack wagon trains. In 1849 the army bought the fort and made it one of its outposts on the Oregon Trail. Later it was the staging area for the campaigns that led to the confinement of the Indians on reservations. When gold was discovered in the Black Hills, soldiers from here protected travelers bound for the gold fields. The fort was abandoned in 1890. The Visitor Center and museum are located in the 1884 storehouse, and an audiovisual program prepares visitors for a tour of the many restored structures at the fort. Open daily.

GREEN RIVER

In 1868, John Wesley Powell started from here on his exploration of the Green and Colorado rivers.

Sweetwater County Historical Museum (80 West Flaming Gorge Way; 307/875-2611). The museum has pioneer artifacts and exhibits on the history of southwestern

Wyoming and Indian tribes, as well as a photography collection. Open daily except Sundays in July and August; Monday through Friday the rest of the year.

JACKSON

Jackson is a determinedly Old West town, and Jackson Hole is one of the best-known ski areas in the country.

Jackson Hole Museum (101 North Glenwood; 307/733-2414). Regional historical and archaeological material. Open daily, late May through October.

The Shootout (Town Square) is a Western melodrama presented nightly from Memorial Day to Labor Day.

Dirty Jack's Wild West Theater and Opera House (140 North Cache St.; 307/733-4775 or 800/443-6133). Western musical comedy is presented here nightly from June through September.

LANDER

Fremont County Pioneer Museum (630 Lincoln St.; 307/332-4137). Exhibit rooms, including a saddle shop and chapel. Also a Plains Indian diorama and a restored cabin. Open Monday through Friday.

South Pass City (32 miles south on WY 28, then 2½ miles west; 307/332-3684). A booming mining town during the gold rush of 1868–69, it is now being restored. By a territorial act introduced from here and passed in Cheyenne in 1869, Wyoming granted women the right to vote and to hold public office.

LARAMIE

Laramie was populated by hunters, saloonkeepers, and rowdies during the building of the Union Pacific Railroad. After the rail-

road builders left, vigilantes were the only law in town for six months.

Laramie Plains Museum (603 Ivinson Ave.; 307/742-4448). A Victorian mansion filled with collections of toys, military memorabilia, and railroad artifacts. Open daily except Sundays.

Accommodations: *Annie Moore's Guest House* (819 University; 307/721-4177). A bed-and-breakfast in a post-Victorian home, close to downtown. *Waystation* (111½ Grand Ave.; 307/742-0619). Guest rooms in an 1893 building decorated in a railroad motif. Breakfast is included in the rates.

NEWCASTLE

Anna Miller Museum (Delaware and Washington Park; 307/746-4188). The museum, housed in a stone cavalry barn, has some 12,000 artifacts relating to the history of northeastern Wyoming. On the grounds

Whoopee-ti-yi-oh, get along, little dogies,
It's your misfortune and none of my own,
Whoopee-ti-yi-oh, get along, little dogies,
For you know Wyoming will be your new home.

—COWBOY SONG, "GET ALONG LITTLE DOGIES"

Butch Cassidy and the Sundance Kid

He was born Robert Leroy Parker and became a protégé of a rustler named Mike Cassidy. After Cassidy went to prison, he was a miner before joining the McCarty gang. He worked briefly in a Wyoming butcher shop, picking up the nickname "Butch," to which he added the name of his mentor. At the Hole in the Wall, a wild region in northern Wyoming, he assembled a gang, the Wild Bunch, which included Harry Longbaugh, known as the Sundance Kid. The gang roamed the West for several years, robbing banks and trains from Wyoming to New Mexico. When the law closed in, Butch Cassidy, the Sundance Kid, and a girl named Etta Place fled the country and lived peacefully for a time in the backcountry of Brazil. Then Etta went home, and Butch and Sundance launched a Latin American crime wave that ended in 1911 in Bolivia, where they were apparently killed by government troops. Their families, however, claimed that Butch and Sundance had escaped and returned home, Butch living as William K. Phillips in Spokane until his death in 1937, Sundance marrying Etta and living until 1957.

Fashion Rides the Range

Cowboys wore practical clothing, made for ranch work and the western climate. It was distinctive, but that was incidental. Most important were hats and boots. A cowboy hat had a flat brim and a tall crown, five to eight inches high, with a decorative belt or band to regulate the fit. Thongs, or "bonnet-strings," helped secure the hat in a high wind. The height and crease of the crown and the roll of the brim varied from place to place; Southwesterners like the high crown and wide brim of the Mexican sombrero, while Northern cowboys preferred a lower, flat crown and narrower brim.

Cowboy hats were a hit-or-miss affair until the 1860s, when a young hatmaker from New Jersey, John Batterson Stetson, out West for his health, saw the need for a practical, broad-brimmed hat for range wear. In 1865 he opened a shop and began designing and selling models for the Western trade. Soon "Stetson" and "John B." were synonymous with Western hats, and by 1906 Stetson employed some 3,500 workers who turned out two million hats a year.

A hat was a tool of the cowboy's trade, protecting him from the sun and rain, serving as a drinking cup and a fan for the campfire. He could use it to signal other riders, or to slap a bucking bronco. It was the first thing he put on in the morning, the last thing he took off at night.

A cowboy's boots were his badge of office. They were made of top-grade leather with a high arched vamp, a rounded toe, and a tapered heel that prevented the foot from slipping through the stirrup. Cowboys preferred handmade boots, and they were the most expensive items in their wardrobes. Spurs were a necessary accessory, and each spur included a rowel, a shank, a heel plate, a spur bottom, and a leather strap to hold the spur in place. In some areas, cowboys never removed their spurs from their boots; on the West Coast, spurs were worn only at work.

What Stetson did for cowboy hats, Levi Strauss did for cowboy pants. Strauss landed in San Francisco in 1850 with a load of merchandise he planned to sell in the mining camps. A large supply of canvas went unsold, and Strauss made it into work pants. They were an overnight success, and he opened a factory in San Francisco, switched from canvas to heavy blue denim, added copper rivets at the stress points, and made a fortune.

Sometimes, however, "Levi's" didn't afford sufficient protection for a cowboy's legs. Large pieces of rawhide, called *armas*, were draped across the saddle horn and tucked over

are a log cabin from Jenney Stockade (the oldest building in the Black Hills) and a vintage rural schoolhouse. Open weekdays.

Accidental Oil Company (4 miles east at 5297 U.S. 16; 307/746-2042). The country's only producing oil well that was dug by hand. Steam-powered drill rig. Restored oilfield equipment. Guided geological tours to the bottom of an oil well. Open daily, Memorial Day to Labor Day.

RAWLINS

Gen. John A. Rollins found a spring near here and said, "If anything is ever named after me, I hope it will be a spring of water." They named the spring and the community that grew up beside it after Rollins, but somehow it came out "Rawlins."

Wyoming Frontier Prison (5th and Walnut; 307/324-4111). In use from 1901 to 1981, the prison is on sixty-five acres. Tours. Open daily, June through Labor Day.

Accommodations: *Ferris Mansion Bed & Breakfast* (607 West Maple; 307/324-3961). A 1903 Victorian mansion with period furnishings.

RIVERTON

The town is surrounded by the Wind River Indian Reservation (see *Dubois*). In the area are oil, natural gas, iron, timber, and phosphate.

Riverton Museum (700 East Park St.; 307/856-2665). Shoshone and Arapaho artifacts. A mountain-man display. A general store, a drugstore, a post office, a saloon, a homesteader's cabin, a church, a dentist's office, a bank, a school, and a beauty shop are re-created. Collections of clothing, quilts, cutters, and buggies. Open daily, May through September; Tuesday through Saturday the rest of the year.

SHERIDAN

The wars with the Cheyenne, Sioux, and Crow were over and ranchers were moving in when Sheridan was founded in 1882, but for years there was trouble with rustlers and acrimony over boundary disputes. The first dude ranch in the country opened here in 1904.

Bradford Brinton Memorial Ranch Museum (7 miles south on U.S. 87, then 5 miles southwest on WY 335; 307/672-3173). Built in 1892, this ranch was purchased in 1923 by Bradford Brinton, who enlarged it to twenty rooms. Excellent vintage furnishings. Collection includes more than 600 Western oils, watercolors, and sketches by American artists, including Remington and Russell. Bronzes, prints, and rare books. Indian artifacts. Open daily, mid-May through Labor Day.

Trail End Historic Center (400 Claredon Ave., next to Kendrick Park; 307/674-4589 or 777-7014). The home of John B. Kendrick, Wyoming governor, then U.S. senator (1917–33), is a Flemish Revival mansion on landscaped grounds, with outstanding woodwork. Family and historic memorabilia. Open daily.

Bighorn National Forest (307/672-0751). U.S. 14 from Burgess Junction passes the Medicine Mountain site of the *Medicine Wheel*, a stone circle seventy-five feet in diameter, with twenty-eight spokes radiating out from a central cairn. There are several theories concerning its origin and construction.

Accommodations: *Spahn's Big Horn Mountain Bed & Breakfast* (off I-90 near Big Horn; 307/674-8150). A log house and cabin in the pine forest high on the mountainside above Sheridan.

The Old Wyoming State Penitentiary in Rawlins, built in 1901, now is open to the public. Visitors can see the death house, the cell blocks, exercise grounds, and other facilities of this frontier prison where convicts paid their debt to society.

the legs like a lap robe. *Armas* evolved into chaps (from the Spanish *chaparras*, meaning "leather breeches").

Shirts were always collarless; a kerchief provided protection for the neck, and could be pulled over the nose and mouth when a cowboy was "eating dust." When a jacket was worn, it was of denim or duck, cut short and loose to give the wearer freedom of movement . Most cowboys, however, wore vests, with pockets for small pieces of equipment and for a pack of Bull Durham tobacco with which to roll cigarettes. For wet weather, a yellow slicker was tied across his saddle cantle. Hot in the summer and cold in the winter, slickers had wide, long skirts with slits and gores that formed a tent over the man and his saddle. Gloves provided warmth and protection against rope burns.

A cowboy might have a silver belt buckle, but generally he was conservative, preferring plain styles and dark colors. He wouldn't know what to make of the elaborate designs and bright colors of modern Western wear.

12

Colorado

ALAMOSA

Fort Garland State Historic Monument (25 miles east on U.S. 160 at Fort Garland; 719/379-3512). Built in 1858 to protect settlers in the San Luis Valley and the roads running south to Taos from Ute and Apache attacks, this fort was commanded in 1866–67 by Col. Kit Carson. He and Gen. William T. Sherman held a council with the Ute chief Ouray, which led to a treaty that kept the tribe peaceful, even during the western Colorado Ute uprising of 1879. Despite the treaty, though, two years later troops from Fort Garland removed the local Utes to Utah. Today there are seven restored adobe buildings: five officers' quarters, the cavalry barracks, and the infantry barracks. A museum displays fort and Indian artifacts and a collection of folk art. Open daily, Memorial Day to Labor Day.

Cumbres & Toltec Scenic Railroad (28 miles south in Antonito; 719/376-5483.). The 1860 narrow-gauge steam train *Colorado Limited* makes a scenic excursion, passing through the Phantom Canyon and Toltec Gorge. Daily, mid-June to mid-October.

ASPEN

Aspen Historical Society Museum (620 West Bleeker St.; 303/925-3721). Artifacts and exhibits relating to local history. Open daily, early June through September and mid-December to mid-April.

Marble (30 miles northwest on CO 82, then some 23 miles south on CO 133, then 3 miles east on a gravel road). Marble mined in this near–ghost town was the source of stone used in the Lincoln Memorial in Washington and the Tomb of the Unknown Soldier in Arlington National Cemetery.

Ashcroft (10 miles south). A preserved ghost town with circa-1880 buildings. Open June through October; the road is closed the rest of the year.

BOULDER

University of Colorado Museum (on campus; 303/492-6892). Relics of life in the state, from prehistory to modern times. Open daily.

Boulder Historical Society and Museum (1206 Euclid Ave.; 303/449-3464). In the 1899 Harbeck house, this museum has exhibits tracing the history of the area since 1858. Open Tuesday through Saturday.

Accommodations: *Briar Rose* (2151 Arapahoe Ave.; 303/442-3007). Eleven guest rooms in an 1897 English country-style home decorated with antiques. Breakfast and afternoon tea included in rates.

BRECKENRIDGE

In 1859, gold was discovered in the Blue River, and soon Breckenridge was a booming ghost town. Now it is a ski resort and a good place from which to explore nearby ghost towns, including *Lincoln City*, Swandyke, Dyersville, and others. Inquire locally for directions and road conditions. Some can only be reached by four-wheel-drive vehicles or on horseback.

Accommodations: *The Fireside Inn* (in the historic

Prospectors face a new day on King Solomon Mountain during the Colorado gold rush in the 1870s. A few struck it rich, but thousands never saw the sparkle of gold in their pans. Mining soon became big business, requiring expensive equipment to dig gold out of the ground.

district; 719/453-6456). A bed-and-breakfast in a turn-of-the-century house.

BURLINGTON

Old Town (South 14th St.; 719/346-7382). A historical village with sod house, school, saloon, and jail. Open daily.

CANON CITY

At the mouth of the Grand Canyon of the Arkansas River, this was a Ute camping area. Zebulon Pike was probably the first white man to camp here. The poet Joaquin Miller held various town posts here in gold-rush days. (He proposed changing the town's name to Oreodelphia, but the miners said they could neither spell nor pronounce it.) In 1868 the town was offered its choice of the state penitentiary or the state university. The miners chose the penitentiary, saying they thought it would be better attended.

Canon City Municipal Museum (612 Royal Gorge Blvd.; 719/275-2368). The museum has Indian artifacts, pioneer and early railroad displays, and gun and doll collections. Behind the museum is the 1860 Anson Rudd cabin and his 1881 stone house, which contains Victorian furnishings and glassware. Open daily.

Royal Gorge (8 miles west on U.S. 50, then 4 miles southwest; 719/275-7507). Here cliffs rise more than a thousand feet above the Arkansas River. The Royal Gorge Suspension Bridge, 1,053 feet above the river, is the highest in the world. The Royal Gorge Incline Railway takes passengers from the top to the bottom of the canyon on a forty-five-degree incline. A 2,000-foot aerial tramway ride crosses the gorge. Restaurant. Open late spring to fall, weather permitting. The *Royal Gorge Scenic Railway* (719/275-5485) runs a three-mile trip along the rim of the gorge, with panoramic views of the gorge and its suspension bridge. Daily from April to October. On the grounds is the *Steam Train and Antique Car Museum*, which includes the famed McAllister steam locomotive collection.

Buckskin Joe (8 miles west via U.S. 50; 719/275-5149). A replica of a mining town, with staged gunfights and hangings. Coach rides. Restaurant and ice cream parlor. Open daily, May to mid-October.

Zebulon Pike

Seeking fame as a soldier, Zebulon Pike found it as an explorer. His chance came when he was ordered to lead an army reconnaissance of the upper Mississippi in 1803. His maps were an excellent portrayal of the area. Heading west again, he crossed Kansas into Colorado, and in freezing weather tried unsuccessfully to climb the peak that now bears his name. On a later expedition to the Southwest, Pike was arrested by a Spanish patrol and taken to Mexico before being released. His narrative of his journey brought him recognition but little money. A general in the War of 1812, he was killed leading the attack on Toronto.

CENTRAL CITY

The first important discovery of gold in Colorado was made here in Gregory Gulch in 1859, and the boomtown was known as "the richest square mile on earth." More than $75 million worth of gold and other minerals came from here and neighboring mining towns.

Gilpin County Historical Society Museum (228 East High St.; 303/582-5283 or 582-5251). Housed in an 1869 schoolhouse with exhibits of gold-mining days in the county, the museum includes a Victorian home, an opera house, and period shops. Open daily, Memorial Day to Labor Day. The society is also restoring the 1863 Lace House on Main Street.

Thomas-Billings Home (209 Eureka St.; 303/562-5093). This house has been restored to Victorian elegance and furnished appropriately for the period. Open daily, May to October.

Central City Story (Armory Bldg., Main St.). Dioramas of the town's history. Open daily, May through October.

Old 71 (Main St.). A narrow-gauge train on permanent display.

Central Gold Mine and Museum (126 Spring St.; 303/582-5574). Mementos of mining days are on display. Mine tours are conducted daily from May through September, weather permitting. The *Lost Gold Mine* (231 Eureka St.; 303/642-7533) also has tours on weekends, May through September.

Accommodations: *Golden Rose Hotel* (102 Main St.; 303/825-1413). Built in 1874, the hotel has twenty-six guest rooms with Victorian-era furnishings and decorations.

COLORADO SPRINGS

Gen. William J. Palmer and the Denver & Rio Grande Railroad founded a health resort here at the foot of Pikes Peak in 1871 and the city grew up around it.

Pikes Peak. There are two ways to go to the top of this mountain: the toll road (10 miles northwest to Cascade, then 19 miles on a toll road to the summit), which is open daily May through October, and the cog railway (8 miles west to 515 Ruxton Ave. in Manitou Springs; 719/685-54 01), which makes eight trips daily, May through October.

Pikes Peak Ghost Town (400 South 21st St. at U.S. 24, then 2 miles west; 719/634-0696). A *faux* Old West town, with a general store, a blacksmith shop, a jail, a firehouse, a livery stable, a saloon, and Victorian houses. The *Magellan,* a bulletproof railcar used by President Franklin D. Roosevelt, is on display here. Memorabilia of President Chester A. Arthur. Shooting gallery. Nickelodeons. Open daily, mid-May to mid-October.

Pioneers' Museum (215 South Tejon St.; 719/578-6650). The museum has material relating to the history of the Pikes Peak region. There are three reconstructed rooms of the Helen Hunt Jackson home, with original furnishings. Open daily.

El Pomar Carriage House Museum (Lake Ave.). Carriages and other vintage vehicles. Turn-of-the-century artifacts. Open daily.

American Numismatic Association (818 North Cascade; 719/632-2646). Displays of vintage coins, medals, tokens, and paper money. Library. Open Tuesday through Saturday.

McAllister House Museum (423 North Cascade Ave.; 719/635-7925). An 1873 six-room Gothic Revival cottage with vintage furnishings. Tours. Open Wednesday through Sunday, May through August; Thursday through Saturday, September through April.

Hall of Presidents (1050 South 21st St.; 719/635-3553). Mme. Tussaud wax figures of all U.S. presidents are displayed in room-size sets. Open daily.

Museum of the American Cowboy and Pro Rodeo Hall of Fame (101 Pro Rodeo Dr., I-25 exit 147; 719/593-8847). Paintings, bronzes, and memorabilia of the cowboy and the rodeo. The Hafley-Shelton Wild West Show exhibit. Two multimedia theater presentations. Open daily, Memorial Day to Labor Day; daily except Mondays the rest of the year.

Old Colorado City (3 miles west on U.S. 24; 719/577-4112). The historic district, with shops and restaurants.

White House Ranch Historic Site (3202 Chambers Way, 4 miles west via I-25, Garden of the Gods exit to 30th St., then south to Gateway Rd. at east entrance of Garden of the Gods; 719/578-6777). An 1895 working ranch, an 1868 homestead, and a 1907 mansion. Living-history program. On the site is the Rocky Mountain Arboretum. Open Wednesday through Sunday, June through August.

Garden of the Gods Trading Post (near Balanced Rock at the north end of the park; 719/685-9045). A gallery, established in 1910, of Hopi kachinas, Santa Clara pottery, and contemporary Indian jewelry. Open daily.

Flying W Ranch (3330 Chuckwagon Rd.; 719/598-4000). A working ranch with numerous restored buildings, offering a chuckwagon supper and a Western stage show. Reservations required. Daily, mid-May to September; Fridays and Saturdays the rest of the year.

National Carvers Museum (14960 Woodcarver Rd., 21 miles north on I-25, in Monument near the Air Force Academy; 719/481-2656). The museum has exhibits of the carver's craft and demonstrations. Open daily.

Seven Falls (7 miles southeast on Cheyenne, in South Cheyenne Canyon). The only completely lighted canyon and waterfall in the world. Indian dances are presented daily in the summer.

Accommodations: *Holden House, 1902* (1102 West Pikes Peak Ave,; 719/471-3980). An antique-filled Victorian bed-and-breakfast near the historic district. *Hearthstone Inn* (506 North Cascade Ave.; 719/473-4413). Two circa-1885 houses joined by a carriage house, with twenty-five guest rooms, all with private bath. Breakfast is included in the rates.

CORTEZ

Thirty-eight miles southwest of here, a simple plaque 100 yards from U.S. 160 (the Four Corners Highway) marks the exact point where four states (Colorado, New Mexico, Arizona, and Utah) and two Indian nations (Ute and Navajo) meet.

Hovenweep National Monument (20 miles northwest on U.S. 666 to Pleasant View, follow signs 5 miles west on County BB, then 20 miles south on County 10; 303/882-4811). In the desolate country north of the San Juan River are mesas and small canyons where the Anasazi once lived. They were part of a large group of Indians who occupied the Four Corners until almost A.D.

1300. Their culture was similar to the people who lived in what is now Mesa Verde National Park, and their descendants are probably the present-day Pueblo Indians of New Mexico and Arizona.

Some 2,000 years ago, the people in this region began to farm. Before long they built pit houses in the valleys or on the mesa tops, later building surface rooms in contiguous rows. In the 900s they started to use stone masonry. From the late 11th century to the present, Pueblo Indians have built multistoried dwellings. The Anasazi raised corn, beans, and squash in small fields. They also gathered wild plant foods, hunted and trapped animals, including birds, and domesticated the turkey. They were expert artists and craftsmen, producing a variety of tools, utensils, ceremonial objects, jewelry, and clothing. They lived in peace and security in

The first major dwelling to be discovered at what now is the Mesa Verde National Park was the Cliff Palace. Protected under a huge brow of sandstone, it contains more than 200 living rooms, 23 kivas, and numerous storage rooms. Hundreds of Anasazi once lived here.

small, scattered villages, but by the early 12th century they had left their villages for larger pueblos. By 1200 they had moved to the heads of the Hovenweep (the Ute word for "deserted valley") canyons, which contain springs. In the late 13th century a long period of drought began here. Failing crops and diminishing water supplies forced the Anasazi to abandon their homes and drift south to the Rio Grande and Little Colorado drainages. They never returned.

Today the monument consists of six groups of ruins: *Square Tower Ruins*, the best preserved and most impressive; *Cajon Ruins* in Utah; and the *Holly, Hackberry Canyon, Cutthroat Castle,* and *Goodman Points Ruins* in Colorado, all noted for square, oval, circular, and D-shaped towers. All the ruins except Square Tower are isolated and difficult to reach. Pueblo and tower

walls are constructed of excellent coursed-stone masonry. Though most of the mortar has long since disappeared, some walls still stand more than twenty feet high. Ports at strategic points in these walls command the approaches to the buildings. A trail leads through the Square Tower Group. Open daily, though facilities are limited in the winter. Limited wheelchair access

Mesa Verde National Park (10 miles east on U.S. 160; 303/529-4465). This is the Anasazi showcase of the Four Corners, with some 4,000 dwellings spanning nearly every stage of their development, from pit houses to mesa-top pueblos to sprawling cliff cities. Here too is the best display of Anasazi pottery, tools, and everyday implements to be found in the West. The ruins cover a series of mesas separated by deep, narrow canyons. The Anasazi were in the area in the 6th century, and by A.D. 600 they were living in mesa pit houses, hunting and farming small plots. By 800 the pit houses had given way to aboveground pueblos, and the Anasazi were building reservoirs and check-dams to hold rain runoff. By 900 they had domesticated turkeys for food and dogs as sentries and a source of fur. By the middle of the 12th century, some 5,000 Anasazi lived atop Mesa Verde in "apartment houses" of several hundred rooms, but less than a hundred years later something happened—invasion of the area by enemies, internal strife, a change in the climate—because the Anasazi abandoned the mesa tops and built new pueblos in the large caves in the sides of the canyons. This involved great hardship, because drinking water and building stones had to be carried into the caves. Then around 1275 the drought came, and the Anasazi migrated south.

Prospectors probably stumbled on the ruins, but in 1874, William Henry Jackson, a photographer, was the first white man to record them. In the 1880s, Richard Wetherill and Charles Mason, whose ranches were nearby, found Spruce Tree House and other major ruins. Thousands of artifacts were

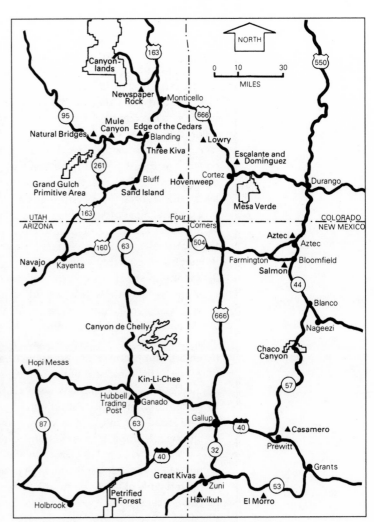

The Four Corners Area

removed before Mesa Verde became a national park in 1906.

The Fair View Center is seventeen miles south of the park entrance, and four miles farther is the museum, with exhibits describing the daily life of the Anasazi and their arts and crafts. Two six-mile self-guided loop drives go to ten mesa-top ruins and give views of some twenty-five cliff dwellings from vantage points on the rim of the canyons. Bus tours lasting four hours leave several times daily from the Visitor Center.

Five cliff dwellings may be visited at specific hours during the summer, but only Spruce Tree House can be visited in the win-

Prospectors

There is mining and there is prospecting. Mining is big business; prospecting is a craft, requiring little money but a soldier's eye for terrain, an artist's sensitivity for color, and a gopher's ability to dig. In the Old West, the prospector was as distinctive as the cowboy, trapper, or lumberjack: behind the façade of an eccentric loner lurked a shrewd, enterprising, and perceptive brain.

A prospector usually worked at an unskilled job to make enough money—called a grubstake—to buy equipment, pack animals, and supplies for a season of exploration. Or he might get a grubstake by giving someone a share of what he found. Horace W. Tabor, a Leadville grocer, made a fortune grubstaking prospectors. Most prospectors honored their grubstake agreements.

James Marshall found gold at Sutter's Mill by accident, but most strikes were the result of prolonged search by experienced prospectors. Cowboy Robert Womack searched for twelve years before finding gold at Cripple Creek. Edward S. Schieffelin spent a year locating the lodes of Tombstone, Arizona.

A prospector in the field would look for rock formations with black-stained strata, "rusty" outcroppings, or quartz dikes. If nothing looked promising, he would check streams by panning, following upstream whatever fork showed the most "color," and if the color ceased, he knew he had passed its origin. He looked for colors other than gold: the green and blue of copper, the rust red of iron, the lilac of cobalt, the dead black of manganese. Spongy-looking bits of maroon-stained quartz in streambeds were called "float," and half the prospector's life was spent tracing float upstream to its point of origin.

If he found a possible lode, a prospector would make a variety of tests. First he would detach chips, pulverize them, and pan out the residues. Mercury or nitric acid would detect gold or silver. He would make a rough calculation of the value per ton of the rock, and if it was high enough he would set boundary markers and do the ten days of work required by law before making a claim. There were other considerations; sometimes high-grade ore can be deceptively concentrated on the surface of a low-grade lode, a condition called "having its big end up."

Claim law was simple. A prospector had a right to what he found, regardless of the rights of the owner of the land. He could register a claim of a certain size around the lode, then work it or sell it as he pleased. A claim was usually a thousand feet in length; claim shares were sold as so many "feet."

Prospectors often made mistakes, squandering time and money on a low-yield site or abandoning a good site to join a new gold rush. Yet with crude equipment they often discovered riches in places that gave no outward signs of their valuable contents. A prospector's proverbs were a reflection of his folk wisdom: "Iron rides a gold horse" (gold is often found in iron-stained formations), and "A copper penny will stain a mile" (a minute amount of copper will produce enough color to excite the inexperienced). The prospector was proud of his craft, and his spirit and determination were largely responsible for discovering the mineral riches of the West.

ter. Ruins open to the public include the following:

Spruce Tree House (in the canyon behind the museum). The best preserved of the ruins contains 114 living rooms and eight ceremonial kivas.

Cliff Palace (on Ruins Rd., a 10-minute drive from the Visitor Center). The first ruin to be discovered, this is the largest and most famous. More than 200 living rooms, twenty-three kivas, and many storage rooms. Closed in the winter.

Balcony House (on Balcony Rd., a 15-minute drive from the Visitor Center). Accessible only by a thirty-two-foot ladder, this is a small but dramatic structure, noted for its defensive features. Ranger-led tours from late May to late September.

Long and Step houses (on Wetherill Mesa, 12 miles from the Visitor Center). These are open from mid-June to Labor Day. Ranger-led tours are available to Long House, self-guided tours to Step House.

Park Point Fire Lookout (halfway between the park entrance and the Visitor Center). Spectacular views of the area may be seen from the point's elevation of 8,572 feet. The access road is closed in the winter. From early June to Labor Day, a campfire program features talks by rangers on the Anasazi and the natural history of the Four Corners. The park is open daily. Limited wheelchair access. Phone ahead for weather advisories and tour schedules.

Ute Mountain Tribal Park (15 miles south via U.S. 666; 303/565-3751). On the southern edge of Mesa Verde National Park, in Mancos Canyon, are hundreds of Anasazi cliff and surface dwellings, some as large as those in Mesa Verde. The Ute tribe is developing this 125,000-acre park on their tribal lands and opening many of the largely unexcavated ruins to the public. Ute guides give tours of the ruins on weekdays, starting at Ute Mountain Pottery. Some hiking is involved. The park offers backcountry trips of one to four days, led by Ute guides. Open daily, June through September. Limited wheelchair access.

Lowry Pueblo Ruins (21 miles northwest on U.S. 666 to Pleasant View, then 9 miles west on a county road; 303/247-4082). Built in the same period as the Mesa Verde and Ute Mountain pueblos, these structures contain forty excavated rooms, including one great kiva and nine small ones. Open daily, weather and road conditions permitting. Limited wheelchair access.

Anasazi Heritage Center and Escalante Ruins (8 miles north on CO 145 to Dolores, then 2 miles northwest on CO 184; 303/882-4811). A museum contains artifacts from excavations in southwest Colorado by the Dolores Archaeological Program. Near the center are the Dominguez and Escalante ruins, discovered by Franciscan friars in 1776. Museum and ruins are open daily in the summer, weekdays in the winter. Limited wheelchair access.

Accommodations: *Kelly Place* (15 miles southwest at 14663 County Rd. G; 303/565-3125 or 882-4943). A bed-and-breakfast in the Four Corners that offers a unique educational experience. The house, an adobe ranch built by George Kelly, the horticulturist who designed the Denver Botanic Garden, is at the foot of Sleeping Ute, the tribe's sacred mountain, and there are five Anasazi sites on the property. Week-long programs include archaeological excavation, pottery-making and weaving taught by Navaho instructors, and nature photography. Overnight covered-wagon trips are available to Mesa Verde or Monument Valley. Evening lectures. Full meals. Five guest rooms with private baths.

CRAIG

Moffat County Museum (Court House, on West Victory Way in center of town; 303/824-6360). Indian artifacts, a barbed-wire collection, local history exhibits, and memorabilia of Edwin C. Johnson, former Colorado governor and U.S. senator. Open weekdays.

Marcia (333 East Victory Way). This was the private railroad car of tycoon David Moffat. Open weekdays, May through August.

CRIPPLE CREEK

Bob Womack was brought to Colorado by his father in 1861 to avoid conscription in the Civil War and to hunt for gold. The Womacks had a small silver mine near Georgetown for a while, but the father felt his health was being ruined by mining, so he sold the mine and bought a nearby cattle ranch. Bob hated ranching and spent most of his time drinking. He told anyone who would listen that he believed there were rich lodes of gold in Cripple Creek. One day he found some rocks here that assayed at $200 a ton, but his find was discounted. Womack wasn't reliable, and a gold hoax had fooled residents a few years before. A dentist loaned him $600 and he made another strike, but he still wasn't taken seriously. Then James Portales, a German count living in Colorado Springs, struck gold not far from the Womack mine. Cripple Creek became a boomtown overnight. By 1889, Cripple Creek mines had produced $21 million in gold; they went on to yield $23 million in 1900 alone. By then this was a city, served by seven railroads and an electric trolley. By contrast, the current population is about 750. Cripple Creek made some thirty millionaires, but Bob Womack wasn't one of them. He died in 1909, sixty-six years old and penniless. However, his unshakable belief in gold at Cripple Creek had led to a $400-million bonanza.

Cripple Creek District Museum (on CO 67; 719/689-2634). Artifacts of the town's glory days. Mining and railroad displays.

Heritage Gallery. Assay Office. Open daily, Memorial Day to October 10; weekends only in winter and early spring.

Old Homestead (353 East Myers Ave.). An opulent 1896 brothel with original furnishings. Open daily, Memorial Day through October.

Cripple Creek–Victor Narrow Gauge Railroad (719/689-2640). Pulled by an antique locomotive, a train departs the Cripple Creek District Museum for a four-mile round trip past deserted mines. Daily, late May to early October.

Victor (7 miles south on CO 67). Once known as "the city of mines," Victor has streets paved with low-grade gold ore.

Accommodations: *Imperial Hotel* (123 North 3rd St.; 719/689-2713). Thirty-three guest rooms in a three-story 1896 brick building. The dining room is the best restaurant in town. The *Imperial Players* (719/689-2922) perform Victorian melodramas in the hotel's Gold Bar Room Theatre, afternoons and evenings except Mondays, June to mid-September.

DENVER

Prospectors settled this "Mile High City" in 1858, and two years later it still comprised only sixty-odd cabins and the state's first saloon. Denver began to boom when silver mines were opened nearby in the 1870s. By 1890 its population topped 100,000, and it soon became the most important city in the state.

State Capitol (East Colfax Ave. and Sherman St.; 303/866-2604). Built of Colorado granite, the building has a dome covered with Colorado gold leaf. The dome may be visited for a panoramic view of the city. In the capitol complex, the *Colorado History Museum* (1300 Broadway; 303/866-3682) has exhibits and dioramas depicting the state's history, and a display of mining equipment. Open daily.

Denver Public Library (1357 Broadway; 303/571-2000). An outstanding Western history department comprising some 1.5 million volumes. Exhibits. Open daily.

Denver Art Museum (100 West 14th Pkwy.; 303/575-2793). A large collection of Indian art. Changing exhibits. Open daily.

Museum of Western Art (1727 Tremont Place; 303/296-1880). Works of Remington, Russell, Blumenschein, O'Keefe, and some fifty other artists are on display, housed in the historic 1880 Old Navarre building, which has been at one time or another a girls' school, a bordello, and a restaurant. Open Tuesday through Saturday.

Denver Museum of Natural History (2001 Colorado Blvd., in City Park; 303/370-6363). The museum has an American Indian collection in addition to natural history material. The Charles C. Gates Planetarium is in the building. Open daily.

United States Mint (320 West Colfax Ave.; 303/844-3582 or 844-3332). Established in 1862, the mint offers thirty-minute tours weekdays.

Denver Firefighters Museum (1326 Tremont Pl.; 303/892-1426 or 892-1436). Housed in Fire House No. 1, the museum displays firefighting equipment from the mid-1800s. Open weekdays.

Forney Transportation Museum (1416 Platte St., near I-25 exit 211; 303/433-7444). A collection of more than 300 vintage automobiles, locomotives, and other vehicles. Open daily.

Molly Brown House Museum (1340 Pennsylvania St.; 303/832-4092). Built circa 1889, this was the home of the "unsinkable" Molly Brown, a poor girl who became a socialite and a heroine of the 1912 *Titanic* disaster. Tours. Displays of city and Brown family history in the carriage house. Open daily, Memorial Day to Labor Day; daily except Mondays the rest of the year.

Grant-Humphreys Mansion (770 Pennsylvania St.; 303/866-3508). This three-story Victorian, built in 1902 for Governor

John Wesley Powell

Scholar, teacher, soldier, explorer, geologist, anthropologist, conservationist—John Wesley Powell had as many facets as a diamond. A protégé of George Crookham, a naturalist, he taught in country schools to put himself through college. He lost an arm in the Civil War, then was a professor, making several trips to the Rockies with his students. On an 1869 expedition he made the first boat trip through the Grand Canyon. In 1873, Powell published his *Exploration of the Colorado River*, a classic in the field. Appointed director of the U.S. Geological Survey, he became a leader in the conservation movement, promoting irrigation projects in the West to reduce the area's economic dependence on mining. Powell was a pioneer in the rational use of natural resources, and was vindicated by the passage of the Newlands Reclamation Act shortly before his death in 1902.

Grant, is beautifully furnished. Tours. Open Tuesday through Friday.

Larimer Square (Larimer St. between 14th and 15th). A gaslit restoration of the city's first street, featuring Victorian architecture.

Comanche Crossing Museum (30 miles east in Strasburg; 303/622-4668 or 622-4322). Area artifacts and memorabilia of the completion of the intercontinental railroad are displayed. On the grounds are a restored 1891 schoolhouse, the Strasburg Union Pacific depot, a caboose, and an 1880 windmill. Open daily, June through August.

Accommodations: *Victoria Oaks* (1575 Race St.; 303/355-1818). A bed-and-breakfast housed in an 1894 rooming house. Nine guest rooms furnished with antiques.

DURANGO

This was the southeast gateway to Colorado for Indians, fur traders, miners, ranchers, and railroad builders. The town, founded by the Denver & Rio Grande Railroad in 1880, quickly developed a rowdy reputation. Local vigilantes once engaged the notorious Stockton-Eskridge gang in an hour-long gunfight in the main street. In the 1890s the Durango *Herald-Democrat* was noted for the profane wit of editor Dave Day, who once had forty-two libel suits pending against him. Will Rogers once said of Durango, "It's out of the way and glad of it."

The Silverton (Durango & Silverton Railroad) (479 Main Ave.; 303/247-2733). In service since 1882, the country's last regularly scheduled narrow-gauge passenger train runs between Durango and Silverton with original coaches and steam engines. The trip goes through the canyon of the Animas River, with spectacular mountain scenery. Runs daily.

Southern Ute Tourist Center (23 miles southeast via U.S. 550/CO 172 in Ignacio; 303/563-4531). Owned and operated by the Southern Ute Tribal Council, the Sky Ute Lodge contains the Sky Ute Gallery, which sells traditional and progressive artwork by local tribal artisans.

Jarvis Suite (125 West 10th St.; 303/259-6190). A restored 1888 hotel with twenty-two kitchen suites.

ESTES PARK

Rocky Mountain National Park (2½ miles west on CO 34; 303/586-2371). Joel Estes build a cabin on Fish Creek, here on one of the higher sections of north-central Colorado. Though he moved away, later settlers called the area Estes Park. The noted landscape artist Albert Bierstadt described this as America's finest landscape for the painter. The area to the west of Estes Park became Rocky Mountain National Park in 1915. *Headquarters Building* (just inside the east entrance station, 3 miles west of Estes Park on U.S. 36) has information on the park, guided walks, and evening educational programs daily during the summer. The *Moraine Park Museum* (1 mile into the park from the Beaver Meadows entrance) has exhibits on the park's history.

Estes Park Area Historical Museum (200 Fourth St.; 303/586-6256). The museum has exhibits on the history of Rocky Mountain National Park and the surrounding areas. One building here was the park headquarters from 1915 to 1933. Open daily, May through September; daily except Mondays in March, April, and December.

Enos Mills Cabin (9 miles south on CO 7; 303/586-3675). At the foot of Longs Peak, this cabin, the home of the famed naturalist who was "the Father of Rocky Mountain National Park," contains his notes, documents, and photographs. Nature trails. Open daily.

Never Summer Ranch (10 miles north of the Grand Lake entrance on Trail Ridge Rd.; 303/627-3471). A preserved 1920s dude ranch, with a pioneer homestead nearby. Open daily, mid-June to Labor Day.

Aerial Tramway (420 Riverside Dr., 2 blocks south of Elkhorn St.; 303/586-3675). The tram goes up Prospect Mountain to its 8,896-foot summit, with a view of the Continental Divide during the trip. Daily, mid-May to mid-September.

FAIRPLAY

Gold was discovered in a stream here in 1859 on a Ute hunting ground. When news of the strike spread, newcomers arrived but were treated badly by the miners. One bitter group moved on to the South Platte itself, where they found gold. They started a camp of their own, naming it Fairplay. Today Fairplay is a collection of original buildings, buildings moved from other old mining towns, and a few reconstructions. One of the nearby ghost towns is *Buckskin Joe*, named after "Buckskin Joe" Higganbottom. A smallpox epidemic struck the town in the

1860s, and a beautiful dance-hall girl named Silverheels nursed the miners after the other women had fled. The grateful miners wanted to reward her, but she couldn't be found. She had contracted smallpox and, her beauty gone, had quietly left town. Mount Silverheels was named in her memory.

South Park City Museum (4th and Front streets; 719/836-2387). The restoration of a mining town, with some thirty original buildings and 60,000 artifacts. Exhibits on mining, trades, and social aspects of the mining era. Open daily, mid-May to mid-October.

Prunes Monument (Front Street). A memorial to a faithful burro named Prunes who packed supplies to the mines in Fairplay for more than half a century.

FORT COLLINS

Fort Collins Museum (200 Matthews St.; 303/221-6738). The museum has a model of the army post that gave the city its name, and a collection of Folsom points and other Indian and pioneer artifacts. Three historic cabins. Changing exhibits. Open daily except Monday.

Accommodations: *Elizabeth Street Guest House* (202 East Elizabeth St.; 303/493-2337). A historic brick home filled with antiques. Breakfast is included in the rates.

GEORGETOWN

Gold was discovered here in 1859, but it was silver that built Georgetown. Until the strike at Leadville in 1878, it was the most important silver camp in the state. For years it was famous for the Hotel de Paris, the creation of Louis Dupuy, a Frenchman who squandered his inheritance before coming to America. He joined the army, served in Wyoming, deserted, was a reporter for a

Doc Holliday

A consumptive dentist from Valdosta, Georgia, John Henry Holliday went west for his health and became a drifter, a heavy drinker, a gambler, and a cold-blooded killer. Aware that his tuberculosis was terminal, he welcomed gunfights, swearing that he wouldn't die in bed. Somewhere in his drifting, he married Mary Katherine Michael, known as Kate Elder. In Dodge City he became friends with Wyatt Earp, and later joined him in Tombstone. He was with Earp and his brothers in the gunfight at the O.K. Corral and the ensuing vendetta. Later he was arrested for murder in Denver, but Bat Masterson arranged his release. He was in the Dodge City war in 1883, and the next year killed a gambler in Leadville. He entered a sanatorium in Glenwood Springs, where, at the age of thirty-six, he died in bed.

Denver newspaper, quit, and became a miner, but was injured in an explosion. He became a cook here, eventually buying the bakery, then in 1875 opened his hotel. The Hotel de Paris was known throughout the West for its cuisine, elegant furnishings, and unusual owner. Only guests who met with M. Dupuy's personal approval were allowed to stay in his hotel.

Hotel de Paris Museum (409 6th Ave.; 303/569-2311). Elaborately decorated, with original furnishings, the museum is open daily, May through September; daily except Mondays the rest of the year.

Hamill House Museum (3rd and Argentine streets; 303/569-2840). An early Gothic Revival house with period furnishings. It was once owned by William A. Hamill, Colorado silver magnate and state senator. A partly restored carriage house contains Hamill's office. Open daily, June through September, daily except Mondays the rest of the year.

Georgetown Loop Historic Mining and Railroad Park (train leaves from Devil's Gate Viaduct, west on I-70 to exit 228, then a half-mile south on U.S. 6; 303/279-6101). The reconstructed Georgetown Loop Railroad carries passengers on a scenic seven-mile round trip. Used in the late 1800s to haul ore, it crosses itself once, turns nearly three and a half circles, crosses bridges and the Devil's Gate Viaduct, and in its time was considered an engineering marvel. The train stops to allow a tour of the mine area. Six rounds trips daily.

GLENWOOD SPRINGS

Doc Holliday, the famous gunman who fought at the O.K. Corral, died in a tuberculosis sanatorium here in 1887. The inscription on his tombstone in a local cemetery, decorated with carvings of poker hands and crossed sixguns, notes, "He died in bed," something he swore he would never do.

GOLDEN

Golden, once the rival of Denver, was the capital of the Colorado Territory from 1862 to 1867.

Buffalo Bill Memorial Museum and Grave (Lariat Trail to the summit of

Lookout Mountain, 5 miles west off U.S. 6; 303/526-0747). This is the last resting place of William F. Cody, Pony Express rider, Indian scout, buffalo hunter, and master showman. The museum has an outstanding collection of memorabilia, firearms, documents, and artifacts of his Wild West show. Spectacular view. Open daily, May through October; Tuesday through Sunday the rest of the year.

Colorado Railroad Museum (17155 West 44th Ave., 2 miles east of I-70, exit 265; 303/279-4591). The museum has the oldest narrow-gauge locomotive in the state, as well as a large collection of vintage locomotives, cars, and memorabilia, and a vintage depot. Open daily.

DAR Pioneer Museum (City Hall, 911 10th St.; 303/279-3331, ext. 299). Early gold-mining artifacts, documents from Golden's territorial capital days, guns, photographs, rare newspapers, and Indian dolls. Open daily except Sundays.

Territorial Capitol (Loveland Building, 12th and Washington streets). Legislative sessions were held here on the upper floor.

Accommodations: *The Dove Inn* (711

A room for the night didn't cost much—if one didn't insist on privacy. In this engraving, customers of a saloon bed down on the floor for the night. In the Old West, having a bed, bath, shave, and clean clothes were not a daily event but rather an occasional luxury.

14th St.; 303/278-2209). An 1889 Victorian, furnished with antiques, with six guest rooms and a view of Pikes Peak. Breakfast is included in the rates.

GRAND JUNCTION

Museum of Western Colorado (4th and Ute streets; 303/242-0971). The museum has a small-arms collection and displays depicting the history of the Western slope. Open daily except Mondays, June through August; Tuesday through Saturday the rest of the year.

Cross Orchards Living History Farm (3073 Patterson/F Rd.; 303/434-9158). An outdoor complex interpreting the area's agricultural heritage. Railroad exhibit, tours, demonstrations, and special events. Maintained by the Museum of Western Colorado, along with two natural-history facilities: the Dinosaur Valley Museum and the Rabbit Valley Trail through Time. Open Wednesday through Saturday, mid-May through October.

GREELEY

Greeley was founded in 1870 as a Utopian agricultural settlement named Union County, the brainchild of Horace Greeley, editor of the *New York Tribune*, and supervised by Nathan Meeker, the newspaper's agricultural editor.

Meeker Home (1324 9th Ave.; 303/353-6123). An 1870 house containing many of the town father's belongings and other historical memorabilia. Open Tuesday through Saturday.

Municipal Museum (919 7th St.; 303/353-6123). Pioneer artifacts; lectures and demonstrations. Open Tuesday through Saturday.

Fort Vasquez (1 mile south on U.S. 85; 303/785-2832). A reconstruction of an 1830s fur-trading post. Visitor center and museum. Maintained by the state historical society. Open daily, Memorial Day to Labor Day.

Centennial Village (North 14th Ave. and A St.; 303/353-6123). A collection of restored buildings with period furnishings that reflect the history of the area from 1860 to 1920. Open daily in the summer; Tuesday through Saturday, Labor Day to mid-October.

GUNNISON

Gunnison Pioneer Museum (U.S. 50 at edge of town; 303/641-9963). The museum has town and county artifacts, an old schoolhouse, and a narrow-gauge railroad. Open daily, Memorial Day to Labor Day.

Tincup (36 miles northeast via U.S. 50 and County Rd. 765). An old mining camp. The *Gunnison Visitor Center* (500 East Tomichi Ave.) has maps of the "20-Circle Tour" of area ghost towns.

IDAHO SPRINGS

Utes once bathed in the radium springs here, near the side of one of Colorado's earliest gold strikes. The longest mining tunnel in the world ran from here five miles to Central City.

Argo Town, USA (23rd Ave. and Riverside Dr.; 303/567-2421). A reproduction of an early mining camp. The Argo Gold Mill, first operated in 1913, supported mines on the Mighty Argo Tunnel. Self-guided tours from the mill. The Clear Creek Mining and Milling Gold Mine is accessible from the mill. Open daily, Memorial Day to Labor Day.

Saint Mary's Glacier (12 miles northwest via I-70, Fall River Rd. to Alice). A true ghost town. Park about a mile northwest of Alice and walk a half-mile to the town's ruins and a spectacular view.

If you were in the West in the 1840s, you visited Bent's Fort. John C. Fremont used the fort as a supply base. General Stephen Kearney rested his Army of the West there in 1846, as did General Sterling Price, on his way to Mexico in 1847.

LA JUNTA

The Santa Fe and the Old Navajo trails met here. La Junta (*la HUN-ta*) is Spanish for "the junction," and the town is the home of the Koshare Indian Dancers, a group of Explorer Boy Scouts who perform traditional Indian dances throughout the country.

Bent's Old Fort National Historic Site (6 miles northeast on CO 109 and 194E; 719/384-2596). In the early 19th century, this fort was a stop on the Santa Fe Trail and a gathering place for fur traders and Indian tribes. The founder, William Bent, married Owl Woman, the daughter of Cheyenne chief Gray Thunder. The first white woman to travel the Santa Fe Trail, Susan Magoffin, stopped here in 1846 . Today the reconstructed adobe fort looks as it did in the 1840s. A film at the Visitor Center recounts the fort's history. Open daily.

Koshare Indian Kiva Museum (115 West 18th St.; 719/384-4801). A replica of a Southwestern ceremonial kiva. Displays of baskets, arrowheads, and paintings and carvings by Southwestern Indian artists. Dances are performed here from mid-June to mid-August and the last two weeks in December. Open daily.

Otero County Museum (2nd and Anderson streets; 719/384-4801 or 384-7121). Artifacts relating to county and railroad history. Open daily, June through September.

LEADVILLE

A booming gold camp in the 1860s, twenty years later Leadville was the silver capital of Colorado. In the bonanza, which produced $136 million in a decade, millionaires were made and destroyed in a day. In the lusty brawling boom, a large tent pitched on a vacant lot was advertised as "the best hotel in town," a barrel of whiskey sometimes cost $1,500, and as much as $1,000 was often bet on the turn of a card in the gambling halls.

Prominent in Leadville's history is the rise and fall of H. A. W. Tabor and his two wives, whose story is told in the opera *The Ballad of Baby Doe*. "Unsinkable" Molly Brown made her fortune here, as did David May, Charles Dow, and Meyer Guggenheim. In 1950, Leadville's citizens began rejuvenating the decaying mining town, building a hospital, schools, and recreational facilities, and preserving its Victorian architecture. At an elevation of 10,152 feet, just below the timberline, Leadville is one of the highest towns in the country.

The Matchless Mine (2 miles east on East 7th St.; 719/486-0487) once produced $100,000 a month in silver. The cabin where Baby Doe lived for thirty-six years is a museum. Open daily, June to Labor Day.

H. A. W. Tabor Home (116 East 5th St.; 719/486-0551). Tabor and his first wife, Augusta, lived here until they moved to Denver in 1881. Open daily, Memorial Day to mid-October; Wednesday through Saturday the rest of the year.

Tabor Opera House (308 Harrison Ave.; 719/486-1147). Built in 1879, when Leadville's population was 30,000, this theater was host to the Metropolitan Opera, the Chicago Symphony, and many of the famous stage personalities of the period. Many original furnishings, summer shows. Open daily except Saturdays, Memorial Day through October.

Healy House–Dexter Cabin (912 Harrison Ave.; 719/486-0487). An 1876 Victorian home with vintage furnishings. Costumed guides describe life here in the 1890s. On the site is a two-room cabin with a luxurious interior, built by James V. Dexter, an early mining millionaire. Both buildings are Colorado Historical Society properties. Open daily, Memorial Day to Labor Day.

Heritage Museum and Gallery (9th St. and Harrison Ave.; 719/486-1878). Local artifacts and memorabilia of mining days, exhibits of American art. Open daily, Memorial Day through September.

National Mining Hall of Fame and Museum (120 West 9th St.; 719/486-1229). The museum celebrates mining innovators. Historical and technical exhibits. Open daily.

House with the Eye (127 West 4th St.). This house, now a museum, has a stained-glass "all-seeing eye of God" in its roof. Period furnishings, old musical instruments, bottles, miners' tools, model of the Matchless Mine. A carriage house has a fire wagon and a hose cart. Open daily, early June to early September.

Leadville, Colorado & Southern Railroad Train Tour (old depot, 327 East 7th St.; reservations, 719/486-0189). A fifteen-mile scenic tour over 11,120-foot Fremont Pass to the Climax molybdenum mine. Two departures daily, Memorial Day to Labor Day; weekends, Labor Day through October.

MANITOU SPRINGS

Manitou Cliff Dwellings Museum (on U.S. 24 Bypass; 719/685-5444). An outdoor display of Anasazi architecture and culture. Open daily, May to early October.

Miramont Castle Museum (9 Capitol Hill Ave.; 719/685-1011 or 685-9554). A forty-six-room Victorian mansion with private collections, a railroad museum, and a garden. Tea room and soda fountain. Open daily.

MONTROSE

Ute Indian Museum (Ouray Memorial Park, 17253 Chipeta Dr., 3 miles south on U.S. 550; 303/249-3098). Much of the state was Ute country, and Ute bands have a large reservation in the area near Mesa Verde National Park. The museum documents the Ute contribution to the area with displays of craftsmanship, clothing, and photographs. Maintained by the Colorado Historical Society. Tours. Open daily, May through September.

Horace and Baby Doe Tabor

It was fun while it lasted for the Vermont farmboy who became Colorado's bonanza king. Horace A. W. Tabor was living with his wife and children in Kansas when he learned of the Pikes Peak gold rush. He moved there and opened a store. In the late 1870s, Tabor grubstaked two prospectors who struck it rich. The grubstake brought Tabor a third of the prospectors' profits. Other mining properties, including the Matchless Mine, soon made him a multimillionaire.

Tabor divorced his wife, married a young blond divorcée, Elizabeth McCourt Doe, known as "Baby Doe," built hotels, opera houses, and office buildings, was elected lieutenant governor, and went to the U.S. Senate. He and Baby Doe scandalized society wherever they went. Tabor made a number of bad investments and went bankrupt in the crash of 1893. Friends made him postmaster of Denver. He died the next year, admonishing Baby Doe to "hold on to the Matchless." She returned to Leadville and lived in poverty in a shack at the mine, where she was found frozen to death.

Montrose County Historical Museum (Depot Building, West Main St. and Rio Grande; 303/249-2085). Archaeological artifacts, vintage farm machinery, a pioneer cabin, and local newspapers from 1896. Open daily, May through September.

OURAY

Named for a Ute chief, Ouray was a mining town until the turn of the century.

Ouray County Historical Museum (420 Sixth Ave.; 303/325-4576). Area memorabilia are displayed in this former hospital. Open daily, May through October.

Bachelor-Syracuse Mine (1 mile north via U.S. 550, Dexter Creek Road exit, on County Rd. 14; 303/325-4500). A mine train takes visitors 3,350 feet horizontally into Gold Hill to see the work areas of a mine that has operated continuously since 1884. Gold panning. Open daily, late May through September.

San Juan Scenic Jeep Tours (480 Main St.; 303/325-4444). Guided trips to old ghost towns, mines, and mountain passes, many above the timber line. Daily, June through October, weather permitting.

Accommodations: *St. Elmo* (426 Main St.; 303/325-4951). Eleven guest rooms in an 1898 building furnished with antiques. Hot tub, sauna. Breakfast is included in the rates.

PAGOSA SPRINGS

The mineral springs here are 153 degrees Fahrenheit, and are used to heat the town's houses and public buildings.

Fred Harman Art Museum (2 miles west on U.S. 160, at junction with Piedra Rd.; 303/731-5785). This was the home of the western artist and comic illustrator who created Red Ryder and Little Beaver. Original paintings and drawings. Rodeo, Western, and movie memorabilia. Wheelchair accessible. Open daily, late May to early October.

Treasure Mountain (just east of the

summit of Wolf Creek Pass). In 1890, the story goes, 300 men mined $5 million in gold here and melted it into gold bars, but were forced to leave it behind when Indians drove them off the mountain. The gold never has been found.

PUEBLO

Settled in 1842, Pueblo was a crossroad for Indians, Spaniards, and fur traders. By the time the Rio Grande Railroad came in 1872, it was the largest producer of coal and steel west of the Mississippi.

Rosemount Victorian House Museum (419 West 14th St.; 719/545-5290). A thirty-seven-room mansion with original furnishings, the museum houses artifacts collected by explorer Andrew McClelland. Open daily except Mondays.

Fred E. Weisbrod Aircraft Museum (Pueblo Memorial Airport; 719/948-3355 or 948-4032). An outdoor static display of vintage airplanes. Open daily.

SALIDA

Salida Museum (U.S. 50 at "I" St.; 719/539-2068). Displays of Indian artifacts, pioneer household goods, railroad and mining material. Open daily, late May to early September.

Ghost Town Scenic Jeep Tours (11150 U.S. 50; 800/525-2081 outside Colorado, 800/332-9100 in Colorado). Full-day and half-day trips to deserted towns and abandoned mines. Guests pan for gold.

Accommodations: *The Poor Farm Country Inn* (8475 CR 160; 719/539-3818). A bed-and-breakfast with five guest rooms in a historic Victorian home.

SILVER PLUME

The ghost of a young Englishman named Griffin haunts this once-bustling mining camp. One of the first to arrive, Griffin discovered a mine rich in silver and gold. Despite his good fortune, he made no friends and didn't frequent the saloons or brothels. A visitor brought the rumor to Silver Plume that the night before Griffin was to have been married in England, his fiancée was found dead in his room. Griffin neither confirmed nor denied the story. Soon afterward, Griffin began to sit in front of his cabin on the mountain every evening, playing the violin, the music drifting down to the town. One evening the music ended and a shot rang out. Some townspeople went to investigate. They found Griffin lying facedown in a grave he had dug himself. He had killed himself with a bullet in his heart.

Accommodations: *The Brewery Inn* (in the Silver Plume National Historic District; 303/674-5565). A Victorian bed-and-breakfast with four guest rooms. Fireplaces, antiques, down comforters.

SILVERTON

San Juan County Historical Society Museum (Main St.; 303/387-5838). This museum, located in the old city jail, has mining and transportation artifacts from the town's early days. Open daily, Memorial Day to October.

Circle Jeep Tour (for map and information, phone 303/387-5654). A mapped route for four-wheel-drive vehicles to ghost towns and abandoned mines.

Accommodations: *Fool's Gold Inn* (1069 Snowden; 303/387-5879). An 1883 Victorian overlooking Silverton. Breakfast is included in the rates.

STERLING

Overland Trail Museum (21053 County Rte. 260; 303/522-5070). Indian artifacts, cattle brands, a one-room schoolhouse, a fire engine, and other items of interest. Open daily, May through September.

TELLURIDE

Life was hard in the mining camp here. The winters were severe, and men outnumbered women about fifty to one. There were ample sporting houses, but many men wanted a more permanent relationship. For years there was a brisk business in mail-order brides. Butch Cassidy and his gang robbed their first bank here, but another story involving a local bank is much more revealing of the character of the town. When the Depression was causing bank failures, the head of a Telluride bank went to New York with papers he had carefully doctored, and borrowed enough money to pay all his depositors in full. He was found out, tried, and sentenced to a stiff prison term. Unrepentant, he told the judge, "Those big-city banks can afford to lose money a lot easier than my people back home." All of Telluride is a National Historic District.

TRINIDAD

This was a busy trading post on the Santa Fe Trail. Kit Carson was a frequent visitor, and later Bat Masterson was the sheriff.

Baca House (300 East Main St.; 719/846-7217). This was the 1869 adobe home of a wealthy Hispanic sheep rancher. In the outbuildings is the *Pioneer Museum,* which has artifacts and memorabilia of the Santa Fe Trail and the open-range cattle days. Next door is the *Bloom House,* a restored 1882 Victorian mansion. Guided tours. Open daily, Memorial Day to Labor Day.

A. R. Mitchell Memorial Museum of Western Art (131 West Main St.; 719/846-4224). Paintings by Arthur Roy Mitchell, Harvey Dunn, Harold von Schmidt, and other artists. Indian artifacts, Hispanic religious folk art. Open daily, May through September.

A million years ago the Great Basin was an inland sea, but when the white men came it was a vast desert surrounded by mountains. Indians had learned the secrets of desert survival, but Americans wanted only to get through it and reach California. The route across the desert was called the "highway of the West." The hardy Mormons built a home at the Great Salt Lake and had the Great Basin to themselves until prospectors discovered a mountain of silver in Nevada.

PART V
THE
GREAT
BASIN

A Mormon wagon train nears Utah.

13

Utah

BLANDING

With a population of some 3,000, this is the largest community in an area as large as Connecticut, Delaware, and Rhode Island put together. It is a gateway to Glen Canyon and Lake Powell and many nearby Anasazi sites. Within a fifty-mile radius of Blanding, practically every cliff or canyon slope has some sign of ancient occupation.

Hovenweep National Monument (13 miles south on U.S. 191, then east on UT 262 and county roads to Hatch Trading Post, then 16 miles following signs to Square Tower Ruins; 303/529-4465). The desolate country north of the San Juan River, where Colorado and Utah meet in the Four Corners, was a major center of Anasazi activity between A.D. 800 and 1300. The largest ruin here is the *Square Tower Group*, consisting of thirteen major dwellings in or along the edge of Ruin Canyon, most of them fully excavated. The most impressive is Hovenweep Castle (*Hovenweep* is Ute for "deserted valley"), a two-story, C-shaped structure. On the canyon floor is the Square Tower, a twenty-foot spire. Other buildings are along the canyon's edge, extending eastward for about a mile. Ruin Canyon contains permanent springs, and the Anasazi were farmers. The long draws draining into the canyons could be terraced to hold back the soil and provide irrigation for crops. A long period of drought began in the late 13th century, forcing the Anasazi to abandon their homes. They drifted south to the Rio Grande and Little Colorado drainage areas and never returned.

In the monument within ten miles of the Square Tower Group are five other major sites that can be reached by unpaved road: *Holly Ruin, Hackberry Ruin, Cutthroat Castle, Horseshoe Ruin,* and *Cajun Ruin*. There are several curious structures in these groups. A building at Holly Ruin is round on the outside but square inside; another, at Horseshoe Ruin, consists of two concentric circles. Some buildings, including the Square Tower, have been identified as primitive observatories. During the summer and winter solstices and the autumnal and vernal equinoxes, but at no other time, light coming through narrow windows would strike particular points inside. This was probably the signal for the Anasazi to perform various ceremonies to ensure good growing seasons.

The Visitor Center at Square Tower has drinking water, rest rooms, and books for sale, but no exhibits. Open daily. Limited wheelchair access.

The pre-Hispanic ruins in Hovenweep National Monument in the rolling canyon country on the border of Utah and Colorado are remarkable for their round towers. One tower, Holly Ruin, is round on the outside, square on the inside. No one knows what they were used for.

Buried Treasure

The Lost Dutchman Mine, in the Superstition Mountains near Phoenix, is only one example of buried treasure in the Old West. Here are some others:

Montezuma's Lost Treasure Caravan. According to legend, Montezuma, the Aztec ruler, stripped his buildings of their gold, silver, and jewels and sent them north, rather than let them fall into the hands of Cortés. One account says the caravan went 275 leagues, turned west, and hid the treasure in a cave in a canyon. Other versions have the caravan going much farther north, into present-day Arizona, New Mexico, or Utah. In 1876 a young Mexican arrived in Taos, New Mexico, to look for the treasure. While townspeople watched, he called from a cliff that he had found the treasure in a cave. Then a powerful gust of wind blew him off the cliff to his death. Kanab, Utah, also believes the treasure is nearby. In 1914 a prospector told a wealthy rancher that he had found an old book in Mexico with drawings of symbols that supposedly had been carved on rocks near Kanab. The rancher grubstaked him, and he vanished into the mountains, reappearing eight years later. The prospector said he had found the treasure, but needed more time to get it out. In a canyon on White Mountain, he showed the rancher the symbols, and a nearby tunnel that had been carefully sealed. After three months of preparatory work, the prospector said he was going to Mexico for more information, and was never seen again.

Maximilian's Millions. Shortly before his death, Emperor Maximilian of Mexico supposedly sent $5 million in gold, silver, and jewels out of Mexico. Aides packed the treasure in forty-five flour barrels and took it north, crossing into Texas near El Paso. They were warned of the dangers awaiting them by some ex-Confederate soldiers, whom they hired as guards. Learning of the treasure, the soldiers killed the Mexicans and took what they could carry in their saddlebags, burying the rest at Castle Gap. None of the Confederates lived to recover the treasure. On his deathbed, one told his doctor about the treasure and drew him a map. The doctor searched for the treasure some years later, but could not match the landmarks on the map with those in the area. (Castle Gap is in the King Mountains, north of El Paso.)

Wells Fargo Gold. A stagecoach bound for Salt Lake City in 1865 was attacked by bandits. The passengers were robbed and killed, the driver knocked unconscious, and the

Edge of the Cedars State Park (311 North 5th St. West; 801/678-2238). Excavated Anasazi dwellings and ceremonial chambers. Pictographs and artifacts. A museum has displays relating to Indian history and culture. Visitor Center. Open daily. Limited wheelchair access.

Accommodations: *The Old Hotel* (118 East 300 South; 801/678-2388). In the same family for four generations, the hotel offers seven guest rooms with private baths and color television. Assistance is available for arranging jeep trips, scenic flights, and tours of local attractions. Breakfast included.

BLUFF

On U.S. 163, the scenic route between the Grand Canyon and Mesa Verde, this tiny town of some 120 people still has pioneer homes and other reminders of the first Mormon settlers.

Tours of the Big Country (Box 36, Bluff, UT 84512; 801/672-2281). From April to October, Jim Hook, a naturalist, gives four-wheel-drive tours from April through October to Monument Valley, Old Monarch Cave, Moon House, and Cedar Mesa, operating out of his Recapture Lodge. Half-day, full day, and overnight trips.

Wild Rivers Expeditions (Charles M. DeLorme, P.O. Box 118; 801/672-2244, or 800/422-7654 outside of Utah). Trips on the San Juan River and the Cataract Canyon of the Colorado to see geological formations, fossil beds, and sites ranging from 12,000-year-old Paleo-Indian dwellings through the Anasazi complexes to modern Navaho villages.

Recapture Lodge (on U.S. 191; 801/672-2281). The base for Mr. Hook's tours (see above). Slide shows. Library.

Accommodations: *Bluff Bed & Breakfast* (801/672-2220). A Frank Lloyd Wright–style house on seventeen desert acres, with two guest rooms with private baths.

BRIGHAM CITY

Brigham Young made his last public address here in 1877, and the town was renamed for him.

Golden Spike National Historic Site (23 miles west via UT 83 to Promontory Junction, left 2 miles to next junction, then right five miles; 801/471-2209). On May 10, 1869, Governor Leland Stanford of California took a swing at the traditional golden spike and missed. But the telegrapher touched his key anyway, and the message went out to the nation: "The last rail is laid. The last spike is driven. The Pacific Railroad is finished." Long a dream, Congress authorized and funded the "Forty-second-Parallel Route" in 1862. Soon the Union Pacific was pushing west from Omaha with thousands of immigrant Irish workers. Eastward from Sacramento came the Central Pacific (now the Southern Pacific) with thousands of Chinese coolies. A town sprung up at Promontory, but it was short-lived; the completion of the Lucin Cutoff across the Great Salt Lake in 1903 doomed this section of track. But the ceremony here ensured the continental development of the country and, in the words of the Park Service, gave "added reality to the decision of the Civil War that the Union was indissoluble." The Visitor Center has a film on the railroad. A daily summer interpretive program includes operating replicas of the steam locomotives *Jupiter* and *119*. Open daily.

Brigham City Museum-Gallery (24 North 3rd Street West; 801/723-6769). Exhibits of furniture, clothing, photographs, books, and documents relating to the history of the area since 1851. Open Tuesday through Saturday.

Mormon Tabernacle (251 South Main St.; 801/723-3931). This is one of the state's most architecturally interesting buildings, and it has been in continuous use since it was built in 1881. Tours. Open daily, May through October.

strongbox stolen. The take was $180,000, nearly half of it in gold bullion. When the driver arrived at McCammon, Idaho, a posse was formed and tracked the bandits to the Mud Lake area. When the bandits saw the posse, they threw the sacks into the lake and escaped. The posse tried to retrieve the sacks, but failed. Around the turn of the century, two treasure hunters searched the lake for years and found several gold bars. Townspeople believe the rest of the treasure is still there, probably buried in the lake bottom. (Mud Lake is in Jefferson County, about thirty miles northwest of Idaho Falls.)

Jesse's Missing Millions. Along the Rio Grande in the 1870s, Jesse James and his gang relieved a Mexican insurgent general of a caravan of gold. They headed north and buried their loot in the Wichita Mountains. After Jesse's death, Frank James bought a farm near Lawton, Oklahoma, and openly searched for the gold. Jesse had left a marker of two pick handles and a bucket with a code scratched on it. Frank was convinced that the gold was within a few miles of his farm, but died before he found it. In the 1950s a man named Hunter Pennick found a brass bucket, two old pick heads, and an iron wedge. Scratched on the bucket was an undecipherable code. Pennick combed the area, digging many holes, but found nothing more. (Lawton is in southwestern Oklahoma, about a hundred miles from Oklahoma City.)

A crowd near Promontory, Utah, watches the golden spike being driven to mark the completion on May 10, 1869, of the first transcontinental railroad. The task took six years, the Central Pacific building eastward from Sacramento, the Union Pacific, westward from Omaha.

CEDAR CITY

The first blast furnace west of the Mississippi was built here in 1852. Although it was not very successful, iron is still mined in the area.

Iron Mission State Park (north edge of city on I-15; 801/586-9290). The site of the first iron foundry west of the Mississippi, the park has an extensive collection of horse-drawn vehicles and wagons from pioneer days. Indian artifacts. Open daily.

Accommodations: *Paxman Summer House Bed & Breakfast* (170 North 400 East; 801/586-3755). Four guest rooms in a large Victorian house. Open May through September. *Meadeau View Lodge* (P.O. Box 345, Cedar City 84720; 801/672-2220). An attractive bed-and-breakfast surrounded by pines and aspens.

FILLMORE

Settled in 1851, Fillmore was the territorial capital until 1856, and is now the trading center for farmers and ranchers in Millard County.

Territorial Statehouse State Park (50 West Capitol Ave.; 801/743-5316). Built of red sandstone in the 1850s, the first territorial capitol is now a museum with an excellent collection of pioneer and Indian artifacts, photographs, and documents. Rose garden. Open daily, June to Labor Day.

HEBER CITY

Heber Creeper (6th West and Center streets; 801/654-2900). This charmingly named train makes a three-and-one-half-hour tour from Heber Valley through Provo Canyon to Vivian Park and Bridal Veil Falls, dropping several thousand feet as it goes.

Around the railroad station is *Heber Pioneer Village*, a charming collection of old-time buildings that capture the feel of Utah a century ago. In the background rise the Wasatch Mountains. The train operates on weekends, early May to Memorial Day; daily from then to mid-October.

Accommodations: *Homestead* (700 North Homestead Dr., 5 miles west in Midway; 801/654-1102; reservations, 800/327-7220). A country inn catering to sportsmen. Indoor and outdoor pool. Sauna, whirlpool, and hot tub. Tennis. Bicycles and snowmobiles. Hay and sleigh rides. *Dearden Bed & Breakfast Inn* (830 South Main St.; 801/654-2236). A charming cottage with two guest rooms.

KANAB

If the area looks familiar, it's because the lakes, sand dunes, and canyons have been the setting for more than a hundred movies. Fort Kanab was here, but Indians forced its abandonment in 1864. Mormon missionaries later made a permanent settlement. Zane Grey lived here when he wrote *Riders of the Purple Sage*. Kanab is within a ninety-minute drive of three national parks (Bryce Canyon, Zion, and the North Rim of the Grand Canyon) and three national monuments (Cedar Breaks, Pipe Spring, and the Glen Canyon National Recreation Area).

Movie sets. Several movie locations are in the area, including a false-front Western town. Inquire locally for directions. Some sets are on private property.

Old Barn Theater (801/644-2015). Melodramas are presented here from late May to late September.

Accommodations: *Miss Sophie's Bed & Breakfast* (Ronald and Aprile Barden, 30 North 200 West, Kanab, UT 84741; 801/ 644-5952). A restored late-1800s house in town. Guest rooms are decorated with antiques. Open May through October.

LOGAN

Mormon Temple (175 North 3rd St. East). Brigham Young chose the site and broke ground for this massive, castellated limestone temple in 1877. The temple is closed to the public, but its grounds are open daily.

Ronald V. Jensen Historical Farm, and Man and His Bread Museum (5 miles south on U.S. 89/91; 801/245-4064). Exhibits, displays, and demonstrations relating to the development of agriculture from the mid-1800s to today. The farm is a re-creation of a typical Cache Valley farmstead. Costumed interpreters. Collection of pioneer artifacts and machinery. Open Tuesday through Saturday in the summer.

Daughters of the Utah Pioneers Museum (Civic Center, 52 West 2nd St. North; 801/752-2161). Exhibits tracing the state's past. Open Monday through Friday, June through August.

Hardware Ranch (8 miles south via UT 165 to Hyrum/Blacksmith Fork Canyon, then 17 miles east on UT 101; 801/245-3131). Hundreds of wild elk come here in the winter for a "handout." A horse-drawn sled carries hay around the grounds for several hours every day. Feeding can be seen from the Visitor Center; when there is sufficient snow on January and February weekends, sleigh rides are available into the midst of the herds. Open Wednesday through Sunday, September through March.

Accommodations: *Center Street Bed & Breakfast* (169 East Center St.; 801/752-3443). Six guest rooms in two buildings, a twenty-two-room mansion, and a carriage house.

MEXICAN HAT

A rock formation that looks like an upside-down sombrero gave this town its name. Mexican Hat, across the river from the Navajo reservation, has enjoyed several gold

Brigham Young

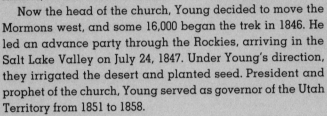

The state of Utah is a monument to the vision and dynamism of Brigham Young, who led the Mormons to prosperity in the promised land. Born in Vermont, the ninth of eleven children, he met Joseph Smith, the founder of Mormonism, in 1832 and became a missionary. They were together during the years when the Mormons were forced to move from New York to Ohio to Missouri, and finally to Illinois, where Smith was slain.

Now the head of the church, Young decided to move the Mormons west, and some 16,000 began the trek in 1846. He led an advance party through the Rockies, arriving in the Salt Lake Valley on July 24, 1847. Under Young's direction, they irrigated the desert and planted seed. President and prophet of the church, Young served as governor of the Utah Territory from 1851 to 1858.

Young, who had more than twenty wives and fifty-seven children, was a prodigious builder. He helped found what are now Brigham Young University and the University of Utah, sent pioneers throughout the West, established more than 350 communities, built railroads, and delivered thousands of sermons.

and uranium booms, but its current population is about 100.

Monument Valley Navajo Tribal Park (22 miles southwest on U.S. 163; Tribal Visitor Center, 801/727-3287). Monument Valley has become the quintessential symbol of the American Southwest. Called "the Eighth Wonder of the World," it has buttes nearly a thousand feet tall, mesas studded with juniper, and twisted hobgoblins of stone, changing color throughout the day in the clear desert light. In the valley are several hundred Anasazi dwellings, most of

The Guns That Won the West

The Colt .44 revolver, the "equalizer" of the Old West, began in the inventive mind of a sixteen-year-old boy on a sailing ship bound for India. Samuel Colt noticed that when the ship's wheel was turned, a clutch aligned the spokes and locked the wheel in position. Applying the principle, he invented the first practical revolver when he was twenty-four. To raise money for manufacturing, he toured the country giving exhibitions of laughing gas. His guns were first used by the Texas Rangers, which led to a government contract in 1847. Although sympathetic to the South, he produced hundreds of thousands of Colt revolvers for the Union in the Civil War.

The Winchester Model M1866, "the gun that won the West," was invented by John Browning, the son of an Ogden, Utah, gunsmith. Known as "the father of modern firearms," he was granted 128 patents, designing guns for Winchester, Colt, Savage, and other manufacturers. Noticing how shooters were rocked back by the recoil of their guns, he devised a way to use the expanding gas that caused recoil to automatically eject spent shells and reload. By 1897 he had developed a semiautomatic pistol, which became the army's standard sidearm for nearly a century. Browning's .30-caliber machine gun was mass-produced for American troops in World War II.

them in Mystery Valley in the southwest part of the park. All but a few are small cliff dwellings in isolated canyons away from the park's roads, and it takes an Indian guide to reach them (unaccompanied backcountry exploring is forbidden). The Anasazi were here by A.D. 900, farming small plots, hunting game, and collecting wild plants. Sometime in the middle of the 12th century, the Anasazi moved away, to places where there was more water. Today several hundred Navajos live in Monument Valley, raising sheep and doing a little farming, their lives virtually unchanged in two centuries. A sixteen-mile unpaved loop road begins at the tribal park headquarters, which straddles the Arizona-Utah border. The road can be negotiated in a passenger car in good weather.

Full-day commercial tours are offered by Goulding's Trading Post, near the park headquarters. Open daily. Limited wheelchair access.

MOAB

Pioneers tried to settle here in 1855, but the Indians drove them away, and Moab was not permanently settled until 1880. This is one of the most scenic areas of the state, on the Colorado River at the foot of red cliffs and the La Sal Mountains.

Moab Museum (118 Center St.; 801/259-7985). Exhibits relating to the history, archaeology, and minerals of the area. Open daily.

Canyonlands Field Institute (P.O. Box 68-MG, Moab, UT 84532; 801/ 259-7750). The institute offers summer educational adventure seminars and trips featuring Indian culture, Southwestern literature, and landscape photography. Guided backpacking and nature walks. Canyonlands and Arches are used as outdoor classrooms.

Hollywood Stuntmen's Hall of Fame (111 East 100 North; 801/259-6100). Stunt-related artifacts including costumes, weapons, and the footprints of some 200 stunt people. Action photographs, films, and videos. Open daily except Monday, March through October.

Canyonlands by Night (leaves dock two miles north on U.S. 191; 801/259-5261). A two-hour boat trip with a sound-and-light presentation highlighting the history of the area. Sails daily at sundown, May to mid-October, weather permitting.

Miners Basin (17 miles northeast on UT 128, then south 10 miles on a dirt road to Castleton, then south 4½ miles on the La Sal Mountain Loop Rd., then east 3½ miles on a steep, four-wheel-drive road). Gold was discovered here in 1888, and until the early 20th century some seventy-five people lived in the town, where there were two saloons, a hotel, and a post office. Several log buildings still stand in the high mountain meadow.

Accommodations: *Canyon County Bed & Breakfast* (590 North 500 West; 801/259-7882 or 800/635-1792). A ranch house with five guest rooms. Hosts Chuck and Judy Nichols can help plan sightseeing trips.

OGDEN

In the early 19th century, this was a rendezvous and winter camp for fur trappers. In 1846 the first white settler, Miles Goodyear, built a cabin and trading post, Fort Buenaventura, but sold out to the Mormons the next year. Settlers were harassed by floods, droughts, disease, and Indian attacks until the coming of the railroad in 1869. Later it was a typical frontier town with gambling halls and saloons, and friction developed between the Mormons and the "gentiles." Among Ogden's native sons are the novelist Bernard De Voto and John M. Browning, inventor of the automatic rifle.

Daughters of Utah Pioneers Visitor Center and Relic Hall (2148 Grant Ave. in Tabernacle Square; 801/621-5224, 394-7211, or 825-0983). Old handicrafts, pioneer clothing, household items, furniture, and photographs of pioneers. Miles Goodyear's cabin, the first permanent home built, is on the site. Open daily except Sundays, June through August.

Union Station (2501 Wall Ave.; 801/629-8444). The station has several interesting features. A railroad museum has an elaborate model railroad, films, and guided tours by "conductors." The *Browning-Kimball Car Museum* displays classic American automobiles. The *Browning Firearms Museum* houses the reconstructed original gun shop and the inventor's models. A 500-seat theater presents musicals and dramas. Art gallery. The Visitors Bureau for Northern Utah also is here. Open daily, June through August.

Fort Buenaventura State Park (2450 A Ave.; 801/621-4808). The reconstructed fort and stockade of mountain man Miles Goodyear, on the original thirty-two-acre site. Open daily, April through October.

Accommodations: *Rogers Rest* (Mr. and Mrs. Frank Rogers, 914 29th St., Ogden, UT 84403; 801/393-5824). An intimate bed-and-breakfast in an eclectically decorated ranch-style house.

PANGUITCH

Anasazi Indian Village State Park (50 miles south via UT 12 at the city limits of Boulder; 801/676-2311). A partially excavated settlement that was inhabited from A.D. 750 to 1150. Archaeologists believe this was the largest Anasazi community west of the Colorado River. A museum displays Anasazi artifacts. Visitor Center. Open daily during the summer.

Upper Kanab (some 33 miles south on UT 89, then east 3 miles to Alton, then 2½ miles on a dirt road). A ranching village was established here in 1882, and the ranchers later imported African antelope and a herd of buffalo. The residents left in the early 1900s during a severe drought. Today the ruins of the town are particularly photogenic.

The coming of the railroad to Ogden in 1869 was commemorated by the handsome gothic Union Station, which now attracts visitors to its museums of the railroad, classic automobiles, and firearms. The old station also houses a 500-seat theater and an art gallery.

After a mining strike, towns sprang up overnight, and when they did, they usually looked like this: A street in Corinne, Boxelder County, Utah, 1869. When the mines played out, however, such settlements could become ghost towns just as quickly.

-+-

"The Mormon emigrants usually start from Council Bluffs [Iowa], on the left bank of the Missouri River.... According to 'Overland Guide,' Council Bluffs is the natural crossing of the Missouri River, on the route destined by nature for the great thoroughfare to the Pacific. This was the road selected by 'nature's civil engineers,' the buffalo and the elk, for their western travel. The Indians followed them on the same trail; then the travellers; next the settlers came."

—SIR RICHARD F. BURTON, the City of the Saints, 1861

PRICE

During the 1930s this quiet town was one of the stopping-off places of the notorious Robbers' Roost gang. Within thirty miles are more than thirty coal mines, and oil and natural-gas fields.

College of Eastern Utah Prehistoric Museum (City Hall, Main and 1st North streets; 801/637-5060). Archaeology exhibits, dinosaur displays, and geological specimens. Open daily except Sundays.

Geology Tours. Maps describing self-guided automobile tours in the area to Indian dwellings and pictographs, Nine Mile Canyon, San Rafael Desert, Little Grand Canyon, and Dinosaur Pit are available at the Chamber of Commerce in the Municipal Building (801/6 37-2788).

Cleveland-Lloyd Dinosaur Quarry (30 miles south off UT 10; 801/637-4584). More than 12,000 dinosaur bones have been excavated here since 1928. Visitor Center with exhibits. Open Thursday through Monday, Memorial Day to Labor Day; weekends from Easter to Memorial Day.

PROVO

Two Spanish priests in 1776 were probably the first Europeans to visit this area. Provo got its name from Etienne Provost, a French-Canadian who explored the valley with a party of trappers in 1825. The city's setting is magnificent. To the east is Provo Peak, to the north is Mount Timpanogos, both over 11,000 feet; to the south is the Wasatch Range, and to the west is Utah Lake, and behind the lake are more mountains.

Brigham Young University (North St. and University Ave.). With 27,000 students, this is one of the largest church-affiliated universities in the world. Tours given weekdays by the Hosting Center (801/378-4678). Of interest on the campus are the *Harris Fine Art Center,* with the Lotta Van Buren collection of rare instruments and music, and the *Museum of People and Cultures* (Allen Hall), which displays material from the Southwest, South America, and the Near East. Both buildings are open weekdays.

McCurdy Historical Doll Museum (246 North 100 East; 801/377-9935). More than

3,000 dolls, antique toys, and miniatures are on display. Documentary film. Doll shop and doll hospital. Tours. Open Tuesday through Saturday.

Pioneer Museum (500 West 600 East; 801/379-6609). An important collection of Mormon pioneer relics and Western art. Pioneer Village. Open daily, June to early September.

Springville Museum of Art (126 East 400 South; 7 miles southeast via I-15, exit 2 in Springville; 801/489-9434). A permanent collection of state art from 1860 to the present, as well as the work of California and East Coast artists. Open daily except Mondays.

John Hutchins Museum of Natural History (635 North Center St., 17 miles northwest in Lehi via I-15 or UT 89; 801/768-8710). Six main collections: archaeology, ornithology and zoology, paleontology, mineralogy, and pioneer artifacts. Most items are from the Great Basin area. Some Indian artifacts. Open daily except Mondays.

Camp Floyd and Stagecoach Inn State Parks (north via I-15, then 21 miles west of Lehi on UT 73; 801/768-8932). From 1858 to 1861, Camp Floyd quartered the largest concentration of troops in the nation. Some 400 buildings were built for army personnel deployed here to quell a threatened Mormon rebellion. Only the cemetery remains. Nearby, the Stagecoach Inn has been restored and has vintage furnishings. Visitor Center. Open daily, mid-March through November.

Eureka (45 miles southwest on UT 6). This was the center of the Tintic mining district, one of Utah's richest. In 1909, 80 percent of the stocks traded on the Salt Lake Stock Exchange were Tintic properties. Unlike most mining towns, Eureka had a reputation for quiet law and order. In 1890 a flash flood destroyed the business district, and three years later it had a disastrous fire. Some 700 people still live in Eureka, which has the look and feel of an old mining camp.

Mammoth (3 miles south of Eureka on UT 6, then a paved road east for 2 miles). In 1873 the owners of the mine here were becoming disillusioned, so when the McIntyre brothers came through, driving a herd of Texas longhorn steers to market, they traded the mine for the cattle. The brothers soon hit a rich body of ore that produced gold, silver, lead, copper, and bismuth for seventy-five years. Today only twenty or so dilapidated, ghostly buildings remain. The mine is on private property.

Accommodations: *The Pullman* (415 South University Ave.; 801/374-8141). This 1898 Victorian mansion built by a railroad magnate, and now listed in the National Register of Historic Places, has six guest rooms.

RICHFIELD

Brigham Young sent a group of Mormons to settle here, and today the area grows some of the world's best beef. Hunters and fishermen like the rugged mountains and well-stocked lakes.

Fremont Indian State Park (20 miles southwest at 11000 Clear Creek Canyon Rd. in Sever; 801/527-4631). The Fremont Indians lived here from A.D. 300 to 1300,

The reality of Indian warfare is evident as a young lieutenant and an army scout examine the body of a man scalped and left to die on the plains. Scalps were to Indians what medals were to soldiers, tangible evidence that they were mighty warriors.

This historic Santa Clara house, built in 1862 by Jacob Hamblin—pioneer and missionary to the Hopi and Navajo—has been restored to its original appearance and furnished with handmade pine furniture of the pioneer period.

then mysteriously vanished. An interpretive center explains the evolution of their culture. There is a collection of artifacts, and a nature trail leads to petroglyphs and a reconstructed pit-house dwelling and granary. Open daily. Limited wheelchair access.

ST. GEORGE

The Mormons called this hot, arid corner of the state "Dixie" and for a while tried to grow cotton here. The first Mormon temple in the state was built at St. George, and its story is worth retelling. Brigham Young selected the site, and although it turned out to be a bog, construction proceeded. Hundreds of tons of rock were pounded into the bog to create a stable foundation. Some 17,000 tons of rock were quarried by hand, and hauled to the site by teams of oxen. Timbers were freighted eighty miles from Mount Trumbull. Mormons from the northern part of the state came on forty-day missions to work on the temple. Mormons in the south gave one day's labor in ten. Begun in the 1860s, the temple was finished in 1877.

Temple Visitor Center (444 South 300 East; 801/673-5181). Tours of the grounds and an indoctrination film. Open daily.

Tabernacle (Main and Tabernacle streets; 801/673-5181). A New England–style church. Open daily.

Brigham Young Winter Home (22 North 100 West; 801/673-5181). A two-story adobe structure built in 1873, with period furnishings and a garden. Young spend the last nine winters of his life here. Open daily.

Daughters of Utah Pioneers Collection (Memorial Building, 133 North 100 East; 801/673-5170 or 628-0943). Regional memorabilia. Open daily except Sundays.

Jacob Hamblin Home (5 miles west off I-15 in Santa Clara; 801/673-5151). The 1863 home of a Mormon missionary to the Indians, furnished in period style. Weaving and spinning demonstrations. Open daily.

Snow Canyon State Park (7 miles northwest on UT 18; 801/628-2255). A flat-bottomed gorge cut into sandstone, with some interesting Indian petroglyphs. Open daily.

Pine Valley Chapel (30 miles north via UT 18, Central exit). Ebenezer Bryce, a former shipbuilder, built this white-frame meeting house in 1868. The walls were completed on the ground, then raised and joined with wooden pegs and rawhide. The chapel is still in use. Open daily, Memorial Day to Labor Day.

Grafton (7 miles northeast on I-15, then 35 miles east to Rockville, then inquire locally). One of the few ghost towns in Utah, Grafton once produced high-quality silk, but was plagued with spring floods and Indian raids. Its population slowly dwindled, and now it is deserted. The movie *Bride of Short Creek* was filmed here. The quality of construction of the buildings and the way the town was laid out are unmistakably Mormon, much different from ghost towns that once were mining camps. Do not explore the well-preserved buildings; much of Grafton is now privately owned.

Accommodations: Green Gate Village Historic Inn (62-78 West Tabernacle; 801/628-6999). A cluster of four restored pioneer homes, circa 1872. The Bentley House has Victorian decor; the Supply Depot is decorated in a style reflective of its origin as a shop for wagoners on their way to California; the Orson Pratt House and the Carriage House also are carefully restored. Sixteen guest rooms. *Seven Wives Inn* (217 North 100 West; 801/628-3737). The innkeeper's great-grandfather had seven wives, hence the name. The attic, concealed by a secret door, is thought to have been a refuge for polygamists. It is now the Jane room, with a skylight and stenciling. Fifteen guest rooms. Breakfast is included in the rates.

SALT LAKE CITY

Brigham Young and his followers arrived here in 1847 and named the desert wilderness Deseret, which means "beehive." They were harassed by drought, by a plague of grasshoppers (which were eaten by seagulls just in time to save their crops), and by the surge of people heading for the California gold fields, but they survived and built Salt Lake City. The Mormon farmers made social experiments throughout Utah, and many were successful. In 1850 they founded the University of Deseret, now the University of Utah. Three blocks south of the state capitol here is Temple Square, with the Mormon Temple and Tabernacle. In the next block is the headquarters of the Church of Jesus Christ of Latter-day Saints. This is a beautiful city: ten-acre blocks, tree-lined streets 132 feet wide, with mountains to the east and west. Seventeen miles to the west is the Great Salt Lake, ninety miles long and forty miles wide, and nearly twice as salty as the ocean. Like other Mormon communities, Salt Lake City was laid out in a grid pattern with the temple at the center; the address "7th East" is seven blocks east of the temple,

Salt Lake City is built around Temple Square. To the right is the Temple, where sacred Mormon rites are performed. The domed building to the left of it is the Tabernacle, home of the famous Mormon Tabernacle Choir. On the far left is the spire of the beautiful Assembly Hall.

"This is the place," said Mormon leader Brigham Young when he entered what now is Emigration Canyon and first saw the land that would become Salt Lake City. The monument pictured here is in Pioneer Trail State Park, which contains a restored pioneer village and other historic buildings.

for example, and is usually written "700 East."

Temple Square. There are a number of points of interest here in the heart of the city. *Visitor Center* (South Temple and North Temple streets; 801/240-2534) has exhibits, information, and gives tours of the square daily. The *Tabernacle* has an elongated, self-supporting dome and an organ with 11,623 pipes. The acoustics of the 1867 building complement the organ beautifully. Organ recitals are given daily. Visitors may hear the Mormon Tabernacle Choir in rehearsal Thursday evenings. The *Temple* (closed to non-Mormons) is an imposing 1893 granite building with six spires, used for the observation of such rites as baptism and marriage. The *Assembly Hall*, built in 1893, is open to tours and has special events on Friday and Saturday evenings. The *Seagull Monument* commemorates the saving of the crops from grasshoppers. The *Museum of Church History and Art* (45 North West Temple) has exhibits of church history from 1820 to the present. Art and artifacts from around the world. Open daily.

Lion House and Beehive House (67 and 63 East South Temple at State Street; 801/240-2671). Built in the mid-1850s, these were the Brigham Young family residence, his office, and the social centers for his nineteen wives and 56 children. Later the Beehive House was the first governor's mansion. Period furnishings. Tours during July and August. Open daily.

Capitol (head of State Street; 801/538-3000). A handsome, Corinthian-style edifice built in 1912 of Utah granite and Georgia marble. Exhibit hall with art. Gold Room decorated with Utah gold and bird's-eye marble. Open daily.

Council Hall (Old City Hall, Capitol Hill; 801/538-3000). Built in the 1860s and reconstructed at its present location in 1963, this was the meeting place of the territorial legislature and later the city hall. It now houses the *Visitor Information Center* of the Utah Travel Council. Open weekdays.

Governor's Mansion (603 East South Temple; 801/538-1005). Originally this was the 1902 mansion of Thomas Kearns, a wealthy U.S. senator in the early 1900s.

Open Tuesdays and Thursdays, mid-May through December.

Pioneer Memorial Museum (300 North Main St. near the capitol; 801/538-1050). Pioneer artifacts and manuscripts. Nearby is the *Carriage House,* with Brigham Young's wagon, transportation exhibits, and Pony Express items. Both are open daily, June through August; daily except Sundays the rest of the year.

ZCMI (Main and South Temple streets; 801/321-6000). Brigham Young established ZCMI (Zion's Cooperative Mercantile Institution) in 1868, and it was the first department store in the country.

Marriott Library (University of Utah; 2½ miles east at the head of South 2nd St.; 801/581-8558) has an important collection of Western Americana. Open daily except Sundays.

Pioneer Trail State Park (2601 Sunnyside Ave.; 801/584-8391). Mormon pioneers first entered the valley here at the mouth of Emigration Canyon. The restored living-history *Old Deseret Pioneer Village* displays life in the valley from 1847 to 1869 and includes Brigham Young's Forest Farm Home and the Mary Fielding Smith Home. Nearby is the *"This Is the Place" Monument,* on the spot where Young spoke these words when he first saw the valley. The Visitor Center is open daily. The village is open daily, May through September.

Pioneer Village (Lagoon Amusement Park, 17 miles north on I-15; 801/451-0101). A re-creation of a 19th-century town with forty-one buildings. Steam train and stagecoach rides. Village and amusement park are open daily, Memorial Day through August; weekends mid-April to late May and in September.

Fort Douglas Military Museum (3 miles northeast, Bldg. 32, Potter St.; 801/521-4154). The museum traces the military in Utah from the arrival of Johnston's army during the "Utah War" in 1857 to Vietnam. Open Tuesday through Saturday.

Bingham Canyon Mine (25 miles southwest on UT 48; 801/322-8270). An open-pit mine two and a half miles wide and a half-mile deep. Now owned by Kennecott, the mine has been operating since 1906. Visitor Center. Open daily) April, through mid-October.

Accommodations: *The Spruces Bed & Breakfast* (6151 South 900 East; 801/268-8762). Built about 1903 for a cabinetmaker and his family, this Victorian Gothic is set among tall spruces and decorated with folk art. A quarter-horse breeding farm is next door. Seven guest rooms.

VERNAL

Daughters of Utah Pioneers Museum (5th West and 2nd South streets; 801/789-0288). Regional artifacts, a miniature frontier village, and a restored 1887 tithing house with period furniture. Open daily except Sundays, June through August.

Thorne's Photo Studio (18 West Main St.; 801/789-0392). A museum with regional artifacts, including weapons and a 1,500-year-old mummy. Open weekdays except Wednesdays.

Bullionville (23 miles north on UT 191 to Red Cloud Loop Rd., west 3 miles to the East Park Reservoir Rd., north 1½ miles to Kane Hollow Rd., then nearly 2 miles to a faint set of tracks leading north, then a quarter-mile or so to the ghost town). Gold was discovered here in 1800, and copper ten years later at the 10,000-foot level in the Uinta Mountains. More than $3 million in ore had been mined when the major vein played out in 1901.

Ignatio (24 miles east on UT 40, then 23 miles south on UT 45 to Bonanza; Ignatio is 3 miles south of Bonanza). This was the river crossing for shipping Gilsonite to Vernal from the mining towns of Rainbow, Dragon, and Watson. The old toll bridge and several miners' cabins remain.

14

Nevada

AUSTIN

Formerly one of the most important towns of central and eastern Nevada mining, with eleven ore-reduction mills and a population of 4,000, Austin now has a population of 300, although the residents deny it is a ghost town. Many of its old buildings have fallen down or are in disrepair. The town is a relic of the glory days of mining.

Lander County Courthouse. This is the oldest courthouse in the state and one of the plainest.

Reese River Reveille. This newspaper has been published continuously since May 16, 1863, now edited out of Tonopah. Complete files of the paper are kept in the courthouse vault.

Hickison Petroglyph Recreation Site (24 miles east on U.S. 50; 702/635-5181). Indian drawings carved in stone, circa 1000 B.C.–A.D. 1500. The site is near a former Pony Express trail. Open daily.

CALIENTE

Delamar (16 miles west on U.S. 93, then 13 miles south). A ghost town complete with cemetery, standing desolate in the desert.

CARSON CITY

This was Eagle Ranch until it was renamed for Kit Carson. In the late 19th century it was notorious in the silver stampede. In 1897, Bob Fitzsimmons knocked out "Gentleman Jim" Corbett here for the world heavyweight boxing title.

State Library Building (401 North Carson St.). Files of Nevada newspapers and books about the state. Open weekdays.

Nevada State Museum (North Carson and Robinson streets; 702/885-4810). A former U.S. Mint, this museum has exhibits of guns, coins, minerals, and pioneer artifacts, and life-size displays of a ghost town and an Indian camp. A 300-foot mine tunnel with displays runs beneath the building. Open daily.

Warren Engine Company No. 1 Fire Museum (111 North Curry St.; 702/887-2200). The museum has old photographs, vintage firefighting equipment, an 1863 Hunneman hand-pumper, an 1847 four-wheel fire cart, and the Currier and Ives series "The Life of a Fireman." Open daily.

Nevada State Railroad Museum (South Carson St. at Fairview Dr.; 702/885-5168). Twenty-two freight and passenger cars and two steam locomotives, once the property of the Virginia & Truckee Railroad, are on display. Weekend steam train and motorcar rides. Open Friday through Sunday, June through October.

Bowers Mansion (10 miles north in Washoe Valley; 702/849-0201). Sandy Bowers, a Missouri muleskinner, described by his friends as "an honest, kindhearted soul and miraculously ignorant," had a claim on a ten-foot strip of mining property, and the owner of the boardinghouse where he lived, Elley Orrum, owned the claim next to his. The bonanza came, and they found their claims were netting $18,000 a month. They married, and soon their claims were paying $100,000 a month. They built

this $200,000 granite mansion and went to Europe on a buying spree to furnish it: custom-made furniture, specially designed and woven carpets, silver sets, morocco-bound books. Back home, the new society leaders chose to snub the Bowerses. The good times didn't last long. The mine was becoming exhausted; new machinery was needed. Soon after it was installed, the mine was flooded. Sandy died. His widow, now penniless, became the "Washoe Seeress," telling fortunes for a living. There are half-hour guided tours of the sixteen rooms, many with original furnishings. Open daily, Memorial Day to Labor Day, weekends in September and October. Limited wheelchair access.

Accommodations: *Winters Creek Ranch* (1201 U.S. 395 North; 702/849-1020). A bed-and-breakfast in a New England Colonial with Victorian furnishings. Four guest rooms. Deer, wild turkeys, and eagles are often seen on the property. Hors d'oeuvres and wine are served in the evening. *The Edwards House* (204 North Minnesota St.; 702/882-4884). An 1877 Victorian in the heart of the historic district. Three guest rooms. Breakfast is included in the rates.

ELKO

Northeastern Nevada Museum (1515 Idaho St.; 702/738-3418). Three galleries with Indian and nature exhibits, art, and theater-in-the-round. Displays of an 1860 Pony Express cabin and vintage vehicles are on the grounds. Open daily.

ELY

Ely (pronounced *eely*) started as a silver-mining camp, and silver and gold are still mined here, but its true growth began in 1907 with the discovery of copper. The mountains around here attract hunters and fishermen.

Nevada Northern Railroad Museum (11th St. East and Ave. A; 702/289-2085). The museum is in the 1906 Nevada Northern Railway Depot, furnished as it was in the old days. The railway was built by Nevada Consolidated Copper and operated later by Kennecott Copper until 1963. Nothing was

Stokes Castle was a landmark in Austin, the mother town in the eastern Nevada mining area. By 1867, 6,000 claims had been filed in Austin, although it was eclipsed by Virginia City. Austin has deteriorated badly, but its 300 residents deny that it is a ghost town.

Unchanged from the day it opened in 1906, this depot houses the Nevada Northern Railway Museum in Ely, which commemorates a short line that served nearby copper mines until 1983. A treat for visitors is touring the area in a 1910 steam passenger train.

Ladies of the Evening

Prostitution was an integral part of the Old West, a necessity, perhaps, in a land of lonely men. Some 65,000 men came to California in the Gold Rush, but only 2,500 women. Seattle was founded as a logging camp, and was short of women for years. The Kansas cow towns Dodge City and Abilene were heavily male.

A double standard applied to prostitution: wrong for white women, acceptable for women of other races. In Santa Fe, the easy virtue of the Hispanic girls was legendary. Indian and black women were fair game. Many San Francisco prostitutes were Chinese, forced into the profession by the Mafia-like crime organizations known as tongs.

Prostitution had four levels: the streetwalker was the lowest; a step up were saloon girls; next were the "cribs," in larger cities often filled with more than a hundred women of all colors and origins; the elite were the women in "parlor houses," which catered to an exclusive, well-heeled clientele.

The parlor houses, often referred to as "girls' boardinghouses," were found only in cities and rich mining towns. But every town had a saloon and saloon girls, and most medium-sized towns had at least one embarrassingly well-known crib. Towns with army posts had their "hog farms."

Prostitution was much more visible in the West. Denver once passed an ordinance requiring that prostitutes wear yellow ribbons on their arms. When madams had their girls wear yellow everything, from shoes to bonnets, the ordinance was repealed. A Seattle writer noted that Eastern vice was "silent, muffle-footed, velvet-gloved, and masqued-faced," while Western vice went about "openly, unclad, unpolished, and open-handed."

The law tolerated red-light districts and tenderloins. San Francisco had its Barbary Coast, Portland its Skidroad, Denver its Market Street. Many smaller towns made sin pay. Ellsworth, Kansas, for example, paid for all its municipal expenses from taxes collected on saloons, gambling houses, and prostitution.

Most prostitutes were in debt to somebody, either to the madam who boarded and clothed them or to the vice lord who owned the madam. Many took their own lives to end their hardship; disease and violence killed others; and many died in poorhouses. A few were able to settle down and raise families.

Some became famous. Mammy Pleasant and Madame Atoy of San Francisco; Julia Bulette, "Queen of the Comstock"; Mattie Silks and Jennie Rogers of Denver; and Cattle Kate of Wyoming. Calamity Jane was probably a prostitute for a while in a "hog farm" near Fort Laramie. All have a host of stories associated with them, some of them probably true.

ever replaced on the Nevada Northern, which makes it one of the best preserved short-line railroads in the country. Rides to old mining towns are conducted on an original steam passenger train with wooden coaches. Open daily.

White Pine Public Museum (200 Aultman St.; 702/289-4710). Vintage railroad steam engines and coaches, and artifacts of the early days in Ely. Open daily.

Ward Charcoal Ovens State Historic Monument (5 miles southeast on U.S. 6, then 11 miles west on an unnumbered gravel road). During the 1870 mining boom, charcoal was made in these six beehive ovens. Open daily.

GARDNERVILLE

Mormon Station State Historic Monument (4 miles north via U.S. 395, then 4 miles west on NV 57 in Genoa). In the fort stockade is a museum displaying relics of the first white settlement in Nevada. Open daily, mid-May to mid-October.

Accommodations: *Sierra Spirit Ranch* (3000 Pinenut Rd.; 702/782-7011). A bed-and-breakfast in a ranch house on thirty-six acres of green fields, sage, and piñon and juniper trees, with a creek flowing into a pond. Pond swimming. Hot tub. Several guest rooms in the house and fully equipped studio cabins. *The Reid Mansion* (1431 Ezell St.; 702/782-7644). The 1910 home of a prominent local banker. Breakfast is included in the rates.

HAWTHORNE

Miners once flocked to the beautiful mountains near this desert town, now a good starting point for exploring the area southeast of Reno.

Aurora (about 35 miles southwest, then take NV 359 and turn off on an unpaved road about 25 miles from Hawthorne). In 1864, a booming mining camp of 10,000 people, now completely abandoned. Mark Twain is supposed to have mined for gold here.

Rawhide (about 42 miles northeast near NV 359; inquire locally about the best road to take). Some 4,000 people arrived here in three months after the 1908 discovery of gold, but the boom was short-lived, and only ruins remain.

HENDERSON

Midway between Las Vegas and Boulder City, Henderson was created during World War II to house workers at a magnesium plant, and is now the fastest-growing city in the state.

Clark County Heritage Museum (1830 South Boulder Hwy.; 702/455-7955). An exhibit center houses artifacts of mining days in the county, and a farming display. "Time Line Railroad" on the grounds. Open daily.

Searchlight (7 miles southeast on U.S. 93/95, then 36 miles south on U.S. 95). A few people still live in this old mining town where burros roam the streets.

LAS VEGAS

In the beginning, this area was a camping place for wagon trains following the Old Spanish Trail from Santa Fe to Mexico. In 1855, Brigham Young sent thirty settlers to build a fort and stockade here. The Mormons left two years later. They had tried mining, but found the ore hard to smelt and the metal unsuitable for bullets. Later the galena ore was found to contain silver. It was a ranch from 1862 to 1899. The coming of the railroad in 1905 created a tent town, then streets were laid out and permanent buildings constructed. Las Vegas slumbered until after World War II, when gambling turned it into a booming entertainment center, glitter-

"Beautiful as the country is, the silence and desolation reigning over it excite irrepressible emotions of sadness and melancholy."

—EDWIN BRYANT, *Journal of a Tour by the Emigrant Route and South Pass, Across the Continent of North America, the Great Desert Basin, and Through California*

Boot Hill Epitaphs

He called
Bill Smith
a liar

—Cripple Creek, Colorado

Here lies Butch
We planted him raw
He was quick on the trigger
But slow on the draw

—Silver City, Nevada

Here lies
Johnny Yeast
Pardon me
For not rising

—Ruidoso, New Mexico

"I love the land
and the buffalo
and will not part
with it."

—SATANTA, KIOWA

ing with plush hotels, casinos, nightclubs, and recreational facilities.

Nevada State Museum and Historical Society (700 Twin Lakes, in Lorenzi Park; 702/486-5205). Exhibits showing the growth of the area from the Spanish explorers to the present. Open daily.

Ripley's Believe It or Not (Four Queens Hotel, 202 East Fremont at Casino Center Blvd.; 702/385-4011). Nine theme rooms display more than a thousand artifacts collected by Robert Ripley, relating to quirky phenomena, both natural and man-made. Fifty-four wax figures. Open daily.

Imperial Palace Auto Collection (on fifth-floor parking area of the Imperial Palace Hotel, 3535 Las Vegas Blvd. South; 702/731-3 311). More than 200 antique and classic automobiles are on display, including ones belonging to Hitler, Eleanor Roosevelt, the King of Siam, and Howard Hughes. Open daily.

Bonnie Springs Old Nevada (20 miles west via West Charleston Blvd.; 702/875-4191). A gussied-up old mining town with museums, shops, a theater, riding stables, a petting zoo, restaurants, and a narrow-gauge railroad. Open daily.

Ghost towns: The town of *Goodsprings* (30 miles southwest via I-15, then west 7 miles on the Jean-Goodsprings turnoff) still has a few inhabitants, and there are other ghost towns in the Sandy Valley area, 11 miles west of here. *Rhyolite* (112 miles northwest on U.S. 95 to Beatty, then 4 miles southwest on NV 58, then follow signs), at the height of the boom in 1907, had a population of 6,000; by 1920, one. Some intrepid settlers have moved in, and the town may have a new life. *Johnnie Mine* (67 miles northwest on U.S. 95, then 11 miles south on

NV 16, then 3 miles east). *Leadfield* (2 miles off the Rhyolite turnoff, then 15 miles west, watch for signs). *Chloride Cliff* (3 miles past the Leadfield turnoff, then 14 miles south). *Carrara* (104 miles northwest on U.S. 95, just off the highway). *Lida* (162 miles northwest on U.S. 95, then 19 miles southwest on NV 3).

LOVELOCK

Prospectors stopped in the valley here to rest their animals and repair their wagons before the thirty-six-hour dash across forty miles of desert to Hot Springs. The area later had its own mining boom, as evidenced by its nearby ghost towns, *Seven Troughs* (northwest on NV 399) and *Rochester* (25 miles northeast on I-80 to Oreana, then east on an unnumbered road).

OVERTON

More than 1,200 years ago, this was the site of an ancient Indian civilization that extended along the Muddy River for thirty miles. Overton started its present life as a Mormon settlement.

Lost City Museum of Archaeology (1 mile south on NV 169; 702/397-2160). This museum, part of the Nevada State Museum, is on a restored part of the Pueblo Grande de Nevada. It has extensive collections of prehistoric Indian artifacts, fossils, and semiprecious stones. Open daily.

PYRAMID LAKE

Pyramid Lake Indian Reservation (36 miles north of Reno on NV 33; 702/574-8140). Pyramid Lake, now thirty miles long and seven to nine miles wide, is a remnant of Lake Lahontan, which, in a prehistoric era, covered 8,400 square miles in what is now western Nevada and northwestern California. John C. Frémont named the lake for its pyramid-shaped islands when he visited the Paiute Indians here in 1844. According to Paiute tradition, one island, 475 feet high, is a basket inverted over an erring woman. Though turned to stone, her "breath"— wisps of steam from a hot spring—can be seen. Another island is called Stone Mother and Basket. This is the homeland of the Paiute and has been a reservation since 1874. Excavations at nearby Astor Pass uncovered a horse skull and fragmentary remains of an elephant, a bison, and a camel, all believed to have lived by the lake in prehistoric times. The lake abounds in cutthroat trout and the rare cui-ui, still a part of the Paiute diet. Some Paiute women continue to make their magnificent traditional baby cradles, woven baskets with a finely decorated leather covering.

RENO

First known as Lake's Crossing, Reno, an overland campsite before the California Gold Rush, grew rapidly after the discovery of the Comstock Lode, becoming a city in 1868. Known as "the Biggest Little City in the World," Reno was synonymous with divorce until other states reformed their divorce laws. It is between the steep slopes of the Sierra and the low hills to the east. The bright lights of the casinos and nightclubs are in contrast with the city's commercial importance.

Nevada Historical Society Museum (1650 North Virginia St.; 702/789-0190). The museum has collections of prehistoric and present-day Indian artifacts, ranching, mining, and gambling paraphernalia, and material from the Carson City Mint. Open Tuesday through Saturday.

William F. Harrah Foundation National Automobile Museum (downtown at 10 South Lake St.; 702/355-3500). Hundreds

Behind Them Swinging Doors

As America moved west, drinking became common and saloons with it. The saloon was the center of the hearty, male-dominated frontier society. A visitor from Britain, Frederick Marryat, observed that in the West, "Americans can fix nothing without a drink. If you meet, you drink; if you part, you drink; if you make acquaintance, you drink; if you close a bargain, you drink; they quarrel in their drink, and they make it up with a drink. They drink because it is hot; they drink because it is cold. If successful in elections they drink and rejoice; if not they drink and swear. . . ."

Western saloons were often ugly and violent; Wild Bill Hickok and John Wesley Hardin were both shot dead in saloons. The saloon was an informal men's club, with steady drinking through the week and heavy drinking on Saturday and Sunday. Aside from drinking and the ubiquitous free-lunch counter, men gambled and made sexual liaisons with dance-hall girls and prostitutes.

They also were everywhere. In San Francisco in 1890, there were 3,117 licensed drinking places, one for every ninety-six inhabitants, and some 2,000 "blind tigers," as illegal saloons were called. Many were dangerous, and some were degenerate; the Boar 's Head was named for its special attraction: sexual activity between a woman and a boar. A typical saloon offered a long bar, bare tables, and sawdust on the floor. Whiskey was one bit (12½ cents), beer ten cents.

Things went too far in the Red Hot Bar in Richmond, Texas, one night in 1889. Some patrons savagely beat David Nation, sending his irate wife, Carry, on a hatchet-wielding, bar-smashing crusade, the start of the prohibition movement that eventually would end the old-time saloon.

The Luck of the Draw

Most Western towns big enough to have a name had a place to gamble. Gambling fever began in New Orleans early in the 19th century, spread up the Mississippi on steamboats, then infected the West. Many Mississippi gamblers went to California during the Gold Rush to ply their trade, and San Francisco soon had a number of gaming houses. The games of chance were poker (usually five-card draw with no wild cards), twenty-one (blackjack), faro (a nearly forgotten game in which the players bet against the dealer on the order in which certain cards will show up), and roulette.

Two notable gamblers in San Francisco were William C. Ralston, a leading banker, and U.S. Senator William Sharon, who was said to have won more than a million dollars at the Pacific Club over fifteen years. In Kansas City, gamblers led by Albert Showers and Bob Potee steadily fleeced cattle barons and free-spending cowboys. Doc Holliday and John Dougherty made gambling reputations in Tombstone, Arizona. In Deadwood, South Dakota, Wild Bill Hickok was killed while playing poker. In 1885, Denver had more than 200 gaming houses, and the city's king of chance, Ed Chase, left a $650,000 estate when he died in 1879.

of beautifully restored vehicles are on display. Theater presentation. Open daily.

Sierra Nevada Museum of Art (549 Court St. [Hawkins House] and 160 West Liberty St. [E. L. Wiegland Museum] 702/329-3333). Western art is well represented in the museum's two locations. Open daily except Mondays.

TONOPAH

"Big Jim" Butler, a rancher who spent his spare time prospecting, stopped for the night in the desert at an old Indian camp called Tonopah—the Shoshone name for a small desert shrub. In the night, one of his burros strayed, and Butler found it under a ledge on Mount Oddie. He took some ore samples and gave them to a young lawyer friend, saying, "I'm broke. Get this assayed and I'll give you a quarter of my claims." The lawyer was also broke, and traded away half of his quarter-claim for an eight-dollar assay. The analysis showed a potential yield of 640 ounces of silver, and $206 in gold per ton of ore! Butler started a number of mines, leasing them for a quarter of the gross. A town quickly sprang up, and Wyatt Earp served for a time as marshal. By 1906 the mines were producing $10 million annually. In the mid-1920s the mines petered out. In 1969, Howard Hughes bought up more than a hundred of the original mines, but nothing came of it. Tonopah now has a population of some 2,000.

Mizpah Hotel (100 Main St.; 702/482-6262). A 1907 hotel named after one of Butler's mines, restored to its original condition.

Goldfield (25 miles southeast on U.S. 95). Like Tonopah, Goldfield is a semi–ghost town with an interesting history. Two young miners, Billy Marsh and Harry Stimler, heard in Tonopah that an Indian had found some gold at Columbia Mountain, thirty miles to the south. They got a grub-stake and headed there on a buckboard drawn by a mule and a horse. They struck gold on the mountain, and by the spring of 1903 a tent camp had sprung up, first named Grandpa in hopes that it would prove to be the grandpa of all the mining camps. The strikes kept getting richer, and by 1904 it was a community of 8,000. A railroad linking Goldfield to Tonopah was built in 1905. To spur the growth of the town, saloon owner "Tex" Rickard promoted the Joe Gans–Battling Nelson lightweight championship fight with a $30,000 purse, displayed in $20 gold pieces in the window of the local bank. Rickard had found his calling and went on to be one of the greatest fight promoters of all time, the principal architect of the career of Jack Dempsey. The peak year here was 1910, with a mine production of $11 million in bullion. Then Goldfield went into decline, plagued by flash floods. The big mines shut down in 1919. A few people still live here.

VIRGINIA CITY

Silver had been discovered here in 1850, but the prospectors were bound for California and gold. It wasn't until 1859 that Peter O'Riley and Pat McLaughlin struck a rich vein on Mount Davidson. Then along came a fast-talking con man named Henry Comstock. After accusing O'Riley and McLaughlin of claim-jumping, Comstock allowed himself to become a partner in return for forgetting about his bogus claim. He later cajoled and blustered his way into a piece of so many claims in the area that it became known as the Comstock Lode. James Finney, known as Old Virginny, and his partners struck a rich deposit at what was to become Gold Hill. Finney is credited with naming the town after his native state.

The early winners ended up losers. Comstock sold out for $11,000 and later committed suicide. Peter O'Riley sold out and ended up in an insane asylum. Pat

McLaughlin was buried in a pauper's grave. Finney sold his share for a bottle of whiskey and a blind horse. The big winner was George Hearst. The Hearst family fortune, expanded by his son William Randolph Hearst, had its beginnings here at the Ophir Mine. Four men—James Fair, James Flood, John Mackay, and William S. O'Brien—secretly bought up stock in the area of their holdings at distress prices before announcing their bonanza. This netted them an estimated $160 million.

Other fortunes were made in Virginia City. William Sharon loaned money to miners and mill owners, taking over their property when a recession came. Adolph Sutro parlayed his scheme of building tunnels to drain and ventilate the mines into millions. Others became rich backing the Virginia & Truckee Railroad. Virginia City was the richest city of its size in the world, and it lived up to its reputation. In the 1870s, Virginia City had a population of 30,000, and boasted four banks, six churches, 110 saloons, an opera house, numerous theaters, and the only elevator between Chicago and San Francisco. Mark Twain was a newspaper reporter here. The mountain of silver ran

Miners once met at the union hall on this now-deserted street in Virginia City, Nevada. The air is so clear here that visitors can see the mountains rising 175 miles away behind the green fields and cottonwoods along the Carson River and the Forty Mile Desert.

the guests. Several guest rooms with baths. Garden patio. Breakfast is included in the rates.

WINNEMUCCA

A Frenchman set up a trading post here in 1850, and the town grew up around it to be one of the largest mining and agricultural communities in the area. A number of Basques live in the area.

Humboldt Museum (Jungo Road and Maple Avenue; 702/623-2912). Indian artifacts, pioneer home items, antique automo-

Built in the late 1870s, Piper's Opera House in Virginia City was the social center of the Comstock and a construction marvel, with a sloping stage and spring-supported dance floor. The performers here included Maude Adams, Edwin Booth, Lillie Langtree, and Buffalo Bill.

Before the Comstock Lode was exhausted, Virginia City was one of the richest cities in the country, with four banks, six churches, an opera house and many theaters, the only elevator between Chicago and San Francisco, and 110 saloons.

out eventually, but what a run they had! The best estimates say that from 1859 to the end of the century, the Comstock Lode yielded a billion dollars in silver and gold.

Today some of the old mansions have been restored and can be toured (open Easter week, then daily from Memorial Day through October). A few old saloons are open. There is gambling, and interesting shops and galleries. Visitors can ride on the old Virginia & Truckee Railroad. There are a number of undistinguished restaurants. The *Visitors Bureau* (South C Street; 702/847-0177) shows an eighteen-minute film, "The Story of Virginia City," and has information on tours to mines and other points of interest.

Accommodations: *Edith Palmer's Country Inn* (416 South B St.; 702/847-0707). Built in 1862 by a wine merchant, the inn's wine center is a popular place for parties. Guest rooms. Breakfast is included in the rates. *Chollar Mansion* (565 South D St.; 702/847-9777). Built in 1861, this was the office of a mine superintendent, and there is a large vault that once held gold and silver and now holds wine and cheese parties for

Only the adobe walls of the original buildings still stand at Fort Churchill State Park in Nevada. The fort was built during the rush to the Comstock in Virginia City to protect against Paiute raids. Near the fort were Pony Express and Overland Stage stations.

biles, and local history memorabilia. Old country store. Open daily except Sundays.

YERINGTON

The original name of the community was Jack Wilson. But some called it Pizen Smith because the whiskey sold here was so bad, and the Paiute called it Wovoka because their messiah grew up in the area. In 1889, Wovoka said he had a vision in which he was instructed to teach a new dance that would force out the white intruders and restore the land to the Indians. The Ghost Dance cult spread, and an Indian uprising appeared imminent. Federal troops moved in 1890 to control the Sioux. Contrary to Wovoka's prophecy, the "ghost shirts" failed to protect the wearers during the massacre at Wounded Knee, and the Ghost Dance cult died out.

Fort Churchill Historic State Monu-

ment (25 miles north on U.S. 95A, then 1 mile west on NV 28; 702/463-3721). When the rush to Virginia City began, this post was established to protect prospectors from the Paiutes, who were avenging white brutalities. It was active from 1860 to 1869. A Pony Express station was nearby, and the Overland Stage came through here. Today only adobe walls remain. The Visitor Center has displays on the fort's history. Open daily.

Lyon County Museum (215 South Main; 702/463-3341, ext. 255). Exhibits depicting early life in the Mason Valley. The museum complex includes a general store, a blacksmith shop, and a schoolhouse. Open weekends.

Accommodations: *Robric Ranch* (5 miles west of town; 702/463-2998 or 463-3515). A house brought over the mountains from the old mining town of Aurora and put on a 160-acre alfalfa farm. Breakfast is included in the rates.

Francisco Vásquez de Coronado explored the Southwest looking for gold in 1450, Father Eusebio began building missions in 1692, and settlers came a few years later. By the time it became part of the United States at the end of the Mexican War, the Southwest was a blend of Hispanic and Indian cultures, a tradition that continues today. Prospectors found the gold and silver that had eluded Coronado, but the area was bedeviled by the Apache until the end of the 19th century.

Acoma Pueblo, New Mexico.

PART VI

THE SOUTH WEST

15

New Mexico

ALBUQUERQUE

Seeking better pastureland, the Spanish governor of New Mexico, Don Francisco Cuervo y Valdes, in 1706 moved thirty families to a spot some fifteen miles south of here on the Rio Grande, naming the settlement for the Duke of Albuquerque, then Viceroy of New Spain. The settlement prospered, and by 1790 it was the largest in New Mexico, with a population of some 6,000. From 1846 to 1870, Albuquerque was an important military post. When the Santa Fe Railroad came, there were problems purchasing land, so the railroad chose a route several miles to the east. A new town grew up on the railroad, New Albuquerque, that soon subsumed Old Albuquerque.

Old Town (1 block north of Central Ave.). This area, all that is left of Old Albuquerque, retains its Spanish flavor. Shops and restaurants.

Albuquerque Museum (200 Mountain Rd. Northwest; 505/243-7255). A regional museum of history, art, and science. Open daily except Mondays.

Maxwell Museum of Anthropology (University of New Mexico, Rome Ave. NE and University; 505/277-4402). Artifacts of Southwestern Indian cultures. Open daily except Sundays.

Indian Pueblo Cultural Center (2401 12th St. Northwest; 505/843-7270). The center, owned and operated by the nineteen Indian pueblos of New Mexico, tells the story of the Pueblo Indians and their crafts and arts. A restaurant serves traditional pueblo fare. Gift shop. Open daily, mid-May to mid-October; daily except Sundays the rest of the year. Limited wheelchair access.

Telephone Pioneer Museum (1209 Mountain Rd. Place NE; 505/256-2105). Displays that trace the telephone in the Southwest from 1876 to the present. Early equipment, directories. Open Tuesday through Friday.

National Atomic Museum (Kirtland Air Force Base, 2½ miles south of I-40 on Wyoming Blvd.; 505/844-8443). Nuclear weapons and artifacts. Science center. Film on the birth of the Atomic Age. Tours. Open daily.

Indian Petroglyph State Park (9 miles west on Unser Blvd. in West Mesa area). Petroglyphs carved on lava formations between A.D. 1100 and 1600 by ancestors of the Pueblo Indians. Open Tuesday to Saturday.

Coronado State Monument (15 miles north on I-25, then 2 miles west on NM 44; 505/867-5351). Coronado, accompanied by 1,200 soldiers and Indian allies, arrived at the Rio Grande near present-day Albuquerque in 1540, eighteen months after leaving Mexico. He sought the fabled Cities of Gold, but found adobe pueblos. He wintered in the valley while members of the expedition traveled east, returning in the spring with shattered dreams. Coronado went back to Mexico in 1542. One of the villages where some of the Spaniards stayed was Kuaua, which means "evergreen" in the Tiwa Language. Founded about 1300, the pueblo had a population of several hundred people, but by the early 1600s it was abandoned. The site of Kuaua is now the Coronado State Monument, considered "the Plymouth Rock of the West." The village has been partially reconstructed, and an interpretive trail winds through the site. The Visitor Center has exhibits telling the story of early settlement in the Rio Grande Valley and of European exploration and colonization. Open daily.

Turquoise Trail. A back route between Albuquerque and Santa Fe through spectacular scenery and three ghost towns. The 150-mile trip takes a full day. Drive east out of Albuquerque on I-40 about 17 miles to NM 14, turn north and go six miles to NM 44, then go west through the Cibola National Forest. Eight miles beyond the forest, follow the Sandia Crest sign, turning left about six miles, and drive to the top of Sandia Mountain (road open from April through November). Then return to NM 14 and go north to *Golden*, the first of the ghost towns. Continue north on NM 14 to *Madrid*. The *Coal Mine Museum*, in an old company building, has vintage equipment and a restored steam locomotive. The opera house presents melodramas on summer evenings. Madrid is now a community of artists, craftsmen, writers, and filmmakers. Turn north on NM 14 again and take the turnoff to *Cerrillos*, a booming mining camp in the 1880s, now a tree-shaded village. Return to NM 14 and exit at I-25N to go to Santa Fe, I-25S to return to Albuquerque.

Accommodations: *Casita Chamisa* (850 Chamisa Rd. Northwest; 505/897-4644). An 1850 adobe home with three guest rooms, owned by an archaeologist. Pool. Breakfast is included in the rates. *W. E. Mauger Estate* (701 Roma Ave. Northwest; 505/242-8755). A restored Victorian boardinghouse, now on the National Register of Historic Places, with six guest rooms. Tours of pueblos and petroglyphs. Breakfast is included in the rates.

AZTEC

Aztec Ruins National Monument (northeast of town, near the junction of U.S. 550 and NM 44; 505/334-6174). The first Anasazi to settle here came from Chaco, sixty-five miles to the south, a large pueblo community that flourished from A.D. 1050 to 1150. A forty-foot-wide "highway" once connected this community with Chaco Canyon. The first Anasazi built the original pueblo and lived in it for some 500 years before moving away. A few decades later, other Anasazi came and settled here. These later arrivals were culturally similar to the cliff-dwellers of Mesa Verde, forty miles to

the northwest. They remodeled the old pueblo and built others nearby. They, too, stayed 500 years, then left. The first white man to see the ruins was probably the geologist John S. Newberry, in 1859. Then pot hunters and looters descended. When Lewis H. Morgan, an anthropologist, came in 1878, he estimated that a quarter of the pueblo's stones had been carted away by nearby settlers for building material. A few years later some boys broke through a wall and found a room with burials and a trove of baskets, beads, ornaments, and other artifacts. In 1916, the archaeologist Earl H. Morris came and spent five years working here. He supervised the reconstruction of the Great Kiva, which now stands virtually as it did 600 years ago. It is the only restored great kiva in the Southwest.

Aztec is misnamed. Like Montezuma Castle in Arizona, it has no connection with the Aztecs, who flourished much later in central Mexico.

The Visitor Center displays Anasazi artifacts. A trail from the center leads to the main ruins. *West Ruin* once had from 350 to 400 rooms and stood three stories high. *Hubbard Site* is one of a few tri-wall structures in the Southwest. The inner space was a kiva, built on the site of an earlier kiva. Open daily. Limited wheelchair access.

BLOOMFIELD

Chaco Culture National Historic Park (36 miles south on NM 44 to Blanco, right on Rte. 57, then 20 miles to the park; 505/988-6727). This valley was a major center of Anasazi life a thousand years ago. They farmed the lowlands and built masonry towns, linking them together with a network of roads. They began to flower culturally in the early 900s, reaching heights never surpassed in the Four Corners region. They used the same building technique as their forebears—walls one stone thick, held

Pueblo Bonito in New Mexico's Chaco Canyon National Monument is a look into America's pre-Hispanic past. Anthropologists puzzle over the great Anasazi civilization that flourished and fell here, leaving spectacular ruins of multistoried buildings.

together with mud mortar—but they built much larger, multistory villages. Six large pueblos were constructed first—Pueblo Bonito, Chetro Ketl, Una Vida, Penasco Blanco, Hungo Pavi, and Kin Bineola—and eventually there were seventy-five such pueblos, most of them linked by more than 400 miles of roads. The longest ran forty-two miles north toward the towns now known as Salmon Ruins and Aztec Ruins. Between A.D. 1130 and 1180, a prolonged drought sent Chaco into decline. Even the irrigation methods used by the Chacoans were to no avail, and the people began to move to better watered regions.

Today seven sites are easily accessible to visitors. *Una Vida*, only partially excavated, looks much as it did when it was discovered in 1849. There are five kivas and some 150 rooms in the structure. Anasazi petroglyphs are on a canyon wall near the site. *Pueblo Bonito* is the largest and best known of the great houses and the core of this Anasazi complex. In its final form, Pueblo Bonito contained some 600 rooms and forty kivas

and rose four stories high. It is considered the "type" site for the Classic Bonito Phase. *Chetro Ketl*, begun about A.D. 120, completed by 1054, was remodeled and enlarged in the early 1100s. It has about 500 rooms and sixteen kivas. *Pueblo del Arroyo* has about 280 rooms and more than twenty kivas. *Kin Kietso* nearby is believed to have been built in two stages, the first in 1125, the second in 1130 or later. This pueblo had about a hundred rooms and five enclosed kivas. *Casa Rinconada* is the largest "great kiva" in the park. The great house called *Tsin Kietsin* offers a panoramic view of the area.

Hiking trails lead to other ruins: *Pueblo Alto*, on top of the mesa, at the junction of several prehistoric roads; *Casa Chiquita* and *Penasco Blanco,* which may be reached from the central canyon; and *Wijiji*, remarkable for its symmetrical layout and rooms of uniform size. Exhibits in the Visitor Center explain Chaco and its people. In the summer, rangers lead tours and give evening programs. Open daily.

The Santa Fe Trail

The Santa Fe Trail ran some 780 miles from Westport (now Kansas City), Missouri, to Santa Fe, connecting with El Camino Real, which led into central Mexico. Large caravans of freight wagons moved over the trail, carrying American manufactured goods and returning with silver, fur, and mules. It was more a beaten track over the tough Plains grass than a road, and though it had its dangers, Indians virtually never attacked a well-organized caravan. Only eight men died on the Santa Fe Trail during its first ten years of use.

CARLSBAD

Explorers Cabeza de Vaca and Antonio de Espejo passed by here as they made their way down the Pecos River in the 16th century. More than 300 years later, Carlsbad was a stop for cowboys driving herds on the Goodnight-Loving Trail.

Carlsbad Museum and Art Center (Fox St., 1 block west of Canal; 505/887-0276). Pioneer and Indian artifacts, Pueblo pottery, the McAdoo painting collection, and Jack Drake birds. Open daily except Sundays.

Presidents' Park (1 mile east via U.S. 62/180; 505/867-0276). The park offers rides on the 1880 narrow-gauge train *Abraham Lincoln* along the Pecos River and the paddlewheeler *George Washington* on Lake Carlsbad. Daily from Memorial Day to Labor Day.

Million Dollar Museum (20 miles southwest on U.S. 62/180 to White's City, then west on NM 7; 505/785-2291). A hodge-podge collection of antique European dollhouses, dolls, the first automobile west of the Pecos, and the Whittlin' Cowboys Ranch. Open daily.

CHAMA

Cumbres & Toltec Scenic Railroad (505/756-2151). An 1880s narrow-gauge steam railroad offers excursions to Osler, Colorado, on the *New Mexico Express*. Another trip goes to Antonito, Colorado; passengers stay overnight and return by van. Daily, mid-June to mid-October.

CIMARRON

This old town was a stop on the Santa Fe Trail. Among the historic buildings still standing is the 1872 jail and the St. James Hotel, where Buffalo Bill Cody organized his Wild West shows.

Old Aztec Mill Museum (NM 21 south of U.S. 64 in Old Town; 505/376-2913). An 1864 gristmill displays local artifacts including mill wheels and a chuck wagon. Open daily except Thursdays, May through September.

Philmont Scout Ranch (4 miles south on NM 21; 505/376-2281). This 138,000-acre summer camp for Boy Scouts has several thousand Indian artifacts, drawings, and paintings in the Kit Carson Museum, seven miles south of headquarters. Buffalo, deer, elk, and antelope. Open daily, mid-June to late August.

DEMING

Deming-Luna-Mimbres Museum (301 South Silver St.; 505/546-2382). Indian and Hispanic artifacts. Mimbres Indian pottery and baskets. Quilt room. Chuck wagon and equipment. Open daily.

Columbus Historical Museum (32 miles south on NM 11, in Columbus; 505/531-2217 or 531-2214). In an old Southern Pacific depot, the museum has memorabilia of the 1916 raid by Pancho Villa and of General Pershing's expedition into Mexico. Open daily.

Pancho Villa State Park (35 miles south on NM 11, near Columbus). The park commemorates Villa's raid into American territory on March 9, 1916. The park is the site of Camp Furlong, from which "Black Jack" Pershing pursued Villa into Mexico, the first American military action to employ motor vehicles and airplanes. Some original buildings. Open daily.

DULCE

Jicarilla Apache Indian Reservation (15 miles south on U.S. 64; 505/759-3442). Unrestored ruins. A museum displays arts and crafts, including basketry, buckskin tanning, leatherwork, and beadwork. Reservation open daily, museum open on weekdays.

ESPANOLA

Ghost Ranch Living Museum (22 miles northwest on U.S. 84, near Abiquiu; 505/685-4333). Operated by the U.S. Forest Service, the museum displays animals native to the area, including bears, mountain lions, and snakes. Also here is the *Florence Hawley Ellis Museum of Anthropology,* with displays and relics of Indian and Spanish history. Both open daily, May through September; daily except Mondays the rest of the year.

Galeria Plaza del Cerro (10 miles northeast via NM 76 in Chimayo; 505/351-4889). An example of an old Spanish colonial village, this gallery displays and sells work of northern New Mexico artists. Nearby is *Ortega's Weaving Shop* (505/351-4215), where generations of weavers make blankets, coats, purses, and rugs. Open daily except Sundays.

El Santuario de Chimayo (10 miles northeast via NM 76 in Chimayo; 505/351-4889). This old church, visited by pilgrims, especially at Easter, has a legend of healing powers. Open daily.

FARMINGTON

Once the home of the Anasazi, Farmington (the Navajos call it Totah) is now the largest city in the Four Corners area, a center for the Navajo, Ute, Apache, and Pueblo.

Salmon Ruins (2 miles west of Bloomfield on U.S. 64; 505/632-2013). To ease overpopulation at Chaco Canyon, fifty miles south of here, Anasazi migrants built a satellite pueblo here around A.D. 1100, linking it to Chaco Canyon by a forty-foot-wide "highway." The pueblo, a four-story structure containing some 250 rooms, abandoned about 1130, was reoccupied in about 1230 by Anasazi from Mesa Verde. Fire swept the pueblo in 1250. It was rebuilt, but was nearly destroyed by another fire twenty years later and abandoned. The ruins are named after George Salmon, who protected them from pot hunters when he and his family homesteaded nearby in the 1870s. The Visitor Center displays Anasazi artifacts. A short trail leads to the ruins.

GALLUP

Once a railroad town, Gallup now serves a large area, including the Navajo Reservation north and west of town.

"There are all kinds of beauty in the world, but for a greatness of beauty I have never experienced anything like New Mexico."

—D. H. LAWRENCE

Eagle dancers perform during the Intertribal Indian ceremonial in August at Gallup, New Mexico. More than fifty tribes from the United States, Canada, and Mexico participate in rodeos, games, and dances. Gallup is a trading center for Navajo, Zuñi, and Hopi Indians.

El Morro, a sandstone mesa in New Mexico, jutting up like the prow of a ship, was a landmark on the early trails. Beginning with Indian petroglyphs, hundreds of inscriptions have been carved on its base. The oldest Spanish one was made on a 1605 expedition.

Red Rock State Park (10 miles east via I-40 and NM 566). The park has an 8,000-seat auditorium where the Intertribal Indian Ceremonial is held. The nearby **Red Rock Museum** (505/722-6196) displays Navajo, Hopi, and Zuñi artifacts. Open daily in summer, weekdays the rest of the year.

GRANTS

In 1950 a Navajo named Paddy Martinez discovered uranium ore and woke up this sleepy town. More than half of the known domestic reserves of uranium are in the area.

Chamber of Commerce Museum (100

North Iron St.; 505/287-4802). The only uranium-mining museum in the world. Also Indian relics and a display of minerals. Open daily.

El Morro National Monument (43 miles west on NM 53; 505/783-4226). El Morro is a striking landmark, a massive mesa of sandstone rising 200 feet above the valley floor. It was named by Spanish conquistadors who often camped here in the 17th century because of a large natural rain basin at its base. It was later a stopover for Americans traveling to the West. El Morro is also known as Inscription Rock, because many travelers cut a record of their passage into the soft sandstone, the first such inscription having been carved by Don Juan de Onate in April 1605. On the top of El Morro are the ruins of Zuñi pueblos, largely unexcavated, that were abandoned long before the Spanish came. The Zuñis left hundreds of petroglyphs carved on the sides of the mesa. In a unique way, El Morro is a symbol of the cultural mixture of the Southwest.

Visitor Center exhibits depict the history of the surrounding area. A trail leads from the center to and along the base of the mesa, past the historic inscriptions, and continues on to the top of the mesa and the pueblo ruins. The altitude here is 7,200 feet, and overexertion may be dangerous. Open daily. Limited wheelchair access.

HOBBS

James Hobbs and his family were in their covered wagon crossing the Llano Estacado bound for Alpine, when they met a family leaving Alpine because they couldn't make a living there. Hobbs turned his wagon north and settled here.

Western Heritage Center and Lea County Cowboy Hall of Fame (New Mexico Junior College campus; 505/392-4510). Local memorabilia and relics of the Indian, cowboy, and oil eras. Open weekdays.

Confederate Air Force Flying Museum (5 miles west on U.S. 62/180 at Lea County Airport; 505/393-7543). The Confederate Air Force is an organization that restores and flies World War II military aircraft, and they are displayed here. Many have been used in films. Open daily.

LAS CRUCES

Apaches massacred a party of travelers here. The crosses that marked their graves gave the town its name.

Mesilla (2 miles southwest). A historic village that was the Confederate capital of the Territory of Arizona. The Gadsden Purchase was signed here. Billy the Kid escaped from the local jail after being convicted of murder. La Mesilla State Monument comprises the original plaza and the adobe buildings that surround it.

Gadsden Museum (2 miles southwest on East Barker Rd. in Mesilla; 505/526-8911). Memorabilia of the Gadsden Purchase, which in 1853 added 29,640 square miles to the United States. Indian and Civil War artifacts. *Santo* collection. Open daily.

Fort Selden State Monument (12 miles north on I-25; 505/526-8911). Fort Selden, established in 1865 to protect settlers of the area from Apaches and desperadoes, consisted of flat-topped adobe buildings arranged about a parade ground, and was garrisoned by two companies, one of infantry and one of cavalry. Units of the famed "buffalo soldiers," black cavalry, were stationed here. In the early 1880s the post was commanded by Capt. Arthur MacArthur. His son, Douglas, who later became Supreme Commander of Allied Forces in the Southwest Pacific in World War II, spent several childhood years at this desert post. The Visitor Center displays artifacts. Open daily.

Meson de Mesilla (1803 Avenida de Mesilla; 505/525-9212). A thirteen-room adobe inn furnished with antiques. Break-

fast is included in the rates. *Lundeen Inn of the Arts* (618 South Alameda Blvd.; 505/526-3355) is a bed-and-breakfast in an adobe house.

LAS VEGAS

Fort Union National Monument (20 miles northeast on I-25 to Watrous–Fort Union exit, then 8 miles northwest on NM 477; 505/425-8025). Fort Union was built in 1851 to protect settlers in the territory from the Apaches who attacked the villages in the mountains to the north and menaced the Santa Fe Trail. Jicarilla Apaches ambushed and nearly wiped out a cavalry company, but were driven into the mountains west of the Rio Grande and routed. Other military operations were conducted against the hostile Utes of southern Colorado in 1855, and a few years later against Kiowas and Comanches who were raiding the plains to the east of the fort. With the coming of the Civil War, the regular troops were withdrawn from such frontier posts as Fort Union and replaced with volunteers. Fearing a Confederate invasion of New Mexico, the army built a second fort here, a star-shaped earthen fortification. The Confederates were turned back at the Battle of Glorieta Pass,

At one time wagon trains thundered into the protecting walls of Fort Union, chased by Comanche raiders. Near the end of the Santa Fe Trail, the New Mexico fort was one of the largest and most important in the West and a supply depot for fifty other forts.

For more than 50 years, the Cavalry protected wagon trails and pioneer settlements from the Indians. The life of a typical trooper, such as the one in the photograph far right, was hard—a blend of boring fort life, long periods in the field, and deadly skirmishes with hostile Indians. Many troopers left the army when their enlistment was up for safer, more profitable occupations.

and the new star fort was abandoned. A new fort was built here in 1863–69. In the late 1860s and 1870s, troops from here fought the Indians almost continuously. The supply depot at the fort ceased operation in 1879, when the Santa Fe Railroad replaced the Santa Fe Trail, and was abandoned in 1891.

Today a number of restored buildings may be visited. The Visitor Center has interpretive exhibits. There are living-history demonstrations in the summer. A nearly ten-mile trail leads through the ruins and to the remains of the star fort. Across the valley to the west, the ruins of the ordnance depot are visible on the site of the first fort. Open daily. Limited wheelchair access.

Theodore Roosevelt Rough Riders' Memorial and City Museum (Chamber of Commerce Bldg., 727 Grand Ave.; 505/425-8726). Artifacts and memorabilia of the future president's regiment in the Spanish-American War. Also local history material. Open daily except Sundays.

LORDSBURG

Steins Old Railroad Town (20 miles west on I-10, exit 3; 505/542-9791). Lordsburg was a Southern Pacific railroad town in the

late 1800s, and when the railroad closed its depot, the water supply was cut off and the town died. On the main street once stood saloons, a grocery store, the Hotel Steins, an assay office, and boardinghouses. Portions of the old section crews' houses have been restored and authentically furnished. Tours. Open daily.

Shakespeare (1½ miles south; 505/542-9034). During its lifetime, this ghost town had more ups and downs than a jack-in-the-box. At first it was called Mexican Springs, for the water supply that made it a stop on the way to California. A prospector named W. D. Brown stopped here and found some promising ore in the nearby Pyramid Mountains. He interested William C. Ralston, the organizer of the Bank of California, who laid out a town here called Ralston City, keeping the best parts for himself. The scheme fell apart. A few years later an improbable pair, Philip Arnold and John Slack, turned up at Ralston's bank with diamonds they said they found here. A mining expert vouched for the claim. Ralston bought Arnold and Slack out for $600,000, only to find that they had salted the mine. The pair was nowhere to be found. A number of old buildings are still standing. The cemetery on Main Street, one of the oldest in the state, contains the graves of early settlers and outlaws. Tours are given the second Sunday of each month.

Pictured at right is the assay office in Shakespeare, New Mexico, one of the state's classic ghost towns. Once a stop on the Butterfield Trail, the town boomed and busted during various silver strikes and a diamond hoax. Shakespeare had its share of saloons and brothels, lawmen and outlaws.

LOS ALAMOS

In 1942 the government took over a boys' school here and used it for nuclear research. Scientists from all over the country labored in secret on the Manhattan Project, which developed the atomic bomb.

Bradbury Science Museum of the Los Alamos National Laboratory (Diamond Dr.; 505/667-4444). Materials relating to the history of the laboratory, nuclear fission, and the bomb are on display. Open daily.

County Historical Museum (Fuller Lodge Cultural Center, 1921 Juniper; 505/662-4493 or 662-6272). Pueblo ruins and a homesteader's log cabin. Manhattan Project exhibit. The culture center displays arts and crafts of northern New Mexico. Both open daily.

Bandelier National Monument (6 miles south, then 6 miles east via NM 4 to signs; 505/672-3861). The Pajarito Plateau is a beautiful mesa slashed with canyons, extending eastward from the slopes of the Jemez Mountains. A group of Anasazi came here late in the 12th century, began to farm, and built hundreds of small dwellings. In the late 14th century, they began to consolidate their agricultural units, and by 1450 most of them were living in large pueblos, farming the fields at the bottoms of the canyons, irrigating them with canal systems. Less than a century later the area was abandoned. In the 1880s, Adolph F. A. Bandelier, the distinguished Swiss-American anthropologist for whom the park is named, surveyed the ruins.

The most easily accessible ruins are *Tyuonyi Ruin, Long House Ruin,* and *Tsankawi Ruin.* Tyuonyi and Long House are in Frijoles Canyon, and Tsankawi, an unexcavated pueblo of some 350 rooms, is eleven miles north on NM 4. The Visitor Center has Anasazi exhibits. Guided walks and campfire programs in summer. Open daily. Limited wheelchair access.

Jemez State Monument (31 miles west on U.S. 4, then 9 miles south in Jemez Springs; 505/829-3530). Some 600 years ago, the ancestors of the people of the Jemez Pueblo built several villages in the mountain valley and on the high mesas around it. A mission was built in the early 1620s, but was later abandoned. Today the ruins of the village and church of San José de los Jemez are among the most impressive in the Southwest. The Visitor Center displays Jemez Indian artifacts. Open daily.

MESCALERO

Mescalero Apache Reservation. Some 2,400 Apaches live on this beautiful reservation. The store, museum, and fish hatchery are worth visiting. On the Fourth of July Mountain Spirit dancers perform, arts and crafts are sold, and a rodeo takes place. On the reservation is the *Inn of the Mountain Gods,* an excellent resort owned and operated by the tribe. The reservation is open daily.

"No secret was ever better kept than that of Los Alamos. The schoolboys had it that they were moving out for the Ethiopian Ski Corps or the Scandinavian Camel Artillery. Santa Feans saw lights against the Jemez peaks, but knew nothing. Only the veteran reporter, Brian Dunne, dared write in the *Santa Fe New Mexican* that "buses were coming in loaded with Indians, people jabbering Spanish, and Nobel Prize winners."

—ERMA FERGUSON

◆✦◆

In Frijoles Canyon at Bandelier National Monument in New Mexico there is a mile of cave dwellings carved out of the soft turf and houses built out from the cliff. On the floor of the canyon is a great circular pueblo ruin. All the dwellings were occupied by Anasazi from A.D. 1200 to 1400.

"I am the Captain
General of the
province of New
Mexico for the
King our Lord,
passed by here on
the return from the
pueblo of Zuñi on
the twenty-ninth of
July the year of
1620, and put them
at peace at their
humble petition,
they asking favor
as vassals of his
Majesty and
promising anew
their obedience,
all of which he did,
with clemency,
zeal, and prudence
as a most Christian
like [gentleman]
extraordinary and
gallant soldier of
enduring and
praised memory."

—GOVERNOR EULATE,
INSCRIPTION AT EL
MORRO NATIONAL
MONUMENT,
NEW MEXICO

MOUNTAINAIR

Salinas National Monument (25 miles south on NM 14; 505/847-2770). Two cultural traditions, Anasazi and Mogollon, overlapped in the Salinas Valley to produce Abo, Gran Quivira, and Quarai. By the 10th century the Mogollon were here, living first in pit houses, then in aboveground *jacales* of adobe-plastered poles. By the late 1100s the Anasazi were making their presence felt. Their stone-and-adobe homes were the earliest stage of the pueblo society. Over the next several centuries the Salinas Valley became a trading center and one of the most populous parts of the pueblo world, with some 10,000 inhabitants. Major trade routes went through here, and the villagers became middlemen between the Rio Grande villages and the Plains tribes to the east. Anasazi culture was dominant by 1300, although it wasn't as advanced as that in the Anasazi heartland to the north. The brush-and-mud *jacales* had evolved into large stone complexes, some with hundreds of rooms and surrounding plazas. In 1596, Juan de Onate led an expedition to start a permanent colony in New Mexico. Relations with the Indians soured when soldiers attempted to collect tribute. Many of the missionaries had good intentions, but the overlapping privileges granted to the church and to civil authorities led to conflict.

The Spanish used the *encomienda* in dealing with pueblos. In this system, ranking citizens were allowed to collect tribute in return for providing protection, aid, and education to the Indians and military support for the government. In addition, the missionaries placed heavy demands on the pueblos to support the missions. Finally, cultural conflict and natural disaster spelled the end of the Salinas pueblos. The Apaches, once trading partners, now raided the pueblos. Drought came in the 1660s and 1670s, accompanied by famine. Some 450 Indians starved to death at Gran Quivira alone.

European diseases came with the Spanish, and epidemics devastated the pueblos. The Salinas pueblos and missions were abandoned in the 1670s, and the surviving Indians went to live in other pueblos. In 1680 the pueblos north of Salinas revolted and drove the Spanish from New Mexico. In the general exodus, the Piro and Tompiro survivors of the Salinas pueblos moved south to the El Paso area and were absorbed by Indian communities there, becoming the only Pueblo Indian group to lose both its homeland and its language.

Three major sites may be visited. The *Abu Ruins* (9 miles west of Mountainair on U.S. 60 and one-half mile north on NM 513; 505/847-2400) are the ruins of a Spanish church, San Gregorio de Abo, and a large unexcavated pueblo. *Gran Qivira Ruins* (25 miles south of town on NM 14; 505/847-2770) has a museum with exhibits of pueblo life. On the site are two churches, *San Buenaventura* and *San Isidro,* and excavated Indian structures. *Quarai Ruins* (8 miles north of town on NM 14 and 1 mile west; 505/847-2290) has the most complete Salinas church, *Nuestra Señora de la Purisima Concepción de Cuarac.* All sites are open daily. Limited wheelchair access.

RATON

Folsom Man Site (25 miles east on U.S. 72 to Folsom). A wandering cowboy found a distinctive and very finely chipped projectile point near the skeleton of an extinct bison, and the discovery revolutionized theories about the length of time man had been in America. In 1928 an American Museum of Natural History expedition found more points and proved that they were from 8,000 to 10,000 years old. (Previously, it had been believed that mankind had been resident in America for no more than 2,000 years.)

Folsom Museum (216 South 1st St.; 505/445-8300). Indian and Hispanic artifacts

Trading posts, like this one in Ruidoso, New Mexico, were the commercial link between whites and Indians in the Southwest. Indians swapped baskets, blankets, and jewelry for the necessities of life. The trader often served as an ombudsman, helping the Indians get fair treatment.

and materials relating to ranching, railroading, and mining in the state. Open Tuesday through Saturday, April through October; Friday through Sunday the rest of the year. Closed January.

Capulin Mountain National Monument (29 miles east on U.S. 84/87 to Capulin, then 3½ miles north; 505/278-2201). Here, one can drive to the rim of an extinct volcano that last belched lava 10,000 years ago. The Visitor Center has a museum with geology exhibits. Open daily.

RUIDOSO

Smokey the Bear Historical State Park (22 miles north via NM 37/48, on U.S. 380 near Capitan; 505/354-2748). A baby bear, orphaned by a fire in the Lincoln National Forest, was found near here in the 1950s and became Smokey the Bear, the symbol of forest fire prevention. Smokey is buried here within sight of the mountain where he was found. The *Smokey the Bear Museum* (505/354-2612) has memorabilia of the famous bear. Visitor Center. Open daily.

Lincoln State Monument (30 miles east on U.S. 70, then 10 miles west on U.S. 380; 505/653-4372). Lincoln was the focal point of one of the bloodiest episodes of the Old West—the Lincoln County War, a clash of rival businessmen vying for economic control of the area. On one side were John Tunstall, Alexander McSween, and John Chisum. Their rivals were L. G. Murphy and James J. Dolan. Hostilities began with the killing of Tunstall in early 1878. McSween's hired gunmen, including William Bonney (Billy the Kid), set out to avenge the killing. A bloody trail of ambushes and killings culminated in a five-day shootout that left several men dead, including McSween.

Several historic structures are in Lincoln. The *Tunstall Store Museum* contains much of its original stock. The *Lincoln County Courthouse* was where, in 1881, Billy the Kid made his escape, only to be hunted down by Sheriff Pat Garrett. Food and lodging are available at the state-owned *Wortley Hotel* (505/653-4500). Tours. Open daily. Limited wheelchair access.

White Oaks (10 miles north of Carrizozo on NM 349). By 1887 the gold mines were booming here and White Oaks, with two banks and two newspapers, felt that all it lacked was a railroad. The citizens felt that the Kansas City, El Paso & Mexican Railway would pay top dollar for the privilege of coming through their town, and set right-of-way prices accordingly. The railroad went to Carrizozo instead. The mines played out in the 1890s, and White Oaks died.

Fort Stanton (5 miles southeast of Capitan, then south on a secondary road). Built in 1855 to control the Apaches, the fort was abandoned at the start of the Civil War and temporarily occupied by Confederates. The Apaches, meanwhile, were raiding through central New Mexico. Kit Carson's forces brought them under control and a reservation was established here in 1871. The army abandoned the fort in 1896, and it was made into a hospital. Many of the original stone buildings are still in use. Open daily.

SANTA FE

In 1610, Don Pedro de Peralta laid out the plaza here and built the Palace of the Governors. Seventy years later, the Pueblo Indians revolted and drove out the Spanish. Troops led by General Don Diego de Vargas made a peaceful return in 1692. The Santa Fe Trail opened in the 1820s. Gen. Stephen W. Kearney led his troops into the town without resistance in 1846 and raised the American flag.

The Plaza. At the southeast corner, the *End of the Trail Monument* marks the end of the Santa Fe Trail. In the center, the *Soldiers Monument* is dedicated to the Union soldiers killed at the Battle of Glorieta Pass, fought on the trail seventeen miles to the south in 1862. The plaza is the scene of markets and fiestas.

Palace of the Governors (plaza; 505/827-6460). The oldest public building in continuous use in the country. Built in 1610, it was the seat of government in New Mexico for more than 300 years. Now a museum of Southwestern history, it has exhibits relating to the Santa Fe Trail. Indians sell arts and crafts in the shade of the covered walkway outside. Open daily, March through December; daily except Mondays the rest of the year.

New Mexico Museum of Fine Arts (Lincoln Ave.; 505/827-4455). Designed by John Gaw Meem in classic Pueblo Revival style, has works of well-known Indian artists, known as the Taos masters, Georgia O'Keeffe, and other contemporary artists. Open daily.

Cathedral of St. Francis (Cathedral Place; 505/982-5619). This French Romanesque church was built in 1869 under the direction of Archbishop Jean-Baptiste Lamy,

Mission San Miguel in Santa Fe, New Mexico, is sometimes called "the oldest church in America." It isn't, but it stands over the foundations of a church built around 1636 and burned in the 1680 revolt. The mission has been rebuilt and remodeled five times.

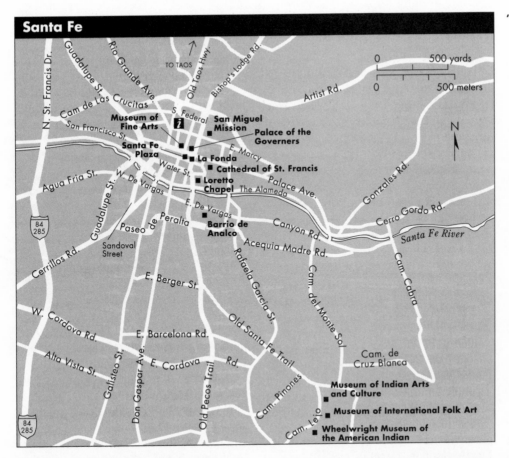

Santa Fe

TO TAOS

Rio Grande Ave.
Guadalupe St.
Cam. de Las Crucitas
N. St. Francis Dr.
San Francisco St.
Old Taos Hwy.
Bishop's Lodge Rd.
Artist Rd.
S. Federal

Museum of Fine Arts
San Miguel Mission
Palace of the Governors
E. Marcy
Santa Fe Plaza
La Fonda
Cathedral of St. Francis
Loretto Chapel
Water St.
W. De Vargas
The Alameda
Palace Ave.
Gonzales Rd.
Cerro Gordo Rd.

Agua Fria St.
Guadalupe St.
E. De Vargas
Canyon Rd.
Santa Fe River

Peralta
Paseo de
Barrio de Analco
Acequia Madre Rd.
Cam. Cabra

Sandoval Street
Cerrillos Rd.
E. Berger St.
Rafaela Garcia St.
Cam. del Monte Sol

W. Cordova Rd.
E. Barcelona Rd.
Old Santa Fe Trail
Cam. de Cruz Blanca

Alta Vista St.
Galisteo St.
Don Gaspar Ave.
E. Cordova Rd.
Old Pecos Trail
Cam. Piñones
Cam. Leío

Museum of Indian Arts and Culture
Museum of International Folk Art
Wheelwright Museum of the American Indian

84 285

0   500 yards
0   500 meters

N

---

the city's first archbishop and the inspiration for Willa Cather's *Death Comes for the Archbishop*. A tiny chapel, built in 1718, holds La Conquistadora, a wooden statue of the Virgin Mary, the oldest Marian statue in the country, which was returned to Santa Fe by Don Diego de Vargas during the reconquest. Open daily.

La Fonda Hotel (100 East San Francisco St.; 505/988-4455). Known as "the Inn at the End of the Trail," the hotel was built in 1920. Its one-story predecessor witnessed the arrival of William Beckness, "the Father of the Santa Fe Trail," in 1821. Later its gambling tables gave it a lurid reputation. John P. Slough, a hero of Glorieta Pass, was shot dead in the lobby in 1867. The hotel's public spaces display Mexican tin art and the work of Indian artists.

Loretto Chapel (Chapel of Our Lady of Light) (Old Santa Fe Trail; 505/988-5531). When Archbishop Lamy brought six nuns of the Order of Loretto across the trail in 1852, they opened a convent and a girls' academy. Inside this tiny 1874 Gothic-style chapel is the famous *Miraculous Staircase*. Built by an unknown carpenter to give access to the choir loft, this circular stairway, twenty-two feet high with thirty-three steps, makes two complete turns. It was constructed without a central support and is held together with wooden pegs.

San Miguel Mission (Old Santa Fe Trail and De Vargas St.; 505/983-3973). This is the oldest church still in use in the country. Open daily. Next door is the *Oldest House*, built by Indians more than 800 years ago. Other historic houses, not open to visitors,

"Santa Fe, the capital of the province of Nuevo Mejico, contains about three thousand inhabitants, and ... is a wretched collection of mudhouses, without a single building of stone, although it boasts a palacio— as the adobe of the Governor is called—a long low building, taking up the greater part of one side of the plaza or public square.... The appearance of the town defies description, and I can compare it to nothing but a dilapidated brick-kiln or prairie-dog town."

—GEORGE FREDERICK RUXTON, *Wild Life in the Rocky Mountains*, 1846

The east side of the plaza in Santa Fe, the bustling terminus of the Santa Fe Trail, as it looked in 1866. The city was founded by Don Pedro de Peralta, who laid out the plaza and built the Palace of the Governors in 1610, ten years before the Pilgrims landed in Plymouth, Massachusetts.

on De Vargas Street include the *Blanche Boyle House*, the *Gregorio Crespin Home*, the *Crespin Hacienda*, and the *Adolph Bandelier House*.

Museum of Indian Arts and Culture (Canyon Rd.; 505/827-8350). An outstanding anthropology collection. Indian basketry, pottery, weaving, jewelry. Open daily, March through December; daily except Mondays the rest of the year. Across the yard is the *Museum of International Folk Art* (505/827-8350), containing some 125,000 wood carvings, toys, textiles, jewelry, paintings, and religious articles. Open daily, March through December; daily except Mondays the rest of the year.

Wheelwright Museum (704 Camino Lejo; 505/982-4636). Navajo textiles, silver, baskets, and pottery. Open daily, May through September; daily except Mondays the rest of the year.

Sanctuario Nuestra Señora de Guadalupe (100 Guadalupe St.; 505/988-2027). A restored 1795 mission with exceptional hand-painted *reredos*, executed in 1783. Open daily.

Old Cienega Village Museum (10 miles south, off I-25; 505/471-2261). Exhibits of colonial village and agricultural life. Open by appointment only, Monday through Friday, April to October.

Institute of American Indian Arts Museum (1369 Cerrillos Rd. 505/988-6281). Displays Native American and Aleut arts and crafts. Open daily.

Pecos National Monument (25 miles southwest via U.S. 25 to Glorieta exit, then right on NM 63 for 2 miles; 505/757-6414). Anasazi from the Rio Grande Valley migrated eastward around A.D. 1100 and settled in the Pecos Valley near the Sangre de Cristo Mountains. Coronado's expedition visited this pueblo, then called Cicuye, in 1541. Priests came in the early 1600s and built a church, the *Mission de Nuestra Señora de los Angeles de Porcinucula*. In the Pueblo Revolt, the Spanish were driven out and the mission was partially destroyed. The Spanish returned and rebuilt the mission. Plains Indians raided the pueblo repeatedly in the 18th century, and a smallpox epidemic killed many Indians in 1781. The last seventeen Pecos survivors moved in 1836 to live with kinsmen at the Jemez pueblo in Texas. The deserted pueblo became a landmark on the Santa Fe Trail.

Today the most interesting site is the mission church, which resembles a fortress, nearly 170 feet long, ninety feet wide at the transept, and thirty-nine feet wide inside the nave; in some places the walls are seven feet thick. Only eighteen such structures are known to have been built in the Americas; this is the only one north of Mexico City. A small museum at the Visitor Center displays Anasazi and Spanish artifacts. In the summer, Indians, many of them descendants of the original inhabitants, demonstrate the making of baskets, pottery, bread, and their unique turkey-feather blankets. Open daily. Limited wheelchair access.

Puye Cliff Dwelling (U.S. 285 north to Pojoaque, west on NM 4 to NM 30, then north 5 miles; dwellings are 9 miles up the Santa Clara Canyon; 505/753-7326). These ruins are on the Santa Clara Indian Reservation portion of the Pajarito Plateau. The Santa Clara Indians are believed to be the descendants of the Anasazi who lived here. On a cliff overlooking the Santa Clara Canyon is *Top House Ruins*, a partially exca-

vated pueblo that once contained some 2,000 rooms. Directly below are the remains of a cliff village with a few restored buildings. Archaeologists believe Top House was built between 1450 and 1475, reached its peak about 1540, and was deserted about 1550, like Bandelier and other Anasazi villages in the area. The cliff dwellings were probably used as winter quarters by the residents of Top House.

Short but steep trails lead to the cliff village from the canyon floor. Top House can be reached by trail or an unpaved road from the parking area. The Puye Ceremony is held annually on the last weekend of July, and consists of two days of tribal dancing and an extensive display of arts and crafts. Open daily, April through October. No wheelchair access.

Accommodations: *Pueblo Bonito Bed & Breakfast Inn* (138 West Manhattan; 505/984-8001). Fourteen quiet *casitas* on a century-old estate, a five-minute walk from the plaza.

SANTA ROSA

Fort Sumner State Monument (3 miles east on U.S. 54/66; 505/355-2573). The Apache and Navajo fiercely resisted the flood of settlers that came to the territory in the early 1860s. The army was ordered to put the Indians under guard on military reservations. Kit Carson invaded the Mescalero Apache and Navajo homelands, destroyed their homes, crops, and livestock, and starved them into submission. The captives were forced to march here, in some cases more than 400 miles. By the end of 1868, 500 Apaches and nearly 9,000 Navajos were held at the nearby Bosque Redondo. The reservation experiment was a disaster. Crops were destroyed by cutworms, drought, and hail. The water from the Pecos River was bad, and wood was scarce. After five years of deprivation, the Indians were

Pecos National Monument, near Santa Fe, New Mexico, contains the ruins of two large Spanish mission churches, shown at left. Once the home of 2,000 Indians, the pueblo was occupied for 500 years. When it was abandoned in 1838, there were only seventeen survivors.

Billy the Kid

Pulp fiction transformed a vicious hired killer named William Bonney into Billy the Kid, a likable lad forced by evil men into a life of crime. Bonney was arrested at a tender age in New Mexico for stealing clothes from two Chinese. He escaped, fled to Arizona, and soon shot a blacksmith who was bullying him. He went back to New Mexico and stayed briefly with John Chisum, a cattle baron involved in a fight for the economic dominance of Lincoln County. He then became a hired gun for John Tunstall, whose murder touched off the Lincoln County War. Riding with a vigilante group, he killed two men and helped ambush and kill the sheriff and a deputy. Despite more killings, a deal was offered Billy: a pardon in return for evidence against the other killers. He surrendered, but grew tired of waiting for his pardon, and rode out of Lincoln. He began to rustle cattle, killed a man in a saloon fight, and was nearly captured,

Pat Garrett

but escaped, killing a lawman. After a gunfight, Billy was captured by Pat Garrett, the new sheriff, and was tried and convicted of murder. Before he could be hanged, he killed two deputies and escaped. On the night of July 14, 1881, Garrett was waiting in the bedroom of a ranch where Billy was hiding out. When Billy stepped into the darkened room, Garrett fired twice. Three weeks later, a fanciful biography of Billy the Kid was on sale around the country.

allowed to return to their homelands, where they remain today.

Fort Sumner was abandoned by the military and purchased by Lucien Maxwell, a cattle baron. He converted one of the officers' quarters into a spacious home, where, on July 14, 1881, William Bonney, alias Billy the Kid, was shot dead by Sheriff Pat Garrett. Bonney is buried by the fort gate. The Visitor Center has exhibits that depict life on the reservation. Open daily.

Billy the Kid Museum (44 miles southeast via U.S. 84; 505/472-3763). The museum has some 60,000 items relating to Billy the Kid, the Old West, and Fort Sumner. Open daily in the summer; daily except Sundays the rest of the year.

SILVER CITY

The foothills of the Mogollon (*MUGGY-yone*) Mountains once were dotted with mining camps, but the gold and silver are now almost gone.

Fleming Hall Museum (Western New Mexico University campus; 505/538-6386). Displays showing the contributions of Native American, Hispanic, European, and African-American cultures to the region. Mimbres Indian artifacts. Photography collection. Open daily.

Silver City Museum (312 West Broadway; 505/538-5921). The museum is in the restored 1881 home of mine owner H. B. Allman. Antiques and vintage furnishings. Casa Grande Indian artifacts. Memorabilia from the mining town of Tyrone. Open daily except Mondays.

Santa Rita Copper Mine (12 miles southwest on NM 90; 505/537-3381). The open-pit copper mine has an observation point where visitors may view operations. A mining museum has exhibits of operations since the mid-1800s, and mineral displays. Open daily except Mondays.

Phelps Dodge Copper Mine (12 miles southwest on NM 90; 505/538-5331). Each day, 50,000 tons of ore are mined here; the mine also has an observation point. Tours. Open weekdays.

Gila Cliff Dwellings National Monument (42 miles north on NM 15; 505/536-9461). The best preserved Mogollon ruins in the Southwest are in five adjacent caverns high in the side of a narrow canyon on the southern edge of the Gila Wilderness. The single-story dwellings are made of a distinctive cream-colored rock, with original wall supports and roof timbers. The earliest ruin here is a pit house of a type made from A.D. 100 to 400. The Mogollons hunted, grew corn and beans, and gathered wild plants for food. Some years later the cliff dwellings were built, along with pueblos on terraces overlooking the West Fork of the Gila River. Mogollon pottery was superb; a ceramic piece of the Mimbres Period will fetch $20,000 or more.

The Visitor Center displays Mogollon ceramics and artifacts. A one-mile loop trail leads to and through the cliff dwellings. Open daily.

Pinos Altos (7 miles north on NM 15; 505/388-1882). In 1860 a prospector named Three-Fingered Birch found gold in Bear Creek, and in a few months 700 men were panning gold in the stream near here. A few months later a gold vein was struck, the Pacific Vein. The camp, however, was on Apache hunting grounds. One day Chief Red Sleeves rode up to the camp and told the miners that if they would leave, he would take them to a great gold deposit in the south. The miners seized Red Sleeves, whipped him, and threw him out of camp . He went to Cochise and they attacked the camp with 400 warriors. The miners fought off the attack, although seven of them were killed. By the 1890s, Pinos Altos was a sizable town with two hotels, a drugstore, and a Turkish bath. In 1906 a railroad spur reached town to take ore to the smelters in Silver City. However, the mines soon petered out and Pinos Altos wound down to almost a ghost town. Today there is a general store and a small museum.

Mogollon (75 miles northwest via U.S. 180 and NM 78; 505/539-2841). James Cooney, a cavalry sergeant on a scouting expedition, discovered rock ledges rich in gold near here. He told no one, and when he was discharged in 1876, he and some friends began mining. Apaches drove them off, but they came back two years later and restaked their claims. Apache raids continued, however, and grew worse after the miners killed

the son-in-law of Chief Victorio. Cooney and a friend were slain in an Indian ambush. The camp survived, though, and was for a while a hideout of Butch Cassidy and his gang. A big strike came in 1889, and the mine, the Little Fanny, helped the area produce 18 million ounces of silver. The town is surrounded by the Gila National Forest.

SOCORRO

Once the home of Piro Indians, Socorro had a Franciscan mission as early as 1598. A Spanish land grant in 1817 attracted the ancestors of many of the current residents.

Old San Miguel Mission (303 Bernard; 505/835-1620). Constructed in the early 1600s, the mission has been rebuilt. The south wall was part of the original 1598 mission. The church features carved corbels and ceiling beams. The office displays early artifacts. The church is open daily, the office on weekdays.

TAOS

Spanish colonists in the area built a church in 1617. After the Pueblo Revolt and De Vargas's reconquest in 1692, Taos was plagued by marauding Apaches and disagreements with the Taos Indians. Today it is really three towns—the Spanish-American settlement that is Taos proper, Taos Pueblo, two miles to the north, and Ranchos de Taos, four miles to the south—each distinct, but all closely allied. The first artists came in the 1880s, and today the town is a flourishing art colony.

Taos Pueblo (2½ miles north on Pueblo Rd.; 505/758-9593). When the Spanish soldiers first saw the golden brown, multistoried apartmentlike architecture of Taos Pueblo, they thought they had discovered one of the fabled Cities of Gold. The pueblo has survived much: the invasions of the

One of the most photographed mission churches in the Southwest, San Francisco de Asis, still serves the parish.

Spaniards in the 1540s, the Pueblo Revolt and the reconquest, and a rebellion of their own. In 1847, warriors from the pueblo, refusing to recognize American authority, killed Charles Bent, governor of New Mexico, and several other Americans. U.S. troops arrived to restore order, and 700 Indians barricaded themselves in the San Geronimo mission and refused to surrender. Artillery blew the church wall apart, killing 150 Indians. Peace was restored after seven Indians were executed for taking part in the uprising. For more than one thousand years, the Tiwa-speaking Indians of this pueblo have maintained their deep-rooted culture and religion. The pueblo looks much the same as it did before the Spanish came. By choice, there is neither electricity nor indoor plumbing; water is drawn from the Rio Pueblo, which runs through the village. This is one of the most traditional of the pueblos and one of the most beautiful, nestled at the foot of 13,160-foot-high Wheeler Peak. The dancing is extraordinary. Photography by permit only. Open daily.

Ranchos de Taos (4 miles south on U.S. 68; 505/758-2754). The town has three of the most beautiful mission churches in the Southwest. The *San Francisco de Asis Mission Church* has huge buttresses, twin belfries, and an exquisite interior. Open daily except Sundays.

Harwood Foundation (25 Ledoux St.; 505/758-2754). A research and public library on the history and culture of the Southwest. Collection of books by and about D. H. Lawrence. Art library. Gallery with more than a hundred paintings by Taos artists. Open daily except Sundays.

Taos Art Association (220 Paseo del Pueblo Norte; 505/758-2052 or 758-2036). Paintings, sculpture, and graphics of Taos and other Southwestern artists. Performing arts center. Open daily.

Kit Carson House (just off the plaza on Kit Carson Rd.; 505/758-4741). From 1843 to 1868, Christopher "Kit" Carson, fur trapper, trader, guide, Indian agent, general and hero in the Indian Wars, lived in this adobe house. Four rooms of the 1825 house are original, and three—the parlor, kitchen, and bedroom—are authentically furnished. The fourth features displays associated with Carson's life and Indian artifacts. Carson and his wife are buried in Kit Carson Memorial State Park, at the end of Dragoon Lane. Open daily.

Ernest L. Blumenschein Home (18 Bent St.; 505/758-0330). Mementos and paintings by the Blumenschein family and other early Taos artists. Open daily.

Governor Bent House Museum and Gallery (8 Bent St.; 505/758-2376). This was the home of the first American territorial governor and the scene of his death in 1847. Family possessions, Indian artifacts, Western art. Open daily, March through December.

La Hacienda de Don Antonio Severion Martinez (2 miles west on NM 240; 505/758-1000). A Spanish colonial hacienda with period furnishings that was once used as a fortress in Indian raids. Two large patios. Open daily, March through December.

Millicent Rogers Museum (4 miles north on NM 3; 505/758-1000). Indian and Hispanic arts and crafts. Open daily, May through October; Wednesday through Sunday the rest of the year.

D. H. Lawrence Ranch and Shrine (15 miles north on NM 3, then 5 miles east on a gravel road; 505/776-2245). This was the home of the British author for several years after World War I. The shrine contains his tomb. The 160-acre ranch now is a conference facility maintained by the University of New Mexico. Shrine open daily. Limited wheelchair access.

Fort Burgwin (8 miles south on NM 3; 505/758-8322). A restored frontier fort that was occupied by the First Dragoons of the U.S. Cavalry from 1852 to 1860. A museum displays archaeological, Indian, and Spanish-American relics. By appointment only.

Accommodations: *Hacienda del Sol* (Morada Lane; 505/758-0287). Mabel Dodge, a patron of the arts, and her Indian husband, Tony Luhan, used to entertain the likes of D. H. Lawrence and Georgia O'Keeffe in this circa-1800 adobe hacienda at the base of the mountains. Three guest rooms. Breakfast is included in the rates. *La Posada de Taos* (309 Juanita Lane; 505/758-8164). This adobe lodge in the historic district has five rooms. Breakfast is included in the rates.

TRUTH OR CONSEQUENCES

In 1950, Hot Springs renamed itself to honor the tenth anniversary of the radio program "Truth or Consequences," hosted by Ralph Edwards, who also created "This Is Your Life." No one now seems to remember why.

Geronimo Springs Museum (325 Main St.; 505/894-6600). Indian artifacts, pioneer relics, and exhibits of local history. Open daily.

TUCUMCARI

Tucumcari Historical Museum (416 South Adams; 505/461-4201). A mélange of Indian artifacts, gems and other minerals, local mementos, a restored caboose, and a firetruck. Open daily in the summer, daily except Mondays the rest of the year.

PUEBLOS OF NEW MEXICO

The promise of riches drew the Spanish to the Southwest. The first expedition left Mexico City in 1526. After a disastrous battle with Indians in present-day Florida, the survivors escaped in makeshift boats, and a storm washed four ashore in Texas. Naked, more dead than alive, they were captured by Indians. After a while they became shamans (witch doctors) to the tribe. One, Alvar Núñez Cabeza de Vaca, was noted for his healing powers. He and his companions were passed from tribe to tribe until they reached the border of Mexico, then called New Spain, and released. They walked home across hundreds of miles of desert, arriving eight years after their departure.

From the Indians, the Spaniards had

Taos Pueblo in New Mexico has multilevel adobes facing one another across its plaza. This was the northern frontier of the Spanish province, and Plains Indians came here to trade.

heard of pueblos called the Seven Cities of Cibola, the Cities of Gold. This excited the Viceroy of New Spain, Antonio de Mendoza, who sent an expedition to find the golden cities. It returned empty-handed after its guide, one of Cabeza de Vaca's men, was slain at Zuñi Pueblo.

Several other small expeditions failed. Then, in 1540, Francisco Vásquez de Coronado, a provincial governor, headed north with 300 soldiers and 800 friendly Indians. Instead of the golden cities, Coronado found the mud-walled pueblo of Hawikuh, "a little, crowded village, looking as if it had been crumpled all up together." Coronado explored as far north as present-day Kansas before returning to Mexico City.

The first permanent Spanish settlement in what is now New Mexico was founded in 1598 by Juan de Onate near San Juan Pueblo. Other settlements grew up along the Rio Grande, and in 1609 Don Pedro de Peralta founded the provincial capital of Santa Fe. A goal of the settlements was to Christianize the Indians and make them productive servants of New Spain. Each settlement was built around a Jesuit mission, and the missionaries wielded great power over the natives. The missions, which resembled fortresses, became centers of farming, commerce, and education. The Indians were forced to give up their religion and give a large part of their crops to the mission.

The Spanish were beset by troubles in New Mexico: droughts, epidemics, attacks by the Apache, jurisdictional conflicts between civil and religious officials, and, most dangerous of all, a growing unrest among the Pueblo Indians. As Antonio Barreiro later wrote: "At the exact moment when they became convinced that their conquerors were merely searching for idols of gold and had an insatiable desire to own slaves, the pueblos of New Mexico unleashed a truly heroic war on their cruel oppressors."

In the Pueblo Revolt of 1680, the Pueblo Indians, aided by Apaches, drove every Spaniard—soldier, civilian, and priest—out of New Mexico, destroyed most of the missions, and returned to their traditional ways. Twelve years later, in 1692, Don Diego de Vargas reconquered the province without resistance. All the pueblos suffered in the reconquest, and some were destroyed.

Today the pueblos are scattered among

Pumpkins ripen in front of a Zuñi adobe in this 1879 photograph. The Zuñi, descendants of the Mogollon, were the first Pueblo tribe to encounter the Spanish. On his famous expedition, Coronado mistook Zuñi pueblos for the fabled Seven Cities of Cibola.

the cities and Hispanic villages of the northern Rio Grande in New Mexico. Sixteen are described here. The Taos Pueblo is described in the Taos section (page 207), the Hopi pueblos in the Arizona chapter. The pueblos contain the largest and most culturally intact Indian groups in the Southwest.

Visiting Pueblos

- Visitors to pueblos are guests and should behave like guests.
- Alcohol and drugs are prohibited on pueblos.
- Some pueblos charge admission.
- Photographing, sketching, and recording are strictly prohibited, unless permission is granted by the tribal office. A fee may be involved. If photography is prohibited, do not carry a camera. An unauthorized camera may be confiscated by tribal police.
- If photography is permitted, ask residents for permission before taking their pictures.
- Obtain permission before spending a prolonged amount of time on a pueblo.
- Disturbing a site or removing artifacts is an offense punishable under both civil and tribal law.
- Pueblos are closed to visitors during most religious ceremonies.
- Pueblos do not have special facilities for wheelchairs. Phone the tribal office at the pueblo to inquire about access.

Acoma Pueblo (from Albuquerque, 40 miles west on U.S. 60 to exit 108, left on NM 23, then 12 miles south; 505/552-6604). This pueblo, whose name means Sky City, was built around A.D. 900 and may be the oldest existing community in the country. It is atop a steep, 365-foot mesa, and until recently the only access was a narrow path carved from the rock. In 1558, Juan de Zaldivar, the provincial governor, toured the pueblo, later sending his nephew to exact tribute. Acoma warriors killed him and thirteen of his soldiers. More soldiers came, killed 800 Indians, burned the pueblo, and took 600 captives to the Santo Domingo Pueblo for trial. All surviving Acoma men were sentenced to twenty years in prison and the amputation of one foot. The elderly were sold as slaves to the Plains Indians. Acoma was rebuilt around 1603 by the few survivors. After the reconquest, Acoma held out much longer than the other pueblos before allowing priests to return. Today, Acoma is one of the friendliest pueblos. Only a handful of the 3,000 Indians here live in the old village. A road now goes up the mesa, and visitors may park there. Artisans are famous for their black-on-white and black-on-red pottery, usually decorated with geometric designs. Photography fee. Visitors must be accompanied by Indian guides. A tribal museum has Acoma artifacts. Open daily.

Cochiti Pueblo (from Albuquerque, 40 miles north on U.S. 25, left on NM 16, then right at junction of NM 22; 505/465-2255). The Mission of San Buenaventura here was burned in the Pueblo Revolt. Fearing reprisals, the Indians took refuge in the mountains. Diego de Vargas besieged them in the reconquest, killing twenty warriors and capturing some 300 women and children. He permitted them to return to Cochiti to help build a new mission. A few original structures still stand around the central kiva, but most of the 800 Indians now live in modern homes. The mission has excellent statuary and paintings. Cochiti "storyteller" pottery, clay figures of Indians and animals, is popular but not traditional. No photography. Open daily.

Isleta Pueblo (from Albuquerque, U.S. 25 south 14 miles to exit 209, left 1 mile, then right on NM 45, then left 1 mile on U.S. 85; 505/877-0370). This is one of the few pueblos where the priests got along well with the Indians. Isleta did not take part in the Pueblo Revolt, and the governor came here when he was forced out of Santa Fe. A

"From the Indian also learned . . . that they [the Jemez] have priests to administer their own religion which they like better than the Roman Catholic, which he says has been forced upon them, and which they do not understand."

—LT. JAMES H. SIMPSON, 1849

year later, though, an expedition from Mexico took 365 Indians prisoner and destroyed the pueblo. They were later given land near El Paso and built a pueblo, naming it Isleta del Sur. Isleta was rebuilt twenty years after the reconquest by Indians from Isleta del Sur and other pueblos. Today it is the largest pueblo in New Mexico. Many original structures stand on the large plaza, but modernization has taken its toll. One side of the plaza is dominated by the mission of Saint Augustine. Visitors are free to roam the pueblo, and photography is permitted. Open daily.

Jemez Pueblo (from Albuquerque, 18 miles north on U.S. 25, left on NM 44 to exit 242, then 23 miles to NM 4, left 5 miles; 505/834-7479). Coronado found ten pueblos in the foothills of the Jemez Mountains, but the Spanish later persuaded the Indians to concentrate in the three largest, Astiolakwa, Gyusiwa, and Patoqua. By 1622, Spanish missionaries claimed that more than 6,000 Indians had been converted. In the Pueblo Revolt, the Indians killed 300 settlers, then went to live in the mountains. After the reconquest, they built a new pueblo called Walatow, now Jemez Pueblo. Today it is a pueblo of 2,100 people, most of whom live in around the central plaza. They still tend farms near the river, and raise cattle and

sheep. Artisans make silver and turquoise jewelry, willow baskets, and pottery. Permission from tribal headquarters is necessary before walking around the plaza. The only photography permitted is of the mission. Open daily.

Jemez State Monument (20 miles north of Jemez on NM 4; 505/829-3530). This is the site of the ruins of Gyusiwa Pueblo and the original San Diego Mission. The museum at the Visitor Center displays a collection of Jemez artifacts, The ruins and the setting are serenely beautiful. Open daily.

Laguna Pueblo (from Albuquerque, 40 miles west on U.S. 40 to Exit 114, 1 mile west on frontage road; 505/552-6654). The pueblo actually consists of six villages, Old Laguna and five satellites: Seama, Mesita, Encinal, Paguate, and Paraje. They were built after the reconquest by refugees from Santo Domingo and Zia pueblos. Others were from Cieneguilla, one of the mountain strongholds destroyed by Diego de Vargas. Old Laguna, a small cluster of stone and adobe structures, sits on a mound overlooking the San Jose River, and is now surrounded by house trailers and modern homes. The San Jose Mission in Old Laguna has an exceptional interior. The walls in the sanctuary are covered with religious murals, and the altar is decorated with Indian sym-

Some Indians fought against the U.S. Army in the Southwest, while others fought for them alongside the soldiers. The army found that Apaches, shown here clad in makeshift uniforms and armed with army carbines, were generally more useful as scouts and trackers than as soldiers.

bols. A painting in the church once touched off a feud. King Charles II of Spain presented a painting of St. Joseph to Juan Ramírez, a New Mexican priest, who, in turn, gave it to this church. The Acomans came to believe the painting had miraculous powers. In 1800, Laguna Pueblo, plagued with drought and sickness, asked to borrow the painting for a month, then another month, and finally refused to return it to Acoma. The painting stayed at Laguna for half a century. In 1852, after years of litigation, a court ordered the painting returned. When warriors went to pick up the painting, they found it leaning against a tree on the trail between the two pueblos. Acomans believe that when Saint Joseph heard of the court's decision, he started home on his own. Today Laguna is a wealthy pueblo with an industrial park. As a result, there are few artisans at work here. Photography permitted. Open daily.

Nambe Pueblo (from Santa Fe, 15 miles north on U.S. 84/285, right on NM 4, after 3 miles turn right again; 505/455-7692). Coronado's conquistadors visited this pueblo several times, and Gaspar Castano de Sosa came in 1591 to erect a large cross to remind the Indians that this was part of the province of New Mexico and they were expected to pay tribute. The Indians tore the cross down as soon as Castano left. A large mission was built early in the 1600s, but was destroyed in the Pueblo Revolt, and a priest was murdered. After the reconquest, a second church was built but later collapsed while being repaired. Only about twenty pre-Hispanic structures still stand, and most of them have been modernized. Few of the 400 members of the tribe live in the pueblo. Artisans make woven belts, pendants, and beaded hair clips. Photography by permit from tribal headquarters. Open daily.

Picuris Pueblo (from Espanola, 17 miles north on NM 68 to NM 75, right 24 miles, then left onto Indian Road 120, then 1 mile north; 505/587-2519). The first Spanish to come here found the inhabitants aggressive and warlike. In the revolt, some twenty Spaniards were slain at Picuris, the mission was demolished, and a band of Picuris warriors went to Santa Fe to fight there. The Picuris did not resist the reconquest, but rose up again in 1696. Abandoning the pueblo, the 3,000 Picuris Indians joined the Apache. Only 500 were still alive when they returned to their pueblo ten years later. Today only 200 Indians live here and most of the pueblo is gone, but what remains is fascinating. In the 1960s, archaeologists unearthed several 700-year-old kivas, which now are open to visitors. A mission built about 1775 is on the plaza. A museum displays recently unearthed artifacts. Artisans produce bead and leather work and one of the few types of Indian pottery that can be used for cooking. Tours in the summer. Photography by permit from the the tribal office. Open daily.

Sandia Pueblo (from Albuquerque, 14 miles north on U.S. 85; 505/867-2876). One of the cluster of twelve pueblos of Tiguex, near the site of present-day Albuquerque. Wintering here, Coronado's conquistadors began stripping the pueblos of food and clothing and raping the women. Violence flared, and Coronado ordered all the villages burned. A new pueblo grew up around the Mission of San Francisco, but it was destroyed in the revolt. The Sandia moved westward to Hopi country and built the village of Payupki on Second Mesa, returning here in 1742 to rebuild the pueblo. A new mission, dedicated to Saint Anthony, was built on the site of the old mission. Today, except for the saint's feast day, June 12, there is little here for the visitor. Most of the old structures have lost their distinction through careless remodeling. Photography is not permitted. Permission to walk in the pueblo must be obtained from the tribal office. Open daily.

San Felipe Pueblo (from Albuquerque, 22 miles north on I-25, left at the San Felipe sign, then 3 miles; 505/867-3381). A mis-

"There was so much sky, more than at sea, more than anywhere else in the world. The plain was there, under one's foot, but what one saw when one looked about was that brilliant blue world of stinging air and moving cloud. Even the mountains were mere ant-hills under it. Elsewhere the sky is the roof of the world; but here the earth was the floor of the sky. The landscape one longed for when one was away, the thing all around one, the world one actually lived in, was the sky, the sky!"

—WILLA CATHER,
Death Comes for the Archbishop

"The Indians all directed their attack against me because my armor was gilded and glittering."

—FRANCISCO VÁSQUEZ DE CORONADO, 1540

sion was built here in 1605, but destroyed in the Pueblo Revolt, and the pueblo was abandoned. The Indians joined other refugees in the mountains, and later built a new village atop Tamita Mesa. They returned about 1700, and a new mission was built a few years later. San Felipe surrounds a central plaza, which has two large kivas. Many of the 2,500 Indians farm small plots in the bottomland of the nearby Rio Grande. Except for feast days and dances, there isn't much for the visitor. Photography is not permitted. Open daily.

San Ildefonso Pueblo (from Santa Fe, 15 miles north on U.S. 84/285 to the junction of NM 4, then left 6 miles; 505/786-5382). The large mission here was built about 1617. In the Pueblo Revolt, the Indians spared the mission, but helped burn Santa Fe. In 1694, after the reconquest, they joined with Santa Clara and Tesuque Indians on a mesa to the north. They withstood a two-month Spanish siege that killed forty, but later signed a peace treaty and returned to their pueblos. They rose up again two years later, this time burning the mission before going to the mesa. Spanish cavalry routed them, and they returned to the pueblo and have been there ever since. Today more than 200 historic structures surround the large plaza. Many have been reconstructed but, in contrast to some other pueblos, the work was done carefully to retain the traditional architecture. In the late 1950s the old mission, which the tribe considered ugly, was demolished and replaced with a handsome replica of the mission burned in the third San Ildefonso revolt. The tribal office has a collection of pueblo artifacts and contemporary arts and crafts. San Ildefonso is well known for its pottery. The most famous potter was Maria Martinez, who died in 1980. She and her husband developed a method of making matte black designs on polished black pottery. Photography by permit. Open daily.

San Juan Pueblo (from Espanola, 1 mile north on NM 68, then left onto U.S. 285 for one-half mile; 505/852-4400). This is believed to be the third pueblo built here after the coming of the Anasazi. The other two, both named O'ke, were destroyed by floods centuries ago. In 1598, Juan de Onate chose O'ke to be the capital of the province. The Indians were forced out, and the pueblo was renamed San Juan de los Caballeros. In 1675, forty-seven Indian religious leaders from several pueblos were charged with witchcraft. Some were hanged, some flogged. One survivor was Po Pay of San Juan, who became the leader of the Pueblo Revolt in 1680. Today San Juan is a progressive pueblo, a leader in forming Indian policy and in the production of pueblo arts and crafts. The Eight Northern Pueblos Council displays of pueblo artifacts are here. San Juan artisans produce pottery, coral and turquoise jewelry, embroidery, beadwork, weaving, and baskets. Photography by permit only. Open daily.

Santa Clara Pueblo (from Espanola, 1.3 miles north on NM 5; 505/753-7326). After the reconquest, the Santa Clara Indians joined with refugees from other pueblos on Black Mesa. They later fled to the Zuñi and Hopi pueblos to the west, returning here in 1702. Today, quite a few of the old buildings in the pueblo have been torn down and replaced by new construction. Santa Clara pottery is well known, consisting of both polychrome and black-on-black ware. Photography is permitted. Open daily.

Santo Domingo Pueblo (from Albuquerque, U.S. 25 north 30 miles to the junction of NM 22, left 4 miles to the junction of Indian 84, then right 2 miles; 505/465-2214). This Santo Domingo Pueblo was built in the late 19th century, its predecessors having been washed away by floods. The original pueblo was called Guipui. In the reconquest, Santa Clarans retreated into the mountains. The Spanish attacked, killing ninety warriors and capturing most of the women and children. The survivors fled west and founded the Laguna Pueblo. Today, although

Buffalo dancers in action at the Santo Domingo Pueblo in New Mexico. On feast days, dancers from two to eighty years old perform the Corn Dance. This pueblo is known for its jewelry, particularly heishi, *small shells polished to a silky smoothness.*

the pueblo is open daily, Santo Domingo is considered by most to be unfriendly to non-Indian visitors, except on August 4, the annual feast day. Photography is not permitted.

Tesuque Pueblo (from Santa Fe, 9 miles north on U.S. 64/84/285; 505/983-2667). The Pueblo Revolt started here. Two Tesuque served as secret messengers between the plotters. Betrayed to the governor, they were arrested. The chiefs sounded the alarm and the uprising began. Tesuque warriors killed a Spanish civil servant on August 9, 1680, a priest the next morning, the first casualties of the revolt. Tesuque was later abandoned, and the inhabitants lived for fourteen years in the mountains to the west. In the reconquest, they joined the Santa Clara and San Ildefonso Indians and fought at Black Mesa. They returned here in 1700 and built a new pueblo. Today the pueblo has a large central plaza dominated by a church dedicated to San Diego, which was built in 1915 on the ruins of an earlier church. Some Tesuque potters make a fine black-and-red-on-white ware, but most produce what is called

"tourist pottery." Photography by permit, and only on the plaza. Open daily.

Zia Pueblo (from Bernalillo, 19 miles west on NM 44; 505/867-3304). A conquistador, García López de Cárdenas, visited here in 1540 and noted that the houses were whitewashed and trimmed in bright colors. Priests arrived around 1598 and built a mission using forced Indian labor. It was destroyed and the priests slain in the Pueblo Revolt. Soldiers found 3,000 warriors defending the pueblo. Two days of fighting left 600 Indians dead, fifty Spanish wounded, and the pueblo in flames. Seventy Indians were taken captive, and the other survivors took refuge in the mountains. By the time Diego de Vargas arrived in the 1692 reconquest, the Indians were back at the pueblo. They swore allegiance to the crown, and the Spanish helped them rebuild the mission and the church. The pueblo, atop a 300-foot-high hill, is relatively unchanged today, though a little the worse for wear. Zia pottery is excellent, black and dark brown on white, usually depicting the long-necked Zia bird. Photography is not permitted. Open daily.

Descendants of the Zuñi, who made these pictographs, live on the Zuñi Pueblo in New Mexico, one of the "Seven Cities of Cibola" that Coronado thought were built of gold. The Zuñi are famous for their Shalako dance, performed in late November or early December.

Zuñi Pueblo (from Albuquerque, 75 miles west on U.S. 40 to junction of NM 53 at Grants, left and 75 miles on NM 53; 505/782-4481). The Zuñi have been here for more than 1,000 years and their history is the most fully recorded of all the pueblos. Estevan, a former Moorish slave, and Fray Marcos arrived at Hawikuh (fifteen miles south of the present pueblo) in 1539. Estevan was killed by the Indians, but Fray Marco made it back to Mexico, where he told of golden cities to the north. In 1598, the Zuñi came under Spanish domination. In 1632 they killed two priests and, fearing Spanish wrath, fled to Corn Mountain, southwest of the pueblo, returning three years later. Hawikuh was abandoned in 1670 after an Apache attack killed many Zuñis and destroyed the mission. They again fled to Corn Mountain during the Pueblo Revolt, and returned peacefully during the reconquest. Instead of reoccupying the old villages, they built a new pueblo atop the site of Haloes. The Zuñi Pueblo today has only a few of the original structures left, and the new buildings are not attractive. Visitors may arrange at tribal headquarters for a guide to the ruins of Hawikuh and other nearby old pueblos. The Zuñi are famous for their black-and-red-on-white pottery and sil-ver jewelry decorated with turquoise, jet, and coral. Photography by permit. Open daily.

Pueblo Festivals

Candelaria Day Celebration. San Felipe, Cochiti, and Santo Domingo pueblos. Buffalo and other dances. Early February.

Spring Corn Dances. Cochiti, San Felipe, Santo Domingo, and other pueblos. Also races and contests. Easter weekend.

Fiesta and Green Corn Dance. San Felipe Pueblo. Early May.

Riverman Day. Cochiti Pueblo. Early May.

Folk Art Festival. At Old Cienega Village Museum. Exhibits, crafts demonstrations, music, and dancers. Spring Festival, first weekend in June; Harvest Festival, first weekend in October.

War Dances and Foot Races. San Juan and Santo Domingo pueblos. Late June.

Santa Fe Rodeo. Four days in mid-July.

Fiesta at Santo Domingo Pueblo. The largest and most famous of the Rio Grande pueblo fiestas. Corn dance. Early August.

Santa Fe Horse Show. Early August.

St. Lawrence Feast. Cochiti Pueblo. Mid-August.

Indian Market. Santa Fe Plaza. Tribes from all over the United States display arts and crafts. Dances. Two days in mid-August (505/983-5220).

International Antique Indian Art Show. Hilton Inn., Santa Fe. Pre-1935 items in the largest show of its kind in the country. Mid-August.

Christmas Eve Celebrations. Street fires and *farolitos* (paper bag lanterns) "to guide the Christ Child," candlelit *nacimientos* (nativity scenes), and other events in Santa Fe and nearby villages. December 24. Santo Domingo, Tesuque, Santa Clara and other pueblos have Christmas dances the following three days.

16

Arizona

BISBEE

Copper was discovered here in 1877 by an Indian scout who, with a partner, founded the Copper Queen Mine. Phelps Dodge purchased land nearby, and the two companies merged to form the Copper Queen Consolidated Mining Company. They named the town Bisbee after an Eastern stockholder. By 1885 the mine was "the Queen of the Copper Camps." Operations continued until 1975—a record of longevity few mines in the country can equal. Now a semi-ghost town, Bisbee waits, hoping for an increase in the price of copper that would make the mine profitable again. The idle mine is on one side of the canyon, the public buildings line the main street at the bottom, and the town clings to the other slope in a haphazard manner.

Bisbee Mining and Historical Museum (5 Copper Queen Plaza; 602/432-7071). In 1895 this was the office of the mine. Exhibits explain early mining techniques and recount the town's history. Historical photographs. Open daily. The museum also operates the *Muheim Heritage House* (207B Youngblood Hill). Open Friday through Monday.

Bisbee Restoration Association and Historical Museum (37 Main; 602/432-4106). Indian relics and pioneer artifacts. Open daily except Sunday.

Town and Mine Tours (602/432-2141). Visitors are taken on a narrated tour through the historic sections of Bisbee and two mines. Inquire about wheelchair access.

Queen Mine (U.S. 80; 602/432-2071). A mine-train tour goes 1,800 feet into the mine. Tours daily.

Lavender Pit (U.S. 80; 602/432-2071). A 340-acre open-pit mine. Tours available. Open daily.

Accommodations: *Copper Queen* (11 Howell Ave.; 602/432-2216; reservations, 800/247-5829). This 1902 hotel has been charmingly restored. *Bisbee Inn* (45 OK St.; 602/432-5131). The inn is decorated with antiques. Breakfast is included in the rates.

CASA GRANDE

Casa Grande Ruins National Monument (about 14 miles east on AZ 84, then 9 miles north on AZ 87; 602/623-3172). Casa Grande is a mysterious, four-story structure built of unreinforced caliche mud. Archaeologists have no idea of its original purpose. Around it are the ruins of a prehistoric Indian village of some sixty dwellings, several unexcavated mounds, and parts of a seven-foot-high encircling wall. The Hohokam Indians lived here until they abandoned the area in the late 1300s. Casa Grande was in ruins when Father Eusebio Kino, a Jesuit priest, was led to the site by Indians in 1694. In 1891, archaeologists conducted initial excavations. The Visitor Center has Hohokam displays and artifacts. Open daily.

Casa Grande Valley Historical Society and Museum (110 West Florence Blvd.; 602/836-2223). Local history artifacts, period furnishings, and clothing. Exhibits. Open daily except Mondays, mid-September to mid-June.

CHANDLER

Gila River Indian Reservation (15 miles south at the juncture of AZ 93 and I-10; 602/963-3981). The reservation has an outdoor museum with reconstructed houses of the Pima, Apache, Papago, and Maricopa Indians. The

Living Off the Desert

The Apache knew and used the desert. They survived there by using desert plants for food, drink, medicine, and narcotics. The fruit of the cholla cactus was a source of water and energy-giving glucose. Boiled into a potion, the roots of the tall ocotillo cactus relieved fatigue; powdered, they reduced painful swelling. The fruit and flower of the Spanish bayonet yucca were a major food source, and the ground-up roots were used as a detergent to wash clothing. Apache needs were also met by ripe sunflower seeds, prickly-pear cactus, mesquite seeds ground into flour, even portions of milkweed, primrose, and cattail.

Gen. George Crook noted in his 1883 annual report that "the country [the Apache] inhabit is larger than New England, and the roughest on the continent, and though affording no food upon which soldiers can subsist, provides the Indian with everything necessary for sustaining his life indefinitely. The agave [a plant, also called mescal, used for food and liquor] grows luxuriantly in all their mountains, and upon this plant alone the Indians can live. They have no property nor settled habitations of any kind, but roam about like coyotes, and their temporary resting places are chosen with all the experience gained by generations of warfare. The Indian knows every foot of his territory; can endure fatigue and fasting, and can live without food or water for periods that would kill the hardiest mountaineer."

Gila Arts and Crafts Museum gift shop sells the work of more than thirty tribes in the Southwest, California, and Mexico. The restaurant features Indian food.

Accommodations: *Cone's Tourist Home* (2804 West Warner; 602/839-0369). This lodging offers guests kitchen and barbecue facilities in a contemporary home on two acres. Breakfast is included in the rates.

COTTONWOOD

Montezuma Castle National Monument (20 miles southeast on AZ 279, then north and east off I-17; 602/567-3322). In a shallow cave nearly a hundred feet above the bottom of Beaver Creek Canyon is one of the best-preserved cliff dwellings of the Southwest, a five-story, twenty-room structure built by the Sinagua more than 800 years ago. Originally believed to have been built by the Aztec, it was misnamed Montezuma's Castle. The dwelling is built of chunks of rough limestone cemented together with clay mortar and plastered over with mud. The Sinagua who lived here farmed on the banks of the creek. By 1300 the cave dwelling was the center of a large community that lived in the canyon, but by 1400 the area was deserted. The residents probably relocated south to the Gila Valley. Eleven miles northeast is *Montezuma Well*, a 470-foot-wide, 55-foot-deep limestone sinkhole fed by a spring at a rate of one and a half million gallons a day. Several cliff dwellings, a pit house, and the ruins of a pueblo are around the rim of the well. An irrigation canal built by the Sinagua leads from the spring. The Visitor Center has examples of Sinagua pottery and handicrafts and exhibits explaining the ruins. There is no access to the ruins themselves. Open daily, June to September.

FLAGSTAFF

Army scouts helped Thomas McMillan build the first shack here in 1876. When it was finished, they stripped a tall pine of its branches, tied a flag to it, and gave the town its name. Flagstaff became a railroad town with the arrival in 1882 of the Atlantic & Pacific Railroad.

Lowell Observatory (1 mile west on Mars Hill Rd., off Santa Fe Ave.; 602/774-2096). The observatory was founded in 1894 by Percival Lowell, and the planet Pluto was discovered by the observatory in 1930. Telescope viewing, tours, museum. Phone for hours.

Museum of Northern Arizona (4 miles northwest on U.S. 180; 602/774-5211). Exhibits on the contemporary Indian cultures of the area, their arts and crafts, and the geology, archaeology, biology, paleontology, and arts of the Colorado Plateau. Open daily.

Pioneer Museum (2½ miles northwest on U.S. 180; 602/774-6272). Run by the Arizona Historical Society, the museum has material and exhibits on the history of the area. Open daily except holidays.

Riordan State Historic Park (off U.S. 89A at Chambers Rd.; 602/779-4395). The park has homes built in 1904 by Michael and Timothy Riordan, local businessmen and politicians who were instrumental in the development of Flagstaff. Open daily.

Walnut Canyon National Monument (12 miles east off U.S. 66/I-40; 602/536-3367). In about 1125, Sinagua Indians came to this 400-foot-deep canyon and built some 120 cliff dwellings beneath the limestone overhanging the rim. They grew corn and beans along the rim and hunted in the canyon. A century or so later, a drought came and the Sinagua left. Now part of the Coconino National Forest, the canyon takes its name from the Arizona walnut trees that grow here. The cliff dwellings are well preserved, but few of the rooms have been restored. From the Visitor Center, a paved trail leads to twenty-five of the cliff dwelling rooms; others can be seen from the trail. Open daily. Limited wheelchair access.

Wupatki National Monument (15 miles east on AZ 97, then 22 miles on loop road; 602/527-7134). The Sinagua lived here, near the San Francisco Peaks, from 600 to 1065, farming and trading with the Anasazi to the north and the Hohokam to the south. In 1065 a volcano erupted and covered some 800 square miles with cinders and ashes. The Sinagua fled. The eruption, however, turned out to be a blessing; the ash enriched the soil and held moisture from the spring and fall rains. In a few years the Sinagua returned and later were joined by Hohokam and Anasazi. By the end of the century, some 8,000 people were living in the area. The rich soil slowly was farmed out, and then rainfall began to decrease. Some of the Sinagua began moving south into the Verde Valley and Walnut Canyon. Those who stayed built many pueblos, including Wupatki, Lomaki, and the Citadel. Conditions continued to worsen, however, and by 1225 the area was deserted. Within

Flagstaff, Arizona, didn't look too promising until the Atlantic & Pacific Railroad arrived in 1882 and it became a railroad town. Today the city's main industry is tourism. It makes a good base from which to explore the wonders of the Grand Canyon and the Navaho country.

The Spanish

Alvar Núñez Cabeza de Vaca. A born survivor, Cabeza de Vaca was on the Pánfilo de Narváez expedition that cost the lives of 300 men. Cabeza de Vaca and a few others built makeshift boats and set out from present-day Florida. The boats became separated and Cabeza de Vaca's was shipwrecked, probably on Galveston Island. The bedraggled four survivors from the boat were captured by Indians, but Cabeza de Vaca convinced them he was a medicine man and won their release. A few years later they met a Spanish slave hunter near Culiacán in Sinaloa. Cabeza de Vaca's account of his adventures, *Los Naufragios* (*The Shipwrecked*), gave the Spanish a more accurate idea of the east-west extent of North America and stimulated interest in investigating the "northern mystery."

Hernando de Soto. Serving with Pizarro in the conquest of Peru made de Soto rich, and exploring Florida and the Southeast made him famous. Excited by stories of the "northern mystery," he left Spain with seven ships in 1538, landed on the west coast of Florida, and headed north. After traveling through the South, he crossed the Mississippi, passed through Arkansas and into Oklahoma, then headed east again. De Soto died in 1542 and was buried in the Mississippi River. An expedition led by his successor, Luís de Moscoso, went into Texas, probably to the Trinity River, then returned to the Mississippi. They built crude boats, floated down the river and along the Gulf shore until they reached the Río Pánuco in Mexico. Barely half of the expedition survived.

Francisco Vásquez de Coronado. Rumors of golden cities led the thirty-year-old governor of New Galacia, a province in northwest Mexico, to mount the first expedition to the West. He went first to the region along the present New Mexico–Arizona border and came to Cíbola, a Zuñi pueblo. He sent a lieutenant, García López de Cárdenas, west to the Colorado River, where he became the first white man to see the Grand Canyon. Another lieutenant, Hernando de Alarcón, went up the Colorado River as far as California. Indians told of gold far to the east, and the expedition crossed the Pecos and went across the Texas and Oklahoma panhandles into Kansas. He reached the Indian village of Quivira, found no riches, and returned to Mexico, painfully injured and disappointed.

Juan Rodríguez Cabrillo. A Portuguese captain in the employ of Spain, Cabrillo was the first to explore the coast of southern California. In 1542, he sailed from Puerto de Navid (near present-day Manzanillo, Mexico) in search of a water route from the Pacific to the Atlantic. He discovered San Diego Bay, Santa Catalina and San Clemente islands, the Santa Barbara Channel, and the islands of Santa Cruz, Santa Rosa, and San Miguel. He missed the Bay of Monterey, the Golden Gate, and San Francisco Bay, but did find Drake's Bay. Turning south, Cabrillo landed at San Miguel Island and died there. His chief pilot,

Bartolomé Ferrelo, assumed command, went north to a few miles above the California–Oregon border, then returned to Mexico.

Juan de Onate. The founding of New Mexico cost Onate his health and his fortune. The son of a rich mine owner, he married a descendent of Cortez, and in 1595 received a royal warrant to colonize the upper Rio Grande Valley. By 1598 he had founded a settlement in New Mexico, San Gabriel, near San Juan Pueblo. He sent expeditions west to the Sea of Cortez and east to the Plains, but found no gold or silver, which he needed to support his colony. When the Acoma Pueblo revolted, Onate suppressed the rebellion with much bloodshed, then had to cope with a mutiny of his disillusioned settlers. A broken man, he resigned as governor in 1607, and later was tried for mismanaging the colony and acquitted. Onate died in Spain while petitioning the Crown to pay him for past services.

Eusebio Francisco Kino. At least twenty cities in the Southwest began as mission villages established by this indefatigable Jesuit missionary. From 1687 to 1711 he built a chain of twenty-four missions, including San Xavier del Bac, near present-day Tucson. Fra Kino introduced to the villages varieties of European livestock, grains, and fruits. He made numerous explorations, mapping Spain's empire. His maps from a trip to Baja California proved that California was not an island.

Diego de Vargas. The Spanish soldier who recaptured New Mexico after the Pueblo Revolt spent three years in prison before his accomplishment was acknowledged. Vargas came to Mexico in 1673 as a courier of the king, and after holding several minor posts he was made governor and captain general of New Mexico. It was not a choice assignment; the Indians had rebelled, slaying soldiers, missionaries, and colonists, and forcing the survivors to leave. Vargas entered New Mexico only to find the pueblos in a conciliatory mood. Most of the leaders of the revolt had died, and the pueblos needed help in fighting off Apache attacks. Vargas went back to Mexico and returned with colonists, only to be attacked at Santa Fe and the San Ildefonso Pueblo. He prevailed, but several pueblos rebelled the following year, killing twenty-six. Finally he made the pueblos accept Spanish rule. In 1697, however, he was ordered home, where he was charged with misconduct and imprisoned. Three years later he was exonerated and sent back to New Mexico as governor. The next year he was killed while fighting Apaches.

Junípero Serra. The twenty-one Franciscan missions that grace the coast of California were the result of the prodigious labors of a missionary who one day may be elevated to sainthood. Born on the island of Majorca, Serra joined the order and taught philosophy before he was sent as a missionary to Mexico. When Gaspar de Portolá occupied present-day California, Serra went along as his religious counterpart. In 1769, Fra Serra founded San Diego de Alcalá, his first California mission. When Portolá discovered Monterey Bay, a second, San Carlos Borromeo, was built at Carmel, and Fra Serra made his headquarters there for the rest of his life. Despite poor health, he personally founded nine of the missions, and supervised the others. His work was a prelude to the Spanish colonization of California.

the fifty-six square miles of the park are some 800 prehistoric dwellings. *Lomaki* is a half-mile off the main loop road. The *Citadel* and *Nalakihu* are located beside a pullout on the loop road. A three-mile road leads to *Wukoki*. The Visitor Center displays Sinaguan pottery and artifacts. Open daily.

Nearby is the *Sunset Crater National Monument*, an unusual, thousand-foot volcanic cone with subsidiary formations and a visitor center. Open daily.

Oak Creek Canyon (14 miles south on U.S. 89A). From the lookout point at the northern end of this beautiful canyon, the road descends nearly 2,000 feet to the creekbed. At the southern mouth of the canyon is the resort town of *Sedona*.

Accommodations: *Dierker House* (423 West Cherry; 602/774-3249). A charming bed-and-breakfast in the old part of the city.

FLORENCE

Pinal County Historical Society Museum (718 South Main; 602/868-4382). Exhibits relating to Indian and pioneer life in the area. Open Wednesday through Sunday, September through May.

McFarland State Historic Park (5th and Main; 602/868-4331). On the site of the original adobe courthouse, an interpretive center has displays of early state and U.S. legal history, and the personal collections of Governor Ernest McFarland, who also was a U.S. senator and a state supreme court justice. Open Thursday through Monday.

GANADO

Hubbell Trading Post National Historic Site (one-half mile west on AZ 264; 602/755-3475). For generations the trading post was a bridge between the white world and the Navajo, and the Hubbell Trading Post is an example of this. It was founded in 1876 by John Lorenzo Hubbell, who learned the

life, ways, and language of the Navajo as a young man. Navajo traveled miles over dusty trails to reach the post to sell their rugs and turquoise and silver jewelry. Trading was a slow and usually enjoyable process. Little money changed hands; most of the business was carried on by exchanging Navajo products for the trader's goods. The post met other Navajo needs with a blacksmith shop, a bakery, a farm, and a one-room schoolhouse with a teacher hired by Hubbell. It was also a place to meet old friends and relatives, and exchange news and gossip. Hubbell was a trusted friend of the Navajo, translating and writing letters, settling family quarrels, explaining government policy, and helping the sick. During a smallpox epidemic in 1886, Hubbell's home became a hospital. Over the years, Hubbell built a trading empire that included several stage and freight lines. He and other traders functioned as vital intermediaries between the Navajo and the white community. They helped the Navajo obtain government aid for building dams and irrigation projects. Hubbell died on November 12, 1930, and was buried on Hubbell Hill, overlooking the trading post, next to his wife and his closest friend, Many Horses. The trading post is still in business. Exhibits, tours, craft demonstrations. Open daily.

GLOBE

This town began with a silver strike, but copper made its fortune and some of the mines are still in operation. Globe is the starting point of the *Apache Trail*, which loops to Junction and back, a 140-mile, five-hour drive.

Tonto National Monument (3 miles west on U.S. 60/70, then north on AZ 88, 30 miles to a marked turnoff; 602/467-2241). In the part of the Sonoran Desert known as the Tonto Basin are two cliff dwellings in caves on the sides of the steep canyons. They were built by the Salado, a peaceful people who moved here between A.D. 900 and 1000 from the Little Colorado River area. For centuries they farmed the bottoms of the canyons, then abandoned their villages and built new dwellings on the rims of the canyons. Then for some reason they left, perhaps moving to present-day New Mexico or the pueblos along the Rio Grande. The Salado were skilled artisans, noted for dyeing the cloth they made on their wooden looms. The *Upper Ruin* contains about forty rooms, the *Lower Ruin* twenty, several of which have been restored. A steep trail leads to the Lower Ruin. Tours of the Upper Ruin are available from mid-September to mid-May by reservation. The Visitor Center displays Salado artifacts. Open daily. Limited wheelchair access.

Gila County Historical Museum (1 mile north on U.S. 60; 602/425-7385). Relics and artifacts of the Salado Indians and the pioneers. Open daily except Sunday.

Besh-Ba-Gowah Indian Ruins (turn right from end of South Broad St., cross bridge, and continue on Ice House Canyon Rd.; 602/425-0320). Salado Indians lived here from 1225 to 1400. The ruins contain more than 200 rooms. Museum. Visitor Center.

Apache Tears Cave (35 miles west via U.S. 60, near Superior; 602/425-5775). The cave has a digging area where visitors may search for the rounded bits of translucent obsidian called "Apache tears." Open daily.

The Apache, who once peacefully roamed an area encompassing present-day Arizona, New Mexico, and northern Mexico, resisted Spanish colonists and developed a reputation for ferocity. This vintage portrait shows an Apache boy painted in tribal patterns.

miles east on U.S. 180; 602/524-6228). The greatest and most spectacular display of petrified wood in the world is contained in the park's 93,532 acres. Trees from a primeval forest are believed to have been washed into ponds by streams. Buried under sediment and volcanic ash, the wood of the trees rotted away and the cavities were filled solid by mineral compounds; the *Rainbow Forest Museum* shows the process in detail. Throughout the park are thousands of petroglyphs made by the Anasazi. A portion of the Painted Desert is contained in the park, and there are good viewpoints along the park road. Visitor Center.

HOLBROOK

Navajo County Historical Museum (100 East Arizona, in Navajo County Courthouse; 602/524-6558). Exhibits relating to Navajo, Hopi, Apache, and Hispanic and local history. Petrified forest and dinosaur exhibits. Open daily except Sundays, May through September; Monday through Friday the rest of the year.

Petrified Forest National Park (19

JEROME

A thousand years ago, Indians used the colorful ores found here to make warpaint and dyes, and in 1872 an Indian scout found evidence of this early digging. A party of prospectors arrived in Prescott in 1876, heard the stories, and took a look, but were unimpressed. Later that year, two ranchers took out claims but quickly sold them to the

"If we are taken back to our own country we will call you our father and mother. If there was only a single goat there, we would all live off of it. . . . I hope to God you will not ask us to go to any other country but our own. When the Navajo were first created, four mountains and four rivers were pointed out to us, outside of which we not should live. . . . Changing Woman gave us this land. Our God created it for us."

—BARBONCITO, TO GEN. WILLIAM T. SHERMAN

territorial governor for $2,000. Nothing happened until the governor met a New York lawyer who was willing to finance a mining operation. The lawyer was Eugene Jerome, Winston Churchill's American grandfather, and he stipulated that the town be named after him. Not until 1893 was the United Verde Copper Company incorporated and a smelter built, a slow beginning for an area that was to produce $500 million in copper. A strike in 1917 was broken when company men forced several hundred miners and agitators into boxcars at gunpoint, and had them taken into the desert and dropped off. The town had a population of 15,000 in 1929, but production trailed off and the mine was closed for good in 1953. The population now is fewer than 500. Renovated structures house shops and restaurants.

Jerome History State Park (off U.S. 89A; 602/634-5381). The park contains the *Douglas Memorial Mining Museum*, the former home of "Rawhide Jimmy" Douglas, which tells the history of Jerome and mining in Arizona. Open daily.

Tuzigoot National Monument (2 miles northwest on U.S. 89A toward Clarkdale, then one mile north on Broadway; 602/634-5564). On a small hill overlooking the valley of the Verde River is a large, partially restored Sinagua pueblo built of limestone blocks, river stones, and mud mortar that once contained ninety rooms. An unusual feature of the pueblo is the scarcity of doorways. The Sinagua would climb a ladder to the roof, enter through a hatch, and go down another ladder. When the great drought came, Tuzigoot tripled in size as more and more Sinaguas came to the valley from the north. The pueblo was abandoned by 1450, its inhabitants probably moving to Hohokam or Hopi villages. The Visitor Center has an exceptional exhibit of jewelry, ceramics, cloth, and Sinagua artifacts. Open daily. Limited wheelchair access.

Fort Verde State Historical Park (15 miles southeast on AZ 279 in the town of Camp Verde: 602/567-3275). The park contains four original buildings of a major army fort during the Indian campaigns of 1871–91. Two furnished officers' quarters, post officer's office, and military artifacts. Open daily.

KAYENTA

Navajo National Monument (20 miles southwest of town on U.S. 160, then 9 miles north on AZ 564; 606/672-2366). The name is misleading; the ruins in these stark canyons are those of structures built by the Kayenta Anasazi. Centuries after the Anasazi abandoned the area, the ruins were discovered by migrating Navajos, hence the name. They lived here for half a century, at first in temporary brush houses, then in pit houses, which were circular, belowground dwellings. Finally they began to build aboveground houses made of stone or sticks covered with mud, a type of construction called *jacal*. To store surplus crops they built storage chambers and made pottery. By 1200 the Marsh Pass region (which visitors drive through on the way into the park) was dotted with farms. Villages, built as masonry room clusters, were nearby, usually on a rise with a view of the surrounding fields. The inhabitants raised corn, beans, and squash, and traded with other settlements for such things as cotton and turquoise. The Kayenta Anasazi were religious, and their kivas (subterranean ceremonial chambers) were used for ceremonies. When a prolonged drought made farming impossible, the Kayenta Anasazi abandoned their village and moved into the Tsegi Canyons. In an inexplicable change of custom, they built the cliff dwellings that are preserved in the park. This move gave them another fifty years before some combination of problems led them to abandon the whole area in about 1300.

There are three major ruins here: *Betatakin, Keet Seel,* and the *Inscription House,* which has been closed to visitors since 1968 because of its fragile condition. Betatakin ("ledge house" in Navajo) is a deep cave that faces south. At its height, about 1286, some 125 people lived at Betatakin. Keet Seel ("broken pieces of pottery") was occupied much longer, and probably had some 150 inhabitants at its peak.

From May through October, tours led by rangers go to Betatakin, a three-mile round trip with a 700-foot incline, the equivalent of a seventy-story building. The ruin can be seen from the Betatakin Point Overlook, a half-mile from the center. Keet Seel is about eight miles north of the center, and can be reached only on foot or by horseback. Navajo guides lead full-day horseback excursions. The Visitor Center has exhibits, audiovisual programs on Anasazi life, and campfire programs. Open daily. Limited wheelchair access.

Monument Valley Tours, Inc. (602/697-3463). This company offers guided tours in four-wheel-drive vehicles to Monument Valley, Mystery Valley, and Hunt's Mesa. Daily.

Accommodations: *Goulding's Monument Valley Lodge* (23 miles north of Kayenta, then 2 miles west on U.S. 163; 801/727-3231). Open March through October. Restaurant.

KINGMAN

Mohave Museum of History and Art (400 West Beale St., a quarter mile east of I-40 Beale St./Las Vegas exit; 602/753-3195). Exhibits on local and state history, a turquoise display, and a gallery where local artists show their work. Open daily except major holidays.

Bonelli House (310 North 4th St.; 602/753-3195). This was one of the first permanent structures in the city when it was built in 1894. It has been restored and furnished with original pieces and period antiques. Open Mondays and Thursdays.

Oatman (25 miles southwest on U.S. 66; 602/753-6106). This was a tent city in 1906 and grew to a population of 10,000 when the gold mine was abandoned in World War II. Now 125 people live here. The town is authentic and has been the setting for several movies. Wild burros roam the streets, and gunfights are staged on weekends. Old mine sites. Turquoise and antique shops.

MESA

Mesa Southwest Museum (53 North MacDonald; 602/644-2230). The museum is devoted to the history of the area from pre-Hispanic Indians to the Space Age. Territorial jail cells. Indian dwellings. Pioneer and Indian collections. Adobe schoolhouse. Visitors may pan for gold. Open daily.

Champlain Fighter Museum (4636 Fighter Aces Dr. at Falcon Field; 602/830-4540). An important collection of fighter aircraft from the First and Second World Wars, an automatic-weapons display, a gallery of aerial combat art, and a collection of photographs of fighter aircraft. Open daily.

Dolly Steamboat Cruises (602/827-9144). Passengers are taken on a narrated tour that follows the original bed of the Salt River.

Lost Dutchman State Park (14 miles east on U.S. 60 [89] to Apache Junction, then 6 miles northeast via AZ 88); 602/982-4485). Indians told Coronado of gold in these rugged mountains, but after several members of his party were killed here under mysterious circumstances, Coronado called off the search, naming them the Superstition Mountains. In 1845, Don Miguel Peralta of Sonora, Mexico, discovered a rich vein here, but he and all his miners were massacred by Apaches, who believed the miners were defiling the home of their Thunder God. Later a Dutch miner learned the location of the vein from an Apache maiden, who was slain by her tribe for her indiscretion. The

Apaches, who had terrorized the Southwest for years before their capture, pose in 1866 at a rest stop near the Nueces River in Texas, on their way to prison in Florida. In the center of the first row is Chief Natchez, and to his left is the infamous Geronimo and his son in matching shirts.

Dutchman became a recluse in Phoenix, going into the mountains from time to time to bring out ore. Many tried to follow him, but he either lost them in the maze of overgrown canyons and gullies or killed them if they got too close. His mine became famous as the Lost Dutchman Mine. Since his death in 1891, many attempts have been made to find the Lost Dutchman, but all have failed. The park is the supposed site of the mine. Open daily. Limited wheelchair access.

NOGALES

Pimeria Alta Historical Society Museum (223 Grand Ave.; 602/287-5402). Exhibits tracing the history of southern Arizona and northern Sonora. Tours. Open daily.

Tubac Presidio State Historic Park (20 miles east on AZ 82, then 4 miles north; 602/398-2252). A fort was built here in 1752, the first white settlement in the state. In the park

are Spanish Colonial and territorial ruins, and petroglyphs. A museum has displays and an underground view of the remains of the fort's main building. Open daily.

PAGE

Page is at the Glen Canyon Dam on the Colorado River, which forms 180-mile-long Lake Powell, the second-longest man-made lake in the country.

John Wesley Powell Memorial Museum (6 North Lake Powell Blvd.; 602/645-9496). Collections of Indian artifacts, fluorescent rocks, and books, as well as a replica of Powell's boat. Open daily.

PARKER

Parker is on the Colorado River, fifteen miles south of the Parker Dam, which forms

Lake Havasu and is the trade center of the Colorado Indian Reservation.

Colorado River Indian Reservation (2 miles south at 2nd Ave. and Mohave Rd.; 602/669-9211). This is the home of four tribes: the Mojave and Chemehuevi are the original inhabitants of the region; the Navajo and Hopi moved here more recently. A museum features an important collection of ancient and modern Indian arts. Open daily except Sundays.

PHOENIX

As early as 500 B.C., the Hohokam Indians developed an intricate system of canals in the Salt River Valley for irrigating fields of corn, beans, squash, and cotton. In 1868 the remains of that system were taken over and expanded by the Swilling Irrigation Canal Company, the first Anglos to stake claims in the long-deserted valley. The settlement was named Phoenix by an Englishman who saw a new civilization rising like the mythical bird from the ashes of the Hohokam. The first residents of Phoenix were ranchers, miners, and the soldiers stationed at the military outposts. As the canals were expanded, the land was used to pasture cattle and grow cotton, alfalfa, and citrus fruit. Water became plentiful with the construction in 1911 of Roosevelt Dam, still the world's largest masonry dam, on the Salt River, ninety miles away. With the coming of the Santa Fe Railroad in the 1880s, tourists began to arrive, anxious to see Indians and sample Western life on a dude ranch. Phoenix got a boost when it became the state capital in 1889. As the city grew, it attracted Easterners suffering from tuberculosis who found relief in the dry, hot climate.

Arizona State Capitol Museum (West Washington St. and 17th Ave.; 602/542-4581). This four-story restored building of native stone houses re-creations of the original 1912 governor's office and the early

house and senate chambers and galleries. Open Monday through Friday.

Arizona Museum (1002 West Van Buren St.; 602/253-2734). Exhibits depicting 2,000 years of Arizona history. Open Wednesday through Sunday.

The Heard Museum (22 East Monte Vista Rd.; 602/252-8848). Outstanding collections of the arts, crafts, and culture of the Indians of the Southwest from prehistoric times to the present. The Barry M. Goldwater kachina doll collection is here. Open daily.

Arizona Hall of Fame Museum (1101 West Washington St., in the restored Carnegie Library; 602/255-2100). The museum celebrates the people who have made significant contributions to the state. Open daily except Sundays.

Firefighters' Hall of Fame (5810 Van Buren St., in Papago Park; 602/275-3473). The largest collection in the country of antique fire equipment, fire communications, firemarks, artwork, models, and memorabilia. Open daily except Sundays.

Pueblo Grande Museum (4619 East Washington St., 6 miles east off U.S. 60/80/89; 602/275-1897). This museum is on a Hohokam archaeological site. Open daily except Mondays.

Phoenix Art Museum (1625 North Central Ave.; 602/257-3791). Exhibits of Western, European, contemporary, and decorative arts. Open daily except Mondays.

Arizona History Room (First Interstate Bank Plaza, 1st Ave. and Washington St.). A re-creation of a territorial banking office of the 1800s. Exhibits depict life in early Arizona. Open weekdays.

Arizona Historical Society Museum (1242 North Central Ave., in the Ellis-Shackelford home; 602/255-4470). Exhibits on the history of the city and the Salt River Valley. Displays relating to irrigation, the military, and ranching. Open Tuesday through Saturday.

Heritage Square (7th St. and Monroe; 602/262-5071). A historical city park with

I want my boss to draw my roll,
He had me figured out for five dollars in the hole
Me and my boss had a little chat,
And I slammed him in the face with my ten-gallon hat.

—"THE OLD CHISHOLM TRAIL," A POPULAR COWBOY SONG

The Rosson House, an 1895 Victorian, is one of eight early buildings in Heritage Square in Phoenix. Around A.D. 500, Hohokam Indians built an intricate system of irrigation canals here. Remains of that system were expanded in 1868 by early Arizona settlers.

eight turn-of-the-century houses, including the restored 1895 Rosson House and Silva House. Tours. Open Wednesday through Saturday.

Mystery Castle (7 miles south via Central Ave., then east on Baseline Rd., south on 7th St., then east on Mineral Rd.; 602 /268-1581). A unique castle built over a period of eighteen years by a father for his daughter. The castle contains eighteen furnished rooms, thirteen fireplaces, a cantilevered staircase, and a chapel. Open Tuesday through Sunday, October through June. Limited wheelchair access.

PRESCOTT

When President Abraham Lincoln created the Territory of Arizona in 1864, this was its capital. It was moved to Tucson in 1867, then back to Prescott from 1877 to 1889, but after much wrangling it was finally moved to Phoenix.

Sharlot Hall Museum (415 West Gurley St.; 602/445-3122). The museum contains several period houses, including the 1864 Territorial Governor's Mansion, Fort Misery (1864), the William Bashford Home (1877), and John Frémont's home (1875) while he was territorial governor. Pioneer schoolhouse. Rose and herb garden. Museum. All open daily.

Hopi Indian Reservation (67 miles north on U.S. 89, right on U.S. 89/I-40, right at Tuba City on NM 264, and 3 miles to Moenkopi. From Moenkopi, Third Mesa is 49 miles, Second Mesa is 59, First Mesa 75; First Mesa, 602/734-2262; Second Mesa, 602/737-2570; Third Mesa, 602/734-2404). The ancestors of the Hopi had lived in the desert of northern Arizona for centuries before they built Oriabi, the first Hopi mesa pueblo, between A.D. 1020 and 1100. The first white men arrived five centuries later. When Captain Pedro de Tovar, one of Coronado's conquistadors, came here, he found some 3,500 Hopis living in seven pueblos. Tovar attacked the Indians when they refused to pledge allegiance to God and Spain. After he returned to Mexico with Coronado, the Hopis were left in peace until priests and soldiers came here forty-three years later. Five missions were built, the Hopi religion was outlawed, and the use of the ceremonial kivas was forbidden. Farmers were ordered to give a large part of their crops to the priests. The deeply religious Hopis believed everyone must live in peace and harmony with nature. But as the priests learned, the Hopis could be pushed too far. In the Pueblo Revolt of 1680, four priests were killed and all the missions destroyed. When Diego de Vargas reconquered the area in 1692, he received a promise of peace from the Hopis in return for letting them alone. No Catholic church has been built on the Hopi mesas since.

The 1,560,000-acre Hopi Reservation is an island in the Navajo Reservation. There are two parts to the reservation: at the core,

631,000 acres are totally Hopi; around the core is land shared by Hopi and Navajo. Three pueblos are on each of the three mesas that run north to south across the reservation, little changed from the days of Spanish rule. Around the pueblos, the soil is mostly sand and rock, and less than a foot of rain falls in a year. The winter brings deep snow; summer temperatures reach 120 degrees. Despite this, there are fields of corn, beans, cotton, and melons, and small herds of cattle, sheep, and goats.

On First Mesa, the mesa farthest east, *Walpi* was founded the year of the Pueblo Revolt; *Sichomovi*, about seventy years later; and *Hano* by Tewa Pueblo Indians who came here from New Mexico at the time of the revolt. On Second Mesa, *Shungopovi* was rebuilt on the top of the mesa when an earlier village was destroyed in the revolt; *Mishongnovi* and *Shipaulovi* were rebuilt after the revolt. On Third Mesa are *Oriabi*, the oldest of the pueblos; *Hotevilla*, founded in 1906 by a faction of Hopis from Oriabi; and *Bababi*, built by dissidents from Hotevilla. The Hopi farming community of *Moenkopi* is forty miles west of Third Mesa.

The Hopi make pottery, silver jewelry and serving ware, baskets, weavings, paintings, and kachina dolls. Their pottery is usually dark brown and red on a light brown background. Most is inexpensive, though large bowls may cost several hundred dollars. Hopi baskets are made from hilaria grass and yucca and are very popular. Kachina dolls represent Hopi spirits who possess great powers and join the mortal world each year from November to July. Hopi pueblos should be visited when dances and public ceremonies are being held on summer weekends, and the best place to start is at the *Hopi Cultural Center* (Second Mesa; 602/737-2570), which displays artifacts, vintage photographs, and arts and crafts. The center has a motel and a restaurant that serves Hopi dishes. The pueblos are open daily except during religious ceremonies.

Canyon de Chelly National Monument (east on I-40, then north on AZ 191 at Chambers, turning west at Gando on AZ 264, north on AZ 191 to entrance; 602/674-5436). There are three canyons here: Canyon de Chelly (*de-SHAY*), Canyon del Muerto, and Monument Canyon, each 500 to 700 feet deep, and they meet a few miles east of Chinle. Within them are nearly 2,000 archaeological sites, of which sixty are major dwellings, although only three are easily accessible to visitors. The most spectacular and best preserved is *White House Ruin*, three miles up Canyon de Chelly, which has two sets of dwellings. Sixty rooms and several kivas are on the canyon floor near the river; ten more rooms are thirty-five feet above, in an alcove in the cliff that rises 500 feet. Five miles up Canyon del Muerto is *Antelope House Ruin*, a fifty-room, multistoried pueblo, named for the four antelope painted on a nearby cliff. The largest ruin in the canyons is *Mummy Cave*, seventeen miles up Canyon del Muerto. It has ninety rooms in two adjacent caverns several hundred feet above the river. Its name comes from two mummified Anasazi found here in the late nineteenth century.

At one time the territorial governor's mansion, Sharlot Hall is now a museum in Prescott, the first capital of the Arizona Territory. Other attractions here include Fort Misery, the Bashford Home, the John C. Frémont House, a pioneer schoolhouse, and a museum.

At the White House Ruin at Canyon de Chelly, one of the most spectacular in the Four Corners area, the sheer cliff soars 500 feet to meet the sky. White House was built around 1060 and abandoned by 1275. At its zenith some 100 Anasazi are believed to have lived there.

The Anasazi abandoned the area in the 11th century, and many years later Indians slowly returned, first the Hopi, who farmed the canyon bottoms in the summer, and in the 18th century the Navajo. In 1864, Kit Carson drove nearly all the Navajo out of the canyons, marching them on foot 300 miles to the Bosque Redondo in eastern New Mexico. Today Canyon de Chelly is considered the heartland of the Navajo Reservation. Roads with numerous outlooks on the north rim of Canyon del Muerto and the south rim of Canyon de Chelly give good views of the canyons and many of the major ruins. A steep trail goes to White House

Ruin. To visit other ruins, visitors must be accompanied by a Navajo guide or a park ranger. The Visitor Center displays Anasazi and Navajo artifacts. Both the *Thunderbird Lodge* and the *Canyon de Chelly Motel,* near the park, offer tours into the canyons in four-wheel-drive vehicles. The monument is open daily from mid-May to October. Limited wheelchair access.

Accommodations: *Marks House Inn* (203 East Union; 602/778-4632; reservations, 800/822-8885). A Victorian mansion, now on the National Historic Register, built in 1894 by Jake Marks, a cattle rancher and miner. Five rooms. Breakfast is included in the rates. *Prescott Pines Inn* (901 White Spar Rd.; 602/445-7270). A 1902 dairy farm with four cottages for the farmhands is now a pleasant thirteen-room bed-and-breakfast.

SCOTTSDALE

Taliesin West (2 miles north off Shea Blvd. and Via Linda, on 100th St.; 602/860-2700). A historic landmark designed by Frank Lloyd Wright, and the campus of the Frank Lloyd Wright Foundation. Tours. Open daily, October through May.

McCormick Railroad Park (7301 East Indian Bend Rd.; 602/994-2312). A railroad buff's dream: a Baldwin steam engine, a baggage car, and a Pullman car that was once owned by Roald Amundsen. Exhibits by model railroad clubs. Rides on the half-sized, steam-powered *Paradise and Pacific.* Open daily.

Wild West Jeep Tours (602/941-8355). This company takes passengers on a desert tour that includes pistol shooting and visits to a working gold mine and Indian petroglyphs. Daily.

Accommodations: *Squaw Peak Inn* (4425 East Horseshoe Rd.; 602/990-0682). Five guest rooms and a pool. Breakfast is included in the rates. Clark Gable used the inn as a hideaway.

SIERRA VISTA

Coronado National Memorial (25 miles south on AZ 90/92; 602/366-5515). In a futile search for the fabled Seven Cities of Cibola, Coronado wandered the Southwest in the early 1540s. His expedition did, however, introduce the horse to the Indians. This mountainous park on the border between Arizona and Mexico lies within sight of the valley through which the Spanish explorer passed. The short trail to Coronado Peak in the Huachuca (*wha-CHOO-ka*) Mountains affords a view of the countryside. This is bird-watching country, with some fifty resident species. The Visitor Center has a special alcove with a fourteen-foot window wall to facilitate taking photographs of the birds. Center exhibits include Spanish armor, swords, and equipment. Open daily. Limited wheelchair access.

Fort Huachuca (just west of the city; 602/538-7111), founded in 1877, was one of a chain of forts established to protect southern Arizona from the Chiricahua Apache. Troops from here chased Geronimo through the wilds of Mexico's Sierra Madre in 1886. Still active, Fort Huachuca is the home of the Army Strategic Communications Command. Large adobe houses on officers' row, built in the 1880s, are still in use. A row of eight adobe huts, north of the parade ground, was built around 1900 to house Apache scouts. A museum has artifacts and displays of fort history. Open daily.

TOMBSTONE

After searching in vain in California and Nevada, Ed Schieffelin was prospecting for silver in Apache country in southern Arizona. Passing soldiers laughed at him. One said, "All you're going to find is your tombstone." But Schieffelin found not one but several rich veins, naming the first the Tombstone. Unlike most prospectors, he managed to hold on to his claims, develop them, and grow rich. Tombstone grew rapidly, and its reputation as a wide-open town attracted such men as Wyatt Earp, Doc Holliday, Bat Masterson, the Clantons, and the McLowerys. Much of Tombstone's fame came from an incident on October 27, 1881. There was bad blood between the Earp brothers and the Clanton and McLowery families. Deciding to settle things once and for all, Marshal Earp confronted them at the O.K. Corral, ordering them to throw down their guns. Frank McLowery drew on Earp—who shot him. The ensuing barrage of gunfire left three of the Clantons and McLowerys dead. Only Doc Holliday was left uninjured. By 1890, Tombstone had a population of 15,000, but by the turn of the century the mines were playing out, and they closed for good in 1914. But Tombstone was called "The Town Too Tough to Die"—and it never really did. It survived, after a fashion, because it held an irresistible attraction for tourists, a living museum of Arizona frontier life. In 1962 it was designated a National Historic Landmark.

Tombstone Epitaph (5th St. near Allen St.; 602/457-2211). The oldest continuously published newspaper in Arizona, founded in 1880, is now a monthly journal of Western history. The office has a collection of early printing equipment. Open daily.

Bird Cage Theatre (6th and Allen streets; 602/457-3421). This establishment was known in its heyday as "the wildest and wickedest spot between Basin Street and the Barbary Coast." Girls plying their trade in the upstairs "cages" inspired the song "She's Only a Girl in a Gilded Cage." Original fixtures and furnishings. Open daily.

Boothill Cemetery (northwest of town on U.S. 80; 602/457-3348). The last resting place of many desperadoes, some with fanciful epitaphs. Open daily.

Rose Tree Inn Museum (4th and Toughnut streets; 602/457-3326). The museum, in the oldest house in town (1860),

"The Canyon de Chelly I scouted from its beginning to its mouth. It is the fort on which the Navajo Indians have based their hopes of making themselves invincible . . . and as it is . . . fortified by nature with the cliffs that form it, that hope is not without reason."

—LT. COL. NARBONA, 1805

◆-I-◆

Here lies
Lester Moore
Four slugs
From a forty-four
No Les
No Moore

—INSCRIPTION AT BOOTHILL CEMETERY, TOMBSTONE, ARIZONA

I have fallen in
   love with
   American names,
The sharp names
   that never get fat,
The snakeskin-
   titles of mining
   claims,
The plumed war-
   bonnet of
   Medicine Hat,
Tucson and
   Deadwood and
   Lost Mule Flat.

—STEPHEN VINCENT
   BENÉT,
   "American
   Names"

contains vintage furniture, artifacts, and historic dioramas. Outside is a 7,500-square-foot rosebush, the largest in the world, which blooms in April. Open daily.

O.K. Corral (Allen St. between 3rd and 4th streets). The gunfight site is surrounded by a restored stagecoach office and other buildings, including Fly's Photography Gallery, which has a collection of vintage photographs by the famous frontier photographer. Life-sized figures of the participants in the shootout are in the corral. Open daily.

Tombstone Historama (Safford and North 3rd streets, next to the O.K. Corral). A presentation of the Tombstone story with a film and a diorama. Shows daily.

Tombstone Courthouse State Historic Park (3rd and Toughnut streets; 602/457-3311). Exhibits of the town's early days and Cochise County history. Gallows in back. Open daily.

Silver Nugget Museum (6th and Allen streets; 602/457-3310). The museum has a number of authentic vintage room settings, old gambling equipment, and pioneer and ranching items. Open daily.

St. Paul's Episcopal Church (Safford and North 3rd streets). The oldest Protestant church still in use in Arizona. Open daily.

Crystal Palace Saloon (Allan and 3rd streets). The famous saloon has been restored and has dancing on weekends. Open daily.

TUCSON

Arizona State Museum (University of Arizona campus, Park Ave. and University Blvd.; 602/621-6302). Exhibits depicting Southwest Indian culture from 10,000 B.C. to present. Open daily.

Arizona Historical Society Museum (949 East 2nd St. at Park Ave.; 602/628-5774). State history exhibits, a costume room, a mining hall, and a photography gallery. Collection of 19th-century glass. Open daily.

Frémont House Museum (151 South Granada Ave.; 602/0956). The 1880 home of John C. Frémont's daughter, Elizabeth, when Frémont was the territorial governor. Tours. Open Wednesday through Saturday.

Tucson Museum of Art (140 North Main Ave.; 602/624-2333). Housed in six buildings in El Presidio Historic District, the museum has pre-Hispanic, Spanish Colonial, and Western artifacts, art of the Americas, contemporary arts and crafts, and a Mexican heritage collection. Open daily except Mondays.

Fort Lowell Museum (2900 North Craycroft Rd., in Fort Lowell County Park; 602/885-3832). A supply depot and administrative center in pioneer days, the fort occupied two sites: a tent city established in 1862 by California Volunteers who had captured the town from the Confederates; and a permanent garrison built in 1873. The Santa Rita Hotel is on the first site; the surviving ruins in the park include those of the old hospital and three barracks. The commanding officer's house has been reconstructed and contains exhibits and period furniture. Open Wednesday through Saturday.

Old Pueblo Museum (7401 North La Cholla Blvd.; 602/742-7191). Displays of history, culture, and genealogy of the Southwest. Mineral collection. Paleo-Indian rock shelter. Open daily.

Arizona–Sonoran Desert Museum (Tucson Mountain Park, 12 miles west via AZ 86; 602/883-1300). The museum houses live creatures of the desert, such as jaguars, mountain lions, bighorn sheep, prairie dogs, snakes, and tarantulas. Nature trails lead through desert botanical gardens. Open daily.

Old Tucson (201 South Kinney Rd.; 602/883-6457). This artificial town was created in 1939 as the setting for the first big outdoor movie of its time, *Arizona*, starring Jean Arthur and William Holden. Set designers studied old maps and photographs, and with the help of the Arizona Pioneers Historical Society, they laid out stores, houses, a saloon, a mission church, and other buildings to conform exactly to how Tucson looked in the 1860s. For nearly twenty years the set lay abandoned, then a promoter took it over, expanded it as a movie location, and developed a family amusement park around it. Since then, more than a hundred movies and television shows have been filmed here. Five gunfights and stunt shows daily. Narrow-gauge train and stagecoach rides. Movies. Entertainment. Sound-stage tours. Open daily.

Tumacacori National Monument (45 miles south on I-19; 602/467-2241). The ruins of the Spanish mission San José de Tumacacori, built in stages from 1803 to 1825, is near the spot visited by Father Eusebio Kino, the Jesuit who explored and mapped much of southern Arizona and Mexican Sonora in the 17th century. Ramón Liberos, a Spanish priest, supervised most of the construction, but was forced to leave in the Pueblo Revolt of 1828. The chapel at Tumacacori was the center of a mission with housing, classrooms, workshops, granaries, an orchard, and a cemetery. Mexico cut off the funding of this and other northern missions in 1848 and left it at the mercy of the Apache.

The Visitor Center has an audiovisual program on Indian culture and life in the early Southwest, also a self-guided tour and living-history programs. Mariachi Mass the first Sunday in December. Open daily.

Accommodations: *La Posada Del Valle* (1640 North Campbell Ave.; 602/795-3840). A 1920 adobe house that wraps around a courtyard with a fountain. Five guest rooms open onto the patio. Breakfast and afternoon tea are included in the rates. *Ford's Eastside Bed & Breakfast* (1202 North Avenida Marlene; 602/885-1202). Two guest rooms.

WICKENBURG

In the early 1860s, Henry Wickenburg picked up a rock to throw at a stubborn burro

The Earps

Wyatt Earp

Wyatt was the famous Earp, but there were four other brothers: James, Virgil, Morgan, and Warren. They moved around the West a lot, doing a lot of things. Wyatt was a gambler who worked both sides of the law. In Dodge City, where he was an assistant marshal, he killed his first man and became friends with Doc Holliday, who also was handy with a gun. Wyatt grew restless and persuaded his brothers to join him in Tombstone, where they became law officers and made enemies of the Clantons, a family of cattle rustlers. Warned that the Clanton gang was gunning for them, Wyatt, Virgil, Morgan, and Doc Holliday met them at the O.K. Corral. In the gunfight, two members of the Clanton gang were killed, and Virgil and Morgan were wounded. Later Virgil was shot from ambush, losing the use of his left arm, and Morgan was slain. Wyatt killed three suspects in Morgan's murder, then fled with Warren and Holliday. For years Wyatt was a gambler, drifting from mining camp to mining camp, and for a while he ran a saloon in Nome during the Klondike gold rush. In Hollywood in the 1920s, he was a coach for the early cowboy stars William S. Hart and Tom Mix.

and found the richest gold deposit in Arizona, the Vulture Mine. Some $30 million in gold was mined here while the boom lasted.

Desert Caballeros Western Museum (20 North Frontier St.; 602/684-2272). A Western art gallery, dioramas, period rooms, Indian artifacts, and a 1915 street scene. Open daily.

The Jail Tree (Tegner and Center streets). From 1863 until 1890, when a jail was built, prisoners were chained to this tree. Friends and relatives visited and brought picnic luncheons.

Old 761 Santa Fe Steam Locomotive (Apache and Tegner, behind City Hall). A veteran of the run from Chicago to the West.

"There is one God looking down upon us all."

—GERONIMO

—I—

"You must speak straight so that your words may go as sunlight to our hearts."

—COCHISE

Cochise, Nana, and Geronimo

Nana

Cochise. Although he waged a savage war on the whites of the Southwest, Cochise, chief of the Chiricahua Apache, is remembered as a folk hero. An unfortunate incident sent him on the warpath. Renegade Apaches raided an Arizona ranch and kidnapped the rancher's young son. An army detachment went to Cochise, who told them he hadn't been involved. Soldiers attempted to seize Cochise, but he escaped. The Chiricahua Apache killed 150 within two months; 4,000 would die in the next ten years. Settlements were abandoned in the wake of Apache destruction. In 1872, the success of President Grant's Indian policy depended on peace with Cochise. Gen. O. O. Howard, working with Tom Jeffords, an Indian agent who was friendly with Cochise, made peace on the Apache's terms: a reservation of Cochise's choosing, and Jeffords as its agent. After the death of Cochise, the boy who had been kidnapped turned up and confirmed that his captors were western Apaches, not Cochise's Chiricahua Apache.

Nana. Though crippled with rheumatism, this chief and his small band of Apaches went on a rampage in southern Arizona in 1881, killing nearly a hundred settlers. They were pursued by more than 1,500 troops but escaped into Mexico. Three years later, after a treaty allowed U.S. troops to pursue hostile Indians in Mexico, General Crook surprised Nana in the Sierra Madre and returned him and his Apaches to the notorious San Carlos reservation. Nana later escaped and returned to the mountains, where he lived out his life in peace.

Geronimo. No fiercer warrior ever lived than the Apache chief who terrorized the Southwest in the late 1800s. In 1858 Geronimo's tribe was camped near Janos, Mexico, when soldiers attacked without provocation, killing his mother, wife, and children. After years of raiding Mexican towns, Geronimo was arrested and sent to a reservation in Arizona. He broke out and began his reign of terror. Gen. George Crook twice persuaded him to surrender, but both times he escaped and returned to the warpath. In 1886 he surrendered unconditionally to Gen. Nelson Miles and was sent with his small band to prison in Florida. In his old age, Geronimo supported himself by appearing at fairs and expositions.

Geronimo

Frontier Street. A number of buildings preserved from the early 20th century.

WILLCOX

Museum of the Southwest and Cochise Information Center (1 mile north via Circle I Road, just off Fort Grant Rd. exit from I-10; 602/384-2272). Apache exhibits, a display of photographs of Southwestern historic sites, Rex Allen memorabilia, and the Willcox Cowboy Hall of Fame. Heritage Park. Open daily.

Amerind Foundation (about 25 miles southwest via I-10 exit 318 on Triangle T Rd. in Dragoon; 602/586-2272). The foundation has a museum with one of the finest archaeological and ethnological artifact collections in the country. Art gallery with paintings by Native American artists. Open daily.

Fort Bowie National Historic Site (22 miles southeast on AZ 186, then 6 miles northeast on a graded road into Apache Pass, then 2 miles to the trailhead, then a 1½ mile walk to fort; 602/847-2500). This was the hub of the military expeditions fielded by Generals George Crook and Nelson Miles that finally smashed the power of the Chiracahua Apache—Cochise, Mangas Colorado, Naiche, and Geronimo. For the army, the Apache wars of 1861–66 consisted of endless marches under the desert sun with few chances to fight. One soldier wrote home, "Everything that grows pricks, and everything that breathes bites." The fort was near the eastern entrance of strategic Apache Pass. In 1858 the Butterfield Overland Mail started using the pass for its stagecoaches on the St. Louis–San Francisco route. The trouble started in 1861 when George Bascomb, a young lieutenant, attempted to arrest Cochise in the pass, and blood was spilled on both sides. Enraged, Cochise launched an all-out war on the Americans. For years the most frightening word in the territory was

"Apaches!" Consider Nana, an old and sickly chief who led forty Apache braves on a two-month, thousand-mile rampage in 1881. They killed forty whites, wounded another hundred, won eight pitched battles with the army, captured 200 horses, eluded 1,400 troopers and armed civilians, and finally escaped to a Mexican hideaway without losing a single warrior.

Today only rock foundations and adobe remnants mark the site of the original fort. Wall fragments and foundations of more than forty buildings of the second fort dot the slope below Bowie Peak. Well-preserved traces of the stage route may be seen in the pass, and the ruins of the Butterfield stage station are west of the spring. Open daily. Limited wheelchair access.

Chiricahua National Monument (32 miles southeast on AZ 186, then 4 miles east on AZ 181; 602/824-3560). The Chiricahua Mountains were the homeland of the Chiricahua Apache. Led by Cochise and Geronimo, they launched repeated attacks on the tide of pioneers for more than twenty-five years. After peace came, Neil and Emma Erickson, a Swedish immigrant couple, were among the first settlers. Their "little home in the foothills of the Chiricahuas," located in remote Bonita Canyon, included a farm and cattle ranch. The only neighbors were the Stafford family. By the 1920s, one of the Erickson daughters, Lillian, and her husband, Ed Riggs, had turned the homestead into a prosperous guest ranch. Lillian, the strong-willed "lady boss," named it Faraway Ranch because it was so "god-awful away from everything." The Riggses built trails and took guests to see the "Wonderland of Rocks." In 1922 they promoted the idea of a national park here, and two years later the Chiricahua National Monument was established.

The park is full of grotesque rock formations created by erosion. Precariously balanced monoliths, towering pinnacles, and lush vegetation make Chiricahua (Apache for "people of the mountain") a wonderland.

"Why is it that the Apaches want to die—that they carry their lives on their fingernails?"

—COCHISE

Geronimo and other Apaches who followed him terrorized the Southwest in the late 1800s, but even dedicated Indian fighters needed an occasional day off. Here Army officers and their wives enjoy a rare holiday away from the fort with a picnic in a grove of organ-pipe cactus.

An eight-mile paved road leads up Bonita Canyon to the Massai Point overlook. The thirty-one-mile loop through Echo Canyon is one of the most scenic trails in the park. The seven-mile Heart of Rocks trail leads visitors to the Punch and Judy and Big Balanced Rock formations. Visitor Center. Campfire talks and ranger-led walks. Tours of Faraway Ranch are offered daily in the summer, weekdays the rest of the year. The park is open daily. Limited wheelchair access.

WINDOW ROCK

Window Rock is the headquarters of the Navajo Nation, and the eighty-eight-member tribal council meets in the octagonal council building located there. A natural bridge frames the town like a window.

Navajo Tribal Museum (east of intersection of AZ 264 and Indian Rte. 12; 602/871-6673). In the Navajo Arts and Crafts Enterprise Building, the museum preserves Navajo history, art, culture, and natural history. Open weekends except on tribal and other holidays.

Navajo Nation Zoological and Botanical Parks (Tse Bonito Park, east on AZ 264, after junction with Indian Rte. 12; 602/871-6573 or 871-6574). The parks have representative collections of plants and animals of historical or cultural importance in the Navajo tradition. Open daily.

St. Michaels (2 miles west; 602/871-4172). This Catholic mission, established in 1898, has done much for the education and health of the tribe. A museum in the original mission displays area artifacts. Open daily except Saturdays, June through August.

Navajo Indian Reservation. This is the largest Indian reservation in the country, covering 25,000 square miles in three states. The larger portion is in northeast Arizona, the rest in Utah and New Mexico. The most important sites are Canyon de Chelly, Navajo National Monument, Monument Valley Navajo Tribal Park, and the Hubbell Trading Post.

The Navajo moved into the arid Southwest more than 400 years ago and carved out a life that was in harmony with its natural beauty. In the 19th century they were interrupted by white settlers and the cavalry. Finally they were removed forcibly from their ancestral land and made the "Long Walk" to Fort Sumner, New Mexico. The move was not a success, and the Navajo were allowed to return home in 1868.

Today the Navajo practice many of their ancient ceremonies, including the Fire Dance and *yel-bi-chal* in the winter and the Squaw Dances in the summer. Many ceremonies are associated with healing the sick and are primarily religious in nature. Visitors must obtain permission to view these ceremonies. Photography and recording are prohibited. Tribal Rangers patrol the parks and are helpful to visitors. Paved roads cross the reservation. Unpaved roads often are impassable in the July and August rainy season. The reservation is open daily.

YUMA

In 1540, Hernando de Alarcón, a member of the Coronado expedition, passed this point on the Colorado River. In 1699, Father Eusebio Kino came through the area, and the next year Father Francisco Tomás Garces established a mission which was destroyed in 1781. The Yuma Crossing, where the Colorado River narrows between the Yuma Territorial Prison and Fort Yuma, the only natural crossing of the Colorado in the Southwestern desert region, was a major entry route into California.

Yuma Territorial Prison State Historic Park (off I-8, east of Main St.; 602/783-4771). The park contains the ruins of the 1878 prison that had a reputation similar to that of Alcatraz in later years. The prison's adobe walls were eighteen feet high and eight feet thick, with towers mounting Gatling guns. It stood atop a barren cliff overlooking the river. A museum on the site of the old mess hall displays Southwest artifacts and prison relics. Open daily.

Yuma Quartermaster Depot (2nd and Colorado River, behind City Hall; 602/783-4771). The depot served as a supply distribution point for troops stationed at military outposts in the Arizona Territory. Open Thursday through Monday.

Quechan Indian Museum (Fort Yuma; 602/572-0661). Tribal relics of Colorado River Yuman Indians are on display. Fort Yuma, where the museum is located, was established in 1850 to protect prospectors on their way to the California gold fields. Museum open weekdays.

Century House Museum and Gardens (240 Madison Ave.; 602/782-1841). The home of pioneer merchant E. F. Sanquinetti, the museum is a division of the Arizona Historical Society. Arizona Territory artifacts, documents, period clothing, and furniture. A garden with exotic birds surrounds the museum. Open daily except Mondays.

Yuma Art Center (281 South Gila St.; 602/783-2314). Located in the restored Southern Pacific Railroad Depot, the center has changing exhibits of Southwestern art. Open daily except Mondays.

Yuma River Tours (1920 Arizona Ave.; 602/783-9589). Narrated half- and full-day historical tours on the Colorado River. Daily.

Yuma Valley Railroad (8th St. tracks; 602/783-6014). The railroad makes twelve-mile, two-and-a-half-hour trips along the river levee and the Morelos Dam.

These gates lead to the old Yuma Territorial Prison, now an Arizona historic park. Between the prison and old Fort Yuma is the Yuma Crossing of the Colorado. Part of the Coronado Expedition passed by in 1540, and a mission was established here in 1780.

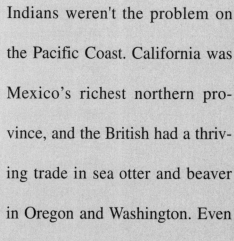

Indians weren't the problem on the Pacific Coast. California was Mexico's richest northern province, and the British had a thriving trade in sea otter and beaver in Oregon and Washington. Even Russia had an outpost at Fort Ross. However, in 1846, American colonists seized control of California and created the Bear Flag Republic, and the United States risked war with Britain to establish a northwestern boundary. Then gold was discovered at Sutter's Mill, and the world turned upside down.

The Columbia River, the route of Lewis and Clark.

17

Washington

ABERDEEN

Aberdeen Museum of History (111 East 3rd St.; 206/533-1976). Pioneer household furnishings and implements, including a general mercantile store, a church, a blacksmith shop, a one-room schoolhouse, and fire trucks. Open Wednesday through Sunday, June through Labor Day, weekends the rest of the year.

Grays Harbor Historical Seaport (813 Huron St., 206/532-8611). The seaport's interpretive center has replicas of the ships *Lady Washington* and *Columbia Rediviva*, and a working shipyard that restores vintage vessels. A museum has exhibits on the history of sailing in the Northwest. Open daily.

BELLINGHAM

Capt. George Vancouver sailed into the bay here in 1792 and named it for Sir William Bellingham. Lumbering, coal mining, salmon fishing, and shipping helped the city grow.

Maritime Heritage Center (1600 C St.; 206/676-6806). The center is devoted to commercial salmon fishing, and has exhibits on salmon development from egg to adult fish. Open weekdays.

Whatcom Museum of History and Art (121 Prospect St.; 206/676-6981). In the former 1892 city hall, the museum has displays of regional history, and art exhibits. Open daily.

Fairhaven District (12th St. and Harris Ave.). A separate city in the late 1800s, Fairhaven dreamed of becoming a second Chicago. Old buildings now house theaters, restaurants, and shops.

Lynden Pioneer Museum (217 Front St. in Lynden, 12 miles north on WA 539; 206/354-5995). In addition to artifacts of the local Dutch community, the museum has farm equipment. Open daily, June through September; weekdays the rest of the year.

Accommodations: *The Castle* (1103 15th St. in Old Fairhaven; 206/676-0974). A small inn with Old World grandeur. *Schauzer Crossing* (4421 Lakeway Dr.; 206/733-0055). Near Lake Whatcom, this lodging has a suite with a fireplace and a Jacuzzi.

BREMERTON

With water on three sides, Bremerton is the home of the U.S. Navy's Pacific Fleet.

Bremerton Naval Museum (130 Washington Ave.; 206/479-SHIP). Displays relating to navy and shipyard history. American and Japanese naval artifacts. Ship models. Open daily except Mondays.

Kitsap County Historical Society Museum (3343 Northwest Byron St., ten miles north in Silverdale; 602/692-1949). In an old-time bank in the area known as Old Town, the museum has local memorabilia. Open daily in the summer; Tuesday through Saturday the rest of the year.

CASHMERE

Chelen County Historical Museum (east edge of town; 609/782-1328). A pioneer village with nineteen cabins, a waterwheel, a railroad depot, and a dining car, as well as pioneer and Indian artifacts and an archaeology exhibit. Open daily, April through October.

Vigilantes

They went by many names—Regulators, Minutemen, White Caps, Moderators—the men who took the law into their own hands. They were not solely a Western phenomenon; vigilante movements were common in Colonial America. Nor were they necessarily bad. There was a need to band together to establish law and order and administer frontier justice where law officers and courts didn't exist or were corrupt or incapable of doing their job. But by the 1880s, as a historian noted, it had become "the lazy way, the careless way, the cheap way by which Americans often dealt with the problem of disorder."

"Lynch law," however, was better than no law at all. The frontier moved too fast for the legal system to keep up with it. In mining camps and cow towns, there were no courts or jails at first. The problem was that lynch-law justice would continue long after the judicial process was in place.

Regulator and Moderator movements appeared in the West in the 1850s. In many cases they were taken over by the criminal element they were formed to combat. There were exceptions. San Francisco vigilantes were unique in that they gave the accused a fair trial. Montana vigilantes brought the notorious Plummer gang to justice. Theodore Roosevelt was among those who openly sympathized with the vigilantes.

During Reconstruction, the Ku Klux Klan and the White Caps were active, particularly in Texas, harassing blacks and Hispanics. In a curious turnabout, Mexican laborers in New Mexico took the name White Caps in their fight against discrimination. Vigilante organizations declined with the close of the 19th century, but lingered on for decades.

CENTRALIA

This small logging city was founded by a black slave named George Washington, who came west with his master from Missouri and was later freed and adopted as a son.

Borst Blockhouse and Joseph Borst Family Farmstead (Fort Borst Park, west of town, south of Harrison Ave., off I-5; 206/736-7687). An 1852 fort, built at the confluence of the Skookumchuck and Chehalis rivers and later moved here. The 1860s farmstead is restored with vintage furnishings and has an early steam locomotive. Open weekdays.

CHEHALIS

Chehalis is an Indian name meaning "shifting sands," and the town is where the Chehalis and Newaukum rivers meet. In 1873 this was a warehouse on the railroad, then the county seat was moved here.

Lewis County Historical Museum (599 Northwest Front St.; 206/748-0831). Pioneer and Indian memorabilia in a restored railroad depot. Pioneer oral history, photographs, family histories. Open Tuesday through Saturday.

Claquato Church (3 miles west via WA 6, on Claquato Hill). Built in 1858, this is the oldest church in the state. Open house on Easter and other holidays.

CLARKSTON

Asotin County Museum (215 Filmore St.; 509/243-4659). Pioneer artifacts, branding irons, pictures, and sculptures. On the grounds are a furnished sheepherder's cabin, a one-room schoolhouse, a pioneer house, a blacksmith shop, a windmill, and a river barge. Open Tuesday through Saturday.

Indian petroglyphs. These inscriptions can be seen from WA129, upriver from Asotin, on the cliffs near Buffalo Eddy.

COLVILLE

Keller Historical Park (700 North Wynne; 509/684-5968). A museum in the park has local artifacts and records, a cabin, the 1910 Keller house, gardens, and carriage house, and a schoolhouse. The museum is open daily; the Keller house, Wednesday through Sunday, May through September.

St. Paul's Mission (12 miles northwest, near the intersection of U.S. 395 and the Columbia River in Coulee Dam National Recreation Area; 509/633-9441). A restored, hand-hewn log chapel built by the Indians in 1847. Open daily.

Fort Colville Monument (east on Tiger Hwy. one-half mile to top of hill, then 1 mile north). The monument commemorates the fort, which was a Hudson's Bay Company trading post from 1826 to 1871. Lake Roosevelt now covers the original site, near Kettle Falls.

COULEE DAM

This small town was established to house workers on the Grand Coulee Dam project.

Fort Spokane (in Coulee Dam National Recreation Area; 509/725-2715). This was the last of the military outposts in the state built to keep the peace between the pioneers and the Indians. Four of the original thirty-five buildings remain. The Visitor Center in the guardhouse has displays and a museum. Living-history programs are presented on summer weekends. Open daily.

Fort Okanogan (46 miles northwest on WA 17; 509/686-7231). A former fur-trading post. An interpretive center has displays relating to the fur trade and the Indian tribes. Open daily.

Grand Coulee Dam (near the junction of WA 155 and WA 174; 509/633-9265). This famous dam, 550 feet high, with a 500-foot-wide base and a mile-long crest, is one of the largest concrete structures in the world. It diverts water from the Columbia River down the deep Grand Coulee ravine, producing electric power and reclaiming more than a million acres of land. A glass-enclosed elevator goes down the face of the third power-plant dam. On summer evenings, floodlights and lasers illuminate the dam's spillway. Open daily.

COUPEVILLE

Thomas Coupe, a sea captain, an early settler, and the only man to sail a full-rigged ship through Deception Pass, gave the town its name. Fortifications here once protected Puget Sound.

Ebey's Landing National Historical Reserve (2 miles south on WA 525; 206/618-6084). On Whidbey Island in Puget Sound are the sprawling Victorian houses and false-front shops of a 19th-century seafaring and farming community. It was named for Col. Isaac N. Ebey, an early settler killed by Indians in 1857. The 17,000-acre reserve includes the land Ebey claimed in 1850, the historic town of Coupeville. The island possesses a raw and rugged beauty, with craggy coasts, high cliffs, pine forests, fields of prairie grass, sheltered lagoons, gentle beaches, and the deep harbor of Penn's Cove. Overlooks provide beautiful views of the water, where seals, gray whales, and killer whales are often seen. A tour leads by the historic buildings in Coupeville. Open daily.

Island County Historical Museum (Alexander St.; 206/678-3310). Pioneer and Indian artifacts. Open daily, May through September; weekends in April.

Building the Grand Coulee Dam created the Franklin D. Roosevelt Lake, a storage reservoir with a 660-mile shoreline, extending 151 miles northeast, almost to the Canadian border. The lake is a popular place for camping, swimming, boating and fishing.

A cowboy is about to be thrown at the rodeo in Ellensburg, a Labor Day tradition and one of the biggest in the state of Washington. Ellensburg was a tough town originally known as "Robber's Roost." The present-day town has a well-established western tradition, and there are many dude ranches nearby.

Alexander Blockhouse (on the waterfront, near Front St.). Built in 1855, this is one of four fortifications constructed on Whidbey Island that protected settlers during the White River Massacre.

Fort Casey State Park (3 miles south; 206/678-4519). The fort has a small museum with displays on the fort's history. Open daily.

Accommodations: *Whidbey Island Guest House* (10 miles south via WA 525 at 835 East Christenson Rd., Greenback; 206/678-3115). A luxury guest log home, four kitchen cottages, and a suite in the main farmhouse. Pool and whirlpool. Breakfast is included in the rates. Twenty-five acres with forest and meadows. Adults only. *Captain Whidbey Inn* (2072 Captain Whidbey Inn Rd.; 206/678-4097). A charming 1907 inn and cottages in a sheltered cove. Restaurant.

ELLENSBURG

When this town was founded in 1867, it was known as Robber's Roost. The tough cow town now has a number of excellent dude ranches.

Olmstead Place State Park–Heritage Site (4 miles east via Kittitas Hwy. on Squaw Creek Trail Rd.; 509/925-1943 or 856-2700). A turn-of-the-century farm, homesteaded in 1875, converted into a living-history farm. Eight buildings, farm machinery. Tours. Open summer weekends.

Wanapum Dam Tour Center (29 miles east on I-90, then 3 miles south on WA 243; 509/754-3541). Displays show the lives of Indians, fur traders, miners, and ranchers. Fish-viewing room. Open daily (fish-viewing room open May through September).

HOQUIAM

Castle (515 Chenault Ave.; 206/533-2005). A twenty-room mansion built by Robert Lytle, a lumber baron. Antique furnishings, 600-piece cut-glass chandelier. Open daily, mid-June to Labor Day; weekends the rest of the year; closed December.

Polson Park (1611 Riverside Ave.; 206/532-1924). A restored twenty-six-room mansion filled with antiques and local memorabilia. Picnicking. Rose garden. Open Wednesday through Sunday in the summer; weekends the rest of the year.

ILWACO

Lewis and Clark Interpretive Center (Fort Canby State Park, three miles southwest of town at Cape Disappointment; 206/642-3029). The mouth of the Columbia River was dominated by the Chinook Indians, who controlled trade with both the Indians and the whites. The center explains the Indian contributions to Lewis and Clark. Annual chinook salmon bake. Chief Concomly, famed leader of the Chinook, is buried in the Ilwaco cemetery.

Fort Canby (206/642-3078). The fort was a strategic base from its founding in 1864 through World War II. The nearby *Lewis and Clark Interpretive Center* depicts the history of the expedition. Displays on local Indians, Fort Canby, and the lifesaving station near the fort. Open daily, mid-May to late September; weekends the rest of the year.

Fort Columbia (6 miles southeast on U.S. 101; 206/777-8221). The site of a former coastal artillery corps post and fortifications protecting the mouth of the Columbia. An interpretive center in the barracks tells the fort's history. Nearby is *Columbia House*, once the home of the fort's commander. Open daily, mid-April through September; Wednesday through Sunday the rest of the year (interpretive center closed in the winter).

MARYSVILLE

Tulalip Indian Reservation (6 miles northwest via WA 506; 206/653-4585). Along the road are St. Anne's Church, built in 1904, the Indian Shaker Church, Indian Agency Superintendent's Office, and the tribal community center.

NEAH BAY

Makah Cultural and Research Center (1 mile east on WA 112; 206/645-2711). The Makah are the southernmost tribe of the Wakashan group. In 1855 the Makah ceded by treaty all their lands at the mouth of the Strait of Juan de Fuca except the land the reservation is now on. The museum, operated by the Makah, has more than 55,000 artifacts found at the Ozette archaeological site, a Makah village buried by a mudslide in the late 15th century. Exhibits on Makah and other Northwest Coast Indians, including canoes and a complete longhouse. Craft shop. Open daily, Memorial Day to mid-September; Wednesday through Sunday the rest of the year.

NORTH BEND

Snoqualmie Valley Historical Museum (320 South North Bend Blvd.; 206/888-3200). Displays and room settings of pioneer life, Indian artifacts, logging exhibits, photographs, reference materials, slide shows. Open weekends, April through November and the first two weeks in December.

Puget Sound & Snoqualmie Valley Railroad (4 miles northwest via WA 202 to town of Snoqualmie; 206/888-3200). A ten-mile vintage scenic railroad that passes the top of the 268-foot-high Snoqualmie Falls. Frequent departures from the restored depot. A diesel engine is used in April and October; a steam engine May through September. Weekends only.

Accommodations: *Salish Lodge* (37807 Southeast Fall City, Snoqualmie Falls, northwest via WA 202; 206/888-2556). A luxury resort at the crest of Snoqualmie Falls, popular with skiers and sightseers. Excellent restaurant.

OLYMPIA

The state capital began life in 1850 as the village of Smithfield. The next year it was chosen as the site of a customs house, and the U.S. Collector of Customs persuaded the settlers to rename their community for the Olympic Mountains. Soon afterward, there was agitation to separate the land north of the Columbia River from Oregon. In 1853 the new territory of Washington was proclaimed, and Olympia became the territorial capital, the first legislature convening the next year despite Indian unrest. A fifteen-foot stockade wall was erected around Olympia, but was later torn down and the wood used to plank the streets.

State Capital Museum (211 West 21st Ave.; 206/753-2580), a 1920s Spanish-style mansion houses Indian culture and art ex-

"Francis Parkman saw them in 1845. Working on a history of LaSalle he reflected that the French explorer, too, must have observed a wondrous spectacle, ". . . the memory of which can quicken the pulse and stir the blood after the lapse of years: far and near, the prairie was alive with buffalo; now like black specks dotting the distant swells; now trampling by in ponderous columns or filing in long lines, morning, noon, and night, to drink at the river—wading, plunging, and snorting in the water—climbing the muddy shores and staring with wild eyes at the passing canoes.'"

—EVAN S. CONNELL, *Son of the Morning Star*

The Logger

He roamed the dark forests with steel calks in his boots, an ax in his hand, a plug of chewing tobacco in his pocket. In myth he was Paul Bunyan, in reality he was the logger. He didn't call himself a lumberjack. Townspeople called him a "bindlestiff" because he went from job to job carrying his bedroll, or bindle, but they didn't call him that to his face.

Logging involved hard, physical, dangerous work. Falling branches, rolling logs, log jams, and falls from trees could kill or maim. Loggers were tough young men who worked hard, knew their jobs, and avoided risks. Some were characters. The legendary Jigger Johnson loved to boast, "I can run faster, jump higher, squat lower, move sideways quicker, and spit farther than any son of a bitch in camp."

Loggers lived a transient life with little security. Life in a logging camp was unvarying. In the early fall, some of the crew would ready the camp, and when the others arrived, logging would begin, continuing through the spring thaw. After the last logs were pulled to the river landing, the big log drives began with the spring runoff. When loggers got to town, whiskey and women looked good indeed.

In camp, loggers lived in crude bunkhouses, sleeping in triple-decker bunks covered with boughs. One logger wrote, "Everybody's clothes got wet from the snow every day and so we needed a lot of racks for drying. When the socks began to send off steams at night, you sure knew you were in a logging camp. When you mix the smell of wet socks with a smell of baked beans and chewing tobacco, you have a smell that a logger never forgot even if he lived as long as Methuselah."

Crews felled and trimmed trees for ten to twelve hours a day, six days a week. In the 1880s the crosscut saw replaced the ax, doubling the production of logging crews. Mechanization made obsolete many of the logger's skills.

Henderson House Museum (south on U.S. 5 to exit 103, in Turnwater Historic Park). A restored 1905 Carpenter Gothic house containing exhibits on local history. Photographic displays. Furnished log home nearby. Visitor Center. Open daily, April through September; weekdays the rest of the year.

Capitol Lake (Deschutes Pkwy.). Starting in mid-August, thousands of spawning salmon may be seen making their way upstream. The lake was formed by a dam at the point where the fresh water of the Deschutes River empties into the salt water of Budd Inlet.

Accommodations: *Puget View Guesthouse.* A waterfront bed-and-breakfast cottage next to Dick and Barbara Yunker's home. Boat outings and cookouts in the summer.

PASCO

Sacajawea State Park (3 miles southwest on WA 12; 509/545-2361). The park has a museum containing Columbia River archaeological specimens and exhibits telling of the historic role played by Sacajawea, a young Shoshone woman, in leading Lewis and Clark across the continent. Open Wednesday through Sunday in the summer.

Kahlotus (42 miles northeast via U.S. 95 and WA 260). A town redone in an Old West motif. Many of the buildings are practically museums.

PORT GAMBLE

A Maine sea captain, William Talbot, in 1853 founded what has become the oldest continuously operated sawmill in North America to build spars for ships. The company, Pope & Talbot, built this community, still owns it, and gave it its New England architectural style. The company has re-

hibits, a gallery, pioneer and natural history exhibits. Open daily except Mondays.

Fort Lewis (11 miles north via I-5 exit 120; 206/967-6277). The army center of the Northwest and home of I Corps, the Ninth Infantry Division, and associated support units. The base museum has exhibits on the military history of the Northwest. Access requires a vehicle permit. Open daily except Mondays.

stored more than thirty houses, commercial buildings, and the St. Paul Episcopal Church. The entire town has been designated a historic district.

Port Gamble Historic Museum (downhill side of the General Store; 206/297-3341). Exhibits that trace the history of the timber company and the town. Replicas of the saw filing room, the office, a ship captain's cabin, other individual rooms. Open daily, Memorial Day to Labor Day.

Of Sea and Shore Museum (uphill side of General Store). A large collection of shells. Bookshop. Open daily except Mondays, mid-May to mid-September; weekends the rest of the year.

PORT TOWNSEND

Capt. George Vancouver came ashore on the Quimper Peninsula, at the northeast corner of the Olympic Peninsula, in 1792 and named this spot Port Townsend after an English nobleman.

Old Fort Townsend (3 miles south on WA 20; 206/385-3102). The site of a fort established in 1856 and abandoned in 1895.

Rothschild House (Franklin and Taylor streets; 206/385-4730). A handsome 1868 structure, furnished in vintage style. Formal and herb gardens. Open daily, May through October; weekends and holidays the rest of the year.

Accommodations: *James House* (1238 Washington St.; 206/385-1238). Twelve guest rooms in an 1889 Victorian with period furnishings. *Manresa Castle* (7th and Sheridan streets; 206/385-5750 or 800/ 732-1281). An 1892 mansion with period furnishings and several guest rooms.

PUYALLUP

After crossing the Plains in a covered wagon, Ezra Meeker named the settlement

he founded here for an Indian tribe in the area. Puyallups still live in the area. Tulip, iris, and daffodil bulbs are big business here.

Ezra Meeker Mansion (312 Spring St.; 206/848-1770). The 1890 seventeen-room Victorian home of the town's founder, who traveled the Oregon Trail six years after Packman. Six fireplaces, stained glass, elaborately carved wood.

Loggers were a hardy lot, but a tree this size would give Paul Bunyan pause. The length of the saw that stretches to where the men are sitting suggests the tree had just been felled and the photograph was taken to preserve the occasion for posterity.

The American Fur Company

Students of American corporate monopolies usually start with John Jacob Astor's American Fur Company, which, through its enormous capital resources and political influence, once controlled three-quarters of the fur business. Astor, an Eastern exporter, founded the company in 1805 to free himself from dependence on Canadian and British suppliers and to expand his market. His political influence got the government out of the fur business and allowed Astor to operate in contested areas during the War of 1812, and to use liquor in trading with the Indians. Astor expanded to the upper Missouri Valley, either buying competing companies or forcing them out of business. An unscrupulous businessman, he also had a canny marketing sense. He foresaw the decline in the fur market, sold out at an enormous profit, and later made another fortune in New York City real estate.

"The true point of view in the history of this nation is not the Atlantic Coast, it is the great West. Even the slavery struggle ... occupies its important place in American history because of its relation to westward expansion."

—FREDERICK J. TURNER, *The Significance of the Frontier in American History*

SAN JUAN ISLANDS

San Juan Island National Historical Park (ferries from Anacortes, 83 miles north of Seattle, or from Sydney, British Columbia, 5 miles north of Victoria; commercial flights leave from Seattle and Bellingham; 206/378-2240). The Americans and the British almost went to war in 1859 over the possession of a portion of the Washington Territory. Eager to lay claim to the region, the British established businesses on the island in the early 19th century at the same time Americans were settling here. The island gave birth in 1845 to the American expansionist slogan "Fifty-four-forty or fight," but the crisis didn't come until an American killed a British-owned pig after it uprooted an American potato patch. In the Pig War of 1859, friction between the seven British and fourteen American inhabitants of the island reached such proportions that in 1859, 461 American troops supported by fourteen cannon opposed five British warships with 2,140 troops and 167 guns. Kaiser Wilhelm I of Germany was called on to act as arbiter,

and he settled the boundary in favor of the United States. During the thirteen years of controversy, the pig was the only casualty. San Juan Island was the last place the British flag flew within the territorial United States.

Today the British Camp, at the northwest end of the island, has a restored wooden barracks, a blockhouse, a commissary, a hospital, and a formal garden. Trails lead from the parking lot to the British cemetery at Young Hill, and along the coast to Bell Point. The American Camp was on a barren, windswept peninsula on the southeastern tip of the island. Two original buildings, an officers' quarters and a laundress's quarters, survive. Nearby are the remains of Robert's Redoubt, the principal American defense. A loop trail leads past the old buildings and the redoubt. Another trail loops through the fir trees along Jakles's lagoon, offering vistas of Mount Rainier, Mount Baker, the Olympic Mountains, and British Columbia. Open daily (information center open daily, June through August; daily except Sundays the rest of the year). Limited wheelchair access.

Accommodations: *San Juan Inn* (50 Spring St., Friday Harbor, a half-block from the ferry dock; 206/378-2070). This restored 1873 building has ten guest rooms.

SEATTLE

In the early days, Seattle had great hopes but a poor supply of women. Civic leader Asa Mercer went east and persuaded eleven young New England women to sail with him around the Horn back to Seattle to take husbands. This all worked out so well that Mercer went back and recruited a hundred Civil War widows. Many of Seattle's first families are descended from these women. In 1897 a ship arrived from Alaska laden with gold, and the Yukon Gold Rush was on. Seattle became a boomtown, ships from here sailing up the Inland Passage, the natural gateway to Alaska. The opening of the

Panama Canal in 1915 was a further stimulus to the city's commerce. Seattle is on Elliott Bay, a natural harbor between Puget Sound, an arm of the Pacific, and Lake Washington, a twenty-four-mile stretch of fresh water. Seattle is on the same latitude as Newfoundland, but is warmed by the Japan Current, shielded by the Olympics from heavy winter rains, and protected by the Cascades from midcontinental winter blasts. Winter temperatures there have never dropped to zero Fahrenheit.

Seattle Center (305 Harrison St.; 206/684-7200). A seventy-four-acre park, the site of the 1962 World's Fair, containing a *Monorail*, the *Space Needle, Fun Forest Amusement Park*, and the *Seattle Center Opera House, Playhouse, Arena,* and *Coliseum,* and the *International Fountain*. Open daily.

Kwakiutl Indian Family House (Seattle Center, Pacific Science Center, 305 Harrison St.; 206/625-9333). Sea Monster House, constructed from a Kwakiutl house from British Columbia, has traditional carvings and paintings. There is a video of a Hamatsa dance and other aspects of Indian culture. Open daily.

Pioneer Square (bounded by 1st Ave. and Pike St.; James St. and Yester Way; 206/682-7453). This is where the city was founded in 1852. Restored buildings now house galleries, shops, and restaurants.

Chinatown, International District (5th to 12th avenues, Yester to Weller streets). Chinese Association buildings, Hing Hay Park, and the Nippon Kan Theater (a national historic site).

Charles and Emma Frye Art Museum (704 Terry Ave. at Cherry St.; 206/622-9250). Collections of American and European paintings from the late 19th century, and a gallery of Alaskan art. Open daily.

Seattle Art Museum (Volunteer Park, 14th Ave. and East Prospect St.; 206/625-8900). Asian, African, and ethnic art. Chinese jade. Open daily except Mondays.

Museum of History and Industry (2700 24th Ave.; 206/543-9186). A re-creation of 1880s Seattle, with machines and tools used by early settlers. The Marine Gallery has a large collection of Pacific Northwest items. Open daily.

Daybreak Star Arts Center (Discovery Park, West Government Way at 36th Ave.; 206/386-4236). Indian owned and operated, the center exhibits work by Native American artists. A dinner theater presents Native American cuisine and entertainment. The center is in a 500-acre virgin wilderness on Magnolia Bluff, the site of a former army post. The center is open weekdays; the theater on Friday evenings.

Sacred Circle Gallery of American Indian Art (607 1st Ave.; 206/233-0072). Owned by United Indians of All Tribes Foundation, the gallery exhibits and sells arts and crafts of Northwest tribes. Open daily.

Museum of Flight (Boeing Field–King County International Airport; 206/764-5700). The museum has exhibits on aviation pioneers. Some thirty-five vintage aircraft are on display. Adjacent is the 1909 *Red Barn,* the original Boeing Aircraft manufacturing building, displaying artifacts of aviation from the beginning to the Space Age. Open daily.

Pacific Northwest Indians have a distinctive totemic art, and the Museum of Native American Cultures in Spokane has outstanding examples. In winter ceremonials, Indians here wore large masks that stood for family totems— similar, in a way, to Scottish clan plaids.

Klondike Gold Rush National Historical Park–Seattle Branch (117 South Main St., Visitor Center in the Pioneer Park district; 206/442-7220). Exhibits and artifacts of the gold rush stampede from here to Alaska in 1897–98. Gold-panning demonstrations. Open daily.

Tillicum Village (Blake Island State Park, excursion from Pier 56, at the foot of Seneca St.; 206/329-5700). Attractions include a narrated harbor cruise, an Indian-baked salmon dinner, and Northwest Coast Indian dancing. Daily, May to mid-October; weekends the rest of the year.

Bill Speidel's Underground Tours (610 1st Ave.; 206/602-1511; reservations, 602/4646). An entertaining and informative guided walking tour of the five-block area where the street level was raised thirty-five feet after the Seattle fire of 1889, leaving many storefronts intact underground. Tours daily.

American Indian Tour and Travel Agency (607 1st Ave.; 206/223-0072). This company offers tours to reservations throughout the West. Open daily except Sundays.

Accommodations: *Chambered Nautilus* (5005 22nd Northeast; 206/522-2536). A

In 1874 at Fort Walla Walla in the Washington Territory, General Frank Wheaton (standing center with white plume in hat) poses with officers in dress uniforms and members of their families.

1915 Georgian house built by an English family, now a bed-and-breakfast with six guest rooms, coved ceilings, fireplaces, and Persian rugs. *Galer Place* (318 West Galer St.; 206/282-5339). Within walking distance of Seattle Center, this is a 1906 shingled house with four guest rooms. Breakfast and afternoon tea.

SEDRO WOOLLEY

Sedro is Spanish for "cedar," and it was the name of this town until it merged with the town of Woolley, which was named for its founder.

Lake Whatcom Railway (11 miles north on WA 9 in Wickersham; 206/595-2218). A steam train with vintage Northern Pacific cars takes passengers on a seven-mile ride through the countryside. Tuesdays and Saturdays during the summer.

SPOKANE

Once an Indian hunting ground, this city began as a sawmill powered by Spokane Falls. Spokane, which means "Children of the Sun," was the only point in a 400-mile-long north-south range of mountains where a railroad could cross the Rockies and reach the Columbia Basin. The Coeur d'Alene gold fields in Idaho helped Spokane grow and survive a disastrous fire in 1889 that nearly razed the city.

Museum of Native American Culture (200 East Cataldo Ave.; 509/326-4550). The largest collection of Indian art and artifacts in the Northwest. Open daily except Monday.

Cathedral of St. John the Evangelist (1125 South Grand Blvd. at Sumner Ave.; 509/838-4277). A splendid sandstone Gothic structure. Imported stained-glass windows and recitals on a 49-bell carillon and Aeolian-Skinner organ. Tours. Open daily.

Eastern Washington State Historical

Society (2316 West 1st Ave.; 509/456-3931). *Cheney Cowles* displays historical collections. *Campbell House* is a restored 1898 mansion of the city's "Age of Elegance." Open daily.

Flour Mill (West Mallon St. near Riverfront Park entrance; 509/838-7970). When built in 1890, this was the most modern mill west of the Mississippi. Now it houses shops and restaurants. Open daily.

Gonzaga University (Boone and Addison streets; 609/328-4220). In the *Crosby Library*, a gift of alumnus Bing Crosby, is a collection of the crooner's memorabilia. Open daily.

Accommodations: *Durocher House Bed and Breakfast* (West 4000 Randolph Rd.; 509/325-4739). A Victorian farmhouse with views of Puget Sound and the Olympic Mountains.

SUQUAMISH

Suquamish Museum (2 miles south of town on WA 305; 206/598-3311). Owned and operated by the Suquamish tribe, the museum has a major exhibit explaining the history and culture of the Suquamish as seen through the eyes of Chief Seattle and other tribal elders. Displays of baskets, a dugout canoe, and fishing equipment. The audiovisual presentation *Come Forth Laughing* is an Indian approach to American history. Open daily. In a church cemetery in town is the grave of Chief Seattle, with Suquamish burial canoes erected over it. Nearby is the site of *Old Man House*, Chief Seattle's home and probably once the largest longhouse in the Pacific Northwest, 500 to 600 feet long and fifty feet wide.

TACOMA

The Hudson's Bay Company built Fort Nisqually in 1833 on the coast near the

Marcus Whitman

The first important figure in the Oregon Territory was Marcus Whitman, a physician and missionary from New York. He toured the Pacific Northwest in 1853 in search of a site for an Indian mission. He and Henry Spalding, accompanied by their wives, moved to Oregon the next year, their wives becoming the first white women to cross the Rockies. They established a mission near Walla Walla, which became a way station for emigrants. Some pioneers arrived ill, however, and their illness spread to the Indians. Whitman, his family, and twelve other whites were massacred by a band of Indians in 1847.

present site of Tacoma. In 1841, Charles Wilkes, the commander of an American expedition, began a survey of Puget Sound and named the bay around which the city is built "Commencement Bay." When the Northern Pacific reached tidewater here in 1873, Tacoma became an industrial center.

State Historical Society Museum (315 North Stadium Way; 206/593-2830). Indian collections and artifacts of Washington history. Open daily.

Tacoma Art Museum (12th St. and Pacific Ave.; 206/272-4258). A collection of American art. Open daily.

St. Peter's Church (2910 Starr St. at North 29th St.; 206/272-4406). This church, the oldest in the city, has an organ and a bell that were shipped around Cape Horn. Open Sundays.

Fort Nisqually (6 miles north in Point Defiance Park; 206/591-5339). A restored fur-trading outpost, this fort was built in 1833 when the British controlled the area and fur pelts were used as currency. The United States purchased the fort in 1869, and it was moved to this location in 1937. Remaining buildings are the 1853 *Factor's House* and the 1843 *Granary*, the oldest buildings in the state. Eight other buildings are reconstructions. Living-history presentations. Open daily, Memorial Day to Labor

"The time has come. England must not get a foothold. We must be first. Act discreetly, but positively. . . . I saw the way opening clear before me. War with Mexico was inevitable; and a grand opportunity now presented itself . . . to make the Pacific Ocean the western boundary of the United States."

—JOHN FRÉMONT

"Salmon is almost the only food used by the Indians on the Lower Columbia River, the two months' fishing affording a sufficient supply to last them the whole year round. The mode in which they cure them is by splitting them down the back, after which each half is again split, making them sufficiently thin to dry with facility, a process occupying in general from four to five days. The salmon are afterwards sewed up in rush mats, containing about ninety or one hundred pounds, and put up on scaffolds to keep the dogs from them."

—Paul Kane,
Wanderings of an Artist Among the Indians of North America,
1859

Day; Wednesday to Sunday the rest of the year.

Camp Six, Western Forest Industries Museum (6 miles north in Point Defiance Park; 206/752-0047). A reconstructed logging camp. The museum has a Dolbeer Donkey steam engine, one of two in existence, a restored water wagon, and bunkhouses. On summer weekends, a ninety-ton Shay steam locomotive is in operation. Open daily.

Pioneer Farm (35 miles southwest via WA 7; 206/832-6300). A replica of an 1837 homestead, log cabin, barn, trading post, and outbuildings. Antiques and animals. Open daily, mid-June to Labor Day; then weekends until November and from mid-March to mid-June.

TAHOLAH

This is the principal town on the Quinault reservation on the Olympic Peninsula. A tribally owned and operated salmon cannery is at the mouth of the Quinault River.

Quinault Reservation (on the shore a few miles north of town; 206/206-8211). Lewis and Clark found this small Salish tribe along the Pacific Coast and estimated their number at a thousand. Open daily.

UNION

This little town once thought it would be the saltwater terminus of the Union Pacific Railroad. A British bank that had invested in the railroad failed, however, upsetting its plans. When its finances were stabilized, the Union Pacific went elsewhere.

Tollie Shay Engine and Caboose No. 7 (5 miles west on WA 101 in Shelton; 206/426-2021). A railroad rarity: a refurbished three-cylinder locomotive and a Simpson

Logging Caboose with a coal-burning stove and a unique side-door design.

VANTAGE

Wanapum Dam Tour Center (5 miles south of I-90 exit 137 on WA 243; 509/754-3541). The center has exhibits on the culture of the Wanapum, a small tribe that still lives in the area. Open daily in the summer.

Gingko Petrified Forest State Park (I-90 exit 136; 509/856-2700). Columbia River rock art is visible along the interpretive trail near the Visitor Center. Open daily.

WENATCHEE

North Central Washington Museum (127 South Mission; 509/664-5989). A culture center with a mélange of exhibits, including Great Northern Railroad artifacts. Open daily, February through December; weekends the rest of the year.

Rocky Reach Dam (on the Columbia River, 7 miles north on U.S. 97; 509/663-8121). The dam's powerhouse has two interpretive museums, Gallery of the Columbia and Gallery of Electricity, and changing art exhibits. Open daily except January through mid-February.

WINTHROP

This town of 1,700 people has a deliberate Old West flavor and holds numerous events to attract visitors.

Shafer Museum (Castle Ave.; 509/996-2125). A log house built in 1897 by Guy Waring, founder of the town. Displays of early farming and mining implements. Open daily in the summer.

18

Oregon

ASTORIA

Partners of John Jacob Astor sailed around Cape Horn and decided to put a fur-trading post on this point of land overlooking the Columbia River, ten miles from the Pacific. A four-mile toll bridge now crosses the mouth of the river.

Fort Clatsop National Memorial (8 miles southwest on U.S. 101A; 503/861-2471). During the winter of 1805–6, Lewis and Clark and thirty-one other members of the Corps of Discovery built a camp here, beset by fleas and constant rain. The site offered excellent hunting, easy access to ocean salt, and protection from the coastal storms. In May 1804, the explorers had begun their famous journey, at the behest of President Thomas Jefferson, in search of a water route to the Pacific. They traveled with Toussaint Charbonneau, a French-Canadian interpreter, and his Shoshone wife, Sacajawea, and the couple's infant son. The first winter was spent near present-day Bismarck, North Dakota. Resuming their journey, they had their first view of the Pacific in November 1805. The expedition left Fort Clatsop on March 23, 1806, and arrived back at St. Louis on September 23 of that year.

The original log encampment has been re-created according to a floor plan etched on the cover of Clark's field book. It consists of a fifty-foot-square stockade with two rows of small cabins separated by a parade ground. A short trail leads to the canoe landing site on the Lewis and Clark River. On a beach fifteen miles southwest of here (now called Seaside), Lewis and Clark set up a small salt-making camp. By boiling seawater, they produced more than three bushels of salt necessary for preserving food on the long trip back east. A me-

morial of boulders with five kettles, known as the Salt Works, is on the spot where the salt was produced. The Visitor Center has exhibits about the expedition. The canoe landing has replicas of dugout canoes of that period. In the summer, people in buckskin and Indian dress demonstrate wilderness crafts and frontier survival skills. Open daily.

Flavel House (441 8th St.; 503/325-2203). An outstanding example of Queen Anne architecture, this house was built by Captain George Flavel, a shipping tycoon, in 1883–87. Antique furnishings, fine art, and a collection of vintage toys. Open daily.

Columbia River Maritime Museum (17th and Marine Dr.; 503/325-2323). Memorabilia and artifacts of the river, its tributaries, and the Northwest coast. The old lightship *Columbia* is moored nearby. Open daily, April through October; Tuesday through Sunday the rest of the year.

Fort Stevens State Park (5 miles west on U.S. 101, then 5 miles north on a county road). On June 21, 1942, a Japanese submarine fired on Fort Stevens, only one shot reaching the land. The Visitor Center at Old Fort Stevens Military Complex has a self-guided tour. It is the site of a Civil War–era fort. The wreckage of the ship *Peter Iredale* is on the beach. Open daily.

Astoria Column (follow scenic drive signs to Coxcomb Hill). The 125-foot-tall tower commemorates the first settlement. It has an observation deck. Open daily.

BAKER

This town was on the Oregon Trail, but is better known as the home of the Armstrong Gold Nugget. Miner

George Armstrong found the 80.4-ounce nugget on June 19, 1913.

Oregon Trail Regional Museum (2490 Grove St.; 503/523-9308 or 523-3449). Period clothing and artifacts of the county, and an outstanding mineral collection. Open daily, early May to mid-October.

Eastern Oregon Museum (9 miles northeast on old U.S. 30; 503/856-3568). Collections of relics and implements involved in the development of the West. Period rooms. Doll collection. Nearby is an 1884 railroad depot. Open daily, mid-April to mid-October.

Sumpter Valley Railroad (30 miles southwest on OR 7). A gear-driven Heisler steam locomotive and two observation cars take passengers on a seven-mile trip on narrow-gauge track through a wildlife area, passing through the Sumpter mining district. Between 1913 and 1954, the district yielded $10 million in gold.

A scene from perhaps the worst nightmare of a traveler in the West: a stagecoach driver whips his horses as Indians attack. Although it is firearms against bows and arrows, the defenders of the stage are badly outnumbered and help is a long way off.

BANDON

Coquille River Museum (Southwest lst St. in the Old Coast Guard Bldg.; 503/347-2164). Exhibits depicting early maritime activities in the area, including shipwrecks and coast guard operations. An extensive Indian artifact collection. Open daily except Mondays.

Dixie Lee (2nd St. at Port of Bandon; 503/347-3942). A sternwheel riverboat offering trips on the river. Historical site narration. Daily, May through October.

BEND

Emigrants found here the first lush, green land and good water in Oregon. An early traveler reputedly looked back at the sweeping curve of the Deschutes River and called, "Farewell, Bend," and the early settlement here was named Farewell Bend. The unsentimental post office shortened the name to Bend.

High Desert Museum (6 miles south on U.S. 97; 503/382-3221). Biological, historical, and cultural exhibits on life in the desert between the great mountain ranges and on the opening of the West. The Visual Arts Center has Western art and artifacts. Open daily.

Accommodations: *Lara House* (640 Northwest Congress; 503/388-4064). A bed-and-breakfast within walking distance of downtown. *Mirror Pond House* (1054 Northwest Harmon Blvd.; 503/389-1680). A small inn at water's edge. Guest canoe. Breakfast is included in the rates.

CORVALLIS

Horner Museum (Gill Coliseum, Oregon State University campus; 503/754-2951). Changing exhibits on the history of the area. Slide programs. Open daily except Saturdays, Memorial Day to Labor Day; daily except Mondays the rest of the year.

Benton County Historical Museum (6 miles west at 1101 Main St. in Philomath). Displays relating to county history. Art gallery. Open daily except Mondays.

Accommodations: *Madison* (660 South-

west Madison Ave.; 503/757-1274). Built in 1897, this inn offers five guest rooms with quilts and antiques. Breakfast is included in the rates.

EUGENE

Lake County Historical Museum (740 West 13th Ave.; 503/687-4239). Changing exhibits relating to county history. Pioneer and Victorian artifacts. Open daily.

Library (University of Oregon campus; 503/686-3065). The largest library in the state, with more than 1.7 million volumes. An Oregon collection is on the second floor. Open daily.

Accommodations: *The House in the Woods.* A bed-and-breakfast in an old home near the downtown area and the university.

FLORENCE

Sluslaw Pioneer Museum (1 mile south on U.S. 101). Exhibits relating to local history. Indian artifacts. Early logging equipment. Open daily except Mondays.

Indian Forest (4 miles north on U.S. 101N; 503/997-3677). Full-size replicas of Indian dwellings. Live deer and buffalo. The gift shop has Indian arts and crafts. Open daily, May through October.

Dolly Wares Doll Museum (36th St. on U.S. 101; 503/997-3391). The museum has more than 2,500 dolls. Open daily except Mondays, March through October; Wednesday through Sunday the rest of the year.

Accommodations: *Johnson House.* A bed-and-breakfast in a restored 1892 Victorian, the oldest house in town.

FOREST GROVE

Trolley Park Museum (16 miles northwest via OR 8 to OR 6, exit milepost 38; 503/357-3574). Restored old trolleys, double-

---

The Oregon Trail

It was the first overland trail, and it stayed open the longest. John C. Frémont was the first white man to travel the route that would become the Oregon Trail, and his precise report on his expedition became a handbook for emigrants. The first settlers on the trail left Independence, Missouri, in May 1841, followed the Platte River, crossed South Pass in the Rockies, then went northward to the Columbia River, a route that became known as the Oregon Trail.

To travel the 2,000-mile trail took from four to six months. Wagon trains would stop at Fort Laramie and Fort Bridger to rest, get fresh oxen (better than horses at pulling wagons and less attractive to Indians), and replenish food supplies. Rivers were the major obstacle on the trail. A wagon could be overturned on the banks, or swept downstream by the current. Wagon trains timed their departure so that livestock could feed on the grass of the Great Plains. The wagons were drawn into a circle when they stopped for the night, the tongue of one placed under the body of the next to make an impromptu stockade. Indians, however, rarely attacked large, well-organized wagon trains.

With the coming of the railroad, the Oregon Trail was used for cattle and sheep drives. In 1880 alone, some 200,000 herd of cattle were herded west along the trail, and between 1885 and 1890, thousands of flocks of sheep were driven east to the stockyards at Omaha and Kansas City.

---

deckers, interurbans. Trolley rides. Open weekends, May through October.

Pacific University Museum (Old College Hall, entrance to campus on College Way; 503/357-6151). Pioneer artifacts. The building is one of the oldest school buildings west of the Mississippi. Open Wednesday through Saturday.

GOLD BEACH

The town got its name when floods in 1861 washed the placer mines on the beach out to sea.

Curry County Historical Museum (fairgrounds; 503/247-6133). Interpretive displays and collections of artifacts of early life in the county. Open Wednesday through Sunday, June through September; weekends the rest of the year.

Accommodations: *Tu Tu'Tun Lodge* (98550 North Bank Rouge; 503/247-6664). A small luxury inn on the Rouge River.

GRANTS PASS

Grants Pass received its name when railroad construction gangs working here learned of General Grant's capture of Vicksburg in 1863.

Grants Pass Museum of Art (Riverside Park, on the Rouge River between 7th and Park streets; 503/479-3290). Paintings, photographs, and art objects. Open Tuesday through Saturday.

House of Mystery at the Oregon Vortex (17 miles east on I-5/OR 234 in Gold Hill). Guided tours describe natural, historic, educational, and scientific phenomena that are found in this former assay office and the surrounding grounds. Open daily, June through August; daily except Thursdays and Sundays, March through mid-October.

Accommodations: *Mount Baldy Bed & Breakfast* (678 Troll View Rd.; 503/479-7998). Two guest rooms within a ranch-style home. *Lawnbridge House* (1304 NW Lawnbridge; 503/479-5186). A bed-and-breakfast in a 1909 home. Antique furnishings.

HOOD RIVER

Hood River County Museum (Port Marina Park; 503/386-6772). The museum has early settlers' artifacts. On display outdoors are a sternwheeler paddle wheel, an aircraft beacon light used in the Columbia Gorge, and a steam engine from the ship *Mary*. Open Wednesday through Sunday, April through October.

Bonneville Dam (23 miles west on I-84; 503/374-8820). The dam has an overall length of 3,463 feet, extending across the Columbia River to Washington. On the Oregon side is the five-story Visitor Center with underwater windows in the fish-viewing area. Tours and tour boats. Open daily June through September.

Accommodations: *Columbia George* (4000 Westcliff Dr., I-84 exit 62; 503/386-5566; reservations: 800/345-1921). A forty-six-room inn in a restored 1920s building with a Jazz Age atmosphere.

JACKSONVILLE

Prospectors flocked here by the thousands when gold was discovered in 1851. When the gold played out in the 1920s, Jacksonville slumbered. A National Historic Landmark, it is one of the best preserved mining towns in the Northwest.

Jacksonville Museum (County Courthouse, 206 North 5th St.; 503/899-1847). Exhibits relating to area history. Indian artifacts, pioneer relics, and photographs. Children's Museum. Railroad depot. Open daily, Memorial Day to Labor Day; daily except Mondays the rest of the year.

Beekman House (352 East California St.). An 1875 Gothic home. Open daily, Memorial Day to Labor Day.

Beekman Bank (California and 3rd streets). Built around 1863, the bank looks as it did when it closed in 1912. Open daily, Memorial Day to Labor Day.

Accommodations: *Livingston Mansion Inn* (4132 Livingston Rd.; 503/899-7107). A shingled manor with two guest rooms and a suite with a fireplace. Breakfast is included in the rates. *McCully House* (240 East California St.; 503/899-1942). Four guest rooms and an excellent restaurant in one of the oldest buildings in town.

The Overland Stage

The Oregon Trail opened in the 1830s, but not until 1850 did the post office award a contract to John Butterfield to carry mail and packages from Missouri to California within twenty-five days. He formed the Overland Mail Company, which also carried passengers. Two stagecoaches started each way each week. The service grew until Butterfield had 160 stage stations, more than 250 stagecoaches, and 1,800 horses. He employed more than a thousand drivers, blacksmiths, herders, veterinarians, and wheelwrights, as well as hostlers to feed his passengers.

The 2,800-mile route from St. Louis to San Francisco swung south through Fort Smith, Arkansas, and El Paso, Texas, to avoid Northern winters and to please Southern politicians. The fare was $200 westward and $150 eastward, because eastward traffic was lighter. A passenger was allowed forty pounds of baggage free.

Until the coming of the transcontinental railroad, stagecoach lines proliferated. Other important companies included the Pioneer Line, Pike's Peak Express, and Wells Fargo & Company. Even after the railroad came, numerous gold strikes in isolated places gave the stagecoach a second lease on life.

Most of the stagecoaches carried nine passengers and were drawn by a team of six horses. The Concord, the Rolls-Royce of stagecoaches, was built by the Abbot-Downing Company of Concord, New Hampshire. It weighed close to 2,500 pounds, cost $1,050, and was a work of art. Multiple coats of paint were applied to the hand-tooled body, rubbed down with pumice, and covered with two coats of spar varnish for polish. Artists then decorated the exterior with ornate scrollwork and gold leaf. A landscape usually was painted on each door. The steps and top railing were shiny black, the running gear yellow, with fine red pinstriping on the spokes.

The Concord took skill to drive. The driver held the reins of the lead horses between the fore and middle fingers of each hand, those of the middle team between the middle and third fingers, and those for the wheelers between the third and little fingers, manipulating each rein by "climbing," alternately gathering it in with the fingers, or letting it slip out the desired amount. Delicate adjustments of the rein length, combined with judicious use of the foot brake and the whip, let the driver control all six horses independently and with apparent ease.

Astoria began as a fur-trading post for John Jacob Astor, whose partners selected this point of land ten miles from the ocean. When fur trading declined in importance, settlers came, attracted by the location and the abundant natural resources.

JOHN DAY

The town, named for a heroic scout on the first Astor expedition, was a Pony Express stop on the trail to The Dalles. Gold was discovered nearby in 1862.

John Day Fossil Beds National Monument (28 miles west on U.S. 26, near the junction of OR 19; 503/575-0721). This rough, colorful landscape chronicles more than 45 million years of plant and animal life. Spread over three sites—Sheep Rock, Painted Hills, and Clarno—the beds contain an extensive record of four prehistoric epochs. Saber-toothed tigers, early horses, and rhinoceroslike creatures roamed the area. Early oak, laurel, and redwood trees grew in the Painted Hills, and the giant beast *Notiotitanops* and the tapir *Helaletes* lived in the Clarno region. Early paleontologists were attracted, starting with the Reverend Thomas Condon in the 1860s. The 14,030-acre site has a remarkable variety of plant life: juniper, sagebrush, and bunch grass cover the landscape at the higher and drier altitudes. Cottonwoods and willows grow along the John Day River banks, and fir and pine forests cover the nearby moun-

tains. The region was named for the Astor expedition scout, whose encounter with Indians in the early 1800s left him alive but naked. He eventually was reunited with the expedition.

Cant Ranch, which serves as the visitor center at the Sheep Rock section, was the farmhouse of a prosperous sheep and cattle rancher. There are twelve historic buildings on the site, including a barn, a bunkhouse, a workshop, and a shed. Exhibits include mammal and leaf fossils, geological time scales, and early expedition photographs. Open daily.

Grant County Historical Museum (2 miles south on U.S. 395 at 101 South Canyon City Blvd. in Canyon City; 503/575-0362). Relics of gold-mining days, the Joaquin Miller cabin, and the 1910 jail. Open daily, June through September.

Kam Wah Chung & Company Museum (250 Northwest Canton, next to city park; 503/575-0028). Built in 1866 as a trading post on The Dalles Military Road, the museum now houses a Chinese shrine, a medicinal herb collection, and a picture gallery. Open daily except Fridays, May through October.

KLAMATH FALLS

Favell Museum of Western Art and Indian Artifacts (125 West Main; 503/882-9996). The museum has contemporary Western art, a working miniature gun collection, and an extensive display of Indian memorabilia. Open daily except Sundays.

Klamath County Museum (1451 Main St.; 503/883-4208). The museum has dioramas of Klamath and Modoc cultures, a model of a Klamath earth lodge, and memorabilia of the Modoc War of 1872, when the small tribe held off the U.S. Army at the Lava Beds in northern California. Open Tuesday through Saturday.

Klamath County Baldwin Hotel Museum (31 Main St.; 503/883-4207). A renovated turn-of-the-century hotel with many original furnishings. Guided tours. Open Tuesday through Saturday in the summer.

Fort Klamath Museum (36 miles northwest via U.S. 97/OR 62 to Fort Klamath; 503/883-4208). The fort was founded in 1863 to protect settlers in the Klamath Basin from Modoc, Klamath, and Shasta Indians. Troops from here sparked the Modoc War in 1872 by trying to force the Modoc leader Captain Jack and his warriors back onto the Klamath Reservation. During the fighting, it was the principal supply and replacement depot and medical receiving station. After surrendering in June 1873, Captain Jack and his followers were imprisoned at the fort, where he was tried and hanged along with three of his lieutenants. The museum, in a log replica of the original guardhouse, has displays of uniforms, equipment, firearms, and other artifacts from the fort. Open daily, June to Labor Day.

MADRAS

This area was explored in the 1820s, but settlement came much later. The Cascades were a wall of separation between the Indians and the settlers, and it wasn't until 1862 that the first road was built across the mountains to provide a passage for traders. Settlement began shortly afterwards.

Jefferson County Museum (503 D St.; 503/475-3928). In an old courthouse, the museum has a collection of artifacts and photographs of the famous Hay Creek Ranch, and antique doctor's equipment. Open Wednesday through Saturday, June through September.

MEDFORD

Crater Rock Museum (north on I-5 to exit 35, then north on OR 99 in Central Point, 2002 Scenic Ave.; 503/474-0965). Indian artifacts and a mineral and fossil collection. Open daily, June to Labor Day; Tuesdays, Thursdays, and Saturdays the rest of the year.

Butte Creek Mill (10 miles north on OR 62 in Eagle Point; 503/826-3531). A working 1872 gristmill grinds grain with original millstones. The museum is open daily except Sundays during the summer; the mill is open Thursday through Saturday.

Accommodations: *Under the Greenwood Tree* (3045 Bellinger Lane; 503/776-0000). A bed-and-breakfast in a circa-1861 house has four guest rooms. Log buildings on the property include an old barn, a granary, and a weighing station. Orchards and a rose garden. Afternoon tea is served.

NEWBERG

Quakers settled here in 1885, their first settlement west of the Mississippi, and founded the Pacific Academy. Herbert Hoover was in the first graduating class.

Hoover-Minthron House Museum (115 South River St.; 503/536-6629). The future president lived here with his uncle, Dr. Henry Minthron. Built in 1881, the house has many original furnishings and Hoover

Meriwether Lewis and William Clark

Their names became permanently linked when Lewis and Clark became the first Americans to cross the continent to the Pacific, yet two more different personalities never entered history as a team. Lewis was an introverted, moody army officer who had the good fortune to be chosen by President Jefferson, a fellow Virginian, as his personal secretary. After completing the Louisiana Purchase, Jefferson and Lewis planned an expedition to explore the new territory. As his co-leader, Lewis chose a fellow officer, William Clark, the younger brother of the noted George Rogers Clark. Surprisingly, Clark, a big, good-natured redhead, complemented Lewis. He was the mapmaker and the negotiator with the Indians; Lewis was the driving force and kept the expedition's journals. They left Illinois in 1803, reached the Pacific in present-day Oregon, spent the winter, and returned home to national acclaim. In recognition of their achievement, Jefferson appointed Lewis governor of the Louisiana Territory and Clark its Indian agent. Lewis was tempermentally unsuited for the post and was recalled. On the way, he died under mysterious circumstances. Clark excelled at his job, enjoying the respect and confidence of the Indians, and had a long, distinguished career.

boyhood memorabilia. Open Wednesday through Sunday, March through November; weekends the rest of the year except in January.

Newberg Visitor Center (8239 Champoeg Rd. Northeast; 503/678-1251). Tours, film, and historical exhibits. Open daily, Memorial Day to Labor Day; weekdays the rest of the year.

Champoeg State Park (5 miles west of I-5; 503/678-1251). The site of an early Willamette River settlement, swept away by an 1861 flood. Visitor information and interpretive center. Open daily. The *Champoeg Historic Drama* (503/245-3922), a musical about the birth of Oregon, is presented in the park amphitheater Thursday through Sunday, early June to mid-August.

Pioneer Mother's Memorial Cabin (town park; 503/633-2237). A replica of a pioneer log home with artifacts, including a collection of weapons dating from 1777 and a fife played at Lincoln's funeral. Open Wednesday through Sunday, February through November.

Newell House (8089 Champoeg Rd. Northeast; 503/678-5537). The reconstructed home of mountain man Robert Newell, with period furnishings, Indian artifacts, and a collection of inaugural gowns worn by Oregon first ladies. On the grounds are an 1850 jail and a one-room schoolhouse. Open Wednesday through Saturday, February through November.

Georgia Fox College (414 North Meridian; 503/678-8383, ext. 220). Originally the Pacific Academy, the college has a Quaker and pioneer museum in Brougher Hall, Hoover memorabilia in the Academic Building. Campus tours. Open daily in the summer, weekdays during the school year.

NEWPORT

Log Cabin Museum (579 Southwest 9th St.; 503/265-7509). Indian artifacts from the Siletz Reservation, also pioneer artifacts and marine exhibits. The Lincoln County Historical Society also runs the *Burrows House Museum* (545 Southwest 9th St.). Both museums are open daily except Mondays.

Accommodations: *Sylvia Beach* (267 Northwest Cliff; 503/265-5428). A twenty-room inn with a large library and rooms named after authors.

OREGON CITY

River steamboats were built here in the 1850s, and locks near the falls opened the upper river to navigation in 1873. Salmon fishing is both a local industry and a sport.

McLoughlin House National Historic Site (713 Center St.; 503/656-6146). Dr. John McLoughlin, known as "the Father of Oregon," lived in this two-story Colonial house overlooking the Willamette River. As chief factor of Britain's Hudson's Bay Company in the territory from 1825 to 1845, he played a key role in the settlement and development of an area that later became the states of Oregon, Washington, Idaho, and parts of Montana, Wyoming, and the Canadian province of British Columbia. McLoughlin helped to develop the local economy by encouraging agriculture, animal husbandry, and lumbering in an area that was then considered solely fur-trapping grounds. But he is best remembered for his kind and generous treatment of American settlers. He sheltered starving travelers at his Fort Vancouver headquarters, giving them supplies and credit so that they could weather the first difficult years in the Northwest. McLoughlin built his house near the falls of Willamette in 1845, where he settled on the land he had purchased from Hudson's Bay for $20,000, and lived in Oregon City until his death in 1857. His house was moved to its present site in 1909. Dr. McLoughlin and his wife are buried next to the house. Furnishings in the house include his desk, dishes, a chest, a melodeon, and a hand-carved four-poster bed. Open daily except Mondays; closed in January.

Holmes Home (Rose Farm) (Holmes Lane and Reliance St.; 503/656-5146). Built in 1847, this is considered the outstanding house in the state. The first territorial governor gave his inaugural address here in 1849, and the ballroom upstairs was the scene of many early social events. Open Sundays except January, February, and holidays.

Oregon Trail Interpretive Center (5th and Washington streets; 503/657-9336). Exhibits on the early days of the Oregon Trail. Open daily except Mondays.

Old Aurora Colony Museum (15 miles southwest via OR 99E, 15018 2nd St. Northeast, Aurora; 503/678-5754). The museum commemorates the German religious communal society founded by Dr. William Kell. The complex includes the 1863 Kraus House, the 1876 Steinbach Cabin, and an herb garden. Exhibits of furniture, quilts, and musical instruments. Tours. Open daily except Mondays, June through August; Thursday through Sunday in January and February; Wednesday through Sunday the rest of the year.

Mertle Stevens House (603 6th St.; 503/655-2866 or 655-6943). A 1907 house with fifteen furnished period rooms. Doll collection. Open Wednesday through Sunday, February through December.

Willamette Falls Locks (on river in West Linn; 503/656-3381). Built in 1873, this is the oldest multilift navigational lock in the country. The four locks, a guard lock, and a can basin are operated by the U.S. Army Corps of Engineers. Information Center open daily.

PENDLETON

Umatilla Indian Reservation (5 miles east on Mission Highway; 503/276-3873). Three tribes live here, the Umatilla, Walla Walla, and Cayuse. The *Mission Market* sells arts and crafts, including beadwork, moccasins, cradleboards, and traditional clothing. Ceremonial longhouse. One of the first Catholic missions in the Northwest. Open daily.

PORTLAND

The Columbia and Willamette (*Wil-AM-et*) rivers come together at Oregon's largest city, a port visited by more than 1,400 ships from around the world.

Oregon Historical Center (1230 Southwest Park Ave.; 503/222-1741). The center has an excellent collection of Northwest and Northern Pacific material. Open daily except Sundays.

Oregon Art Institute (1219 Southwest Park Ave. at Jefferson St.; 503/226-2811). A noted collection of Northwest Coast Indian art. Also 19th- and 20th-century American, pre-Columbian, and other art. Open daily except Mondays.

Police Historical Museum (111 Southwest 2nd Ave.; 503/796-4587). Early police memorabilia: uniforms, badges, photographs. Open Tuesday through Friday.

American Advertising Museum (9 Northwest 2nd Ave.; 503/226-0000). Displays relating to the history and evolution of advertising and its impact on American culture. Print and broadcast memorabilia. Open Wednesday through Sunday.

Howell Park–Bybee House (12 miles north via U.S. 30, on Howell Park Rd. on Sauvie Island; 503/621-3344 or 254-7371). An 1856 pioneer home restored and furnished with period artifacts. An agricultural museum and a pioneer orchard are on the grounds. Phone before visiting. Open Wednesday through Sunday, June to Labor Day.

Crown Point State Park (25 miles east off I-84 on U.S. 30 Scenic Rte.). Historic 1918 Vista House. Pioneer memorial. Visitor information service in the summer.

Accommodations: *General Hooker's B&B* (125 Southwest Hooker; 503/222-4435). A 1900 Queen Anne town house in the historic district, with four guest rooms. *John Palmer House* (4314 North Mississippi Ave.; 503/284-5893). Once a music conservatory, the house is now an opulent Queen Anne bed-and-breakfast, furnished with antiques and offering seven guest rooms.

ROSEBURG

Douglas County Museum of History and Natural History (1 mile south via I-5, exit 123 at fairgrounds; 503/440-4507). Exhibits describing the history of the area. Photographic collection, research library, regional tourist information. Open daily except Mondays.

Historic Oakland (16 miles north via I-5, exit 138). Untouched by modern development, this town was once the largest shipping center between Portland and San Francisco. Many 19th-century houses.

SALEM

Capitol (Court and Summer streets; 503/378-4423). A gold-leafed statue atop the dome of the 1938 Greek Revival capitol symbolizes the state's pioneers. Tours are given daily except Sundays, June through August. Building open daily.

Deepwood Estate (1116 Mission St. Southeast; 503/363-1825). An 1894 mansion of architectural distinction. The garden has a wrought-iron gazebo from the 1905 Lewis and Clark Centennial Exposition in Portland. English teahouse. Open daily except Tuesdays and Saturdays, May through September.

Mission Mill Village (1313 Mill St. Southeast; 503/585-7012). A restored 1889 mill water-power system is now used to generate electricity for the village. On the grounds are the 1841 Jason Lee House, the 1847 John D. Boon House, the 1841 Methodist parsonage, and the 1858 Pleasant Grove– Condit Church, all restored with period furnishings. Tours. Open daily except Mondays in the summer.

Western Antique Powerland Museum (eight miles north on I-5, off exit 263; 503/393-2424). Antique power equipment and farm machinery. Steam engines, tractors, gas and diesel engines. Flour mills and sawmills. Open daily.

Bush House (Bush's Pasture Park, 600 Mission St. Southeast, 6 blocks south of the capitol; 503/363-4714). An 1878 Victorian mansion with original furnishings. Open daily.

Accommodations: *State House B&B* (2146 State St.; 503/588-1340). On the banks of Mill Creek, the house has four guest rooms.

THE DALLES

The Oregon Trail once ended here, and pioneers continued westward by boat on the Columbia River.

The Dalles Dam and Reservoir (3 miles east of town off I-84 and 1 mile east of The Dalles Highway Bridge; 503/296-1181). A two-hour train tour with views of a historic navigational canal and Indian petroglyphs. Daily, Memorial Day to Labor Day; weekdays the rest of the year.

Fort Dalles Museum (15th and Garrison streets; 503/296-4647). Troops from Fort Vancouver founded this fort in 1850, and in two years a town had grown up around it. Fort Dalles was the headquarters for central and eastern Oregon, protecting the Oregon Trail and serving as a key outpost and supply base during the Yakima War in eastern Washington. General Crook used the post for his Snake River campaign in 1866–68. The only surviving building is the frame 1857 Gothic Revival surgeon's quarters. The museum has a rare collection of pioneer equipment as well as stagecoaches and covered wagons. Open daily, May through September; daily except Mondays the rest of the year.

Original Wasco County Courthouse (406 West 2nd St.; 503/296-4798). Now restored, the 1859 building houses a visitor information center. Exhibits, slide shows. Open Tuesday through Saturday, April through October.

Old St. Peter's Church (3rd and Lincoln). A Carpenter Gothic wooden church with pressed-tin ceiling, stenciled walls. Open daily except Mondays.

Accommodations: *William House Inn* (608 West 6th St.; 503/296-2889). A bed-and-breakfast in a circa-1900 Victorian, complete with veranda, gazebo, and belvedere on Mill Creek. Three guest rooms.

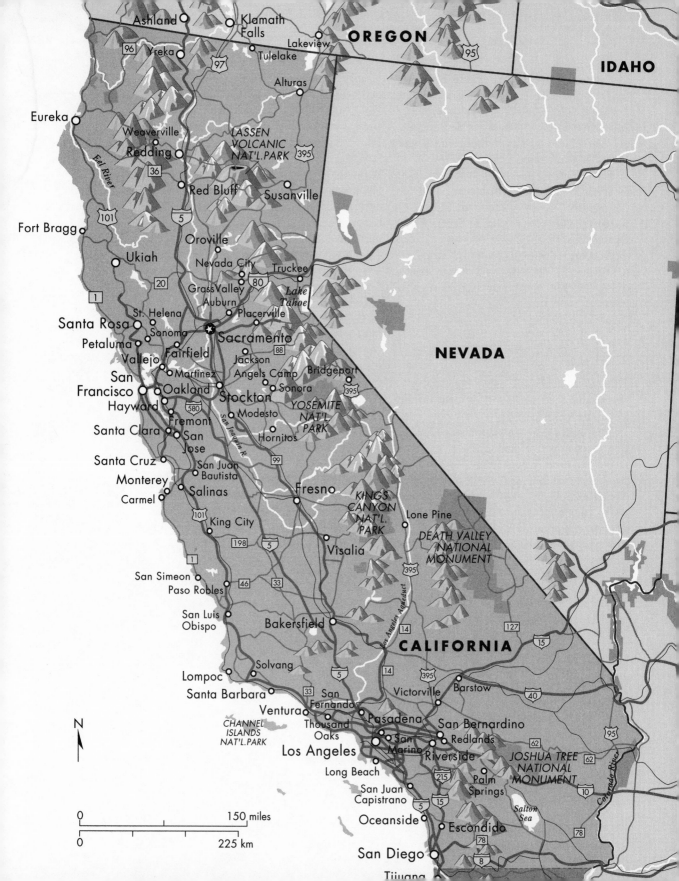

19

California

BARSTOW

Once this was a frontier town, a stopover for wagon trains and an outfitter for Death Valley expeditions. The coming of the Southern Pacific Railroad ensured Barstow's prosperity.

Calico Ghost Town Regional Park (10 miles east via I-15, then 4 miles north on Ghost Town Rd.; 619/254-2122). In 1881, two prospectors found silver here at what became the Silver King Mine, the richest silver strike in California history. Many of the early miners came from Cornwall, England; Cornishmen have the reputation of being the best hard-rock miners in the world. By the end of the decade, Calico had twenty-two saloons, three restaurants, hotels, stores, an assay office, and a school. Calico's end came in 1896, when the price of silver fell from $1.31 to sixty-three cents an ounce, and the mines closed. Walter Knott worked in the mines here as a young man, but his fortune came from what he later created near Los Angeles—Knott's Berry Farm. His heirs purchased the remains of Calico, which had been a ghost town since 1929, and restored it to its former glory. Among the attractions today are the general store, the schoolhouse, the Maggie Mine, Lil's Saloon, specialty shops, a shooting gallery, a narrow-gauge railroad, and tours of the mine. Nearby are the Calico Mountains, which yielded $86 million in silver in fifteen years. Open daily.

Mojave River Valley Museum (270 East Virginia Way; 619/256-5452). Displays of archaeological artifacts, Indian relics, railroad memorabilia, and photographs. Open daily.

Calico Early Man Site (18 miles east via I-15, Mineola Rd. exit, then nearly 3 miles on a dirt road; 619/256-3591). On this site, the only one in the Americas worked by Louis S. B. Leakey, was found the oldest evidence of human activity in the Western hemisphere. In the archaeological digs are visible tools fashioned by early man some 20,000 years ago. Two master pits may be viewed. Small museum. Tours. Open Wednesday through Sunday.

BRIDGEPORT

Bodie State Historical Park (7 miles south on U.S. 385, then 13 miles east on a partly unpaved road; 619/647-6445). One of the legends of the West concerns the "Bad Man from Bodie." Whether the Bad Man was real or fancied, Bodie did have a reputation for being the roughest, toughest mining camp anywhere. With a population of 10,000 at its zenith, Bodie averaged about one killing a day. Two Bodie baddies waylaid the stage from Carson City and relieved it of $30,000 in gold bullion. The culprits were caught a few hours later, and one was killed and the other wounded. But the gold was missing. The second bandit died in jail that night, and more than a century later the gold has yet to be recovered. Bodie had sixty-five saloons and two cemeteries, one for "decent, respectable folks" and the other, far larger, for all the rest. Despite its notoriety, Bodie produced $75 million in gold over the years. Only about 5 percent of Bodie remains today, but it is probably the most awesome ghost town in the West. Self-guided tour. There is a museum in the former Miners Union Hall. Open daily, late spring to early fall. Limited wheelchair access.

Mono County Historical Museum (City Park; 619/932-7911). Local historical items are displayed in an

Chinese Dreams

The Gold Rush brought a flood of Chinese to California in the late 1850s. They dreamed of making money and going home to a life of ease with their families. In reality, they were indentured servants. Chinese merchants paid their passage on the credit-ticket system, and the newcomers were their virtual slaves until the debt was paid, if ever.

The merchants formed the Chinese Consolidated Benevolent Association of San Francisco, popularly known as the Six Companies. It sent Chinese laborers to isolated mining camps and railroads, where regimented labor guaranteed the merchants a handsome return on their investment. The laborers were paid just enough to keep their dream alive, but not to allow it to come true.

A challenge to the rule of the Six Companies came from rebellious factions in the Chinese communities. Secret societies known in Chinese as *tongs* manipulated their countrymen for their own ends. Posing as social clubs and family benevolent institutions, the tongs controlled gambling, prostitution, and opium smuggling through extortion, coercion, and murder. Tong assassins were called "hatchet men." Tong wars were frequent and tarnished the image of the Chinese community.

White resentment of cheap Chinese labor built. In 1871 a mob killed some twenty Chinese in Los Angeles. "The Chinese question" entered politics in the election of 1876. The slogan "The Chinese Must Go" helped turn a pattern of abuse and violence into riots. Rioters in San Francisco in 1877 made the Chinese the scapegoat for the troubles of the workingman, and the idea spread throughout the West. Chinese were driven from the countryside to the towns and from the towns into the country. In 1880 a Chinese was murdered in Denver, and a number of others were killed or wounded in the ensuing riot. Masked men lynched five Chinese in Idaho.

Some 100,000 Chinese were in the West when Congress passed the Chinese Exclusion Act of 1882, ending the immigration of Chinese laborers, but the violence continued. Chinese were driven out of Tacoma and Seattle. For decades, laws restricting the legal and property rights of Chinese were common, further hindering their assimilation as Americans.

1880 schoolhouse. Open daily, May through September.

CARMEL

Spanish settlers named this lovely spot on the coast Carmel for the Carmelite Friars who accompanied them here in the early 17th century. It has attracted artists and writers since the turn of the century.

Mission San Carlos Borromeo del Rio Carlemo (1 mile south off CA 1, then west to 3080 Rio Rd.; 408/624-1271). Father Junípero Serra, who is buried here, founded this mission, the headquarters for the California missions, in 1770. Open daily.

Accommodations: *Cobblestone Inn* (Junipero and 8th avenues; 408/625-5222). The inn has a fireplace in each of its twenty-four guest rooms, complimentary full breakfasts, New England country decor, and a reputation for excellence.

DANVILLE

Eugene O'Neill National Historic Site (tours start in Danville; reservations and information: 510/838-0249). Nobel Prize–winning playwright Eugene O'Neill and his wife Carlotta lived on this isolated property east of San Francisco from 1937 to 1944, gaining the solitude he needed to write his greatest plays, *Long Day's Journey into Night, Moon for the Misbegotten,* and *The Iceman Cometh.* The site includes Taos House, a Spanish-mission-style structure, with white walls and Mexican tile floors, on fourteen acres that include a swimming pool, a bathhouse, and the grave of Blemie, the O'Neills' dalmation. Two rooms of the house have been refurbished, including the playwright's study, which has a view of the San Ramon valley. Park rangers give a ninety-minute tour of the house and grounds. The number of visitors allowed on the site is limited, and reservations are required.

DEATH VALLEY

Death Valley National Monument (U.S. 95 passes east of the monument and connects with NV 267, 374, and 373 to the valley; I-15 passes southeast of the park and connects with CA 127; 619/786-2331). Death Valley is some 140 miles long and four to sixteen miles wide, and the average annual rainfall is less than two inches. Millions of years ago it was part of the Pacific Ocean floor, until violent uplifts of the earth created mountains and drained the water westward. Today 200 square miles of Death Valley are at or below sea level. Badwater, the location of the lowest point on the continent, 282 feet below sea level, is at the base of 11,049-foot Telescope Peak.

The valley is rugged desert in an array of colors ranging from deep purple to rich gold. The colors were formed by the minerals that through the millennia have drained down from the mountains. Death Valley was named when a party of gold hunters in 1849 tried to take a shortcut across the valley and were stranded for several weeks. Later, borax was mined here and hauled out by the famous twenty-mule teams. Mining towns sprang up with such colorful names as Greenwater, Skidoo, and Crackerjack. For more than half a century, until the mines

Scotty's Castle is a monument to Walter "Death Valley" Scott, a prospector, mule-team driver, and trick rider for Buffalo Bill. A character given to tall tales and wild dreams, Scotty was befriended by a rich man from Chicago, who built this mansion for him in 1902.

Western Movies

The first motion picture with a plot was a western, *The Great Train Robbery* in 1903, and the western is the most popular type of movie Hollywood ever produced. At least ten westerns are ranked among the finest movies ever made.

The first western star was "Bronco Billy" Anderson, who wrote, directed, and starred in some 375 short films between 1908 and 1914. His films were eclipsed by Cecil B. De Mille's *The Squaw Man* and *The Virginian*. William S. Hart also wrote, directed, and starred in westerns, introducing such innovations as realistic settings and the reformed badman. His only competitor was Tom Mix, a graduate of Wild West shows, who did simplistic short films.

The first big-budget success was the 1924 epic *The Covered Wagons*, followed by *The Iron Horse*, directed by John Ford, who was to become a master of the western epic. A number of important westerns appeared from 1928 to 1930. Raoul Walsh made *In Old Arizona*, for which Warner Baxter won an Oscar as the Cisco Kid, and *The Big Trail*, which gave John Wayne his first big role. The Depression produced the "B" western: low-budget movies with the likes of Bill Boyd, Johnny Mack Brown, and Ken Maynard; singing westerns with Gene Autry and Roy Rogers; and serials.

Big-budget westerns returned in 1939–40 with John Ford's *Stagecoach, Jesse James,* and *The Westerner,* and the first important western comedy, *Destry Rides Again*. This was the western's classic period, and these films dealt with the code of the Old West in a way that has never been equaled.

After World War II, westerns turned to new themes and gained new vitality. The first was *The Ox-Bow Incident*, a powerful indictment of lynching. With Ford's *My Darling Clementine* and Howard Hawks's *Red River*, the western began to explore male relationships. Sex came in Howard Hughes's *The Outlaw* and King Vidor's *Duel in the Sun.*

Pursued is considered the first "psychological western," and Ford's *Fort Apache* was the initial anti-western, the first to attack preconceptions about the West. Indians were championed in *Broken Arrow*. The aging gunfighter forced to go on one last moral mission was first seen in Henry

played out, miners endured the valley's hardships. Traces of the mining towns can be found in the valley. The climate is pleasant from October to May, but extremely hot in the summer. The record temperature in Death Valley is 134 degrees in the shade.

Scotty's Castle, in the hills near the north end of the valley, is a monument to a most unusual man—Walter "Death Valley" Scot. He was a wrangler in Nevada in the early 1880s, and later a swamper on the twenty-mule teams here; he left to become a trick rider with Buffalo Bill's Wild West Show. Scotty moved back to Death Valley in 1902, becoming famous as a prospector and the owner of a gold mine. With the financial help of an admirer, a Chicago insurance executive, he built his castle from 1922 to 1931 at a cost of $1.5 million. Tours. Open daily.

Harmony Borax Mines. From this processing plant near Zabriskie Point, the first twenty-mule teams set out to carry borax to the railhead at Mojave, 165 desert miles away. Two men made the trip, the driver and a swamper who looked after the mules and did the cooking. The teams pulled 20,000 pounds of borax in two wagons, and 10,000 pounds of water in a tanker. A round trip took about three weeks, and one wagonload filled half a boxcar. The mines closed down in 1888, after borax was discovered closer to the railroad. Remains of the mill and the old mule-team wagons now sit in the desert.

The *Death Valley Visitor Center* at Furnace Creek is open daily, and offers guided walks and evening programs. Parts of Death Valley have limited wheelchair access. Visitors may stay at *Furnace Creek Inn* or *Furnace Creek Ranch*. All are on CA 190. U.S. 395 passes west of Death Valley and connects with CA 190/136.

ESCONDIDO

San Pasqual Battlefield State Historic Park (8 miles east on CA 78; 619/238-3389 or 489-0076). The site of an 1846 Mexican War battle that helped California win its freedom. No traces of the battle remain. Nature trail. Open Thursday through Monday.

Escondido Heritage Walk (321 North Broadway; 619/743-8207). This walk takes visitors through a Victorian ranch house, a blacksmith shop, a vintage barn and windmill, and an 1888 Santa Fe depot. Open Thursday through Saturday.

Antique Gas and Steam Engine Museum (15 miles northwest to Escondido Ave. and Sunset Dr., then left to 2040 North Santa Fe Ave. in Vista; 619/941-1791). The museum has agricultural displays on forty acres of farmland, and a collection of engines and early farm machinery. Open daily.

Palomar Observatory (35 miles northeast on County S6; 619/742-2119). The largest astronomical telescope in the country. There is a visitors' gallery in the telescope dome. A museum explains equipment and displays photographs taken through the telescope. Open daily.

EUREKA

Fort Humboldt State Historic Park (3431 Fort Ave.; 707/445-6567). On a bluff overlooking Humboldt Bay and the Pacific, this fort was active from 1853 to 1867, supplying troops in the second Rogue River War in Oregon in the mid-1850s. Ulysses S. Grant served here as a captain. Military exhibits. Tours. Open daily.

Clarke Memorial Museum (3rd and E streets; 707/443-7331). Baskets made by the Yurok, Karuk, and Hupa are on display, as are firearms, Victorian furniture, and decorative arts. Open Tuesday through Saturday.

Humboldt Bay Maritime Museum (1410 2nd St.; 707/444-9440). Pacific and coastal marine artifacts and memorabilia. Open daily.

Old Town (1st, 2nd, and 3rd streets, C to G streets). On the waterfront, this area has a

King's *The Gunfighter* in 1950, followed two years later by Fred Zinnemann's *High Noon*.

In the 1960s, foreign-made westerns became popular. The first big hit was Sergio Leone's "spaghetti western" *A Fistful of Dollars*, starring Clint Eastwood. More than 200 westerns were made in Europe, mostly in Spain and Yugoslavia, mostly by Italian filmmakers, mostly with amoral heroes, mostly with excessive violence.

The most frequently filmed historical event in westerns is the gunfight at Tombstone's O.K. Corral; *Law and Order*, *My Darling Clementine*, *Wichita*, *Gunfight at the O.K. Corral*, and *Doc*, among others, all featured the famous shootout. Another popular subject is Custer at the Little Bighorn. Among other films depicting this event are *They Died with Their Boots On*, *Fort Apache*, *Custer of the West*, and Arthur Penn's *Little Big Man*. The life of William Bonney has been explored in *Billy the Kid*, *The Outlaw*, *The Left-Handed Gun*, *Dirty Little Billy*, and Sam Peckinpah's *Pat Garrett and Billy the Kid*.

For students of the Old West, a handful of films deserve and reward close attention—the postwar westerns of John Ford, all starring John Wayne, which examine the texture and meaning of the era. At first a believer in bravery in *She Wore a Yellow Ribbon* and *Rio Grande* (these and *Fort Apache* are known as his Cavalry Trilogy), Ford begins to question it in his masterpiece *The Searchers*. In *The Man Who Shot Liberty Valance* he deplores the decline of frontier justice, and in *Cheyenne Autumn* he yearns for the savage wilderness that existed before the coming of the white man.

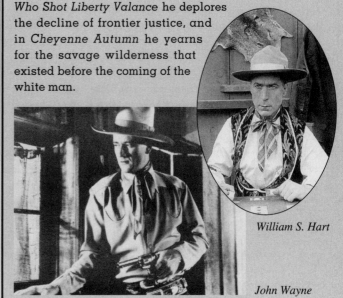

William S. Hart

John Wayne

number of early buildings, antique and specialty shops, restaurants, and a trolley.

Eureka Image Tours (707/442-3738). Five-hour tours of area, including a cruise on the bay and lunch at a logger's cookhouse. Tuesday through Thursday, mid-June to mid-September.

Accommodations: *Gingerbread Mansion* (20 miles south via U.S. 101, at 400 Berdin St. in Ferndale; 707/786-4000). Nine guest rooms in an elaborately decorated 1899 Victorian with an English garden. Bicycles are available to guests. Breakfast is included in the rates.

FAIRFIELD

Western Railway Museum (12 miles east on CA 12; 707/374-2978). A demonstration railroad, a hundred cars and locomotives, and a two-mile electric trolley ride. Bookstore. Picnicking. Open weekends.

FORT BRAGG

A fort was established here in 1857 to control the Mendocino Indian Reservation. The Indians left the reservation by 1864, however, and the army opened up the area to settlement. The town grew up around the old fort, no trace of which remains today.

California Western Railroad (foot of Laurel St.; 707/964-6371). A restored logging railroad known as the "Skunk" takes passengers on a forty-mile, full-day round trip along the Noyo River to Willits. Weekend half-day trips to Northspur are also available. Trips daily.

Guest House Museum (343 North Main St.; 707/964-5325). Artifacts and photographs of pioneer logging in the area. On display are donkey engines and other locomotives. Open Wednesday through Sunday.

Accommodations: *Pudding Creek Inn* (700 North Main; 707/964-9529). Ten guest

rooms in an 1884 Victorian house two blocks from the ocean.

FREMONT

Mission San Jose (43300 Mission Blvd.; 415/657-1797). Built in 1809 and destroyed in an 1868 earthquake, the mission has been reconstructed. A small museum in the padres' living quarters has old vestments, mission-era statues, and the original baptismal font. Open daily except major holidays.

Patterson Farm (Ardenwood Regional Preserve, I-880 to CA 84W, Jarvis-Decoto exit; 415/657-1797). Demonstrations of 1890s farming. Tours of the farmhouse, haywagon rides, and a railcar tour. Open Thursday through Sunday, April through October.

Coyote Hills (I-880 to CA 84, west to Thornton Ave.–Paseo Padre Pkwy., north to Patterson Ranch Rd.). Guided tours of 2,000-year-old Indian shell mounds. Sundays.

FRESNO

When the railroad came through the rich San Joaquin Valley in 1874, the town of Millerton moved to be next to the railroad and renamed itself Fresno.

Metropolitan Museum of Art, History and Science (1555 Van Ness; 209/441-1444). Displays relating to the history and culture of the San Joaquin Valley. Open Wednesday through Sunday.

The Discovery Center (1944 North Winery Ave.; 209/251-5531). Family participatory exhibits, including an Indian room. Open daily except Mondays.

Kingsburg (18 miles south on CA 99; 209/897-2925). The area was settled by Swedes, and the lovely buildings show it. The Historical Society Museum is at 2321 Sierra St.

HAYWARD

McConaghy Estate (18701 Hesperian Blvd.; 415/276-3010). A twelve-room Victorian with period furnishings. There are displays of wagons and buggies in the carriage house. During December the house is decorated for an 1886 Christmas. Open Thursday through Sunday; closed in January.

Hayward Area Historical Society Museum (22701 Main St.; 415/581-0223). Local and area artifacts, including fire engines and costumes. Open daily except Sundays.

JENNER

Fort Ross State Historic Park (12 miles north on CA 1; 707/865-2391). In the early 19th century, this outpost was used by the Russian-American Company of Alaska as a center of the Russian sea otter trade. Captain John A. Sutter purchased the entire Colony Ross of California in 1841. On the site are reconstructions of the 1825 Russian Orthodox chapel, the seven- and eight-sided blockhouses, the officers' barracks, and the stockade walls. Interpretive exhibits. Guided tours. Open daily.

KING CITY

Mission San Antonio de Padua (24 miles southwest on County G14 in Jolon; 408/385-4478). Founded in 1771, this was the third in the chain of California missions. It has a gristmill, a waterwheel, a tannery, and a wine vat. Padres' Garden. Small museum. Open daily.

LOMPOC

Mission La Purisima Concepcion State Historic Park (3 miles northeast at the junc-

tion of Purisima and Mission Gate roads; 805/733-3713). Founded in 1787 and moved from here in 1812, the mission has been restored in its original setting. A museum has mission and Indian artifacts. Living-history tours and craft demonstrations in the summer. Open daily.

LONE PINE

Eastern California Museum (16 miles north via U.S. 385 on Center St. in Independence; 619/878-2411, ext. 2259). Pioneer and Indian artifacts, Indian baskets, and photographs in Little Pine Village. Open Thursday through Monday.

The Commander's House (16 miles north on U.S. 385, 303 North Edwards in Independence; 619/878-2411, ext. 2258). The house was moved from Camp Independence to this site in 1889. Furnished with antiques, some made by soldiers at Camp Independence. Open weekends, late May to early September.

LONG BEACH

British-born W. E. Willmore founded Willmore City here in 1881 as an "American colony." The town's name was changed to

Once an outpost of the Russian empire, Fort Ross was a center for the Russian sea otter trade. Established by the Russian-American Company of Alaska, it functioned for nearly thirty years until the "Colony Ross of California" was purchased by John A. Sutter in 1841.

John Muir

The Sierras, which he called "a range of light," were John Muir's life work. Born in Scotland and raised in Wisconsin, he first visited the Sierras in 1868. He met Ralph Waldo Emerson in Yellowstone Valley and became the transcendentalist's disciple. Nature, to Muir, was a "window opening into heaven, a mirror reflecting the Creator." He founded the Sierra Club in 1892 in San Francisco, and by 1900 he was nationally known as the leading exponent of wilderness values. He later successfully fought against the building of a dam that would have made Yosemite Valley a reservoir.

Long Beach to advertise its five-mile-long, 500-foot-wide beach.

Long Beach Museum of Art (2300 East Ocean Blvd.; 213/439-2119). In this 1912 mansion overlooking the Pacific is a permanent collection of American art. Open Wednesday through Sunday.

Rancho Los Alamitos (6400 Bixby Hill Rd.; 213/431-3541). An 1806 adobe ranch house with six outbuildings and barns. Antique furnishings. Five acres of gardens. Tours. Open Wednesday through Sunday.

Rancho Los Cerritos (4600 Virginia Rd.; 213/424-9423). One of the original land grants that became Long Beach. An adobe building was the headquarters for sheep ranchers in the 1870s. Historic garden. Exhibits. Tours on weekends. Open Wednesday through Sunday.

General Banning Residence (401 East M St. in Wilmington; 213/548-7777). The restored home of one of the original developers of Los Angeles. Exhibits. Tours. Open daily except Monday and Wednesday.

Cruises. *Catalina Cruises* (Catalina Terminal, San Pedro; 213/514-3838) make daily excursions to Catalina Island. *Gondola Getaway* (reservations, 213/433-9595) makes one-hour tours daily around Naples Island in Venetian gondolas.

Accommodations: A historic place to stay is in a cabin on the old pre–World War II Cunard liner *Queen Mary* (Pier J; 213/435-5818), now permanently docked here and used as a hotel, convention center, and tourist attraction. Tours of the ship include the wheelhouse, the officers' quarters, the salons, and the engine room.

LOS ANGELES

On the site of the present city in 1781, Don Felipe de Neve, governor of the Province of California, founded El Pueblo de Nuestra Señora La Reina de Los Angeles de Porciucula. It was a quiet town until 1846, when the acquisition of California by the United States turned it into a vigorous community. During the Gold Rush, Los Angeles was referred to as Los Diablos (The Devils). A tide of new settlers came after the railroads reached here in the mid-1880s, and by 1890, after oil was discovered in the area, the population reached 50,000.

Wells Fargo History Museum (333 South Grand Ave., plaza level; 213/253-7166). More than 136 years of the company's history are depicted through exhibits and displays. Gold collection, stagecoaches, treasure boxes, reward posters, documents, and photographs. Western art collection. A replica of an 1860 Wells Fargo office. Open weekdays except holidays.

El Pueblo de Los Angeles Historic Park (845 North Alameda St.; 213/628-1274). The site of the original settlement of Los Angeles, the park has a number of restored and reproduced buildings reflecting the history and atmosphere of Old Los Angeles. "History of Water in Los Angeles" exhibit. Open daily. *Avila Adobe*, circa 1818, is the oldest house in the city. Open daily except Mondays. *Old Plaza Firehouse* was the city's first firehouse, in 1884. Inside is a museum with 19th-century firefighting equipment and vintage photographs. Open daily except Monday. *Nuestra Señora La Reina de Los Angeles*, built in 1818–22, is still an active parish. Excellent statuary. Open daily. *Olvera*

Street has been preserved as a picturesque Hispanic street market, with restaurants serving traditional food. Open daily. *Sepulveda House* is a partially restored 1887 Victorian. The Visitor Center has a film on the city's early history. Open daily.

Los Angeles County Museum of Art (5905 Wilshire Blvd.; 213/857-6111; recorded message, 857-6000). One of the most important museums in the country, its permanent collection includes Western art. Open daily except Mondays.

Travel Town (Forest Lawn and Zoo drives in Griffith Park; 213/662-5874). A transportation museum. Enter at Arcadia Depot, a Victorian railroad station. Vintage trains, planes, fire engines, cable cars, and steam engines. Open daily.

Lummis Home and Garden State Historical Monument (200 East Ave. 43; 213/222-0546). This was the unusual rock home of Charles F. Lummis (1859–1928), author, historian, and archaeologist. The Historical Society of Southern California is headquartered here. Open Wednesday through Sunday.

Southwest Museum (234 Museum Dr. at Marmion Way, Pasadena Freeway, Ave. 43 exit; 213/222-0546). Indian art and artifacts from prehistoric times to the present. Open daily except Mondays. Nearby is *Casa de Adobe* (4605 North Figueroa St.; 213/221-0468), a re-creation of an early Mexican Colonial hacienda with period furnishings and changing exhibits. Open daily except Mondays.

Los Encinos State Historical Park (16756 Moorpark St. in Encino; 818/784-4849). An early nine-room adobe ranch with exhibits of ranch life. Blacksmith shop. Tours. Open Wednesday through Sunday.

Will Rogers State Historic Park (15 miles west at 14253 Sunset Blvd. in Pacific Palisades; 213/454-8212). This was the humorist's estate while he was a movie star. Rogers memorabilia, Indian artifacts, Western art. Polo on most weekends. Open daily.

George C. Page La Brea Discoveries Museum (5801 Wilshire Blvd., in Hancock Park; 213/936-2230). The museum has more than a million prehistoric specimens recovered from the La Brea Tar Pits. Exhibits. Films. Open daily. Also in Hancock Park is *Rancho La Brea Tar Pits,* with fossils and life-sized dinosaur models. Visitors may observe current excavations. Open daily.

MARTINEZ

John Muir National Historic Site (4202 Alhambra Ave.; 415/228-8860). John Muir, famed naturalist and father of the national park system, lived in the Victorian house on this eight-and-a-half-acre estate from 1890 to 1914. Born in Scotland in 1838, Muir was ten when he and his family moved to Wisconsin, at that time the frontier. After moving here, he wrote some of his most influential books and articles on conservation, his wife and daughter editing and typing his manuscripts. Muir, a hiking companion of President Theodore Roosevelt, defended the environment and promoted the establishment of Yosemite, Petrified Forest, Grand Canyon, and Mount Rainier national parks. In 1892 he started the Sierra Club, an environmental association that is still active today. The house and grounds are little changed today. Palm trees flank the entrance to the seventeen-room house, which is furnished with original pieces and vintage antiques. In Muir's study, which he called his "scribble den," he wrote *Our National Parks*, *Travels in Alaska,* and more than 300 magazine articles. Muir's life is reviewed in a half-hour film. Open daily.

MODESTO

McHenry Museum (1402 I St.; 209/529-3369). Artifacts are displayed in period rooms, including a doctor's office, a blacksmith shop, and a schoolroom. Changing exhibits. Open daily except Sundays. Nearby is the *McHenry Mansion* (15th and I; 209/577-5377), once the Victorian home of one of the city's leading families. Period furnishings. Open Tuesday through Thursday, and Sundays.

Miller Horse and Buggy Ranch (10 miles east on CA 132 at 9425 Yosemite Blvd.; 209/522-1781). A collection of vintage firefighting equipment, a stagecoach, a Wells Fargo Express wagon, a surrey, a 1905 horse-drawn ambulance, and ten antique automobiles and wood-frame bicycles. An old country store, a blacksmith shop, and a barbershop. Open Sundays.

MONTEREY

Spanish explorer Sebastián Vizcaíno sailed into the bay here in 1602 and named it for the Count of Monte-Rey, Viceroy of Mexico. Father Juan Crespi, Father Junípero Serra, and Gaspar de Portolá took possession of the area in 1770, founding the Presidio and the Mission San Carlos Borromeo de Monterey. Five years later, Monterey was recognized by the King of Spain as the capital of California. American whalers and traders called here, planting the seeds of opposition to Mexican rule. In 1846, Commodore John Drake Sloat raised the American flag, and in 1849 a convention met here and drew up California's first constitution. Monterey's sardine fisheries and canneries inspired John Steinbeck, who lived here for a number of years, to write *Cannery Row* and *Sweet Thursday*.

Presidio of Monterey (Pacific St. north of Scott St.; 408/647-5414). Now the home of the Defense Language Institute, the Presidio has twelve historic sites and monuments on Presidio Hill. The fort here was used in 1902 as a cantonment for troops returning from the Philippine Insurrection. Museum exhibits depict the history of the Presidio from the Ohione Indian period through modern times. Open Fridays and Saturdays.

Royal Presidio Chapel (San Carlos Cathedral, 550 Church St.). In continuous use since 1795, this is the only presidio chapel left in California. Its façade is the most ornate of all California missions. Open daily.

Monterey State Historic Park (525 Polk St.; 408/649-7118). Open daily, the park includes a number of historic structures: *Robert Louis Stevenson House* (530 Houston St.) was the home of the author for four months while he courted his future wife, and has a collection of Stevenson memorabilia. There are guided tours daily except Wednesdays. *California's First Theatre* (Pacific and Scott streets; box office, 408/375-4916), now the home of the oldest active little theater group in the country, presented its first production in 1847. Performances are given Wednesday through Saturday in the summer; Fridays and Saturdays, September through June. *Custom House* (Custom House Plaza), built in 1827, was the building over which the American flag was raised in 1846. It has exhibits and gardens. Open daily. *Pacific House* (Custom House Plaza) is a museum of California history, including the Holman Indian collection. Open daily. *Larkin House* (510 Calle Principal at Jefferson St.) was the model for Monterey architecture, and the office of Thomas Larkin, the only American consul here during Mexican rule. Tours are given daily except Tuesdays. *Boston Store* (Scott and Olivier streets), built by Larkin in 1845, is a restored general store with vintage merchandise. Open daily except Tuesdays. *Casa Soberanes* (336 Pacific St.) is an 1842 adobe house with an art collection and displays of Monterey history. Tours are given daily except Thursdays.

Cotton Hall Museum (Pacific St., between Madison and Jefferson streets; 408/375-9944). This building was constructed in 1849 as a town hall and school by the Reverend Walter Cotton, chief magistrate

of Central California during the Mexican War. California's first constitution was written here. A single-story addition to the building contains the 1854 *Old Monterey Jail.* Open daily.

Monterey Peninsula Museum of Art (559 Pacific St.; 408/372-7591). Early California art and Indian art. Open daily except Mondays. The museum also maintains *La Mirada* (720 Via Mirada), the two-and-a-half-acre estate of José Castro, prominent during the Mexican period. Art collection. Saturday tours of the house and garden.

Allen Knight Maritime Museum (550 Calle Principal; 408/375-2553). Ship models, paintings, and maritime artifacts of naval and whaling history. Open daily except Mondays.

Fort Ord Museum (Fort Ord, ten miles north on CA 1; 408/242-4905 or 242-5407). Artifacts and memorabilia relating to the fort and the Seventh Infantry Division, stationed here since its formation in 1918. Open weekdays.

Fisherman's Wharf (on Monterey Harbor). Shops and restaurants in the historic Cannery Row area. Open daily.

Path of History. A self-guided tour to a number of historic houses, several open to the public. All are marked with plaques explaining their history and architecture. A map is available at the Monterey Peninsula Visitors Bureau (380 Alvarado St.; 408/649-1770).

Accommodations: *Jabberwock* (598 Laine St.; 408/372-4777). This lodging has seven rooms and four shared baths in a former convent with gardens and waterfalls. *Old Monterey* (500 Martin St.; 408/375-8284). An exceptional ten-room hostelry in an English-style 1929 country house on a hilltop near the bay. Breakfast and afternoon tea.

OAKLAND

This city across the bay from San Francisco was once part of the Rancho San Antonio, a 48,000-acre fiefdom owned by Luís María Peralta. Horace W. Carpenter acquired the land in 1850 and named his new town for the evergreen oaks that grew here.

Oakland Museum (1000 Oak St.; 415/834-2413). This complex of buildings, covering four city blocks, interprets the land and people of California through exhibits of

Spanish explorer Sebastian Vizcaino sailed into the bay in 1602 and named it for the Count of Monte-Rey, viceroy of Mexico. Monterey became the Spanish heart of California, and in 1775, the King of Spain recognized Monterey as the capital of the province of California.

art, history, and natural science. Tours. Open Wednesday through Sunday.

Camron-Sanford House (1418 Lakeside Dr.; 415/271-6146). A splendid 1876 mansion with period furnishings, paintings, and sculpture. From 1910 to 1967 the home of the Oakland Public Museum, the house is now a resource center for the museum. Library. Tours. Open Wednesday through Sunday.

Jack London Waterfront (bounded by Oakland Estuary, Clay, Franklin, and Embarcadero; 415/444-6400). The author lived and worked here. One of his hangouts was Heinold's First and Last Chance Saloon, at the foot of Webster Street. There is a reconstruction of London's Klondike cabin. At the foot of Alice Street, Jack London Village has restaurants and shops. Open daily.

Joaquin Miller Park (Joaquin Miller Rd.). The site of the poet's home has four monuments erected by the "Poet of the Sierras" to General Frémont, Robert and Elizabeth Browning, Moses, and a symbolic funeral pyre for himself. Open daily.

Northern California Center for Afro-American History and Life (5606 San Pablo Ave.; 415/658-3158). Exhibits tracing African-American history in California, Mexico, and the United States. Open Tuesday through Friday.

Dunsmuir House and Gardens (2960 Peralta Oaks Ct.; 415/562-0328). A thirty-seven-room 1899 Colonial Revival mansion with exceptional grounds and gardens. Tours. Open Wednesdays and Sundays, April through September.

OCEANSIDE

Mission San Luis Rey de Francia (4$\frac{1}{2}$ miles east on CA 76; 619/757-3651). The largest of the twenty-one early California missions. Built in 1798 by Father Lasuen, it was named for Louis IX, king of France from 1226 to 1270, who led a crusade to the Holy Land. Its museum has a collection of Spanish vestments and other artifacts. Indian cemetery. Open daily.

OROVILLE

Miner's Alley is a reminder of the Gold Rush days, when Oroville (City of Gold) was the second-largest city in California.

Judge C. F. Lott Home (1067 Montgomery St., in Loft-Sank Park; 916/538-2497). Built in 1856, the house has been restored and furnished in the period. Picnicking. Open daily in summer; Friday through Tuesday the rest of the year. Closed December to mid-January.

Chinese Temple (1500 Broderick St. at Elma; 916/538-2496). The largest authentic temple in California is all that remains of a Chinatown that once rivaled San Francisco's.

The Pony Express

It only lasted eighteen months, it was a financial flop, but the Pony Express grabbed the American imagination and never let go. It was inaugurated on April 3, 1860, to carry the mail between St. Joseph, Missouri, and Sacramento, California, but its real purpose was to promote mail and passenger service on the central route across the country. The Overland Mail Company had a government mail contract for the southern route, and its promoters thought that speedy mail service might win it away from them.

The Pony Express established 190 way stations at ten-to-fifteen-mile intervals and selected fast horses and daring riders. They cut mail delivery time in half. Even during the hard winter, the Pony Express kept to the eighteen-day schedule.

Although it was a dramatic success, the Pony Express lost nearly $200,000. A government mail contract never came, and the sponsors went bankrupt. The Pony Express ended in October 1861, upon the completion of the transcontinental telegraph. Overland Mail, forced by the Civil War to abandon the southern route, was awarded the mail contract for the central route.

Relic room. Restored tapestry hall. Open daily. Closed December to mid-January.

Accommodations: *Jean Pratt's Riverside Bed & Breakfast* (1124 Middlehoff Lane; 916/533-1413). On the Feather River. Guests can pan for gold on the premises.

PALM SPRINGS

Palm Springs has a habit of being rediscovered. A Spanish explorer came by here in 1774 and named it Agua Caliente, "Hot Water." A century later it was a stagecoach stop. The first rediscoverer was R. S. Williamson, a young army lieutenant in charge of a party seeking the best railroad route to link the Mississippi and the Pacific. He reported passes to a desert ringed with mountains, a band of friendly Indians (the Cahuilla, who still own much of the land here) living in a wild palm grove, and a hot mineral spring. In 1887 the Southern Pacific established service from Yuma to Los Angeles via Palm Springs, and the area, known to the Spanish as La Palma de la Mano de Dios, "The Palm of God's Hand," slowly came to life. The next rediscoverers were the actors Charles Farrell and Ralph Bellamy, who built their Racquet Club here in 1933 and soon were introducing their fellow Hollywood luminaries to the pleasures of the desert. Enough people now have rediscovered Palm Springs to make it America's foremost desert resort.

Palm Springs Desert Museum (101 Museum Dr.; 619/325-7186 or 325-0189). Exhibits of Western art and Indian basketry. Open daily, late September through June.

Village Green Heritage Center (221 South Palm Canyon Dr.; 619/323-8297). The center has two early homes: the 1884 *McCallum Adobe*, the oldest building in the city, which contains an extensive collection of Indian and pioneer artifacts; and *Miss Cornelia's "Little House,"* built in 1893 of railroad ties from the defunct Palmdale Railway, furnished with antiques. Open Wednesday through Sunday, mid-October through May.

PASADENA

Pasadena Historic Society (470 West Walnut St., 818/577-1660). An eighteen-room mansion with antiques, original furnishings, and gardens. Open Tuesday, Thursday, and Sunday, except the third Sunday of the month and the entire month of August.

The Gamble House (4 Westmoreland Pl.; 818/793-3334). An excellent 1908 example of the California bungalow-style wooden house, designed by architects Henry and Charles Greene. Tours. Open Thursday through Sunday except major holidays.

Accommodations: *Dnynmac Irish Inn* (119 North Meredith; 818/440-0066). A bit of Ireland in a turn-of-the-century two-story Craftsman house with three guest rooms.

PASO ROBLES

Mission San Miguel Arcangel (7 miles north via U.S. 101 on Mission Street in San Miguel; 805/472-2311). One of the chain of Franciscan missions, this one has frescoes by Esteban Munras and his Indian helpers. The interior of the church is well preserved. Museum. Open daily.

PETALUMA

Petaluma Adobe State Historic Park (3 miles east of U.S. 101 on CA 116 at 3325 Adobe Rd.; 707/762-2785). The park is the location of a restored adobe ranch house, circa 1840, built for Gen. M. G. Vallejo. The house is a Monterey Colonial building in a traditional Spanish form. Open daily.

Petaluma Historical Library and Museum (20 Fourth St.; 707/778-4398).

Housed in a 1908 Carnegie library with one of the state's few free-standing domes, the museum has artifacts and memorabilia of the area. Open Thursday through Monday.

Winners' Circle Ranch (5 miles southeast, at 5911 Lakeville Hwy.; 707/762-1808 or 762-0220). The ranch breeds and trains miniature show horses, many of them under three feet tall. Tours. Demonstrations. Wagon rides. Open Wednesday through Sunday, May to Labor Day.

RED BLUFF

William B. Ide Adobe State Historic Park (2 miles northeast off I-5, Wilcox Rd. exit; 916/527-5927). A restored adobe home of the only president of the California Republic. Collection of artifacts and memorabilia. Adobe-making demonstrations in summer. Open daily.

Kelly-Griggs House Museum (311 Washington St.; 916/527-5927). A Victorian home from the 1880s, restored and furnished in the period. Indian artifacts and historical exhibits. Pendleton Gallery of Art. Open Thursday through Sunday.

REDDING

Redding was founded in 1872, when the California and Oregon Railroad built its terminus here in the shadow of Mount Shasta. The Sacramento River runs through the city.

Redding Museum and Art Center (56 Quartz Hill Rd.; 916/225-4155). Indian arts and crafts and local artifacts. Rotating art exhibits. Open daily except Mondays.

Shasta State Historic Park (6 miles west on CA 299; 916/243-8194). The park contains a ghost town with several well-preserved buildings, a museum, and an art gallery. Open daily, March through October; Thursday through Monday, November through February.

REDLANDS

Asistencia Mission de San Gabriel (2 miles west, at 26930 Barton Rd.; 714/798-5402). Indian and pioneer artifacts, wishing well and bell tower. Open daily except Mondays.

Lincoln Memorial Shrine (125 West Vine St., in Smiley Park; 714/798-7636). The shrine has a Carrara marble bust of Lincoln sculptured by George Grey Barnard, murals by Dean Cornwell, and paintings by Norman Rockwell. Manuscripts and memorabilia relating to Lincoln and the Civil War. Open Tuesday through Saturday.

San Bernadino County Museum (2024 Orange Tree Lane; 714/793-7636). Pioneer and Indian artifacts, rocks and minerals and a collection of stuffed birds. There is a steam locomotive on the grounds. Open daily.

Kimberly Crest House and Gardens (1325 Prospect Drive; 714/792-1334). An 1897 French chateau–style mansion, the former home of John Kimberly, founder of the Kimberly-Clark Corporation. Italian gardens. Tours. Open Thursdays and Sundays; closed in August.

Accommodations: *Morey Mansion Bed & Breakfast* (190 Terracina Blvd.; 714/793-7970). An 1890 landmark Victorian furnished with antiques, offering five guest rooms.

RIVERSIDE

Riverside Municipal Museum (3720 Orange St.; 714/782-5273). Displays relating to area history. Open daily except Mondays.

Sherman Indian Museum (9010 Magnolia Ave.; 714/369-9434). Rare artifacts and dioramas of leading Native American cultures. Open weekdays.

Heritage House (8193 Magnolia Ave.; 714/689-1333). A restored 1891 Victorian mansion. Open Tuesdays, Thursdays, and Sundays. Closed in July and August.

Mount Rubidoux Memorial Park (west end of 9th St.; 714/782-4787). This mountain, according to Indian lore, was the altar for Cahuilla and Serrano sun worship. A cross on the peak honors Junípero Serra, the founder of the California missions. Open daily, but closed to vehicular traffic Thursday through Sunday in summer.

California Museum of Photography (3824 Main St.; 714/787-4797). A large collection of photographic equipment and memorabilia, maintained by the University of California at Riverside.

March Field Museum (9 miles east via I-215 at March Air Force Base; 714/655-3725). Displays of aircraft, uniforms, and flying memorabilia. Library. Open daily.

Orange Empire Railway Museum (14 miles south via I-215 at 2201 South A St. in Perris; 714/657-2605). More than 250 pieces of railroad equipment are on display, along with railroad and trolley memorabilia. Trolley rides on weekends and holidays. Open daily.

SACRAMENTO

Having secured a land grant from Mexico in 1839, Capt. John Augustus Sutter founded a fort called New Helvetia near here, as a colony for his Swiss compatriots. It was the first outpost of European civilization in inland California. Immigrants came and Sutter prospered, raising wheat, milling flour, distilling liquor, and running a boat service to San Francisco. The discovery of gold at his sawmill in Coloma ruined him. His workers deserted to hunt gold and he lost possession of the fort. His son, who had been deeded family property near Sutter's boat-line terminus, laid out a town there in 1849 and named it Sacramento City. It was the logical entrance to the Mother Lode Country, and within seven months its population was 10,000. In 1854 it became the capital of California. From the early days,

transportation spurred Sacramento's growth. In 1860 it became the western terminus of the Pony Express. Seagoing vessels reached the city through a forty-three-mile channel from Suisun Bay. And Sacramento's Big Four—Charles Crocker, Mark Hopkins, Collis P. Huntington, and Leland Stanford—financed the extension of the Central Pacific Railroad over the Sierras.

State Capitol (10th St. at Capitol Mall; 916/324-0333). Begun in 1854 and completed over twenty years, the capitol building has re-creations of seven historic offices. The Victorian senate and assembly chambers are still in use. There are exhibits in the library and in the state archives on the capitol's history, as well as an introductory film. Tours. Open daily.

Governor's Mansion (16th and H streets; 916/323-0333). This was once the Victorian home of Joseph Steffens, the father of author Lincoln Steffens. Guided tours. Open daily.

"Boys, I believe I have found a gold mine!"

—JOHN MARSHALL, SUTTER'S MILL, 1848

Once owned by the father of journalist Lincoln Steffens, this Victorian has been the Governor's Mansion in California since 1903. Sacramento began as New Helvetia, a Swiss colony founded by John A. Sutter, who was ruined after gold was discovered at his mill.

John Sutter

Unhappily married and deeply in debt, John Sutter fled Switzerland and went to California, where he made a deal with the Mexican governor. In return for some 50,000 acres, Sutter agreed to set up and run a community, which he called New Helvetia. He built Sutter's Fort at what is now Sacramento. The fort attracted American settlers, and he prospered from their trade. Then, on January 24, 1848, James Marshall found gold in the stream beside a sawmill he was building for Sutter in Colema. The subsequent gold rush was Sutter's ruin. His workers ran off to hunt for gold, and prospectors overran his land, slaughtered his cattle, and stole his crops. By 1852, New Helvetia was just a memory. Sutter spent the rest of his life in Washington, D.C., unsuccessfully petitioning the government for compensation.

After gold was discovered on the American River in 1848, New Helvetia was renamed Sacramento, and as the link between the gold fields and the outside world, it became California's first great city. The center of New Helvetia was Sutter's Fort, shown below.

Sutter's Fort State Historic Park (2701 L St.; 916/445-4422). Sutter's restored carpenter, blacksmith, and saddle shops are in the park. Exhibits depict Sutter's life. Living-history demonstrations. Self-guided tour. Open daily.

State Indian Museum (2618 K St.; 916/445-4422). Near Sutter's Fort, the museum displays weapons, dugout canoes, pottery, and basketry. Changing exhibits. Indian leg-

end puppet show and films on weekends. Open daily.

Old Sacramento Historic District (between I-5 and the I St. bridge, adjacent to the central business district; 916/445-4209). The area has twenty-eight acres of historic buildings on the banks of the Sacramento River, restored to the 1850–70 period. Important buildings include the *Hastings Building* (2nd and J streets), the Western terminus of the Pony Express and the original home of the California Supreme Court; the *Old Eagle Theatre* (Front and J streets), which presents period plays on weekends; the *California State Railroad Museum* (111 I St.), which houses twenty-one pieces of rolling stock and some forty exhibits on all phases of railroading. Also here are the *Museum of Railroad History* and the *Central Pacific Railroad Station Museum*. Railroad museums are open daily; most of the other sites are open daily except Mondays.

Sacramento History Center (101 I St. in Old Sacramento; 916/449-2057). Regional artifacts and memorabilia are on display, including gold ore specimens. Hands-on displays and video computers. Open daily.

Crocker Art Museum (3rd and O streets; 916/449-5423). The museum includes the restored 1872 Victorian Gallery and the newer Herold Wing, housing the E. B. Crocker collection of American and European paintings, master drawings, and decorative and Oriental arts. Open daily.

Towe Ford Museum (2200 Front St.; 916/442-6802). A collection of some 150 Ford automobiles from 1903 to 1953. Open daily.

Accommodations: *The Briggs House* (2209 Capitol Ave.; 916/441-3214). Seven individually decorated guest rooms in a 1901 Victorian home with library and garden. Breakfast is included in the rates. *Amber House* (1315 22nd St.; 916/441-3214). Five guest rooms in a 1905 Craftsman-style mansion. Elegant interior. Library. Breakfast is included in the rates.

ST. HELENA

Silverado Museum (1490 Library Lane; 707/963-3757). The museum has an excellent Robert Louis Stevenson collection: first editions, letters and manuscripts, memorabilia, paintings, sculptures, and photographs. Open daily except Mondays and holidays.

Bale Grist Mill State Historic Park (3 miles north on CA 29, 128; 707/942-4575). A restored 1846 water-powered gristmill. Open daily.

Accommodations: *Sutter Home* (225 St. Helena Hwy.; 707/963-4423). An 1884 Victorian with nine guest rooms in the carriage house and water tower. Many antiques. Breakfast included.

SAN DIEGO

This is "the place where California began" when Portuguese navigator Juan Rodríguez Cabrillo landed here in 1542. Since the first mission in California was built here in 1769, San Diego has grown steadily under Spanish, Mexican, and North American influence.

Cabrillo National Monument (10 miles west of I-8 on Catalina Blvd., on tip of Point Loma; 619/587-5450). This 144-acre park commemorates the landing of Cabrillo, the first European to set foot in California, who sailed into what is now San Diego harbor on September 28, 1542. He named it San Miguel, then sailed up the coast as far as Oregon. He prophetically called his next landfall, present-day Los Angeles, "Bahía de los Fumos," for the smoke of Indian campfires.

The Visitor Center has displays on Cabrillo and his expedition, and a large statue of him is nearby. *Old Point Loma Lighthouse*, a beacon for ships entering the harbor from 1855 to 1891, is a good vantage point for observing the annual migration of gray whales from December to mid-March.

Bayside Trail goes by remnants of the artillery that guarded the harbor in two world wars. From here, the most southwesterly point in the continental United States, the view stretches south to Mexico, west across the Pacific, north to La Jolla, and east to the city. Open daily. Limited wheelchair access.

Old Town Historic Park (bounded by Congress, Wallace, Twigg, and Juan streets; 619/237-6770). The park contains several important sites: *Seeley Stable* (Calhoun St.; 619/237-6770), built in 1869, served the stagecoach line; *Casa de Estudillo* (2645 San Diego Ave.), built in 1820–29, is a restored adobe town house with period furnishings; *San Diego Union Historical Restoration* (2626 San Diego Ave.) is the office that first printed the *Union* newspaper in 1868. All open daily except Mondays.

Surrounding the park is *Old Town* (plaza at Mason St. and San Diego Ave.), with more historic adobe buildings. *Presidio Park* (Presidio Drive, off Taylor St.), the site of the first mission, has mounds marking the original presidio (Spanish for a garrison or fortress), inside of which is the *Junípero Serra Museum*, displaying artifacts that trace the city's early history. The *Whaley House* (San Diego Ave. at Harney St.), built in 1856, originally housed a theatrical company and later was the county courthouse. On the

The stores now preserved in Old Sacramento were themselves gold mines of a sort. Merchants got rich charging miners outrageous prices for food and supplies. Here began the fortunes of Collis Huntington and Mark Hopkins, two of the state's richest men.

A monument to Portuguese-born navigator Juan Rodríguez Cabrillo, who landed at present-day San Diego in 1542, marks "the place where California began." Father Junípero Serra established a mission here in 1769, the first of a chain of California missions.

grounds are replicas of a vintage drugstore and gardens. All are open daily except Mondays.

Mission Basilica San Diego de Alcala (10818 San Diego Mission Rd.; 619/281-8449). This was the first California mission when it was built in 1769, and it is still used for services. The mission has a museum with early mission relics. Tours. Open daily.

Gaslamp Quarter (bounded by Broadway, 6th Ave., K St., and 4th Ave.; 619/233-5227). The turn-of-the-century business district is now a National Historic District, with many Victorian buildings. Self-guided tours. Open daily.

San Diego Museum of Art (Balboa Park; 619/232-8322). The museum has American, European, and Oriental paintings and decorative arts. Open daily except Mondays.

Timken Art Gallery (Balboa Park; 619/239-7931). The gallery has 18th- and 19th-century American paintings in its collection. Tours Tuesday through Thursday. Open daily except Mondays. Closed in September.

Museum of Man (Balboa Park; 619/239-2011). Exhibits on California and Hopi Indians, Maya culture, early man. Open daily.

Spanish Village Arts and Crafts Center (Balboa Park; 619/233-9050). Artists and craftsmen work in studios at the center.

The center is open daily.

Seaport Village (West Harbor Dr. at Kettner Blvd.; 619/235-4014). A fourteen-acre re-creation of port life of a century ago, featuring an 1890 carousel and a boardwalk along the waterfront. Open daily.

Villa Montezuma/Jesse Shepard House (1925 K St.; 619/239-2211). Jesse Shepard, author and musician, built this Victorian during the "Great Boom" of 1886–88, Exhibits. Open Wednesday through Sunday.

San Diego Trolley (Santa Fe Depot, Kettner and C streets; 619/233-3004). Two lines: the fifteen-mile South Line to the border across from Tijuana, and the seventeen-mile East Line to El Cajon.

Maritime Museum Association (1492 North Harbor Dr. on Embarcadero; 619/234-4111). Several historic ships are here, including the restored 1863 bark *Star of India,* which sailed under British, Hawaiian, and U.S. flags; the 1839 steam ferry *Berkeley*; and the 1904 steam yacht *Medea.* Open daily.

San Diego Harbor Excursion (foot of Broadway at Harbor Dr.; 619-234-4111). A one-hour narrated sail past Harbor Island, Coronado, and the navy terminals at 32nd Street and North Island. There is also a two-hour sail that adds Shelter Island, Ballast Point, the entrance to the harbor, shipyards, and the submarine base. Sailings daily.

Southern Mission Trail. Several early missions can be visited in a one-day, 159-mile drive. The Serra Mission in Presidio Park is a good introduction to understanding the missions. Start at *Mission Basilica San Diego de Alcala,* then take I-15N forty-four miles to CA 76, turn east, and drive seven miles to *Mission San Antonio de Pala* (not one of the original missions, but an *asistencia* of Mision San Luís Rey de Francia in Oceanside. The present structure is a restoration. Go west twenty-seven miles on CA 76 toward Oceanside; in San Luis Rey follow the sign to *Mission San Luís Rey de Francia.* Then go northwest twenty-nine miles on I-5 to San Juan Capistrano. Just off the road is

Old Mission San Juan Capistrano. Take I-5SE back to San Diego.

Accommodations: *Heritage Park* (2470 Heritage Park Row in Old Town; 619/295-7088). An 1889 Queen Anne mansion with an encircling veranda, vintage furnishings, and nine guest rooms. Film classics are shown nightly in the parlor. *Hotel del Coronado* (1500 Orange Ave., Coronado; 619/435-6611). A handsome landmark Victorian resort hotel that was a setting for the movie *Some Like It Hot* and for Wallis Simpson's first meeting with the Duke of Windsor.

SAN FERNANDO

Mission San Fernando Rey de España (15151 San Fernando Mission Blvd., 818/361-0186). A thirty-five-bell carillon plays a melody once sung in mission days by Indians. An archival center has ecclesiastical and historical documents, relics of Junípero Serra, and Indian artifacts. Open daily.

Lopez Adobe (1100 Pica St., 818/361-5050). The two-story home of early residents Geronimo and Catalina Lopez. Collection of beads, bags, and dolls. Tours. Open Wednesdays and weekends.

SAN FRANCISCO

The ship *San Carlos* sailed through the Golden Gate in 1775 and anchored off what would become this fabulous city. The following March, a site for a mission was selected and dedicated to Saint Francis of Assisi. The little village near the mission was known as Yerba Buena. In 1846, Captain John B. Montgomery and seventy sailors and marines came ashore off the USS *Portsmouth* and raised the American flag, marking the end of Mexican rule. When gold was discovered in 1848, San Francisco had a population of 450; in a year it was a tent city

of 20,000. Some fifty ships were arriving a month, most of them left to rot as the crews deserted to go to the gold fields. It remained a boomtown as America moved west. Trade with the Orient flourished. Chinese laborers helped build 2,000 miles of railroad tracks across the mountains to join with tracks coming from the East. San Francisco was a major city when an earthquake hit on April 18, 1906. In the aftermath of the quake, fires raged unchecked for three days, burning 497 city blocks. Some 2,500 people perished and the damage was estimated at $350 million. Before the ashes had cooled, the city started to rebuild. By 1915 a new San Francisco was able to play host to the Panama Pacific International Exposition.

Mission Dolores (16th and Dolores streets; 415/621-8203). The city began here in 1776 when Junípero Serra established the Mission San Francisco de Asis. It became known as Mission Dolores, taking its name from the nearby Laguna de Nuestra Señora de los Dolores. The cemetery here contains the graves of early pioneers. Open daily.

Society of California Pioneers Museum and Library (450 McAllister St., in the Civic Center; 415/861-5278). Exhibits

It was always an event in San Francisco when the Overland Mail Stagecoach departed on its arduous, often dangerous, 2,000-mile-plus journey east. The stagecoach in the West filled the large gap in transportation between the wagon trains and the railroad.

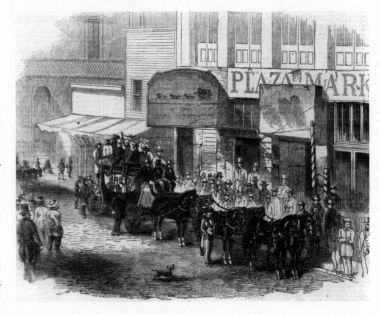

The Big Four

A century ago, everyone in California could name the Big Four—Leland Stanford, Collis Huntington, Charles Crocker, and Mark Hopkins—because there were no richer or more powerful men in the state. Individually and collectively, they were a study in business acumen. Huntington, the biggest of the Big Four, was the son of a Connecticut tinker who left school at fourteen to peddle watches. He went to California in the Gold Rush, spent one day in the mines, then opened a store in Sacramento. Wildly successful, he later took in another merchant, Hopkins, as a partner. Crocker, the son of a liquor merchant in Troy, New York, was a homesteader in Iowa when the Gold Rush called to him. He led a party overland, spent two years in the mines, then opened a store in San Francisco. In a few years he was one of the city's richest men. Stanford, a New York lawyer, went west to Sacramento to join his successful merchant brothers, then later entered politics and became governor.

In 1863 the four men became partners to build the western segment of the transcontinental railroad. Their talents meshed perfectly. Huntington, the most powerful of the four, lobbied for the railroad in Washington. After construction began, he procured equipment and materials, and kept the company solvent during the depression of the 1870s. Stanford provided the political clout in California. Hopkins, in Crocker's words, proved to be "hell on wheels" in matters of economy and efficiency. Crocker, superintendent of construction, found day laborers scarce and hit on the the idea of using Chinese laborers, who didn't know what exploitation meant . He completed the Central Pacific a full seven years ahead of schedule.

depicting state history, and paintings by 19th-century California artists. Open weekdays. Closed in August.

Wells Fargo Bank History Museum (420 Montgomery St.; 415/396-2619). Artifacts of the Gold Rush and the 1906 earthquake. Concord stagecoach. Open weekdays.

Cable Car Museum (1201 Mason St.; 415/474-1887). Vintage cable cars are housed here, including the world's first. There is an underground area to view the machinery that powers the cables. Historic photographs. Open daily.

Palace of the Fine Arts (Lyon St.; 415/561-0360). Built for the Panama-Pacific exposition, the building has been restored. Open Wednesday through Sunday.

California Palace of the Legion of Honor (Lincoln Park, 34th and Clement streets; 415/750-3600). This spectacular building in a 270-acre park has important collections of European art, including a Rodin collection. Open Wednesday through Sunday.

Whittier Mansion (2090 Jackson St.; 415/567-1848). Operated by the California Historical Society, the museum displays California art and local history memorabilia. Library. Tours. Open Tuesday through Sunday.

Haas-Lilienthal House (2007 Franklin St.; 415/441-3004). An 1886 Queen Anne mansion with vintage furnishings. Open Wednesday through Sunday.

Randall Museum (199 Museum Way; 415/863-1339). California Indian and pioneer artifacts, a seismograph, and a model railroad. Open Tuesday through Saturday.

M. H. deYoung Memorial Museum (Golden Gate Park; 415/750-3600). The museum has an excellent collection of American art from Colonial times to the present. Open daily.

Old Mint (5th and Mission streets; 415/567-4761). A fine example of Federal Classic Revival architecture, the building has period rooms, an 1869 coin press, a pyramid of gold bars, and monetary and Old West artifacts. Open weekdays.

Mexican Museum (Fort Mason Center, Laguna and Marina blvds.; 415/441-0404). Pre-Hispanic, colonial, folk, and contemporary Mexican-American and Mexican arts and crafts. Open Wednesday through Sunday.

Treasure Island Museum (accessible from Oakland Bay Bridge, Treasure Island exit; 415/567-1848). Artifacts and memorabilia of the navy and marines in the Pacific from 1813 onward. Exhibits on the 1939–40 Golden Gate International Exposition, for which the island was created. *China Clipper* flying boat. Open daily.

Fort Point National Historic Park (Long Ave. and Marine Dr., under the south end of the Golden Gate Bridge in the Presidio; 415/556-1693). This fort, which guarded the Golden Gate, was one of some thirty built between the end of the War of 1812 and the Civil War as part of a national coastal defense system. Its irregular quadrangle, enclosed by brick walls, was built between 1853 and 1861 on the site of a Spanish fort known as the Castillo de San Joaquín. In the museum are displays of artillery and military equipment, exhibits commemorating the military contributions of African-Americans and women, and living-history demonstrations. Open daily.

Near Fort Point is *Fort Mason Center*, once the army's western headquarters. Old fort buildings and two piers are now a cultural and entertainment center. Moored at Pier 3 is the SS *Jeremiah O'Brien* (415/441-3101), the last surviving World War II Liberty Ship. Open daily.

National Maritime Museum (Foot of Polk St.; 415/929-0202). The five vintage merchant ships berthed here include the *Balelutha*, an 1886 sailing ship restored as a Cape Horn trader. Open daily.

Alcatraz (in the bay; boats to the island leave Pier 41 near Fisherman's Wharf several times daily; reservations, 415/546-9400). Probably the most famous prison in the world, this federal maximum-security facility closed in 1963. Its inmates included Al Capone, "Machine Gun" Kelly, Alvin Karpis, and Robert Stroud, "the Bird Man of Alcatraz." There is a guided tour of the cell blocks, and a self-guided tour of the island. Open daily. Limited wheelchair access.

Chinatown (Grant Ave. and nearby streets). With 80,000 residents, this is the largest Chinese community outside the Orient. The *Chinese Culture Center* (750 Kearny St.; 415/986-1822) offers art exhibits, performances, and themed tours of Chinatown.

Jackson Square (Washington, Jackson, and Pacific streets, from Montgomery to Battery). This area has many buildings that survived the earthquake and fire.

Cow Hollow (Union St. between Van Ness and Fillmore streets). This area, where cows once roamed, has many restored Victorian homes.

Telegraph Hill (Lombard St. above Kearny St.). The hill is topped by the 210-foot Coit Tower, a memorial to the volunteer firemen of the 1850s and 1860s. There is an elevator to the top, from which there is a stunning view. Open daily. Limited wheelchair access.

The Embarcadero. This wide thoroughfare runs three and a half miles from China Basin to Fisherman's Wharf, past the landmark Ferry Building and a promenade at the foot of Montgomery Street.

Fisherman's Wharf (foot of Taylor St.). The picturesque home of the commercial fishing industry.

Accommodations: *Archbishop's Mansion* (1000 Fulton St.; 415/563-7872). Fifteen guest rooms in an antique-filled 1904 mansion. *Queen Anne* (1590 Sutter St.; 415/441-2828). Forty-nine guest rooms in a restored 1890 girls' school. *Spreckels Mansion* (737 Buena Vista West; 415/861-3008). A sugar baron's 1887 Colonial Revival house with a view of the city. Ten guest rooms. Breakfast and afternoon social hour.

SAN JOSE

California's first civic settlement was founded in 1777 as Pueblo de San José de Guadalupe. Before California became a state, San Jose was chosen as the capital, and the state legislature met here for the first time on December 15, 1849.

San Jose Historical Museum (Kelley Park, Phelan Ave. at Senter Rd.; 408/287-2291). The museum has a collection of original and re-created structures: pioneer homes, a print shop, a fruit barn, a doctor's office, a 1927 gas station, a trolley barn, a firehouse, and an operating ice cream parlor. Exhibits trace the city's Spanish and Mexican heritage. Open daily.

Parlata Adobe (186 St. John St.; 408/287-2290). All that remains of El Pueblo de San José de Guadalupe. Open daily.

Winchester Mystery House (110 South Market St.; 408/247-2101). In 1884, Sarah Winchester, the widow of the firearms manufacturer, was told by a spiritualist that she would not die until the house she was building was completed. She kept a crew of carpenters busy until her death in 1922. The cost of the 160-room mansion was some $5.5 million. The house has thousands of doors and windows, and many of its forty stairways go nowhere. Museum of Winchester rifles. Tours. Open daily. Limited wheelchair access.

Accommodations: *Briar Rose* (897 E. Jackson St.; 408/279-5999). A bed-and-breakfast in an 1875 Victorian with period furnishings.

SAN JUAN BAUTISTA

Mission San Juan Bautista (2nd and Mariposa; 408/623-4528). The largest mission built by the Franciscans, begun in 1797 and completed in 1812, is still in use. A museum displays old vestments, music books, a barrel organ, and other artifacts. The cemetery contains the graves of 4,300 Indians. Open daily.

San Juan Bautista State Historic Park (3 miles east of U.S. 101 at 2nd St.; 408/623-4881). Here are the *Plaza Stable*, built in 1861, and the restored *Plaza Hotel* and *Plaza Hall*. Open daily.

A spiritualist told Sarah Winchester, widow of the firearms manufacturer, that she would never die as long as she kept building her California house. For thirty-eight years, she kept crews of carpenters busy on what now is the 160-room Winchester Mystery House.

SAN JUAN CAPISTRANO

Mission San Juan Capistrano (2 blocks west of I-5, Ortega Hwy. exit; 714/493-1424). The mission is famous for its swallows, which depart southward annually on October 23, St. John's Day, and return on March 19, St. Joseph's Day. Built in the shape of a cross, it is one of the most beautiful of the California missions. The roof and belfry collapsed during the earthquake of 1812, and only pillars and arches remain. A tour includes the Serra Chapel, which is still in use, the ruins, and the padres' quarters. A museum has Indian and early Spanish artifacts. Open daily.

O'Neil Museum (31831 Los Rios St.; 714/493-8444). A restored Victorian house with collections of Indian artifacts, period furniture, rare books, and historic photographs. Open Tuesday through Friday and Sundays.

SAN LUIS OBISPO

When Junípero Serra founded this mission in 1772, two nearby volcanic peaks reminded him of a bishop's miter, so he named it after Saint Louis, Bishop of Toulouse. After the thatched roofs of the mission caught fire several times, a tile-making technique was developed that soon set the style for other California missions.

Mission San Luis Obispo de Tolosa (782 Monterey St.; 805/543-6850). This mission still serves as a parish church. A museum contains an extensive collection of Chumash Indian and pioneer artifacts. California's first olive grove was planted here, and two original trees remain. Open daily.

San Luis Obispo County Historical Museum (696 Monterey St.; 805/543-6850). Local memorabilia and decorative arts are displayed in a turn-of-the-century house. Open Wednesday through Sunday.

Ah Louis Store (800 Palm St.; 805/543-0638). The bank and post office of the Chinese community, it was opened by Ah Louis, a community leader who gained prominence when Asians were given few opportunities.

Shakespeare Press Museum (California Polytechnic State University campus; 805/756-0111). A collection of 19th-century printing presses, type, and other equipment. Demonstrations and tours. Open weekends.

Accommodations: *Apple Farm* (2015 Monterey St.; 805/544-2040). A sixty-seven-room inn with antiques, a bakery, and a mill house. Breakfast is included in the rates.

SAN MARINO

Huntington Library (1151 Oxford Rd.; 818/405-2100). This famous library has Gainsborough's *Blue Boy,* a Shakespeare First Folio, the Ellesmere manuscript of Chaucer's *Canterbury Tales,* and the manuscript of Benjamin Franklin's autobiography, as well as a comprehensive collection of 18th- and 19th-century American, French, and British art. There is also a formal garden. Open daily except Mondays.

El Molino Viejo (1120 Old Mill Rd.; 818/449-5450). The first gristmill in Southern California to be powered by water, it contains paintings and prints of California and the West, and is the Southern California headquarters of the California Historical Society. Open daily except Mondays.

SAN SIMEON

Hearst–San Simeon State Historical Monument (42 miles north of San Luis Obispo on the Coast Highway, CA-1; 916/323-2988; 800/952-5580 in California). Publisher William Randolph Hearst was one of the richest men in the country, and he spent money nearly as fast as he made it. In 1919 he began to construct a castle crowning La

"California is a queer place— it has turned its back on the world, and looks into the void Pacific."

—D. H. LAWRENCE

Mission Santa Barbara, the tenth in the California chain, is called the "Queen of the Missions." The present church, completed in 1820, was at one time a beacon for sailing ships. Its twin towers are characteristic of the early Spanish Renaissance architecture.

Cuesta Encantada (the Enchanted Hill), in what he described as a "carefully planned, deliberate attempt to create a shrine of beauty." An army of workmen built a castle with twin towers and surrounded it with formal Renaissance gardens, pools, and tennis courts; they were still at work when Hearst died, decades later. The exteriors of the north and east portions of the buildings are still incomplete. For years Hearst entertained the top stars of Hollywood here, screening new movies for them in his private theater. Until his death, the public could view the castle only through a telescope from the nearby town of San Simeon.

Today, items collected by Hearst can be seen in the castle and on the grounds. Features of the castle include the *Refractory*, a "long, high, noble room" with a hand-carved ceiling and life-sized saints, silk banners from Italy, and stalls from European monasteries; the *Assembly Room*, with tapestries and four marble medallions, each weighing more than a ton; and the lavish *Theater*. The estate includes three luxurious "guest houses," one the residence of Hearst's longtime friend Marion Davies; the *Neptune Pool*, with a pillared colonnade leading to an ancient Greek temple and an array of marble

statuary; and magnificent gardens, pools, fountains, and walks.

The Visitor Center has exhibits on the life and times of Hearst. Buses take visitors to the castle; access to the castle and grounds is by guided tour only. Open daily. Wheelchair access requires ten days advance notice.

SANTA BARBARA

Mission Santa Barbara (2 miles north at East Los Olivos and Upper Laguna streets; 805/662-4713). Known as "the Queen of the Missions" because of its architectural beauty, the twin-towered church and monastery are representative of the earliest phase of the Spanish Renaissance period. There are displays of mission-building arts and crafts, and of Indian and Mexican art. Tours. Open daily.

Santa Barbara County Courthouse (1100 Anacapa St.; 805/962-1601). Resembling a Spanish-Moorish palace, this is considered one of the most beautiful buildings in the West. Tours. Open daily.

Santa Barbara Historical Society Museum (138 East De la Guerra St.; 805/966-1601). Paintings, artifacts, and documents from the Spanish, Mexican, and American eras. Open daily except Mondays.

Santa Barbara Museum of Art (1130 State St.; 805/963-4364). American and European art and sculpture. Photography collection. Tours. Open Tuesday through Saturday.

El Presidio de Santa Barbara State Historic Park (122–129 East Cañon Perdido; 805/966-9719). Original and reconstructed buildings of the last presidio built by Spain in the New World. A museum has artifacts of the Spanish colonial period. Open daily.

Accommodations: *Blue Quail Inn* (1908 Bath St.; 805/687-2300). Nine guest rooms near the beach. Bicycles are available for the use of guests. Breakfast is included in the rates.

SANTA CLARA

Mission Santa Clara de Asis (Santa Clara University campus; 408/554-4023). An enlarged and adapted replica of the 1777 structure, the mission has 12,000 cover tiles salvaged from the earlier missions on this site. Of the four mission bells in the tower, one was a gift from Carlos IV of Spain in 1798, another a gift from Alfonso XIII of Spain in 1929. Gardens. Restored Adobe Lodge. Open daily. Also on the campus is the *de Saisset Museum* (408/554-4528), which houses the California Historical Collection of the pre-Columbian Indian and mission periods. Open daily except Mondays.

Triton Museum of Art (1505 Warburton Ave.; 408/247-3754). Collections of 19th- and 20th-century American and international art. Sculpture garden. Open daily.

Accommodations: *Madison Street Inn* (1390 Madison St.; 408/249-5521). Five guest rooms in a Queen Anne home with a library and a pool. Breakfast is included in the rates.

SANTA CRUZ

Roaring Camp and Big Trees Narrow-Gauge Railroad (6 miles north on Graham Hill Rd. in Felton; 408/335-4400). One old train carries passengers up North America's steepest railroad grades through groves of redwoods on a six-mile round trip, with a stopover at Bear Mountain for picnicking. Another, the *Santa Cruz, Big Trees & Pacific Railway*, runs between Roaring Camp and the beach at Santa Cruz. The two-and-a-half-hour trip goes through tunnels and along the San Lorenzo River Canyon. This historical railroad dates from 1875. A historic town site has an 1880s depot, an old-time general store, and a covered bridge. Trips daily, with additional trips on weekends and holidays.

SANTA ROSA

Sonoma County Museum (425 7th St.; 707/579-1500). Relics and mementos of county and Northern California history. Tours. Open Wednesday through Sunday.

Luther Burbank Home and Garden (Santa Rosa and Sonoma avenues; 707/576-5115). The home has memorabilia of the life and work of the great horticulturist. Burbank's grave is near the greenhouse. Gardens and fountains. Tours. Open Wednesday through Sunday.

Xcelsior Brewery (Railroad Square, 99 6th St.; 707/578-1497). Tours of the restored 1892 brewery home of Acme beer are given by appointment. Open daily except Sundays.

Accommodations: *Hilltop House Bed & Breakfast* (9550 St. Helena Rd.; 707/944-0880). A hideaway on 135 wilderness acres in the Mayacamus Mountains.

SOLVANG

The Danes from the Midwest who founded this town in 1911 created a bit of Denmark with Danish-style buildings and windmills.

Old Mission Santa Ines (1760 Mission Dr.; 805/688-4815). Established by Fray Estevan Tapis in 1804, the mission, an adobe building with a tiled roof, is still used as a church. Artifacts, manuscripts, and vestments are on display, and there is a garden. Open daily.

SONOMA

Mission San Francisco Solano was the most northerly of the missions, and the only one established under Mexican rule. It was secularized by Mariano Guadalupe Vallejo in 1834. Vallejo had been sent by Governor Figueroa to investigate Russian activities at Fort Ross. On June 14, 1848, Sonoma was

"California is a tragic land—like Palestine, like every promised land."

—CHRISTOPHER ISHERWOOD

the scene of the Bear Flag Revolt that established the short-lived California Republic.

Sonoma State Historic Park (West Spain St. and 3rd St. West; 707/938-1519). The park includes the 1823 Mission San Francisco Solano, General Vallejo's house, and an old barracks. Open daily.

Jack London State Historical Park (8½ miles west on CA 12, then 1½ miles west of Glen Ellen on London Ranch Rd.; 707/996-1090). The site of London's "House of Happy Walls," and the author's grave. Also here are a museum, the ruins of Wolf House, the Jack London cottage, a farm building, and the ruins of a winery, in the beautiful Valley of the Moon. Open daily.

Sonoma Depot Museum (210 1st St. West; 707/938-9765). Housed in a replica of an 1880 train depot, the museum displays county memorabilia. The Rand Ross Room has railroad artifacts. Open Wednesday through Sunday.

Train Town (1 mile south on Broadway; 707/938-3912). Twenty-minute trips are given on a miniature steam train, with stops at a petting zoo and a replica of an old mining camp. Runs daily, mid-June to Labor Day; weekends the rest of the year.

This was the ranch home of author, war correspondent, sailor, and rancher Jack London. Located in California's Valley of the Moon, the grounds contain the ruins of Wolf House, the Jack London cottage, and the grave of the author, who died here in 1916 at the age of forty.

Accommodations: *Sonoma Hotel* (110 West Spain St.; 707/996-2996). Seventeen guest rooms in an 1872 boardinghouse with antiques. Breakfast is included in the rates.

STOCKTON

In the Gold Rush, this was "a city of a thousand tents," one of the gateways to the Mother Lode Country. Many failed prospectors settled here after irrigation systems turned the countryside into fertile fields of grain.

Haggin Museum (Victory Park, 1201 North Pershing Ave.; 209/462-4116). Local and state artifacts, 19th-century American and European art and Indian arts and crafts. Open daily except Mondays.

SUSANVILLE

This town was once the capital of the Republic of Nataqua, an area of 50,000 square miles. The town's first settler, Isaac Roop, helped establish the republic, which later became part of the Nevada Territory. An 1864 survey showed that the town was part of California. The residents objected and holed up in Roop's house, but after a day-long gunfight, California won back what is now Lassen County.

Roop's Fort and William Pratt Memorial Museum (110 North Weatherlow; 916/257-2757). Located in Isaac Roop's 1854 fort, the museum has memorabilia of the short-lived country. Open Friday to Tuesday, May to September.

THOUSAND OAKS

Stagecoach Inn Museum Complex (in Newbury Park, at 51 South Ventu Rd.; 805/498-1621). A replica of an 1876 inn, the museum displays Chumash Indian artifacts and has a carriage house with vintage vehicles. *Tri-Village* has a Chumash hut, a Spanish adobe house, and a pioneer house. Gift shop. Nature trail. Open Wednesday to Friday and Sundays.

TRUCKEE

Donner Memorial State Park (2 miles west on old U.S. 40; 916/587-3841). The park is a monument to the Donner Party, stranded here in October 1846 by early blizzards. Only forty-eight of the eighty-one in the party survived. The *Emigrant Trail Museum* has displays on the Donner Party, Indians, construction of the first transcontinental railroad, and Sierra Nevada geology. Open Memorial Day to Labor Day.

TULELAKE

Lava Beds National Monument (30 miles southwest, off CA 139; 916/667-2282). Lava-tube caves, created by volcanic activity over 39,000 years ago, are throughout the park. Cinder cones dot the landscape—one rising 478 feet. Prehistoric pictographs and petroglyphs are on the dark rock walls. This rugged landscape was used as a natural fortress during the Modoc Indian War in 1872–73, one of the last times the army and the Indians clashed in the Pacific Northwest. The war began when the Modocs began attacking the flood of settlers pouring into their homeland on the California-Oregon border. The Modocs were moved to a reservation in Oregon, but fighting broke out between the army and the Modoc braves led by Captain Jack. Captain Jack's forces retreated into the lava beds, repelling the army's attempt to drive them out. Although they had to care for their families and live off the country, the Modocs held off an army more than twenty times their number for five months. At a peace parley, the Modocs

killed Gen. Edward R. S. Canby and the Reverend Eleasar Thomas, both strong advocates of fair treatment of the Indians. Some 650 soldiers launched an attack, but the Modocs escaped, only to be captured days later. Captain Jack and five others were convicted of murder. The army suffered 126 casualties.

In the park are the sites of Captain Jack's stronghold, the army base camp, and the places where Canby was slain and the principal engagements were fought. A visitor center and museum interpret the park's history. Cave trips and campfire programs are held daily, mid-June to Labor Day. The park is open daily. Limited wheelchair access.

VALLEJO

This was the capital of California twice: for a week in 1852 and for about a month in 1853. Prosperity came when the navy purchased Mare Island and built a shipyard, which is now the navy's main Pacific Coast base and repair facility.

Vallejo Naval and Historical Museum (Old City Hall, 734 Marin; 707/643-0077). Galleries here show the city's history from 1852 onward, and navy and Mare Island shipyard models, artifacts, and memorabilia. Open Tuesday to Saturday.

Benicia Capitol State History Park (6 miles southeast in Benicia at 1st and G streets; 707/745-3385). The old capitol has been restored and furnished in the style of 1853–54. Open daily except major holidays.

VENTURA

San Buenaventura Mission (211 East Main St.; 805/643-4318). Founded in 1762 by Junípero Serra, this was his ninth and last California mission. The bell tower has a striped rib dome. Garden with fountain. Museum. Open daily.

Captain Jack

A believer in peaceful coexistence, Captain Jack chose to go to war rather than step down as chief of the Modoc, and died on the gallows. He made friends with settlers in the Lost River Valley in California, and they dubbed him Captain Jack. In 1864, however, the Modoc were removed to an Oregon reservation. They were unhappy there, and Captain Jack led them back and petitioned to have a reservation established in their traditional home. The Indian Office refused and attempted to arrest him, touching off the Modoc War. Captain Jack tried to negotiate a settlement, but his followers feared they would be killed if they surrendered. His leadership threatened, he went along with the murder of the peace commissioners. He was betrayed to the authorities and handed over in 1873. He died bitterly resentful that his betrayers had been given clemency for a war that was forced on him.

"I have said yes, and thrown away my country."

—CAPTAIN JACK, MODOC

and the foundation of an old mission. The museum has Mexican and Chinese artifacts. Open daily except Mondays.

Olivas Adobe (4200 Olivas Park Dr.; 805/654-7837). A restored 1847 house with period furnishings and a garden. The museum is open weekends, the grounds daily.

Ortega Adobe (215 West Main St.; 805/654-7837). On the old Camino Real, the house has vintage rustic handmade furniture. Open daily.

Island Packer Cruises (805/642-7688). Boats leave Ventura Harbor daily for Channel Island National Park.

Accommodations: *La Mer* (411 Poli St.; 805/643-3600). An 1890 Cape Cod Victorian overlooking the coast, with feather beds. Bicycles are available for guests' use. Breakfast is included in the rates.

VICTORVILLE

If this town on the edge of the Mojave Desert induces déjà vu, it's because its been the setting for hundreds of cowboy movies.

Roy Rogers–Dale Evans Museum (15650 Seneca; 619/243-4547). A replica of an old Western fort containing personal and professional memorabilia of the couple who starred in countless oaters in the 1930s and 1940s. Roy's horse Trigger has been stuffed and is on display. Open daily.

Ventura County Museum of History and Art (100 East Main St.; 805/653-0323). Collections of Indian, Spanish, and pioneer relics, and the George Stuart Collection of historical figures. The county's agricultural past is depicted in outdoor exhibits. Open daily except Mondays.

Albinger Archaeological Museum (113 East Main St.; 805/648-5823). The preserved site of a 3,000-year-old Indian culture, a Chumash village settled about 1500,

VISALIA

Tulare County Museum (27000 Mooney Blvd., in Mooney Grove; 209/733-6616). A 150-acre oak grove containing ten historic buildings. On display are James Earl Frazier's "End of the Trail" statue, Indian artifacts, vintage guns, clocks, dolls, and early farm equipment. Open Thursday to Monday.

WEAVERVILLE

Within three years after gold was discovered here in 1849, the population rose to 3,000, half of whom were Chinese miners.

Weaverville Joss House State Historic Park (Main and Oregon; 916/623-5211). A temple built by Chinese miners in 1872, with tapestries and gilded wooden scrollwork. Tours. Open daily, March through October; Thursday to Monday the rest of the year.

J. J. Jackson Memorial Museum (508 Main; 916/623-5284). Local artifacts and memorabilia. Open daily, April to November; Tuesdays the rest of the year.

Scott Museum of Trinity Center (on CA 3 in Trinity Center; 916/266-3378). Exhibits of vintage transportation equipment, barbed wire, farming tools, household items, Indian artifacts and baskets. Open Tuesday to Sunday in the summer.

YOSEMITE NATIONAL PARK

Nestled in the glory of Yosemite are several places of historic interest. The *Pioneer Yosemite Historic Center* (a few miles from Mariposa Grove in Wawona) has historic buildings, a covered bridge, wagons, and exhibits, with tours in the spring and fall. The *Indian Cultural Museum* (behind the Visitor Center at Park Headquarters) has exhibits depicting the cultural history of the Yosemite Indians. Open daily. The *Yosemite Mountain–Sugar Pine Railroad* (4 miles south of the park entrance on CA 41; 209/683-7273) gives rides on a vintage narrow-gauge steam railroad into the Sierra logging country. Museum. Operates from late spring to early fall, weather permitting. Limited wheelchair access. (Yosemite is 67 miles northeast of Merced on CA 140; 62 miles north of Fresno on CA 41; 13 miles southwest of the town of Lee Vining on CA 120; 209/372-0200.)

YREKA

During the Gold Rush, this was known as Thompson's Dry Diggings, later as Shasta Butte City, and since 1852 as Yreka. Many well-preserved 19th-century buildings are in the Miner and Third Street area.

Siskiyou County Museum (910 South Main; 916/842-3836). The museum traces the area's history from prehistoric times, and has period rooms. Open daily in the summer; Tuesday through Saturday the rest of the year. On the grounds is an outdoor museum containing a pioneer cabin, a schoolhouse, a blacksmith shop, a logging skid shack, a miner's cabin, a church, and a general store. The buildings are open weekdays in the summer.

County Gold Exhibit (County Courthouse, 311 4th St.; 916/842-8340). A number of nuggets taken from the mines in the county are on display. Open weekdays.

MOTHER LODE COUNTRY

In the early days, the name "Mother Lode" referred to one rich vein of gold that ran from Melones, near Sonora, in the south to Auburn in the north, 270 miles long but only a few miles wide. This was the scene of the

The miners came in '49,
The whores in '51;
And when they got together
They produced the native son.

—CALIFORNIA SONG, CIRCA 1860

Prospectors search for gold with picks and shovels. As mining became more complicated, prospectors gave way to mining companies. First gold was panned, then dug with picks and shovels, then washed out hydraulically, and finally dynamited loose in deep shafts.

Sutter's Mill

California Gold Rush of the mid-19th century. The discovery of gold in Coloma in 1848 ignited a wave of migration that accelerated the development and population of all the Western states by several decades. The enormous gold-bearing quartz vein was surface-mined until the end of the century. In the first ten years of mining, the Mother Lode yielded $600 million in gold. At the peak, around 1860, there were some 120,000 miners in the Mother Lode country, but by 1873 the number had shrunk to 30,000. The game had changed. Big companies were tunneling hundreds of feet underground, and many miners had come down from the hills and become farmers. Among the miners left were a large number of Chinese, tediously reworking the leftover gravel.

Today the Mother Lode and, at its ends, the Southern Mines and Northern Mines, are transversed by CA 49 and crisscrossed by scenic backroads. Sleepy towns are in a landscape of rolling, grassy foothills. Hundreds of gold camps are now nothing but ghost towns no longer shown on modern maps. All that is left are abandoned mine tunnels and the piles of waste rock called *tailings*. The Southern Mines were particularly wild, with frequent conflicts between "Americans" and "foreigners," and the Chinese waging tong wars between opposing factions. At the other end, just north of Nevada City, CA 49 turns east and climbs to the Northern Mines in the high Sierra. Mother Lode Country has many pleasures for those who explore it. An excellent map of the area is available from the Golden Chain Council of the Mother Lode, Inc., 685 Placerville Dr., Placerville, CA 95667.

Angels Camp

Two writers struck literary gold in this wild-and-woolly mining camp: Bret Harte with "The Luck of Roaring Camp" and Mark Twain with "The Celebrated Jumping Frog of Calaveras County." Harte came to the mines in 1855, taught school for a while, and did a bit of mining. He later confided that he found the camp "hard, ugly, unwashed, vulgar and lawless." Back in San Francisco, he became a successful journalist and author. Mark Twain was twenty-six and still known as Sam Clemens when he accompanied his brother west in 1861. He worked on the *Enterprise* in Virginia City, Nevada, where he first used the pseudonym Mark Twain, before moving to San Francisco in 1864. There he met Harte, and came here and stayed with a family that were friends of Harte. At the Angels Hotel he heard the story of the jumping frog. Twain liked the miner's life. "I know the mines and miners interiorly as well as Bret Harte knows them exteriorly," he later wrote.

Auburn

During the Gold Rush, this mining camp, called North Fork Dry Diggings, was renamed for Auburn, New York. Orchards were planted in the area after the gold played out. Auburn is centrally located in the Mother Lode Country.

Old Town. Many of the historic buildings have been restored in the area bounded by Lincoln Way, Sacramento, Commercial, and Court streets.

Placer County Museum (1273 High St.; 916/885-9570). Old mining equipment, old photographs, minerals, and artifacts of the Gold Rush era. Open daily except Mondays.

Bernhard Museum Complex (291 Auburn-Folsom Rd.; 916/885-9570). A restored 1851 house, an 1874 winery, and an art gallery. Tours and living-history programs. Open daily except Mondays.

Accommodations: *Power's Mansion Inn* (164 Cleveland Ave.; 916/885-1166). Thirteen guest rooms with private baths in a Victorian mansion. Breakfast is included in the rates.

Chinese Camp

In the early 1850s, some 5,000 Chinese miners settled here, and a minor incident at the mines later touched off a tong war. A large stone happened to roll from the diggings of one group of miners to a spot where another group was working, and a fight started. Each group was allied to a San Francisco tong, and each sent for reinforcements. On October 25, 1856, the tongs faced off here, and in the melee four were killed and twelve injured. American law officers took 250 people into custody. Honor had been upheld, however, and everyone later returned to the mines satisfied.

Fiddletown

Prospectors from Missouri were caught by an early winter here, and spent long months confined in their tents. They amused themselves by playing on their fiddles such old favorites as "Turkey in the Straw." When it came time to name their town, Fiddletown seemed the logical choice. The town prospered. It had four hotels, a brewery, and a winery. It also had a Chinatown with its own stores, medicine shops, joss houses, and opium dens. Today Fiddletown is a bit off the main Mother Lode trail and is quiet most of the year. In the summer, however, it hosts an old-time fiddling contest, and thousands crowd its main street.

Grass Valley

Grass Valley emerged from the early Gold Rush days as the most important mining town in the state. It was here that hard-rock mining techniques were introduced and developed, turning mining from a hit-or-miss business into an industry. But for anyone with romance in his soul, Grass Valley was the home of Lola Montez and Lotta Crabtree. Born Eliza Gilbert in Ireland, Lola Montez charmed Europe with her singing and dancing, and scandalized Europe with her affair with King Ludwig of Bavaria. On

Then ho, brothers, ho,
To California go;
There's plenty of gold
In the world we're told
On the banks of the Sacramento

—JESSE HUTCHINSON, JR., "HO FOR CALIFORNIA," 1852

Black Bart

A man wearing a duster and a flour-sack hood, and carrying an empty shotgun, robbed twenty-seven stagecoaches from 1875 to 1882 in the Mother Lode Country, often leaving a poem behind. One read,

I've labored long and hard for bread
for honor and for riches.
But on my corns too long you've trod
you fine haired Sons of Bitches.
(signed) Black Bart, the Po-8

On his last robbery, he was shot at and dropped his handkerchief in his escape. A laundry mark led authorities to Charles E. Boles, a dapper little drifter from New York. Sent to prison, he was asked by a reporter if he would write more poetry. "Young man," he replied, "didn't you hear me say I would commit no more crimes?"

"All sorts of people, from the polished Broadway dandy, who never handled an instrument heavier than a whale-bone walking-stick, to the sturdy labourer who had spent his life wielding the pickaxe and the shovel, had come to California, and all for one common object—to dig gold."

—E. GOULD BURRUM, Six Months in the Gold Mine, 1850

an 1852 American tour, she was not well received in San Francisco, canceled the tour, and retired here, keeping monkeys and a grizzly bear as pets, and giving legendary parties. Lola met and was enchanted by seven-year-old Lotta Crabtree, who lived nearby. Lola took her on as a protégée, teaching her songs and dances. Lotta began performing in a saloon at the age of eight, and the miners showered her with nuggets. She later became an international success, retired early, and lived well. When she died in 1924, she left a $4 million estate. Lola Montez did not fare as well. An 1855 Australian tour was a flop, and so was an American lecture tour. She died in 1861 at the age of forty-three, nearly penniless.

Lola Montez House (248 Mill St.; 916/273-4667). This rebuilt house is the home of the Grass Valley Chamber of Commerce. A small museum has mining artifacts and clothing, photographs, and other memorabilia of the legendary Montez. Open daily except Sundays.

Mining Museum–North Star Powerhouse (Allison Ranch Rd.; 916/273-4255). Displays of the techniques of hard-rock mining. Artifacts include a thirty-foot Pelton water wheel and a stamp mill. Open daily May through October.

Empire Mine State Historic Park (10791 East Empire St.; 916/273-8522 or 273-7714). The Empire, the oldest, largest, and richest gold mine in California, operated continuously from 1850 to 1956, and probably wouldn't have closed if the price of gold hadn't been fixed at $32 an ounce. As many as 800 miners worked here in shifts, digging 5.8 million ounces of gold out of the mine's 367 miles of tunnels. In the park is a baronial cottage surrounded by manicured lawns and formal gardens. There are mining exhibits in the Visitor Center. Tours. Open daily, March through November.

"Rough and Ready" (four miles west on CA 20). Most of the miners who settled here had served in the Mexican War under Gen.

Zachary "Rough and Ready" Taylor, so they named the town after him. The town was founded in 1849 and thrived for twenty years, but its moment of fame came in 1850. A federal miners' tax was passed, and the Territory of California announced its intention to collect it. The town reacted by seceding from the Union and forming "the Great Republic of Rough and Ready." The miners expected trouble, but no soldiers came. After a few months they voted the town back in the Union so that they could celebrate the Fourth of July. Many original buildings remain in this old mining town.

Accommodations: *Annie Horan's Bed & Breakfast* (415 W. Main St.; 916/272-2418). Four rooms with private baths in an elegantly refurbished 1874 Victorian.

Hornitos

Mexican miners founded this town after they were forced to leave nearby Quartzburg. The legendary bandit Joaquín Murieta is said to have made his headquarters here. He swore vengeance against Americans after they beat him, raped his wife, and murdered his brother. To the Mexicans he was a Robin Hood of the Southern Mines in the 1850s. Many historical markers mention his name, but fact and fiction have been hopelessly intertwined.

Jackson

Amador County Museum (225 Church St.; 209/223-6386). Artifacts and mementos of the Gold Rush days displayed in a restored 1859 house. There is a model of the Kennedy Mine. Open Wednesday through Sunday.

Indian Grinding Rock State Historic Park (12 miles northeast via CA 88, Pine Grove–Volcano Rd.; 209/296-7488). A reconstructed Miwok village with petroglyphs and bedrock mortars. The Visitor Center has a museum of regional Indian artifacts. Interpretive trail. Open daily.

Accommodations: *The Foxes* (north on CA 49, 77 Main St., Sutter Creek; 209/267-5882). Six guest rooms with private baths in an 1858 Gold Rush house furnished with antiques. *Sutter Creek* (4 miles north on CA 49; 209/267-5606). Nineteen guest rooms, some with private baths, in an 1859 Victorian. Breakfast is included in the rates.

Nevada City

One of the first of the Gold Rush mining towns, this is still one of the most charming. Two years after gold was discovered here, 10,000 miners were working every foot of ground within a radius of three miles. The town abounds in quality Victorian buildings of historic interest. It also was the first Gold Rush town to see Eleanor Dumont, the lady gambler later known as Madame Moustache. She arrived here in 1854 and opened a blackjack parlor, later moving around the camps. Her beauty began to fade, and she acquired the line of dark fuzz on her upper lip that gave her her cruel nickname. Twenty-five years after arriving in Nevada City, she committed suicide in Bodie.

National Hotel (211 Broad St.; 916/265-4551). This hotel did a prosperous bar business during the 1860s and 1870s, and still operates a saloon and dining room. The three-story building has balconies and balustrades reaching over the sidewalk. Open daily.

Firehouse No. 1. This museum has a hodgepodge of interesting items, including a joss house altar, Donner Party relics, Maidu Indian relics, furniture, clothing, and photographs of early miners. Open daily except winter Wednesdays.

American Victorian Museum (325 Spring St.; 916/265-5804). Located in historic Miner's Foundry, the museum has a collection of Victoriana, including an 1871

Joseph Mayer pipe organ. A cluster of old buildings houses a theater, an educational radio station, and a lounge and restaurant. The museum is open Friday through Sunday.

Malakoff Diggins State Historical Park (27 miles northeast off CA 49 at Tyler Foote Crossing; 916/265-2740). A 3,000-acre recreation area with a museum containing hydraulic mining exhibits. Hiking, swimming, fishing, picnicking, camping, and

This mill race is in Columbia, a restored ghost town. In one morning, a few miners panning a stream here found thirty pounds of gold. At its zenith Columbia had 20,000 residents, almost as many as San Francisco had at the time.

cabins. The museum is open daily, April through October.

Accommodations: *Red Castle Inn* (109 North Prospect St.; 916/265-5135). A Gothic Revival known locally as "The Castle," this lodging offers eight guest rooms, some with private baths. Breakfast is included in the rates. *Downey House* (517 West Broad St.; 916/265-2815). This Victorian, atop the town's Nabob Hill, has six guest rooms with private baths, a pond, and a red barn within walking distance of the historic district. Breakfast is included in the rates.

Placerville

Three great American fortunes trace their beginnings to the mining camp here. From 1853 to 1858, J. M. Studebaker built wheelbarrows in his Main Street shop. When he had saved $8,000, he went home to South Bend, Indiana, and with his brothers built the largest covered-wagon factory in the country. Two fellow tradesmen who became rich were Philip Armour, a butcher, and Mark Hopkins, a grocer. This camp was first known as Dry Diggin's because water was in such short supply. In 1849 the name was changed to Hangtown after a series of hangings, then to Placerville in 1854. After the mines were exhausted, the town became an important stage stop and commercial center for the Northern Mines.

Gold Bug Mine (Hangtown's Gold Bug Park; 916/622-0832). An old, municipally owned double-shaft gold mine with a restored gold stamp mill. Picnicking. Tours by reservation. Open daily, March through November.

El Dorado County Historical Museum (100 Placerville Drive; 916/621-5865). Artifacts of Miwok, Maidu, and Wahoe Indians and of the early Gold Rush days. Open Wednesday through Saturday.

Marshall Gold Discovery State Historic Park (8 miles northwest on CA 49 in Coloma; 916/622-3470). Here, on January 24, 1848, James Marshall, foreman of a sawmill owned by Capt. John Augustus Sutter, saw something shining at the bottom of the mill race. "I reached my hand down and picked it up," he would recall. "It made my heart thump, for I was certain it was gold." Marshall's discovery was ignored at first. A San Francisco newspaper gave it four lines on its back page. But Sam Brannan, who owned a general store near the mill, investigated and found gold there for the picking. He filled a bottle with nuggets and headed for San Francisco. "Gold! Gold from the American River!" he shouted. This time San Francisco believed what it heard and saw. Practically all of its 450 citizens dropped what they were doing and headed for Sutter's Mill. For the first year, the Gold Rush was largely a local phenomenon; a group came from Sonora, Mexico, and some from the Oregon Territory, but most of the miners were Californians. In that year, more than $10 million had been taken from the American River's South Fork. In the East, the first reports of the strike were discounted. The army, however, confirmed the presence of gold. In January 1849, President James K. Polk told Congress in his State of the Union Address, "The accounts of gold in that territory [California] are of such an extraordinary character as would suspend belief." The Gold Rush now had the blessing of the President. Before the year was out, more than 100,000 people had arrived to seek their fortunes.

The park includes the *Gold Discovery Museum, Marshall's Cabin,* the *Thomas House Museum,* an operating replica of Sutter's mill, a blacksmith shop, and several other buildings. Fishing, hiking, and nature trails and picnicking are available. Open daily.

Accommodations: *Chichester House* (800 Spring St.; 916/626-1882). A bed-and-breakfast with three guest rooms and private baths, decorated with antiques. The 1892 Victorian was the first house in Placerville with indoor plumbing. The house has a library and a conservatory, and a pump organ in the parlor. *James Blair House* (2985 Clay St.; 916/626-6136). A 1901 Queen Anne with a three-story turret and wide porches. There is a restaurant, and breakfast is included in the rates.

Sonora

Bad blood between Mexican and American miners marked the early days of this mining camp. After a statewide, twenty-dollars-a-month tax was levied on all foreign miners, the Mexicans left, cutting Sonora's population of 5,000 almost in half. Business suffered until the tax was repealed and the Mexicans returned. Sonora was the richest town in the Southern Mines. In the 1870s, three partners bought a supposedly played-out pocket mine from a group of Chileans. After long digging, the new owners hit a vein of almost solid gold. Within a week, more than $500,000 in gold was mined and shipped. Stretching across seven hills, Sonora, the seat of Tuolumne County, was the setting for several stories by Bret Harte and Mark Twain.

Columbia State Historic Park (4 miles north via CA 49 and Parrotts Ferry Rd.; 209/532-4301). On camping here on a rainy night in March 1850, Dr. Thaddeus Hildreth, his brother, and some others panned for gold. Before they were through, they had found thirty pounds. The area was a geological oddity: a limestone bed full of holes that had captured the gold washed down from the hills over millions of years. Within a month, some 5,000 prospectors were living in a tent town called Hildreth's Diggins. The town, renamed Columbia, quickly grew to a city of 20,000, at that time a population nearly as large as San Francisco's. The boom days lasted twenty years, and what years they were! Edwin Booth played Richard III at the Fallon House theater, followed a few weeks later by Lola Montez and her Spider Dance. An arena was built for fights between bulls and bears. Horace Greeley, editor of the *New York Tribune*, wrote about the fights, likening the contestants to the speculators on Wall Street. "Bulls" and "Bears" quickly found their way into the language of stock trading.

Today Columbia has been restored to its early glory. Among the forty buildings on the self-guided tour are the *Firehouse*, with its elaborately decorated handpumper *Papeete,* made for the King of Hawaii, but stranded in San Francisco when the ship's crew deserted and went to the gold fields; the refurbished 1860 *Schoolhouse,* which was in use until 1930; *Eagle Cottage,* a reconstructed boardinghouse; and *Columbia House*, which has been refitted as a period restaurant. There are tours of an operating gold mine, stagecoach rides, and a museum. The park is open daily in the summer, weekends in the winter.

Railtown 1897 State Historic Park (3 miles south in Jamestown; reservations, 209/984-3953). The park offers a one-hour ride through the Sierra foothills on a steam passenger train, and has a roundhouse museum. Rides daily, Memorial Day to Labor Day; weekends in the spring and fall.

Gold Prospecting Tours (3 miles southwest via CA 49; 209/984-4653). Several hours of instruction are given in the basics of gold prospecting and the use of equipment. Prospecting and river rafting combination tours. Helicopter drop-ins. Five-day campouts. Equipment is provided. Prospecting tours start daily in good weather.

Accommodations: *City Hotel* (3 miles north on CA 49 in Columbia; 209/532-1479). In Columbia State Historic Park, this restored 1850s Gold Rush building has nine guest rooms. Many antiques. Breakfast and afternoon tea. *Jamestown Hotel* (3 miles west on CA 108 in Jamestown; 209/984-3902). An 1856 Victorian Gold Rush hotel with eight guest rooms and four suites.

"Ditches and banks of gravel, denuded hillsides, stumps, and decayed trunks of trees took the place of woodland and ravine, and indicated his approach to civilization. Then a church steeple came in sight, and he knew that he had reached home. In a few moments he was clattering down the single narrow street that lost itself in a chaotic ruin of races, ditches, and tailings at the foot of the hill, and dismounted before the gilded windows of the Magnolia saloon."

—BRET HARTE, *Brown of Calaveras,* 1870

Appendix

STATE TOURIST OFFICES

ARIZONA
Arizona Office of Tourism
1110 West Washington
Phoenix, AZ 85007
602/542-TOUR

CALIFORNIA
California Office of Tourism
Department of Commerce
1121 L Street
Suite 103
Sacramento, CA 95814
800/862-2543, ext. 99

COLORADO
Colorado Tourism Board
Suite 1700
1625 Broadway
Denver, CO 80202
800/422-2656

IDAHO
Division of Travel Promotion
700 West State Street
Boise, ID 83720
800/635-7820

KANSAS
Travel and Tourism
Department of Commerce
400 West 8th Street
5th Floor
Topeka, KS 66603
913/296-2099

MONTANA
Travel Montana/Ski Montana
Deer Lodge, MT 59722
800/541-1477

NEBRASKA
Nebraska Travel and Tourism
Department of Economic Development
Box 94666
301 Centennial Mall South
Lincoln, NB 68509
800/228-4307 (outside Nebraska)
800/742-7595 (in Nebraska)

NEVADA
Nevada Commission on Tourism
Capitol Complex
Carson City, NV 89710
800/NEVADA8

NEW MEXICO
Travel Division
New Mexico Economic Development
    and Tourism Department
Joseph Montoya Building
1100 St. Francis Drive
Room 751
Santa Fe, NM 87503
505/827-0291
800/545-2040 (outside New Mexico)

NORTH DAKOTA
North Dakota Tourism Promotion
Capitol Grounds
Bismarck, ND 58505
800/437-2077 (outside North Dakota)
800/472-2100 (in North Dakota)

OKLAHOMA
Oklahoma Tourism and Recreation
    Department
Literature Distribution Center
215 NE 28th Street
Oklahoma City, OK 73105
405/521-2409 or 800/652-6552

OREGON
Tourism Division
Oregon Department of Economic
    Development
595 Cottage Street, NE
Salem, OR 97310
800/547-7842 (outside Oregon)
800/543-8838 (in Oregon)

SOUTH DAKOTA
South Dakota Department of Tourism
Capitol Lake Plaza
Pierre, SD 57501
800/843-1930 (outside South Dakota)
800/952-2217 (in South Dakota)

TEXAS
Travel and Information Division
P.O. Box 5064
Austin, TX 78463
512/465-7401

UTAH
Utah Travel Council
Council Hall
Capitol Hill
Salt Lake City, UT 84114
801/538-1030

WASHINGTON
State Tourism Development Division
Department of Trade and Economic
    Development
101 General Administration Building
Olympia, WA 98504
206/586-2102 or 800/544-1800

WYOMING
Wyoming Travel Commission
I-25 at College Drive
Cheyenne, WY 82002
307/777-7777 or 800/225-5996

Index

Page numbers in *italics* refer to illustrations and maps